Pasquale J. Simonelli
सत्यशिव चैतन्य

AWARENESS

THE BOOK OF ETHIC, MORALS AND BEHAVIOR

Unicorn on the Church of St George,
Bloomsbury Street Way, London, UK.

Sacer Equestris Aureus Ordo

ISBN-13:978-0615754260
ISBN-10:0615754260
Sacer Equestris Aureus Ordo Inc.
Sacred Texts division
West Long Branch, NJ - Charleston, SC, USA

To my grandchildren
and all the children of the world
"*for theirs is the Kingdom of Heaven.*"
ὅτι αὐτῶν ἐστιν ἡ βασιλεία τῶν οὐρανῶν
Matthew 5:3-10

CONTENT

ABBREVIATIONS......6
ABBREVIATIONS OF WORKS AND AUTHORS......6
TRANSLITERATION......8
VERY FEW AND GENERAL PRONUNCIATION TIPS......8
PREFACE...... 10
PART I A THEORETIC ETHIC
THE QUEST FOR ETHIC, as *Ius Suprēmum*, Supreme Ethic, its Apodictic Epistemic Foundation, AS PERENNIAL ABSOLUTE VALUE, with selected sacred texts' references......14
CHAPTER 1 THE REAL CRISIS 15
CHAPTER 2 DEFINITIONS......17
Philosophy...... 17
Ethic...... 18
Value......18
Morals......19
Liberty......22
Life...... 23
Will...... 26
CHAPTER 3 AWARENESS AS TRANSCENDENCE...... 29
Awareness is Life, Light and Truth......31
Padre Pio......35
"Quid est veritas?" 37
Ramana Maharshi......37
Śaṅkara......39
Superimposition......40
Confutation...... 40
The Real of the Real......40
Certitude...... 41
Consciousness......42
Wakefulness and sleep...... 42
Subconscious...... 43
Super-conscious...... 45
Un-conscious......45
Awareness...... 49
Awareness and mindfulness......58
Consciousness-of the world......63
Destiny......65

CHAPTER 3 RELIGION..68
Apodicticity, conversion and fundamentalism.............. 68
Atheism.. 70
Faith, Certainty and Beliefs.................................... 72
PART I B SACRED TEXTS.. 76
Translation and commentary of the *Kaivalya Upanishad*, the *Bhagavad-Gītā* and other texts.
CHAPTER 1 *KAIVALYA UPANISHAD*....................................77
Veda...77
Upanishad.. 77
Kaivalya INVOCATION... 78
KAIVALYA SECTION I.. 79
THE ESSENCE OF TRANSCENDENCE...........................79
KAIVALYA SECTION II... 96
THE ESSENCE OF ETHIC 96
CHAPTER 2 *BHAGAVAD-GĪTĀ'S KARMA YOGA*.....................107
Mahābhārata 107
Gītā.. 107
The Divine-Song.. 109
Political morality.. 125
PART I C PERENNIAL ETHIC AWARENESS.......................142
New Biblical Exegesis and other sacred texts
CHAPTER 1 THEORETICAL CONSIDERATIONS 143
CHAPTER 2 ETHICAL AWARENESS.......................................146
CHAPTER 3 EMOTIONS..151
Beauty, Love and Truth...153
CHAPTER 4 PRESENT ETHIC 155
CHAPTER 5 CONCLUSION OF PART I 160
PART II THE BOOK OF MORALS
Critical quest for Morals, philosophical views and various sacred texts 163
PREMISE 164
God's Judgment 164
War and Morals 165
Historical Spiritualism 167
CHAPTER 1 METAPHYSICAL MORALS 169
Divine Laws 169
Religions 171
Iusnaturalism 173
Creation and Life 175
Separation between Church and State 176

Equality and Liberty 178
CHAPTER 2 RELATIVISM, RELATIVE MORALS 183
CHAPTER 3 ALTRUISM, UNSELFISH MORALS 188
Laws, Guilt and Sins 192
CHAPTER 4 HEDONISM and UTILITARIAN MORALS 196
Happiness 198
CHAPTER 5 THE GOLDEN RULE 200
CHAPTER 6 CONCLUSION OF PART II 204
PART III THE BOOK OF BEHAVIOR 205
PREMISE 206
Behavioral congregation 207
CHAPTER 1 POWER IN THE POLITICAL AND RELIGIOUS ARENA 210
Ideological power 213
Education 214
CHAPTER 2 LOVE 216
Love's strength 216
The Nature of Love 217
CHAPTER 3 LIFE, SEX AND FAMILY 228
Respect for life 228
Gender 229
Homosexuality 231
Marriage 232
Matrimony 234
Extended-family 236
Monogamy and polygamy 237
Polygyny 238
Polyandry 240
Polyamory 241
Open-family 246
Un-divorce 247
Communal organizations 248
Sex education 249

SELECTED TERMINOLOGIES 257
INDEX 256
ENDNOTES 263
SELECTED and QUOTED BIBLIOGRAPHY and FILMOGRAPHY 342

ABBREVIATIONS

adj. = adjective
cf. = compare, see
comm. = commentator or commentary
ed. = editor or edition
En. = English
ep. = epigraph
ex. = expression
f. = feminine
fol. = following
m. = masculine
n. = noun.
tr. = translator or translation
trlt. = transliteration
viz. = videlicet = that is to say, namely.
vol. = volume

ABBREVIATIONS OF WORKS AND AUTHORS.

B = Brāhmaṇa.
BG = Bhagavad-Gītā
EJVS = Electronic Journal of Vedic Studies
JAOS = Journal of the American Oriental Society
MB = Mahā Bhārata
ŚB = Śatapatha Brāhmaṇa
U = Upanishad
UA = Aitareya Upanishad
UAb = Amritabindu Upanishad
UB = Bṛhadāraṇyaka Upanishad
UC = Chāndogya Upanishad
UĪśa = Īśa Upanishad
UK = Kaṭha Upanishad
UKa = Kaushītaki-Brāhmaṇa Upanishad
UKai = Kaivalya Upanishad
UKe = Kena Upanishad
UM = Māṇḍūkya Upanishad
UMaitrī = Maitrī Upanishad
UMu = Muṇḍaka Upanishad
UNr = Nṛsiṃhottaratāpanī Upanishad
UP = Praśna Upanishad

UŚ = Śvetāśvatara Upanishad
UT = Taittirīya Upanishad
UV = Vajrasūcika Upanishad
UY = Yoga Darshana Upanishad
TB = Taittirīya Brāhmaṇa
V = Veda
VA = Atharva Veda
VṚ = Ṛg Veda
VS = Sāma Veda
VY = Yajur Veda
W = Monier-Williams, Sir Monier, A Sanskrit-English Dictionary
ZDNG = Zeitschrift der Deutdchen Morgenländischen Gesellschaft

TRANSLITERATION

DEVANĀGARĪ ALPHABET							LATIN ALPHABET with diacritic marks			
Vowels Initial/Media/			**Consonants**							
अ		*a*	Gutturals		Cerebrals		Labials		Spirants	
आ	ा	*ā*	क	k_a	ट	$ṭ_a$	प	p_a	श	$ś_a$
इ	ि	*i*	ख	kh_a	ठ	$ṭh_a$	फ	ph_a	ष	sh_a
ई	ी	*ī*	ग	g_a	ड	$ḍ_a$	ब	b_a	स	s_a
उ	ु	*u*	घ	gh_a	ढ	$ḍh_a$	भ	bh_a	ह	h_a
ऊ	ू	*ū*	ङ	$ṅ_a$	ण	$ṇ_a$	म	m_a		
ऋ	ृ	*ṛ*	Palatals		Dentals		Semivowels		*Visarga*	
ॠ	ॄ	*ṝ*	च	c_a	त	t_a	य	y_a		
ऌ	ॢ	*ḷ*	छ	ch_a	थ	th_a	र	r_a	:	*ḥ*
ए	े	*e*	ज	j_a	द	d_a	ल	l_a		
ऐ	ै	*ai*	झ	jh_a	ध	dh_a	व	v_a	*Anusvārsa*	
ओ	ो	*o*	ञ	$ñ_a$	न	n_a			ं ँ	*ṁ* *ṃ*
औ	ौ	*au*								

VERY FEW AND GENERAL PRONUNCIATION TIPS

letter	pronunciation		letter	pronunciation		letter	pronunciation	
ā	aa	***A***merica	ऐ *ai*	aaee	***I***-am	श $ś_a$	sc	di***SC***ipline
इ *i*	ee	***EA***ster	ङ $ṅ_a$	ng	ki***NG***	ष sh_a	sh	***SH***un
ऋ *ṛ*	ri	***RI***ver	च c_a	ch	***CH***urch	: *ḥ*	ha	***H***ave
ए *e*	eh	***E***stimate	ज j_a	j	***J***oin	ं *ṁ*	n^n	ba***N***

~~~

Some of us can
distinctly remember,
almost to the hour,
when, in the midst of
an intense childish play,
we realized, with surprise,
the futility of it all.
Then, we turned away
from the amusement
to pursue serious
mature occupations.
Then, "the sage,
in search for realization,
after studying the scriptures,
should discard them
as the rice sifter
discards the husk."
(*Amritabindu Upanishad*, 18)

~~~

PREFACE

This work, composed of three parts, is the continuation of our book *Beyond Immortality*. The three parts will investigate ethical, moral and behavioral topics. Throughout the course of the research we will examine various philosophical ideas and scientific principles. Furthermore, we will translate and comment several texts from different religions.

I) The first part explores the possibility of a Perpetual Absolute Value. This Supreme Ethic, *Ius Suprēmum*, in order to be valid, must be Universal. To be widespread, it must have a Scientific Foundation. To be exact, it must be Indubitable. To be certain, it must have its precise roots in the epistemic, gnoseological process.

II) The second part will analyze different moral views. Morals and laws will be critically examined in their philosophical, historical, geographical and cultural perspectives. We will also analyze and research the possibility of universal morals will be critically examined.

III) On the grounds of the previous two parts, the third one will examine different social behaviors. Various cultural customs will be investigated and scrutinized. Finally, it will research the possibility for social structures promoting the wellbeing of all individuals.

Regarding ethical perspectives, we will discard all those doctrines that do not stand up to be real, absolute and unbound principles devoid of contingent necessities. That is, we will reject those apparent values that

a) Are relative,

b) Are dictated by self-interest and/or

c) Derive from dogmatic or metaphysical mandates.

For the purpose of this work, we take distance from all dogmatic and religious affiliation, which could take away the integrity and objectivity that we claim for our research. This will not impede that, very frequently, we will quote sacred literature. This is not due to religious zealousness or the necessity to proselytize. Rather, it will be to highlight philosophical, ethical or moral statements. Quotations from sacred texts, in fact, may clarify particular issues or topics. We should not fall in the opposite dogmatic error, namely, to reject sacred texts due to preconceived idiosyncrasies for religions in general. We have encountered many self-proclaimed a-theists who have a *religious* approach regarding their a-theism.

Furthermore, we acknowledge that, on occasion, also secular philosophies, scientific-stances, ideologies and/or political affiliations became dogmas. As an example, Nazism, Communism, Fascism, Capitalism and similar at times were and are revered religiously. In the course of history, similar creeds become the cause of atrocities and persecutions.

We depart from religious believers in general. We deny those who uncritically state dogmas to impose them on others, even with violence. Moreover, we take distance also from those who, blinded by their philosophies and/or politics, erroneously call themselves, *empirical-secular-humanists*. These religious zealots are characterized by an unwillingness to listen or to discuss issues for fear of being critically disproved. They are like the *learned ones* who, in Brecht's *Galileo*, refuse to "look through the" telescopic evidence of heliocentrism claiming *geocentrism* on the authority of Aristotle and the Bible.[1]

Consequently, there must be openness to others' thoughts without preconceived negativity, affirms the Tibetan Buddhist Dalai Lama.

"*I think* [he states] *in many ways narrow-minded attitudes lead to extreme thinking. And this creates problems. For instance... the idea that 'everyone' should be Buddhist is quite extreme. And that kind of extreme thinking just causes problems... Even if we tried to make the whole world Buddhist it would be impractical. Through closer contacts with other traditions you realize the positive things about them... Then it's like going to a restaurant – we can all sit down at one table and order different dishes according to one's own taste. We might eat different dishes, but nobody argues about it!*"[2]

Regarding the interpretation of sacred scriptures, we propose an introspective, psychological and epistemic approach. We will offer a new exegesis and new word analysis. Commonly accepted terms will be reexamined. New word translations will be proposed with accurate adherence to semantic, textual and philosophical meaning. The new rendering will be duly annotated and explained in endnote. The western approach to religion is contrary to the eastern one. For the Western mentality, religion is different from philosophy and science. Finally, it is historically based. All the events described in the sacred text have a reality in history and providentially intervene in history. For the Eastern perspective, religion, science and philosophy are the same. The sacred texts and all the gods are a-temporal paradigms; they have no historical foundation. Any temporal dimension nullifies them. There is a pragmatic approach, by which any religion that is not realized or tested is not so. It is only a *darśana*, a point of view. In fact, the *Bṛhadāraṇyaka Upanishad*, a sacred text itself states that at one point,

> "*the gods* [are] *not the gods, the* [sacred text] *Vedas* [are] *not the Vedas*."[3]

More so, the *Amritabindu Upanishad* declares,

> "*The sage in search for realization, after studying the scriptures, should discard them as the rice sifter discards the husk*."[4]

Both statements are a very different stand from the Middle Eastern adoration of sacred texts.

Throughout various religious metaphorical scripts, there is a consistency that systematically leads to search an internal connection with the transcendent. Beyond all differences, the various religious and scriptural metaphors emphasize the surrender to that Transcendent. Here, we make ours Joseph Campbell's comment on the interpretations of myths, symbols and metaphors present in different religious texts. In his book, *The Power of Myth*, he states, "The reference of the metaphor in religious traditions is to something transcendent that is not literally any thing. If you think that the metaphor is itself the reference, it would be like going to a restaurant, asking for the menu, seeing beefsteak written there, and starting to eat the menu... [We make] a mistake in the reading of the symbol. That is reading the words in terms of prose instead of in terms of poetry, reading the metaphor in terms of the denotation instead of the connotation... [The myth is] that which is beyond even the concept of reality, that which transcends all thought. The myth puts you there all the time, gives you a line to connect with that mystery which you are."[5] Like art, mythology "is a lie that makes us realize truth."[6] "Mythology is psychology misread as cosmology, history, and biography."[7] Mythology is intended for those who have transparent minds[8] and

"*ears to hear*."[9]

Dante writes,[10]

"O you who have sound intellects
observe the doctrine that hides itself
under the veil of puzzling verses."

"*In fact, the gods love the metaphor,*" states the *Aitareya Upanishad.*[11]

Mythology is the echo of Transcendence.

PART I

A

THEORETIC ETHIC
THE QUEST FOR ETHIC,
as *Ius Suprēmum*, Supreme Ethic,
its Apodictic Epistemic Foundation,
AS PERENNIAL ABSOLUTE VALUE,
with selected sacred texts' references

CHAPTER 1

THE REAL CRISIS TODAY IS THE ABSENCE OF CLEAR VALUES

In the world today, generally, money is the only value. While leaders cowardly abdicate their posts, in some parts of the globe, fundamentalists dictate medieval laws. In other locations, martyrdom is regarded as meritorious. Elsewhere, only personal gratification sets the goal. Most of the supporters of relative values enforce that which was imparted to them by their society. In the name of imagined orthodoxy, heretics were burnt at the stake or imprisoned.

Historically, the disagreements present in the world end up in local conflicts. They may expand into full wars with very dangerous international involvement. Each side tries to impose its own worldview upon the other. Relative and dialectically contrasting ideas fight each other. Every perspective declares war against the opposite one.[12] Traditional weltanschauungs clash at the drumming battle cry of my "*God wants it!*"[13] While hedonistic governments incite war with the hymn, *Nature*, or *Our Country*, or *Our National Interest demands it.*[14] Like ancient *Trial by Ordeal or by Combat*,[15] each side lets God or weapons decide who the depository of righteousness is. Wars brake out for the purpose of enforcing one set of morals and laws over others. The American Revolutionary War of Independence (1775–1783) broke out on the Illuminist assumption of *Natural Laws.*[16] An abstract metaphysical *Nature* guarantees three laws: "*Life, Liberty and Pursuit of Happiness.*" These truths are regarded as *inalienable* and *self-evident.* They became the foundation of a *New World Order*[17] established by the American Constitution.[18] The appeal of these morals swept through Europe as wild fire. Consequently, the divine mandate of kings was rescinded.

Eventually, *Nature* and the *Goddess Reason* empowered the revolutionary French People. The People, in the name of *Liberty, Equality* and *Brotherhood*,[19] beheaded the king, in 1793. On November 10, they celebrated the Festival of Liberty or the Cult of Reason.[20] The French National Convention enthroned the actress, "Demoiselle Candeille, of the Opera... on palanquin shoulderhigh," as the "*Goddess of Reason* ... escorted by wind-music... on the high-altar of Notre-Dame" in Paris. In 1886, *she* arrived in New York Harbor as the *Statue of Liberty Enlightening the World*.[21]

Other wars of independence broke out through Europe. In 1848, new constitutional monarchies were established. Even the Italian Papal States were affected. Indeed, in 1870, the Italian army confined Pius IX, the Pope of Rome, in what is now the Vatican City.

After World War I (1914–1918), a great number of crowns fell. Eventually, it took a Second World War (1939-1945) for the *New World Order* to overcome. With alternate vicissitudes, more regional wars consolidated the Western *Pursuit of Happiness* and its economic control over the planet.

However, the ordeal is not over. At the beginning of the second millennium, old and new worldviews are disputing that *Order*. They claim the return of old values imposed by a traditional leadership with heavenly mandate.

In these continuous recurring conflicting events, can peace be really attained without a truly *Ius Suprēmum*, a Universal Supreme Law? Is such ethic achievable? This is the question.

"IS THERE A RIGHTEOUS ACTION TO TAKE?
IF SO, WHICH ONE IS IT?"

It is imperative that new philosophies and new researchers explore the feasibility of deontological and moral disciplines.

CHAPTER 2

DEFINITIONS

For clarity of exposition, it is necessary to state the definitions of specific terms as they are used in this research. The first and most important inquiry is, "*What is philosophy?*"

Philosophy

1) *Philosophy is the holistic, critical and constantly intentionally objective "rethinking of the World."*[22]

Philosophy reexamines reality with an all-inclusive and non-sectorial method. What characterizes the philosopher is his/her search for a logical, critical, and scientific Grand Unified Theory of Everything. A theory, however, that refers and includes not only physics[23] but the entire human being in all its aspects, physical, biological, psychical and spiritual. Obviously, the philosopher must be aware that the conclusion of his/her research cannot be dogmatic. S/he must tend towards an objective outcome. S/he must always keep an open mind to the fact that the inquiry is never concluded. Like any science, philosophy is always in the making. It is enriched by the various new experiences and discoveries that s/he encounters. What may be certain today may be disproved tomorrow. And Philosophy will holistically incorporate the new finding/s.

The staggering multitude of scientific disciplines, each with numerous branches of specializations, constitutes a grave difficulty for the holistic aspect of philosophy. However, advancements in information-technology, artificial-intelligence, cybernetic, and genetic-engineering, can place human knowledge at *fingertip*. Through information technology easing data-processing, "the vast mass of computerized data will" and can improve holistic thinking.[24]

As long as there is a mind there is going to be the need for philosophy as an all-encompassing assessment. The mind works in a holistic, unified way. Different sectors of the brain may light up, depending on the types of experiential stimuli. Nevertheless, the brain remains one. The scientist that studies the physical phenomena is the same person that experiences joy, desire or pain. Therefore, we are made to rethink the world holistically. And the way we reevaluate the world is the way we act in it. Hence,

2)	***Philosophy rethinks Ethic.***

<u>*Ethic*</u>

3)	***Ethic is the scientific search for value.***

Etymologically, Ethics or Morals are synonyms. Both, the Greek *ethics* and the Latin *morals* mean "*customs, practices* or *habits.*"[25]

However, there are two different acceptances of Ethics:

1) Ethic as the behavioral *mean* to reach an absolute reality conceived as a *value*, a *good* and an *end* in itself;

and

2) Ethics as the behavioral *reasons* pursuing an object of desire conceived as a historical *value*.

This second acknowledgment cannot be accepted because does not refer to a value in-itself. Then again, denotes that which is dictated by the pursuit of a relative temporal desire. Therefore, it is not an absolute universal value.

<u>*Value*</u>

4)	***Value is the intrinsic worth of one thing over another.***

The concept of value implies a judgment, an assessment of something placed in relation with something else. In the field of ethic, therefore, a deontological scale determines that which is permissible or good as opposed to that which is not. An Absolute Value implies the foundation of all other values. Metaphorically, value is equated to a

> "*treasure in the that faileth not, where no thief approacheth, neither moth corrupteth.*"[26]

Then, the Absolute Transcendent Value

> *"is like unto treasure hid in a field; the which when a man hath found, he hideth, and for joy thereof goeth and selleth all that he hath, and buyeth that field.*
> *Again, the kingdom of heaven is like unto a merchant man, seeking goodly pearls:*
> *Who, when he had found one pearl of great price, went and sold all that he had, and bought it."*[27]

The Absolute Value implies the absence of any comparison or evaluation. Consequently, all other possible or relative *values-treasures* disappear before the Absolute One. Biblically, this distinction between absolute and relative corresponds to the *value-treasure* brought forth by

> *"a distinguished man out of the wellbeing treasure of his heart...* [and by] *a pain causing man out of the pain and trouble treasure of his heart...*[28]
> *For where your treasure is, there will your heart be also."*[29]

Independently from their etymological identity, we distinguish Ethic, as defined above, from Morals.

Morals

5) *Morals are the relative values of Ethic. They are the inevitable consequences of actions. Namely they are all the changing historical laws and norms directing and disciplining human behavior*.

Physical and social laws determine the inevitable consequences of actions. They are distinguished in,

a) Physical laws, which are relative to their natural dimension/s, and
b) Moral laws, which are relative to their historical society/s.

However, both sets of laws and their inevitable consequences are relative only to their physical and/or social dimension/s regulated by those laws. As a result, morals turn out to be dependent and contingent, not absolute settings. Therefore,

6) *Morals become the movers of History.*

The Ethical Science must be universal. Nevertheless, morals with their norms are only relative to different cultural historical societies and geographical locations. They cannot have an absolute fundamental universal validity. Namely, they cannot enforce one behavior over another, except for strictly contingent, temporal and transitory reasons. In that, what may be lawful for a historical time or society may be unlawful for another.

For example, in the nineteen-fifties, divorce, was unlawful in Italy while lawful in the USA. Adultery, in some parts of the world, was/is punished with stoning, as

"*Moses commanded in the law,*"[30]

while it was perfectly legitimate among the Canela people of Brazil.[31]

Is there a universal law sanctioned by an absolute righteousness? German Philosopher Emmanuel Kant declares, "There is therefore but one categorical imperative, namely, this: 'Act always on such a maxim as thou canst at the same time will to be a universal law.'"[32] However, what makes this maxim an absolute imperative? This norm does not go too far from the fundamentally *egotistic* principle of the *golden rule*, with the addition "of a philosophical pedantry," as Schopenhauer states.[33]

The present book researches the possibility of an apodictic, self-evident, unselfish, free, universal, ethical principle. If discovered, such value cannot depend on the will of an individual, of a ruler or even of a political majority. On the contrary, if that value exists, it must be the foundation of the Will in absolute. In addition, if that norm is proven real, it must be independent from the individual acceptance or rejection of it. More so, what are the implications of actions willed in accordance or in conflict with it?

During our research, we should bear in mind that, in order to be a Real Value valid for everyone, Ethic must be Universal and Absolute. Therefore, It cannot be:

I) *DOGMATIC*.

It cannot derive from metaphysical sources, namely God, Soul and/or Nature.[34] These three ideas are affirmed by dogmas, which think and state them without demonstration. They are neither apodictic, nor self-evident and they are not unquestionably verified. They are simple thoughts, ideas (*εἶδος eidos*) that refer to a Transcendent, which, by definition is unknown. Nevertheless, it is believed to be known. Those thoughts become idolatrized [*εἴδωλον eidōlon (eidos)*][35] as having an objective existence. Since that objectivity can be accepted or negated, therefore, those ideas are not absolute. Moreover, those ideas cannot dictate universal laws.

II) *HEDONISTIC*.

It cannot be hedonistic or pleasure seeking, in which case it would contradict its universality. In fact, that which may be pleasurable for one could be disagreeable for another.

III) *RELATIVE*.

It cannot be relative to a place or a historical time. In that case it would contradict its absolute universal aspect.

IV) *THE GOLDEN-RULE*.

It cannot be the generic norm,

> "*Do to others what you would have them do to you,*"[36] or
> "*Do not do to others what you do not want done to yourself.*"[37]

The rule cannot be ascribed to all. In fact, not always one's own wish can be universally shared, as we will see in our second part.

V) *UTILITARIAN*.

Utilitarianism is not universal. It serves only non-universal personal or group interests.

Furthermore, a Universal Ethical Value must be:

VI) *ABSOLUTE*.

It must be a Value-in-Itself, independent from anything external to that Value itself.

VII) *FREE*.

Ethical value must imply absolute freedom. No ethical value can be recognized where free will is coerced, or where there is a compelling intrinsic ineluctable necessity.

Liberty

"The science of morality is above all a Science of Liberty, namely a science of the I."[38]

7)	***Liberty coincides with the autonomous, innate, pure, permanent state of the Self-in-Itself.***

The Self-in-Itself can be thought as an object but cannot be known as the thinking subject itself. We can almost say that the knower, identifying with the known object, *forgets* its own self. Thought cannot reach the thinker of its own thoughts. The best we can do is to think it as *thought-subject* thinking itself as a *thought-subject* object-of-thought. If the subject would reach itself, it would become its own object, never the subject as such. Nothing can touch it or know it. In one word it is Transcendent. In itself, it goes beyond the subject-object correlation. Yet, that subject in-itself, is always referred to. It is implied, it is the ultimate thinker, which must be completely autonomous. The ultimate perceiver is *there*. It remains a noumenon, thought but unknown. Nonetheless, it is uncaused, self-sufficient, self-ruling, independent, and sovereign. In one word, it is free. It is the subject in-itself. It is liberty itself.

On the other side, the subject-for-itself, apart from its individualized life as an Ego, the subject, the *I-think* is universal and permanent. Metaphorically, we can say it is the "once king and future king."[39] It always belonged, belongs and will belong to all sentient, conscious and living beings.

Metaphorically, *before the fall*, logically, before the I subject, as such, confronts the objective world,

> "*the Transcendent Lord God planted a garden eastward in Eden.*"[40]

As U-topia, *No-place*, the Garden is a metaphor for *Delight*, Eden. It symbolizes the place of the subject-in-itself. No sorrow can be there. It is the Pure-Delight (*eden*) of the Present-Awareness. It is the Present as *Eden*-Delight. There, in that realm, what is good? What is evil? How can one state that good or evil exist if they are not known? How could they be seen if eyes are shot? There, as declared by the *Bṛhadāraṇyaka*

Upanishad, good and evil are not.[41] Only when the subject, the knower *ate* the fruit of knowledge, then

"*the eyes... were opened.*"[42]

Namely, the *consciousness-of* the world *saw* and *knew* the object. The subject becomes the knower for-itself. Then, good and evil took the shape of time flowing towards death[43] and humans become

"*like gods.*"[44]

Morals have an epistemic foundation. Kant stated that "thinking therefore is the same as judging."[45] He meant that any representation or thought is a classification. Therefore, it is a judgment. It is a definition stating or judging the existence and/or non-existence, quality and/or nature of the object.

The same underlining concept is present in the Biblical metaphoric

"*tree of knowledge of good and evil.*"[46]

The expression "*good and evil*" in this context stands for "*everything.*" Thus, it is *knowledge* in general. It denotes the epistemic dichotomy of this world of opposites, when we enter the field of time and space. Thus, it describes the gnoseological process of thinking or distinguishing *this* from *that* or judging *good from evil.*

Teaching in the temple, Jesus tells the congregation,

"*You judge and think*[47] *following the duality of the senses,*"[48]

while, on the contrary,

"*I am the light of awareness...*[49] *the light of life.*"[50]

In Eden, there is another metaphoric tree,

"*the tree of life also in the midst of the garden.*"[51]

This tree is projected internally towards the inner reality, while the tree of knowledge is projected externally, towards the objective world deemed existent.[52] Obviously, being life itself, that one must likewise be the foundation of the tree of knowledge, which could not flourish without life. However, what is life?

Life

We can define life from three different perspectives, α) objective, β) subjective and γ) spiritual.

8) *Physics and Biology are the objective perspectives of life.*

α) Objectively is the general way in which physics and biology look at nature's life.

I) Physics uses mathematics as the language that describes and predicts nature's behavior. The various branches of this science, including quantum physics, agree in discovering universal laws that have a reality independent from the scientist.

Physics investigates the laws of nature[53] as entities separated from the researcher. Four fundamental forces are discovered in the Universe. The Strong Force holds the atom's nucleus together. The Electromagnetic Force holds atoms and molecules together. The Gravity Force joins two masses along their center line. Finally, the Weak Force acts between quarks and between leptons, which are elementary building particles of matter.

II) Biology studies life as opposed to physics and minerals. Consequently, it studies the different organisms by classifying, identifying and naming them.[54]

Biology is the complex study, analysis and understanding of life's characteristics as matter organized in hierarchical levels. It starts with DNA (Deoxyribo-Nucleic-Acid) storing long-term information for molecules, which come together as cells. Cells are the smallest units of life. Millions of them form the tissue that transmits signals and electrical impulses to other cells. Many tissues together form organs, which working collectively, shape organ systems. In turn they form organisms, which are able to eat, gather materials, and work, producing energy. These organisms are homeostatic; they remain fundamentally the same while responding to stimuli. During the reproductive cycle, organisms transmit DNA hereditary information as chemical reactions (metabolism) to new cells. Finally, organisms grow, develop and adapt to the environment according to the natural selection of the evolutionary process.

What makes the primordial amoeba evolve into fish? What makes this one move to dry land? Evolution goes from the Big Bang to the present, from quantum particles to astronomical bodies, from plants to animals and from these to Homo sapiens.[55] The evolutionary process proceeds as if being promulgated by an internal blind-will directed by its incessant adaptability within its own environment. Obsolete forms change into other ones more apt to the circumstances. This is not a process of will or thought, as we understand it. Nevertheless, it is only the mind that has intelligence of it. The whole Universe is like a fetus growing with and within a blind aim to reach its own personal affirmation. Namely, until it stands-firm on its own stability.

Life is the seed. Life is the fetus. Those are the most original states from and in which limbs and organs grow on their own accord. In the flora and fauna kingdom some plants and animals retain that capability of spontaneously regrow themselves. That is because life is the living body itself. Nevertheless, the moment knowledge as thinking process steps in, we become alienated from our own body. As thought, we suffer our body. Thought tries to gain control of the living body. Nonetheless, the alienation persists. The best thought can do is to look at the body's life as physiology, namely studying its physio-bio-chemical functions or intervene invasively. That is the objectivizing quality of thought, which desires life, but is incapable of truly *live life*.

It is easy to argue that these written words are still thoughts. However, this is thought that recognizes its true paternity. It is starting to surrender to its Father-Awareness. Yoga-postures (*āsana*),[56] martial-arts, physiotherapy and Olympic-sports in general are actions that release the mind. It is what the athletes sometime call *second wind*. It is the reconnection with the original desireless spontaneity of life. It is the Buddhist state midway between self-mortification and passionate indulging in the senses. It is the Garden of Eden achieved in the state of Aware-dreamless-sleep.

9)	***Psychology is the subjective perspective of life.***

β) Subjectively, life is intentionality, is consciousness-*of* itself as life.

Without consciousness, the physical-biological-objective aspect of life would be non-existent for the scientist. The whole living being manifests intentionality as a will to experience.[57] Intentionality is the epistemic direction towards the object. It is the willful stream of consciousness directed toward the apprehension of the object of knowledge. The knower assimilates and comprehends the object as a reality established in-itself. Subjectivity manifests itself as Will directed towards the apprehension of the external world.

Will

10) *Intentionality is Will itself.*

Agni, the Indian god of fire, represents, metaphorically, the will (*kratu*)[58] as the wise-bard's-power (*kavíkratu*),[59] the psyche's flight driving and guiding action. Re-echoing from within their own wills, it inspires humans

> "*From you, o Divine fire, derive prophetic inspirations, from you spring thoughts and from you come propitiating hymns.*"[60] "*Indeed, this entire world is the Supreme Transcendent Spirit. All this is produced by That, is breathing in That, and it is absorbed in That. Thus, in peace one should meditate upon It. For verily, a person is made of intention. As is the intention in this world, such is a person and one becomes such after death. Let one shape the intention.*"[61]
> "*For as he thinketh in his heart, so is he.*"[62]

Intentionality is the will; it searches for its origin, its own self. The moment it refers to the other than itself it becomes consciousness-*of* and loses its goal. Then it becomes desire. Recognizing its origin the Will becomes Self-Realization and Liberations.

Medical doctor and scientist Robert Lanza called *Biocentrism* a theory of everything centralizing around biological forces. "Life creates the universe," he states, "not the other way around." In fact, "reality is a process that involves our consciousness."[63]

Kant had declared that space and time are "*a-priori* forms of the external and internal mind-sense intuition."[64] Similarly, Lanza writes, "Space and time are not absolute realities but rather tools of the human... mind... Our external and internal perceptions... cannot be separated from one another... The behavior of subatomic particles... is inextricably linked to the presence of an observer... Without consciousness, 'matter' dwells in an undetermined state of possibility... [No] physical event occur independent of life."[65]

Both the subjective and objective aspects are realities for-itself.

11) Being-for-itself is the continuous *immanent* circular reference of a *subject* to its correlated inseparable *object*.

Reality in-itself is the spiritual aspect of life.

12) Being-in-itself is the absolute independent center of the *immanent* circle set apart from the inseparable *subject-object* circular correlation.

Beyond life and beyond psychology, there is a component which is different from the two preceding ones, namely spirituality.

Life is that mysterious force which, for nine months, made our fetus grow. Science calls it *life*, as an objective reality separated from us. Life is not an external reality that rides us.

We are life.

Life is that perennial fountain which still sustains us and quenches our thirst. Ultimately, life is our supreme bosom reality, our utmost intimate self from which we have lost aware connection. If we truly reconnect with it in full awareness, as we were when growing as a fetus, then, we would regain control of that spring of eternal youth, as

"*a well of water springing up into everlasting life.*"[66]

13) *Transcendence is the spiritual perspective of*

life conceived but not known beyond the subject-object correlation.

γ) Spiritually, life in-itself is the ineffable heart, as the center of the true and certain knowledge. We all know we are alive. We do not need to think of it to know it. We are certain of experiencing it. Life is self-transparent. It is the experience of life itself. However, we cannot really grasp it in itself. Whatever we understand of it is different from its lived aspect. We can only live it. Like a phallic-tree, Life is the power[67] that unites the earth merging it with the sky. Life is the present Awareness, the ineffable transcendent element without which we or physics, or biology and or psychology would not be. Therefore, what is the meaning of life? There is no meaning, replies Campbell, "The mind has to do with meaning. What's the meaning of a flower?... There's no meaning. What's the meaning of the universe? What's the meaning of a flea? It's just there. That's it. And your own meaning is that you're there. We're so engaged in doing things to achieve purposes of outer value that we forget that the inner value, the rapture that is associated with being alive, is what it's all about."[68]

14) *Life is the actuality of Apodictic-Aware-Certitude.*

CHAPTER 3

AWARENESS AS TRANSCENDENCE[69]

The ancient sacred Indian literature (*Vedas*, *Brāhmaṇas* and *Upanishads*)[70] was considered to have been revealed, heard (*śrúti*) and realized by seers during deep introspective meditation (*yoga*). The *Bṛhadāraṇyaka*, one of the oldest *Upanishads*, states,

"*You cannot see the seer of seeing,*
hear the hearer of hearing,
think the thinker of thinking,
nor understand the understander of understanding.
This is your Self, which is in everything.
Apart from this [there is] *evil-suffering.*"[71]

Nevertheless,

"*They who know the life of life and eye of the eye and the ear of the ear, the mind of the mind have realized the ancient primordial transcendent.*"[72]

There are two polarities in the way knowledge or the epistemic process works,

1) On one side there is this subject, this ego here that writes and reads. This subject perceives the world *for-itself*, from its perspective or point of view.
2) On the other side, there is the object, the world as it is perceived by the subject (1). How this world is *in-itself*, namely without the subject, without being known, we do not know and will never know.

Like a two heads Janus,[73] this subject, this ego, looks at this world before us and its own self both as objects. In other words, it cannot catch itself as subject. Therefore it can never know itself as knower. We can see our image in the mirror only as an image *never* as the one who is mirroring. Like king Midas' golden touch, like Medusa's petrifying gaze, the subject transforms everything in objects.

However, if we silence our mind, namely if we suspend our thinking process, we find a transparent mode, where

"*one becomes like water* [and] *who sees* [is aware] *without duality.*"[74]

In that state, there is a certitude that has nothing to do with thought. We do not need to think of our-self to be certain that we are presently here as Self-in-Itself. The I "does not need to think of thinking... because... it is present to itself without the need of mediating itself, that is, to see itself before itself as an object of its own knowledge."[75] Namely, we do not need the mediation of the subject. Of course, *now* that we mentioned it, we are thinking of it, but before we thought of it our awareness was still here in a non-thinking, intuitive mode. The fact that we can refer to an *in-Itself* or a *Transcendent*, as that which goes beyond the immanent subject-object synthetic correlation, proves the persistence of its echo in the epistemic process.

Tolle offers us an interesting test, "Close your eyes and say to yourself: 'I wonder what my next thought is going to be.' Then become very alert and wait for the next thought. Be like a cat watching a mouse hole. What thought is going to come out of the mouse hole? ... As long as you are in a state of intense presence, you are free of thought. You are still, yet highly alert. The instant your conscious attention sinks below a certain level, thought rushes in. the mental noise returns; the stillness is lost. You are back in time."[76]

> Jesus, teaching in the temple, said,
> "*You cannot tell whence I come, and whither I go...*[77]
> *You neither know me* [as Awareness], *nor my Father* [as Transcendent-Self]*: if you had known me, you should have known my Father also...*[78]
> *You think*[79] *according to the craving senses;*[80]
> *I think-of nothing...*[81]
> *And yet if I think, my thinking is Pure-Awareness:*"[82]

Because

> "*I am the universal*[83] *light-of-awareness:*[84] *he that followeth me shall not walk in darkness, but shall have the light of life...*[85]
> *For I am not alone, but I and the Father*
> [the Transcendent-Self] *that sent me...*[86]
> *are one.*"[87]

The Self-in-Itself is Truth-Itself.

Awareness is Life, Light and Truth

The Gospel of John portrays Jesus as he who identifies completely with the One-Universal-Self-Awareness and not with the many-consciousness-*of* the world or with the objects-of-thought.[88] Whosoever identifies with the object of knowledge

"*is the servant of*"[89]

the object, says Jesus.

"*And the servant abideth not in the house* [of the Self-in-Itself] *forever:* [but] *the Son abideth ever* [in Awareness]...
If the Son [*i.e.* Awareness] *therefore shall make you free, you shall be free indeed.*"[90]
"*When he shall appear, we shall be like him; for we shall see him as he is.*"[91]

Therefore, this One-Self is not many. However, many can identify (*avatāra*) with It. It is the only One in all. One is the Self who shines in everyone. "Many are the figures, particularly in the social and mythological contexts of the Orient, who represents this ultimate state of anonymous presence," says Campbell.[92] In other words, the identification is with the Intuitive-One-Universal-Apodictical-Self-Awareness which is Now our True-Self and not with the many historical-egos.

Only Self-Aware-Ceritude is Now.

The historical-ego is dead. It is not Now any longer because it is projected in the knowledge of that which is the past as such. The ego is the one who is here and at this time writing or reading. On the contrary, the Self is the presence of the Transcendent in all historical egos, without which the ego itself would and could not be known. However, the Transcendent-Self does not exist because only that which belongs to the consciousness-*of* is placed into existence. When conceived the Self-in-Itself is non-existent. It is the Zero, the Transcendent-Emptiness (*śūnyátā*) from Which all comes and all goes.

"*In the beginning, there was* (*āsīt*) *no non-being* (*n-āsad*) *nor there was being* (*sád*),"

declares the *Ṛg Veda.*[93]

"*Then said Jesus again unto them, I go my way, and you shall seek me, and shall die having*

missed your mark:[94] *whither I go, you cannot come...*[95]
If a human keeps my saying, s/he shall never taste of death...[96]
For if you are not in that certainty that I am [into], *you shall die having missed your mark...*[97]
You are from beneath, in the temporal succession; I am from above time: you are [identified with the consciousness-] *of this world; I am not* [identified with the consciousness-] *of this world."*[98]

The Self-in-Itself is unknown. However, even if not known, we realize It as this undeniable Apodictic-Awareness we have right Now. Awareness is the only true witness.

"*I am One that bear witness of Myself, and the Father that sent me beareth witness of me."*[99]

Who can deny the certainty we have of this writing or even of the dream we had last night. We may doubt the reality in-itself (*i.e:* without the dreamer) of the oneiric world, but never of having the dream as fantasy. Awareness is always the foundation of everything including doubt as awareness of disbelief. Nevertheless, Awareness is always Certitude-of-Awareness.

Inscribed on the ancient Greek temple of the god Phoebus-Apollo, in Delphi at Mount Parnassus, is his oracle, which declared:

KNOW THYSELF[100]

"*and you shall know the truth, and the truth shall make you free."*[101]

However, the *Īśa Upanishad* states,

"*The mouth of truth is covered with a golden dish, bringer of prosperity remove it so I, who am devoted to the laws of Truth, may behold it."*[102]

Nevertheless, Jesus reiterates,

"*But seek you first the* [Transcendent] *kingdom of The Transcendent, and his righteousness; and all these things shall be added unto you."*[103]

It must be clear that *righteousness* is Awareness. Everything, in fact, is right in the light of Pure Awareness. In the presence of Awareness' light, even *injustice* is illuminated, *i.e.: judged*, as such, without any condemnation,

"*and yet if I judge/think, my judgment/thinking is true.*"[104]

The Buddhist tradition describes *righteousness* as the eight-fold middle-path, which is equidistant between the two extremes of austerity and sensual delight. It alone dissolves all desires and extinguishes all sorrows. The Buddhist eight fold path, *Right-View, Right-Intention, Right-Speech, Right-Action, Right-Livelihood, Right-Effort, Right-Mindfulness, Right-Concentration*[105] are similar to the three Jain jewels of *Right*-View, *Right*-Realization and *Right*-Disposition.[106] Their *righteousness* is given by their constant identification with Self-Awareness, which is focused upon during all of those activities.

The ultimate perceiver is the Self-in-Itself. It is Awareness, Intuition which cannot be perceived. It is Ineffable and Unknown Transcendent. Nevertheless, *through It, in It and with It* we see, hear, think, understand and experience the objective changing world (*jágat*).

"*Jagat (world) means ceaseless movement, and obviously there can be no rest in movement,*"

declares Ānandamayī Mā.[107] Jung states that, "western consciousness is by no means the only kind of consciousness there is: it is historically conditioned and geographically limited, and representative of only one part of mankind."[108]

Transcendence is the Kantian noumenon,[109] which can be thought but never known. In fact, Transcendent is that which is conceived as being beyond the subject-object correlation.

"*You must learn to realize the subject and object as one. In meditating on an object, whether concrete or abstract, you are destroying the sense of oneness and creating duality. Meditate on what you are in Reality. Try to realize that the body is not you, the emotions are not you, the intellect is not you. When all these are still you will find... It will reveal itself. Hold on to that,*"[110]

teaches Ramana Maharshi. Therefore, when Transcendent is thought as such, it is not transcendent but exists only as an immanent concept.

In the Hindu iconography, the Transcendent is represented as god Gaṇeśa, a massive obese elephant-headed man with one-tusk.[111] He rides a mouse (*mush-aka*). Therefore, the quickness of the rat becomes the swift disappearance of the Transcendent Gaṇeśa when it is conceived and thought. Furthermore, the word *mush-aka* means also thief. This gives meaning to the Biblical expression,

> "*the day of the Lord so cometh as a thief in the night.*"[112]

Transcendent falls between the subject-object correlation. Therefore, any affirmation stating the existence of the Transcendent is a dogmatic declaration asserting that which has been defined as unknowable. It may turn out to be a *dogma* (δόγμα). A dogma, in essence, is a tenet, an opinion corresponding to illusion, ignorance (*á-vidyā*)[113] and non-reality. It imposes a belief that, by definition, cannot be experientially or immanently proven. In fact, if it could be known or proven, it would not be a dogma any longer.

On the other hand, if that which was originally presented as a dogma is made true (*satyá*), its dogmatic formulation would be understood only as a metaphor. It would be the admission (*abhyupagama*) of an actually ineffable state universally realizable. It would be, as St. John of the Cross metaphorically calls it, a true and a "*very tasty science.*"[114] Then, the dogma, as a metaphor, becomes the coherent philosophical substratum (*adhikaraṇa*) of a truth received (*siddhānta*) through a specific doctrine (*pratitantram*) or through a philosophical system (*sárvatantra*).[115]

> "*I speak to the world those things which I have heard of him* [the Transcendent],"[116]

said Jesus. He is Awareness present to itself as Certitude.

> "*Then said Jesus unto them, When you have exalted the Son of man, then shall you know that I am* [the Transcendent], *and* [that] *I do nothing of myself; but as my Transcendent Father hath taught me, I speak these things.*"[117]

Similarly, the *Kaṭha Upanishad*[118] describes Naciketa, as the Son of Desirous-man (Uśan). As Jesus, he is the Unknown[119] (*Naciketa*) lifted and realized above all worldly attachments and after all desires (*uśan*) or intentionality have been suppressed.

And Jesus continued,

> "*He that sent me is with me: the Father* [the Self-in-Itself] *hath not left me alone; for I* [who am Its

> Awareness] *do always those things that please him."*[120]

This is a metaphoric expression indicating how Awareness shines in truth and certainty without any attachment. He continues,

> *I know that ... my word hath no place in you... I speak that which I have seen with my Father* [*i.e.:* the Self-in-Itself]*: and you do that which you have seen with your father* [*i.e.:* the objective world]... *You abode not in the truth, because there is no truth in him."*[121]

He is talking to persons whose mind-thought does not want to let go its own thinking process. Nonetheless, the objective world has no ultimate reality in-itself.

Padre Pio

Analyzing the writing of mystics, we find precise descriptions of achievements of a transcendent state beyond the subject-object correlation.

One of such descriptions can be found in the epistolary of the Capuchin monk Padre Pio of Pietrelcina (1887–1968). In a letter dated April 18, 1912 to his spiritual father Agostino da San Marco in Lamis, he writes that while praying,

"*Jesus' heart and mine, if you allow the expression, fused. They were not any longer two pulsating hearts, but only one. My heart disappeared, like a drop of water is lost in the sea."*[122]

Similarly, the *Kaṭha Upanishad* declares,

> "*As pure water poured into pure* [water]
> *becomes the same one, in like manner*
> *becomes the self of the sage*
> *who has the right contemplation."*[123]

The yogic practice of subjugation or re-absorption (*pratyāhāra*) prescribes that the senses should withdraw from the external objects.[124]

Likewise, Saint Pio describes his way of praying,

"*All the internal and external senses, together with the same faculties of the soul*[125] *find themselves in an indescribable stillness. In all this there was a total silence around me and within me; immediately replaced by a great peace and abandonment to the complete deprivation of everything and one laying in the same ruin. All this took place in a flash."*[126]

On November 1, 1913, he continues his description, "*The ordinary manner of my oration is this. As soon as I start to pray, immediately I feel that the soul starts concentrating in a peace and tranquility that cannot be expressed in words. The senses remain suspended, except for hearing, which sometimes is not suspended; however, ordinarily this sense does not bother me, and I must confess that even if around me there were very loud noise, it would not molest me at all. The thought that at any moment I may lose Jesus gives me an anguish that I cannot explain; only the soul that sincerely loves Jesus can know it. Jesus told me,* ['] *how many times, my son, you would have abandoned me, if I had not crucified you.*[127] *Under the cross, one learns to love and I do not give the cross to everybody, but only to those who are dearest to me*[']. *Here, I would want that my mind would not think of other but Jesus, but I realize that often it gets lost! From my side, I would not deny myself to anyone. And how could I, if the Lord himself wants it and nothing that I ask him he denies me? I want to tell you that I willingly sacrifice myself hoping that I may one day in this mortal life sing as the prophet: 'Lord finally you have broken my bounds and I for this reason will offer you a sacrifice of praises for eternity. AMEN! ALLELUIA!'*"[128]

Saint Pio continues,

"*I am all of everyone. Everyone can say: 'Father Pio is mine.' I love very much my brother in exile. I love my spiritual sons as much as my own soul and much more. I have regenerated them to Jesus in pain and in love. I can forget myself, but not my spiritual sons, on the contrary, I assure that when the Lord will call me, I will tell him: 'Lord I stay at paradise's door; I enter when I saw entering the last of my sons.*"[129]

This last approach is similar to the Buddhist *bodhisattva*. S/he is the being full of enlightenment[130] who, on the threshold of final liberation, renounces that deliverance in order to help the entire Cosmos achieve salvation.[131] As we see, mystics of different religions, recounting their spiritual achievements, describe the identical circumstances, occurrences and methods. Awareness is at the root of these realizations. And Awareness is the World's Foundation.

"Quid est veritas?"

"What is truth?"[132]
Pilate, in his ignorance, rhetorically asked Jesus. The Nazarene stated,

> *"I... came... into the world, that I should bear witness unto the truth. Every one that is of the truth heareth my voice."*[133]

That truth, that voice is the same Apodictical-Awareness with which Jesus identifies. All the world's avatars are one with It. Actually they are that Aware-Bliss.

Ramana Maharshi

The Hindu mystic and saint, Sri Bhagavan Ramana Maharshi (1879-1950),[134] was considered a real, true and perfect teacher (*sadguru*) with
"steady abidance in the Self, looking at all with an equal eye, unshakable courage at all times, in all places and circumstances."[135]

> ***BG IX.22 "I bring shelter to those beings that are absorbed in me having no other one and to those who always worship me yoked in permanent devotion."***[136]

Bhagavan, from the moment of his awaken enlightenment on July 17, 1896, lived in a continuous identification with the state of Apodictic-Self-Awareness. He proclaims that
"After negating all of the above mentioned [world] *as 'not this', 'not this',*[137] *that Awareness which alone remains — that I am."*[138]

In Awareness, "he was 'perpetually absorbed, whatever he did, whatever he read, walked, spoke, or rested.'"[139] He stated,
"there is neither... desire, nor change in me... There was nothing which I wanted to obtain. I am now sitting with my eyes open. I was then sitting with my eyes closed. That was all the difference... The fact is I did nothing. Some Higher Power took hold of me and I was entirely in Its hands."
At times, during his uninterrupted state of Self-Awareness, his respiration would stop, his body would become cold and a state

similar to death followed. It seemed he was completely unconscious of his body. He remained in that internal absorption for the rest of his life.

Yet, [recounts Ramana,] *my usual current was continuing without a break in that state also.* [He continued,] *I had formerly some preferences and aversions. All these dropped off and food was swallowed with equal indifference."*[140]

However, confirmed Ānandamayī Mā,

"*Under all circumstances, it is imperative to remain wide awake* [i.e.: aware]*; unconsciousness* [i.e.: non-awareness] *must be strictly avoided."*[141]

This is what is implied in the Biblical injunction,

> "*As you desire to breathe, long after thy Transcendent Certain-True Transcendent with all thine heart, and with all thy soul, and with all thy might."*[142]

On applying this instruction, what room is left for any world attachment?

The ascetic *saṃnyāsin, sādhu* or *śramaṇa,* the religious mendicant monk identifies with Self Awareness and rejects all caste distinction.

> "*This great unborn Self... does not become greater by means of good action nor, indeed, smaller by means of bad ones. This One is the Lord of all... One becomes an ascetic by being conscious of This One. Verily, striving to obtain this dimension, the religious mendicants leave home and wonder forth as eremites. Verily then, the sages of old, being well aware of this, truly did not desire any offspring. And they thought: 'Why should we build a family? Therefore, isn't this Self our own dimension here?' Then, indeed, having turned away from the desire for a son, the desire for wealth, and the desire for worldly affairs, they then walk the path of begging. Verily indeed, the desire for a son is the desire for wealth and the desire for wealth is the desire for worldly affairs. Verily, both these are only desires and the Self is not this, not this. It is incomprehensible because It cannot be comprehended. It is imperishable because It cannot be destroyed. It is unattached*

> *because It does not attach himself. It is unbound, never agitated in the mind, and never harmed. Furthermore, the following two thoughts: 'Certainly, for this reason I have done evil,' or 'certainly, for this reason I have done that which is good,' do not overpower the one who has realized the Self. Indeed, It also overcomes them both and, that, which It has done or not, does not torment him."*[143]

The fundamental message of Jesus is the same,

> "*Every one that hath forsaken houses, or brethren, or sisters, or father, or mother, or wife, or children, or lands, for my name's sake, shall receive a hundredfold, and shall inherit life."*[144]

And, with a stronger accent,

> "*If any man come to me, and hate not his father, and mother, and wife, and children, and brethren, and sisters, yea, and his own life also, he cannot be my disciple...*[145] *He that hateth his life in this world shall keep it unto life eternal."* [146]

In fact, as reported by Shantidas, Ramana Maharshi said,

"*a family is simply a meeting of travelers. You know that it is sinful to become attached and to pour oneself out, and quite vain to flood our near ones with our affection.*"

Furthermore, Ramana continues,

"*When a man cannot learn the truth through wisdom, he has to be taught by suffering."*[147]

Therefore, how can we convey this lifestyle to the merchants' caste, whose aim is to *pursue happiness*?

Śaṅkara

Śaṅkara, the IX century Indian philosopher and mystic, describes the epistemic process as having two moments,

a) superimposition and
b) confutation.[148]

Superimposition

Superimposition is a mistaken judgment deemed correct. If, in darkness, we misidentify a rope for a venomous serpent, we will react fearfully to it. Fear will remain until, with proper lighting, we realize that it was only a rope. While perceiving the rope as a snake, our experience was that of a real serpent. In fact, we were superimposing the memory we have of the coiling animal on the rope.

Confutation

Confutation is the realization of the wrong assessed superimposition. A closer look at that apparent snake confutes the error and makes us perceive the reality of the rope. Both experiences, the serpent and the cord, were real. Only that the first one was a superimposition of a separate previously experienced snake on the present rope. Therefore, the quality of a serpent was attributed to the cord. When we superimpose the memory of an earlier different occurrence on a present one, we incur in an erroneous conclusion. Only the confutation of the incorrect superimposition can lead us to the right judgment.[149]

The Real of the Real

Experiences superimpose on each other and each one remains valid until confuted and negated by the new one. Like dreams followed by wakefulness, each experience is valid and truthful knowledge until the next one arises confuting the first one. Nevertheless, at the end of this uninterrupted epistemic chain lies that Reality which cannot be additionally confuted and which will constitute the foundation of all superimpositions. That is

"*The Real of the Real*"[150]

namely the Awareness, as intuitive certitude, on which all superimpositions are superimposed.

Real is not confutable Certitude
and Certitude is Real.

Certitude

Apodictic Intuitive Certain Awareness always accompanies every experience. In fact, we are certain of dreams or hallucinations as such. In other words, *certainty* is the same either in the presence of the consciousness-*of* any object, real and/or dreamt, or in the presence of consciousness-*of* a scientific experiment or a mathematical equation. If we abstract the certitude from the object or from the scientific/mathematical test, the certitude is absolutely constant and identical in all cases. What changes is the reference to the reality or illusion of the object in-itself, namely without that certitude-awareness. The certainty within the consciousness-*of* an event never changes. Even when we wake up and realize the non-reality of the dream, nevertheless, we are *certain* of having had a dream. As the sun light is not affected by the object on which it shines, while the object cannot be seen without the light it emanates. As the power fueling a computer is not affected by what we input in it, although we cannot input anything without turning the power on. Similarly, *Certainty*, present in the consciousness-*of* the object, is never affected by the object itself, whereas we can never know it without the experience's certitude. It is Certitude that confers intentioned transcendence to the object. It is because of this Apodicticity that we declare the world real in itself. However, of that reality in-itself, namely without our Awareness, we have no certitude. To use a biblical expression,

"*The Transcendent saw*"[151]

His creation. That seeing is Certitude, which creates the World. Without It, *creation* would not be.

> "*And The Transcendent said, 'Let us make persons in our image, after our likeness: and let them have conscious dominion... over all the earth.' In his* [own] *image The Transcendent created persons ... the male* [aspect of consciousness] *and the female* [aspect of intentionality].
> *And The Transcendent with Certain-Awareness saw that everything he had made* [was] *very good.*"[152]

Consciousness

"The mind [is] conscious-of its own rightfulness", says Virgil. The Latin word "con*scious*" means, "I know with," *i.e.:* the object. It is connected with the word "*sc*ience." In this sense, we refer to consciousness always as *consciousness-of* or *with* something. Therefore, as a reflection of something that we re*sc*ind, we separate from something else.[153] Consequently, we are conscious-*of* something that is conceived - but not known - as different, *viz.* transcending, or other than our own consciousness-*of* it.

Consciousness-*of* is *knowledge.*

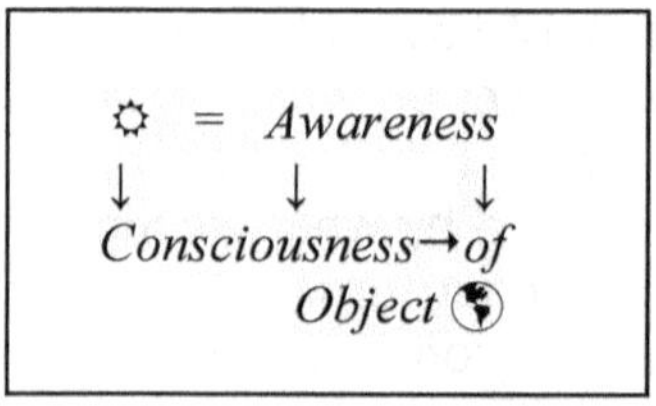

It is the outcome of the epistemic subject-object correlation, when the world is known discursively or intuitively as object *for*-the-subject. What the world is in-itself, apart from the subject, is utterly unknown. However, the objective world in-itself is understood and perceived grounded *in*-transcendence not-*as*-transcendent. We see the wall or the post **out-there**, **not-*as*** out-there. That is, we have the firm belief that the world is out there independent from our perception of it. The world becomes a new god (*theos*) and *atheist* may request the authority of a physicist to deliver the eulogy at funerals. In fact, we believe that the world survives us. Therefore, we take life insurances and write wills. But we will never see if and how that money will be used by our heirs. We have no evidence of it. The fact that others die and the world continues is not proof enough, since we are still here. The answer will be when we too are gone. Let it be clear, we are not stating that the world in-itself is an illusion. We are saying that we do not know anything without our subjective presence.

Wakefulness and sleep

Consciousness articulates on different levels. When awake, we are conscious-*of* the waking-state. When dreaming, we are conscious-*of* the dream-world. In the waking state, the dream state becomes subconscious. However, from the point of view of consciousness, during the dream state the waking state becomes subconscious, while the dream becomes conscious.

Freud explains, "If somebody refers to the Subconscious, I don't know whether he is alluding to it as a *stratum*, that is, something dwelling in the soul beneath the Conscious, or whether he is referring to it as a *quality*, that is, another consciousness, a subterranean one, so to say. To be sure, the greatest probability seems to be that anybody juggling such terms is himself not at all sure of what he really means. The only permissible differentiation is one between Conscious and Unconscious."[154]

Subconscious

Here we use the term Subconscious in both ways. Namely, "it is a stratum" in the sense that when it dwells "beneath the Conscious" of the waking state it is called "*dream*" and when it dwells "beneath the Conscious" of the dream state it is called "*wakefulness*." At the same time, "it has a quality," in that it "is another consciousness," it is now the waking one and now the dreaming one. Consciousness is always consciousness-*of* something that qualifies consciousness itself. At times, in wakefulness, we are conscious of a state called wakefulness, and, in dream, we are conscious of a state called dream. However, in each state the other becomes subconscious.

One consciousness is that present in the waking dimension and the other is that present in the dreaming dimension. Naturally, at this moment, we are analyzing this from the waking consciousness. In addition, each dimension has its own time/space reference different from the other. Therefore, we cannot classify as Unconscious that which, on a different level, becomes conscious during the inevitable process of the "circadian rhythms,"[155] the sleep-cycle that

"*keeps returning again and again to its origin.*"[156]

Consciousness, during the waking state, is not conscious of the dreaming world, which, however, does not disappear in unconsciousness but persist in another dimension that conditions subconsciously the waking state. On the other side, consciousness, during the dreaming state, is not conscious of the waking world, which, however, does not disappear in unconsciousness but persist in another dimension that conditions subconsciously the dreaming state.

The two dimensions are connected to each other through the consciousness of one becoming the subconscious for the other and vice versa. The confusion arises when we are reluctant to confer consciousness to the oneiric state. If the "differentiation is [only] one between Conscious and Unconscious," as stated by Freud, then we must realize that we are not examining the consciousness of the dream dimension, without which we would not be able to remember dreams. In dreams, we have a subconscious memory of the waking world. Between the Conscious and the Unconscious lies the Subconscious as foundation of both dream and waking representations.

Psychology analyzes only half of the human being. Namely, it analyzes the human only from the perspective of the waking state looking at the dream without *living* it. Even when it examines the dream state, it studies it from the waking point of view. A psychological analysis from the other half of our life, that is, from the dream side, is unconceivable for the waking state. Psychology, from the unique standpoint of the dream state, would consider the unchanging rules and limiting laws of the waking state as self-depriving conditions. In them, the *psyche masochistically loves* to confine itself in objective ineluctable laws, contrasting with the dreams' *freedom* of unlimited fantastic possibilities. These ones, as an example, make me defy gravity and make me fly. As a result, from a dreaming perspective, the waking state is not conscious. Rather, it is sub-conscious, while the dream state as such is the conscious one.

From a waking perspective, the dream state is subconscious, while the waking state itself is conscious. From the stand point of any waking or dreaming ($R_{apid}E_{yes}M_{ovement}$) condition, each one views the others as sub-conscious. According to Hobson,[157] "in REM sleep in utero and in early life," there is a "protoconsciousness, a primordial state of brain organization that is a building block for... primary consciousness." This one, "in our dreams... emphasizes perception and emotions at the expense of reason." In turn, this last one, activates a "secondary consciousness," the waking "subjective ... perception and emotion... enriched by abstract analysis (thinking) and metacognitive components of consciousness," the consciousness of consciousness.

Super-conscious

Consciousness, in its purity, namely, apart from its being consciousness-*of*-the-waking or consciousness-*of*-the-oneiric state, becomes Super-consciousness, which implies that it is *consciousness-as-such*, irrespective of being the conscious moment of the waking world or the conscious moment of the dream world. This is the moment in which both consciousness are conscious-*of* consciousness as consciousness-*of*-experiential-representation; it is the thought-that-thinks-itself-as-thought, it is the 'I-think' that thinks itself as 'I-think,' which Kant calls "*apperception.*" In fact, he states, "The 'I think' must accompany all my representations, for otherwise something would be represented in me which could not be thought; in other words, the representation would either be impossible, or at least be, in relation to me, nothing... 'I think,' is an act of *spontaneity*; that is to say, it cannot be regarded as belonging to mere sensibility. I call it pure apperception... because it is self-consciousness... accompanying all our representations."[158]

At this level, we use the term Super-consciousness not "*in an absolute sense... but only* [as] *a higher conscient, something that is conscious to itself and only superconscious to our own limited level of awareness.*"[159]

Nevertheless, Apodictic-Awareness, the Real of the Real is beyond the "*superconscient status in which consciousness seems to be luminously involved in being as if unaware of itself,*"[160] without any thought involvement and beyond Unconsciousness.

Awareness
↓
Un-conscious
↓
Super-conscious
↓
Conscious-of-representations

Un-conscious

Super-consciousness, Consciousness and Sub-consciousness, all spring out from an original Unconsciousness.

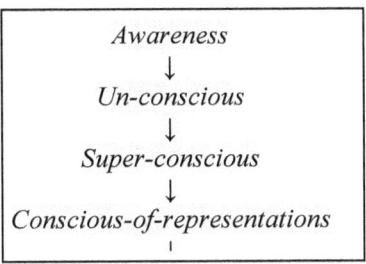

Unconscious is the third stage, the one of deep sleep (N_{on}REM) with no dreams (REM).[161]

The *Bṛhadāraṇyaka Upanishad* states that in the unconscious state one

"does not see, smell, taste, hear, think and know, except that, while not seeing, smelling, tasting, speaking, hearing, thinking and knowing, one is still the seer, smeller, taster, speaker, hearer, thinker and knower. In fact, the seen, smelled, tasted, spoken, heard, thought and known does not separate from the seer, smeller, taster, speaker, hearer, thinker and knower, because it is imperishable. Merely, in that state, there is no otherness and nothing else that one may see, smell, taste, speak, hear, think and know."[162]

The *Māṇḍūkya Upanishad* describes three quadrants, or different stages of consciousness, namely, wakefulness, dream$_{(REM)}$ and dreamless sleep$_{(NREM)}$. In order, they are indicated with the three letters A U M. The first two quadrants (AU) are analogous. They are characterized by the correlation of a subject, the knower/dreamer, and an object, the known/dreamt. The third quadrant (M) is not discursive. The subject and the object are fused in an intuitive synthesis.

> *"Deep-unconscious-sleep is the third quadrant, where one is asleep and does not desire any desire and does not see any dream.*[163] *The state of deep-unconscious-sleep*[164] *stands alone, having become one compact knowledge, made of bliss. Indeed, it is the enjoyer of bliss. It is the source of consciousness and the knower."*[165]

> *Death or unconsciousness for one is living consciousness for somebody else.*

Unconscious is that which we are not thinking-*of* at this moment, which, however, is somehow *unified* and *stored* as a compact flash of intuition. Unconscious is the consciousness of someone else who we believe is conscious of its own thoughts. It seems as if people are "interconnected as their computers… can't help imitating others… similar to spreading germs"[166] among each others. One's death is our consciousness while we are alive. In fact, there would be no unconsciousness or death, as such, if not present to the living Awareness. The existential tragedy takes place when the limitless Awareness is identified with this finite mind of this body, confining the infinite possibilities of consciousness.

The task, throughout all the three stages, wakefulness, dream and dreamless-sleep, is to identify always with Awareness. Also in the moment of unconsciousness, Awareness is present awakening the intuitive moment which is not consciously discursive, therefore is defined non-conscious. Namely it is unconscious to the consciousness-*of*. Even in the state of deep cataleptic sleep, Awareness abides in the not-objectified stillness of complete ineffability and in its transcendent pure bliss without duality. Actually, in that state Awareness is truly so, in that it distinguishes itself from consciousness, which is still connected to the perceived object.

In the Biblical mythological rendering, the limitlessness of Awareness is defined as the depth of the Celestial Waters[167] separated from the lower ones, *viz.* the potentially infinite possibility of the consciousness-*of* the objective world. Therefore,

> "*the Breath of The Transcendent moved... and divided the waters* [as consciousness-*of* the infinite possibilities] *which* [were] *under the firmament from the waters* [as the Infinite-Awareness] *which* [were] *above the firmament.*"[168]

Similarly, the sacred tradition of India states that in the logical beginning there was Emptiness (*śūnyatā*), in the sense of nothing that can be conceived or that can be said. In fact,

> "*Then, there was neither non-being nor there was being... There...were Celestial Waters (ámbhas) of inscrutable depth* [Pure Awareness]*...*
> *By self-power that One-Thing* [Pure Consciousness] *was breathing windless...*
> *In the beginning there was darkness covered by darkness. All this was only an indiscriminate flowing flood (salilá)* [consciousness-*of*]. *By the great power of the sacrificial heat was generated*

that One-Thing, which was hidden in emptiness."[169]

"And the earth was without form, and void;"

declares the *Bible*,

"and darkness [was] upon the face of the deep. And the Spirit of The Transcendent moved upon the face of the waters."[170]

From that nothingness, springs out the Unconscious, says the *Bṛhadāraṇyaka Upanishad*, and calls it Death, Mṛtyu the Creator. He is Hunger, as Desire, which Freud would have described as "an untiring impulsion towards further perfection."[171]

" Verily, nothing at all, was here in the beginning? Indeed, all this was concealed by Death, by Hunger, because hunger is death. Then, he projected the mind: 'Let me be a being for itself.'"[172]

"'Come... come... follow me! You will help me come back to life. I am hungry for existence,' uttered the specter" of death to the living being.[173]

Śūnyátā in Sanskrit means nothingness. It is the Transcendence empty-non-existence. It is the vacuity of the absence-of-mind (*śūnyá*). It is the extinguishment (*nirvāṇa*) of thought as such. It is the absolute void that ensues when the fire of life blows out. Then, the annihilating extinction (*nirvāṇa-śūnya*)[174] results in the disappearance of any virtual individual existence. "Individuals are not stable things, they are fleeting. Chromosomes too are shuffled into oblivion, like hands of cards soon after they are dealt. But the cards themselves survive the shuffling. The cards are the genes. The genes are not destroyed by crossing-over, they merely change partners and march on. "[175] Those who passed away are gone forever. Even if there is resurrection or reincarnation, the regenerated individuals would never be the same individuals as they were. For one, each would have a completely new body, which would be entirely different from the original. If not, any deformities would be preserved for eternity. However, the dead person vanishes forever. That eternal disappearing is the metaphorical hell, the eternal damnation of the individual as such. My Lord, St. Francis of Assisi prays,

"*Blessed are those who* [death] *will find*
in your holiest will,
because the second death will not harm them."[176]

The prenatal and postmortem state is the only reality. It is Heidegger's "being-for-death."[177] That nothingness which precedes birth and follows death is the persistent condition. That is the timeless *era* enveloping and nullifying any validity of-this-world-in-itself. The consciousness-*of*-this-world becomes only a virtual drop of unreality in this ocean of *śūnyátā*. The whole consciousness-*of*-the-world is only a smidge forever lost and melted in that depth.

The Ethic we are searching is the undeniable scientific Truth apodictically present in the detached Awareness, as in undeniable mathematical equations such as 0=0 or 1=1. In that Ethical realm nothingness or *śūnyátā* becomes the perfect calm, the repose or happiness, the highest bliss or the beatitude present in the Apodictical-Self-Awareness beyond life, death or immortality.

"And it is sweet for me to shipwreck in this sea,"
writes Leopardi.[178]

If we look at the Universe as being-in-itself, then we realize that the same nothingness referred to the individual is also true on astronomical scale. The ageless *eons*, figuratively *preceding* the Big Bang and the endless *ages*, imaginatively *following* universal Higgs boson[179] effects, or reabsorptions, or entropies, underscore the original and final zeroness (*śūnyátā*) of the Universe. There it is evident the ultimate illusory nature of all worldly phenomena.

Awareness

After the three quadrants indicated by the letter-sounds AUM, there is a fourth all-encompassing stage indicated by a dot (·). It is an echo sound. That is the silence from which those three come from and to which they go.[180] It is Transcendent Awareness.

The word "*awareness*," derives from the Proto-Germanic or Old English word meaning *collective-on-guard-vigilance (ge-wær).*[181] *While "consciousness-of,"* as such, requires always an object of consciousness to which connect. *"Awareness,"* by itself, is the *flavor* (Latin, sapere-sapor), the sapient-savor that does not require an object to taste or eat.

> "*Ye are the salt of the earth, but if the salt have lost his savour, wherewith shall it be salted?*"[182]

In fact, Awareness is the intuitive, apodictic and power-full foundation on which consciousness itself is founded before it directs its attention towards the world.

Awareness is the building block or the pylon from which the bridge[183] of consciousness departs to reach the other bank of knowledge.

> "*Wherefore also it is contained in the scripture,*[184] *Behold, I lay in Sion a chief corner stone, elect, precious: and he that is certain on him shall not be confounded.*"[185]
>
> "*Ye are the light of the world... men light a candle, and put it ... on a candlestick; and it giveth light unto all that are in the house... Let your light so shine before men... , and glorify your Father which is in heaven.*"[186]

Awareness is not an epistemic moment in-itself. It is the foundation of it.

Awareness is the continuous present intuitive certitude, *realized* beyond the subject-object correlation and beyond good and evil. It is never subject or object. It is neither in-itself nor for itself. It is neither being nor non-being.

The French Philosopher René Descartes, sought to "distinguish Truth from Error." He resolved "to strip... of all past beliefs."[187] He writes, in his *Discourse on Method*, "I ought to reject as absolutely false all opinions in regard to which I could suppose the least ground for doubt, in order to ascertain whether after that there remained aught in my belief that was wholly indubitable. Accordingly, seeing that our senses sometimes deceive us, I was willing to suppose that there existed nothing really such as they presented to us... I supposed that all the objects (presentations) that had entered into my mind

Dreams are always certain, but they are real only until we awake.

when awake, had in them no more truth than the illusions of my dreams. But immediately upon this I observed that, whilst I thus wished to think that all was false, it was absolutely necessary that I, who thus thought, should be somewhat; and as I observed that this truth *I think, hence I am,*[188] was *so certain and of such evidence,*[189] that no ground of doubt, however extravagant, could be alleged by the Sceptics capable of shaking it, I concluded that I might, without scruple, accept it as the first principle of the Philosophy of which I was in search."[190]

When we analyze, with closer attention, Descartes words, immediately we realize that there is an *indubitable certitude* that *precedes* thought, the *cogito,* which too quickly was listed as "*first principle.*" That certitude is the intuition, the Awareness that we have while experiencing and thinking an object. This Certitude comes before we question the reality of the object in-itself. In other words, the experience, whether *physical, abstract, imagined* or *dreamed,* comes ushered by Awareness itself as such. Namely, Certitude enlightens all and every experience before we enquire-*of* them.

Only after awareness, we seek the fallacy of the experience. That is, we inquire about its transcendent correspondence or coherence. Namely, we search for the presence or the absence of an objective reality in itself conceived beyond the I-and-the-world or the subject-and-the-object immanent relationship. In this sense, we must understand the Buddha's earth-touching,[191] when he calls the earth as witness of his awakening.[192] That is, the object, the world is the testimony that presupposes, testifies and follows Awareness. Similarly, we can attempt to read Paul's affirmation,

> "*The invisible things of him from the creation of the world are clearly seen, being understood by the things that are made.*"[193]

Therefore, the world requires and testifies Awareness as its foundation without which it would not be. "A Pawnee Indian said: 'In the beginning of all things, wisdom and knowledge were with the animal. For Tirawa, the One Above, did not speak directly to man. He sent certain animals to tell mankind that he showed himself through the beast. And that from them, and from the stars and the sun and the moon, man should learn.'"[194]

The "wonderful discovery"[195] of existence, in the formula *cogito ergo sum,* was a religious experience for René Descartes.

He perceived it as an epiphany, worthy of a thankful pilgrimage to the house of the Virgin Mary in Loreto, Italy.[196] We do not know if the philosopher ever took that journey. However, there is no doubt that the intuition of the *cogito* was, for him, a sort of metaphysical enlightenment. In fact, by his own admission, "He who says, '*I think, hence I am, or exist,*' does not deduce existence from thought by a syllogism, but, by a simple act of mental vision,"[197] therefore an intuition beyond discursive thought itself.

Nevertheless, what is existence? To exist means *to-stay-out-from* the subject. In other words, the object is extracted, trailed-out-from the subject.[198] Therefore, the subject understands the object as other-than-itself. However, one cannot be without the other. If the subject-knower is missing, there is no knowledge. Similarly, if the object-known is missing there is no subject either. Consequently, there is no knowledge.

However, the intuitive *cogito*, as such, is a *co-agit*ation of the thought with itself.[199] Therefore, it cannot be the source of Descartes' *certitude* of his existence. Indeed, when Descartes declares, "Now I know for *certain* that I am",[200] that certitude does not come from a thought. "*It is Absolute-Aware-Certain-Intuition*" and not a simple "*thought,*" as such, that makes the philosopher affirm, "*Thought is existent* ... and ... I *recognize* ... that I am."[201]

Descartes identified thought with Awareness. Nevertheless, it seems that also in the natural realm and at the cellular level in general, Awareness is ever-present. Contrary to a movie-camera, which only records the event without participation, Awareness may trigger a reaction of mechanical electrical impulses. As spontaneous tear drops, the plant may drip sap when cut. The animal in danger shows an alerted aware response, an *on-guard-vigilance (ge-wær)* that does not necessitate a thinking process to react to danger. "Every animal, even the smallest and lowest... shows clearly how very conscious they are."[202] All martial arts train to enhance those thoughtless moments as responses to an adversary's attack. Yoga itself quiets the mind to reach beyond the thinking process. Awareness is never thought. Thought is the outcome of Awareness. Awareness is Awareness, Intuitive Apodictical Self-Evident Certitude. Thought arises as consciousness-*of* the light of Awareness shone on the perceived objects. That luminescence bounces off them and is reflected back to a thinking subject. When thought confers only to the object the origin of that brightness, then the thought-object becomes *luciferic*, the carrier of light.[203] It becomes like the moon thought to produce its own light.

Awareness is This Certitude.

The Awareness we are referring-to is not the awareness that we are describing with these words, this conceptual presentations of Awareness. They turn out to be a

> "*witness of the Light* [of Awareness], *that all* [men] *through* [it] *might be sure...* [consciousness-*of* is] *not that Light, but* [is meant] *to bear witness of that Light... the true Light, which lighteth every man that cometh ito the world.*"[204]

Biblically, that witnessing was identified with John the Baptist. He identifies with the consciousness-*of*, characteristic of the theological-religious rethinking of Transcendence. Nevertheless, Certain-Awareness remains the basis for theology, philosophy, science, religion and these words. The foundation of the entire world rests on the Awareness we have here and now.

> "*In the beginning The Transcendent created the heaven and the earth... And The Transcendent named the dry* [land] *Earth ... and saw that* [it was] *good.*"[205]

How can we *name* or *see* anything, if the Awareness of the *named* one or the *seen* one is not logically *pre-sent* a-priori? By Awareness, we do not mean the consciousness-*of*-something. Instead, we intend, the Intuitive Apodictic Certitude, as such, which, besides being the foundation of the consciousness-*of*-something, is also the ground-stand of both the subconscious and unconscious. In other words, that founding Awareness is present

A) in the waking stage,

U) during the Rapid Eye Movement (REM) of the dream state, and

M) in the state of deep sleep with no dreams and No Rapid Eye Movement (NREM).

The *Koran* states, that since men

> "*cannot encompass Him* [Allah] *with their knowledge,*"[206]

the children of Israel

"said: 'O Moses, set up for us a god even as they have gods!' He replied: 'Verily, you are people without any awareness!'"[207]

In fact, if we conceive God we must ascribe to It necessarily Awareness. And His Awareness must be conceived as the Supreme and Absolute Awareness, of which we all partake.

"Remembrance of Allah is indeed the greatest [thing you may do]. *And Allah knows all that you do."*[208]

The *Bṛhadāraṇyaka Upanishad* reports that, during the fire-oblation-ritual (*agnihotra*), a conversation took place between sage Yājñavalkya-the-Sacrifice-Speaker and Janaka-the-Progenitor, king of Videha-the-Incorporeal. The Supreme Ruler, symbolizing the 'I,' the a-priori subject logically distinct from its object, questions the source of the light of consciousness.

"Indeed... Sacrifice-Speaker ... came to the King Progenitor of the Incorporeal... for a fire-oblation. The supreme ruler politely asked him.
'O Sacrifice-Speaker, which one is the real light of a person?'
He answered,
'Truthfully, one has the light of the sun, o Supreme Ruler. Indeed, due to the sun, one has light and one stays, moves, performs work and then returns.'
The king replied,
'You are so right, o Sacrifice-Speaker. However, o Sacrifice-Speaker, when the sun has set, which one is the real light of a person?'
He answered,
'The moon, verily, is one's light. Indeed, due to the moon, one has light and one stays, moves, performs work and then returns.'
The king replied,
'You are so right, o Sacrifice-Speaker. However, o Sacrifice-Speaker, when the sun has set and the moon has set, which one is the real light of a person?'
He answered,

'Fire, verily, is one's light. Indeed, due to fire, one has light and one stays, moves, performs work and then returns.'
The king replied,
'You are so right, o Sacrifice-Speaker. However, o Sacrifice-Speaker, when the sun has set and the moon has set and fire is extinguished, which one is the real light of a person?'
He answered,
'The word-idea, verily, is one's light. Indeed, due to the word-idea, one has light and one stays, moves, performs work and then returns. For that reason, o Supreme Ruler, also if one's hand is not seen, when the word-idea is uttered, still one may intend it.'
The king replied,
'You are so right, o Sacrifice-Speaker. However, o Sacrifice-Speaker, when the sun has set, and the moon has set, the fire is extinguished and the word-idea has quieted down, which one is the real light of a person?'
He answered,
'The Self is one's light. Indeed, due to the Self, this one has the light of intelligence, exists, and perceives, acts and returns.'
'Then,' the king asked,
'Which one is the Self?'
Sacrifice-Speaker replied,
'This person, who is composed of knowledge among the vital senses, is the light within the heart. Being serenely centered in itself, It penetrates both worlds [of wakefulness and dream] *as if It were thinking and moving back and forth. Upon entering the dream state, It goes beyond this dimension and the forms of death... It sleeps dreaming by his own light by his own brightness. In this state, the person becomes self-illuminated...*
Being Supreme Brahman-Awareness one goes to Brahman-Awareness...

> *When all desires, which are fastened in one's heart, are shed, then, the mortal becomes immortal. In this manner one reaches the Supreme* [Aware] *Spirit.'"*[209]

> "*Then spake Jesus again unto them* [who were congregated], *saying, I am the light of the world: he that followeth me shall not walk in darkness, but shall have the light of life.*"[210]

The *New Testament* refers to Self-Awareness-in-Itself as

"*Light* [that] *shineth in darkness.*"

That obscurity is the obfuscation of the Self in-Itself, which

"*the darkness comprehended it not.*"[211]

To the question, "*Who am I?*" Ramana Maharshi answered,

"*The gross body which is composed of the... five cognitive sense organs ... I am not... even the mind which thinks, I am not; the nescience too, which is endowed only with the residual impressions of objects, and in which there are no objects and no functions, I am not... After negating all of the above mentioned... that* ***Awareness*** *which alone remains —* ***that I am.***"[212]

From the burning bush, The Transcendent Awareness declares to Moses

> "*I AM THAT I AM.*"[213]

> "*I have come as light* [of Awareness] *into the world, so that everybody who is certain in me may not remain in darkness.*"[214]

From that Awareness derives Consciousness, and creation is consciousness that brings the world into light,

> "*And The Transcendent said, Let there be light: and there was light. And The Transcendent saw* the *light, that* [it was] *good understanding*[215] *... And The Transcendent saw*[216] *everything that he had made, and, behold,* [it was] *very good. And the evening and the morning were the sixth day.*"[217]

The day of creation is a circle that goes from darkness to light, the

"*evening and the morning were the... day.*"

Every one of the six days of creation is an epistemic circle of consciousness. The subject departs from the *darkness of the evening* to *perceive* and *see* the object in the *morning light* of consciousness when it returns again to the subject itself to declare it to be

> "*good understanding...* [218]
> *And on the seventh day The Transcendent ended his work which he had made; and he rested on the seventh day from all his work which he had made.*"[219]

Awareness, as such, is not conditioned by the existence of the object we are conscious-*of*.

Jesus affirms,

> "*As long as I am in the world, I am the light of the world.*"[220]

Awareness, in its precise capacity, is always universal and not individualized. However, individualization takes place in the moment that consciousness receives the reflection of its light shone upon an object. Then, perception identifies with that reflected thing. This is evident in the case of our mind identifying with itself and the body. Therefore, on one side we have Awareness persisting in its own transcendent Reality of reality, never leaving it. On the other side, it projects itself along the entire ladder of reality. The Renascence philosopher Giordano Bruno calls this universal projection the "*Divine Mind*."

The "*Divine Mind*," he declares,[221] "is able to perform all things, not only in the universal but also in the particular."[222]

> "*What woman having ten pieces of silver, if she lose one piece, doth not light a candle, and sweep the house, and seek diligently till she find* [it]?"[223]

The "*Divine Mind*" operates from within, as the universal soul of each natural being. It is always totally aware. Bruno, to emphasize[224] this concept, lists his own old relatives, acquaintances, animals and things. That awareness, he writes, is present from the "red lace of Paolino" Casoria, the Inn keeper, to the gown of tailor "Master Danese." It takes care, as well, of Don "Franzino's melon patch" and each fruit "from the jujube tree" of Filippo's father. It moves the "average size" bug of Costantino's bed. It recognizes each beetle, "born out of the dung" of Albenzio's ox. It also acknowledges the moles "in Antonio Faivano's garden," and each puppy of the bitch of his relative "Antonio Savolino." The "*Divine Mind*" does not forget each hair on the head of "Vasta, the wife of Albenzio," of the poor widow "Laurenza," or of Paolo Alemanno,[225] "Martiniello's son," and the molar of "the old woman of Fiurulo." Nor it overlooks Ambruoggio's semen, derived from "his affair with his wife."[226]

During the consciousness-*of* the world-objects, Awareness in-itself is set aside. We become the subject of our epistemic process and the object becomes a reality believed to be independent from that subject. Therefore, the subject is conceived as being *sub-jugated* to the ineluctability of an *external* world that, as Atlas,[227] it constantly bears on its shoulders.

Awareness puts the world into existence. Biblically, it is described as the

"*tree of life.*"[228]

Outside that Awareness, there can be no affirmation of existence. The realization of Awareness in its purity can transform a life forever. Upon his Enlightenment, on July 17, 1896, Ramana Maharshi declared,

"*some force... arose in me and took possession of me... took hold of me and I was entirely in Its hands.*"[229]

Awareness and mindfulness

Awareness is Timeless-Present Apodictical Certitude.

No awareness can take place outside the present. In fact, Awareness is synonym of Present. Awareness is always Now. Memory, as recollection of the past, has its foundation on the present. It may remember the past, but it is remembrance now of a past that is not any more. In one word is dead except for its living memory, which takes place only in the *now*. More so, Awareness is the foundation on which the entire world and all its memories unfold. The same can be said for the future. The mind projects *now* something that is not. However, that projection has a death-wish imbedded. In fact, the mind desires that projection to become past, an already given, a *done deal*, namely dead to the present. In fact, who wants to have his/her wishes granted in a future that never comes, never becomes past? Through an epistemic deformity, we understand only the past and as such we proceed towards death.

In the Universe, time has no direction. The Cosmos does not distinguish past from future. The World is here and the events are now. They are projections on the great screen of Physical Space. It is the consciousness-*of* the projected object that confers a space-time frame to the Universe, by putting its distant-moments in relation to one another. Thus, the consciousness-*of* the Cosmos conceives a time sequence interwoven with space. Relative to the observing point, the time of an object is measured in spatial distance. When we look at the Universe, we look at its past-present-future all at once. In fact, the grater the distance of a celestial body is from us, the further away it is in the past. And the Earth is directed towards that remote past as if towards its own future. In the present, Consciousness assesses *now* the possibility of an object, its ineluctable past and its inevitable future course.

Mindfulness is Being-Aware.

Therefore, Ethic is not a norm, it is being, namely is freedom.

Ethic is liberty.

Awareness is Autochthonous,

"*Self-Made.*".[230]

Awareness is Apodictical-Certitude. Mindfulness is its Being-Aware.

"And The Transcendent said, 'Let there be light:'
and there was light."[231]

There is Awareness, the Self-enlightening Being Aware. And that Awareness is Now. Metaphorically, the Bible describes Mindfulness as the non-consuming Burning-bush.

In that account, Moses, the one who was drawn out of the many waters of transitory things,[232]

"*kept the flock's multitude of his wealthy,*[233] *father in law,*[234] *priest of the troubled people:*[235] *and he led the flock*[236] *behind*[237] *the desert, and came to the mountain of The Transcendent,* [even] *to the desert."*[238]

Upon leaving behind the flock of the senses, one emerges from the many waters of the immanent world of subject-object correlation. Then, one finds itself in the transcendent high desert where there is no consciousness-*of* objectivity.

> *"And the angel of the LORD appeared unto him in a flashing point of spear of fire out of the midst of a bush: and he intently looked, and, behold, the bush burned with supernatural fire, and the bush* [was] *not consumed or devoured."*[239]

The *Vedas* declare,

> *"Agni-fire was born first from the Sky,"*[240]

thus, the fulgurating fire of Pure Awareness shines of its own accord. It does not turn towards the world to consume it epistemically. Thus, the bush or the world is not consumed or devoured by the fire of Certitude. On the contrary, all levels of realities, conscious, subconscious or unconscious, persist in their own dimensions. For each one, the guarantor of those realms is exactly that Certitude.

> *"And Moses said, I will now reject and turn away from it, and see this great sight, why the bush is not burnt."*[241]

Thoreau asks, "With all your science can you tell how it is, and whence it is, that light comes into the soul?"[242] When Moses rejects the direct connection with the fire and turns away from it to investigate on its origin, he is moving away from the source of everything. He is going back to the consciousness-*of* the world, where he had left his senses-flock. He is trying to conceptualize the Transcendent. However, by divine injunction,

> *"Thou shalt not take the name of the LORD thy The Transcendent in vain: for the LORD will not hold him guiltless that taketh his name in vain."*[243]

In fact, conceptualizing or naming the Transcendent-Awareness implies necessarily losing It by reducing It to a thought, namely to Its contrary, which is the immanent in the subject-object correlation.

> *"And when the LORD saw that he rejected and turned away to see* [and conceptualize and be conscious-*of* the origin of that fiery Awareness]*, The Transcendent called unto him out of the midst of the bush, and said, Moses, Moses. And he said, Here I* [am]*."*[244]

Moses identifies himself as this '*I*' here and at this time. To this the Transcendent

> "*said, Do not approach here: put off thy shoes from off thy feet, for the place whereon thou standest* [is] *the Sacred Transcendent.*"[245]

The '*I*,' as the subject *per-se*, has no stand on this ground. That '*I*' or Ego is the consciousness-*of* or the spirit-of-the-world. It is the principle of individuation, which animates the rational life of the body, the power of thinking, knowing, desiring, feeling and acting. This level is set apart; it transcends this cosmos. In fact,

> *Blessed* [are] *the poor in ego-spirit: for theirs is the kingdom of heaven...*
> *The pure in heart... shall see the Transcendent.*"[246]
> "*My kingdom is not of this world... my kingdom is Now, not from this cosmic place,*"[247]

declares Jesus. It is not the consciousness-*of* this world. His kingdom is Now, the Pure-Present-Apodictic-Awareness, not from the immanent subject-object consciousness-*of* this space-time dimension.

> "*Moreover he said, I* [am] *the Transcendent of thy father, the Transcendent of Abraham, the Transcendent of Isaac, and the Transcendent of Jacob. And Moses hid his face; for he was afraid to look upon the Transcendent.*"[248]

Moses changes his action. Before, he rejected the direct connection with the fire and turned away from it to investigate its cause. Now, he hides his face, because he

> "*cannot see the seer of seeing, hear the hearer of hearing, think the thinker of thinking, nor understand the understander of understanding.*
> [As] *It is your Self, which is in everything*"[249]

and everyone. It is the Eternal-Apodictical-Awareness.

In fact, when Moses asked for His name,[250]

> "*The Transcendent said unto Moses, I AM THAT I AM:*[251] *and he said, Thus shalt thou say unto the children of Israel, I AM hath sent me unto you.*"[252]

He is the '*I*' in-Itself. Then, Moses asks,

> "*Who* [am] *I*,"[253]

and The Transcendent states that he must realize that same *I-in-Itself* as the foundation of his own being.

> "*Because, certainly I am the Self-Evident proof, that I have sent thee: When thou hast brought forth the people out of Egypt.*"[254]

The Hebrew word *Mitsrayim, meaning* Egypt, besides its historical and geographical reference, also means siege, entrenchment, with the sense of limit, enclosure, to bind, besiege, and confine, to shut in, to be an adversary. Therefore, the deliverance from Egypt has here a wider metaphorical reference. It means escape from the world of suffering and enslavement. It means the liberation from the subjugation within the subject-object death enclosure, which derives from the fruit of the tree of knowledge distinct from the divine source of the tree of life.

Following, the foretold metaphor of the Burning-bush, we can distinguish two moments or a double act, Awareness and Mindfulness. Each one implies the other as two sides of the same medal.

1) The first one, named *I AM THAT I AM*, is the Apodictic-Awareness standing firm in *the midst of the bush*. It is the center of the circumference. Awareness is the immutable Eternal-Present-Center, the Timeless-Zero. The Present is not realized in daily occurrence because it is timeless. There is no present in the past or in the future and, when we try to catch it in the present, it is impalpable. The mind, in fact, catches the object as already given, never in the fulguration of the Present. When we think of the now it is already past. Therefore, the Present remains elusive and timeless. Awareness is the unmovable hub of the wheel. On its rim, subject and object travel chasing each other in a time sequence. Awareness is in the World but it is not-*of* the world.[255]
2) The second action is the metaphoric Burning-bush. Namely it is the Being-of-Awareness or Mindfulness.

    > "*In the beginning* [declares the *Ṛg Veda*] *there was darkness covered by darkness* [*the evening of the day*].[256]
    > *All this* [Awareness] *was only an indiscriminate flowing flood. By the great power of the sacrificial heat*[257] *was*

> *generated* [Mindfulness,] *that One-Thing, which was hidden in emptiness* [the Zero of Awareness]."[258]

That One-Thing is Mindfulness. All events are imprinted on the background of Awareness, like film-projections on a movie screen or icons on computer wallpaper. However, those imprints are not in a time sequence, but in the Ever-present-Awareness. In fact, Awareness is always in the Timeless-Present.

> "*Therefore whatsoever you have spoken in darkness shall be heard in the light; and that which you have spoken in the ear in closets shall be proclaimed upon the housetops.*"[259]

In fact, nothing can escape the now. If we time-travel to the Ides (15th) of March, 44 BC in Rome, the assassination of Julius Caesar would be experienced as a given contemporary event. All events are co-eternally present. All events are preserved because they take place only in the present, namely in a non-time. This preservation of data is similar to the holographic principle information encoded on the black hole's surface.[260] Mindfulness is the stillness, which, while containing all the possible objects, does not change and is not qualified nor is taken by them. It does not engage with the object of knowledge. Mindfulness contains the World but it is not-mindful-*of* the world. It is the fire that does not consume the bush. It is what Lao Tzu calls the

"*action without action.*"[261]

We must realize that the above description is completely inadequate to express Awareness and Mindfulness. In fact, it reduces their transcendence becoming a thought, an immanent concept. Only metaphors, like the Biblical Burning-bush, remain the most adequate expressions to convey transcendent references like Awareness and Mindfulness.

Consciousness-of the world

We have seen that Awareness and Being-Mindfulness are not *of* the World and do not *consume* or *devour* the object. Thus, the question: "How does the transition from Mindfulness to consciousness-*of* the world take place?" Where does consciousness-*of* the world spring out from?

Some ancient sacred texts of India have addressed these issues. The oldest one, the *Ṛg Veda* declares,

> "*Then, there was neither non-being nor there was being... Then, there was neither death nor immortality. Nor there was knowledge of night or day. By self-power that One-Thing* [Mindfulness] *was breathing windless.*[262] *Thus, indeed no other seed*[263] *was beyond it, none whatsoever.*"[264]

What was there before the origin of time? No one can state what was *then*, except in negative terms. What was there before the Big Bang or before you were born? You can imagine a realm that predates the Universe or your birth. However, to imagine it or to think of it, you must be born. Without that event, no one can state anything. *Then*, what is there before the idea? Nothing precedes thought as such. There is Light. There is Joy. There is Love. There is Awareness.[265] Beyond being and non-being, there, from that Vast Ocean of Pure Nothingness, surfaces the the 'I,' as the Fire Agni.

> "*In the beginning desire sprung about. Consequently, that desire, that intentionality* (*kāma*) *was the original flowing seed of the mind.*"[266]

It is desire or intentionality as will that generates the mind. It is a tension, a hunger that evolves in a mind capable of having consciousness-*of* the objective World by burning it, consuming it and digesting it. The event of creation, related by another sacred text of India, the *Bṛhadāraṇyaka Upanishad*, describes desire as hunger, the creative forces of Death. Those are "essentially passive ... unknown and uncontrollable forces" by which "we are *lived*" and to which Freud gives "the name of Id."[267]

> "*Verily, nothing at all, was here in the beginning? Indeed, all this was concealed by Death* (also as the god of love-lust), *by Hunger, because hunger is death. Then, he* [Death-Hunger-Desire] *projected the mind: 'Let me be a being for-itself.'*"[268]

This is the same Biblical myth of the tree of knowledge, but with a different metaphor. There, after satisfying their hunger with the forbidden fruit, the original couple's

> "*eyes were opened, and they knew*"

and consequently were subject to death.[269] In that Indian myth, Death creates a mind, which, eventually,

"*set free started thinking.*"[270]

Moses turned "*away from*" the Burning-bush to see and rationalize that great event. Similarly, Death projects a mind (*mánas*)[271] hungry for knowledge that wants to conceptualize its own origin, namely the Transcendent. Nevertheless, the mind cannot accomplish the task and ends in continuous cycles of consciousness. From the subject it flows to the object only to come back to the subject once more. The mind becomes conscious-*of* the World contained in the Present-Mindfulness. However, the mind is conscious-*of* the object as the light of Awareness reflects on it. The object becomes the mirror reflecting the light of Awareness. However, Awareness can never be a known object except as reference, which obviously is not Awareness. Therefore,

> "*the stone which the builders* [the knowers] *rejected, the same is become the head of the corner,*"[272]

namely Awareness.

> "*And Jesus said unto them, I am* [Awareness] *the bread of life: he that cometh to me shall never hunger; and he that is certain in me shall never thirst.*"[273]

"*The one obstacle is the mind*; [proclaims Ramana Maharshi,] *it must be got over whether in the home or in the forest.*"[274]

Destiny

Biologically, our life is predestined *now* in our DNA. "Our future is indelibly written in our genes."[275] Since the Present is the ineluctable reality of what it is, how can it be different from what it is? Change this *now* if you can. Ramana Maharshi wrote, "*The Ordainer controls the fate of souls in accordance with their prārabdhakarma,*[276] [which *concerns only the out-turned, not the in-turned mind.*[277] *Whatever is destined not to happen, will not happen, try as you may. Whatever is destined to happen will happen, do what you may to prevent it. This is certain. The best course, therefore, is to remain silent.*"[278]
Similarly, Ānandamayī Mā stated,

"*All that occurs, good or bad, - if it was predestined to happen – comes about through the mysterious working together of certain forces... Whatever happens was destined to happen.*"[279]

Here, destiny does not refer to something that must happen in the future. In fact, the future does not exist. It has to do with the present. In reality, we should not even speak of destiny as the inevitable necessity for the occurrence of some event, yet to take place. We must realize the inevitability of what is *now* present to awareness. That is destiny. That is accepting the event in the eternity of the present, which no one can change. If we want to ascribe future events to the choices we make today, then we must consider what makes us select one thing in place of another. We are our intrinsic physiological nature and our sociocultural environment. Nature, in its evolutionary process, forces us one way or the other. How can the male buck not choose the female doe during the rut season?[280] Who we are compels us to choose how and what we choose. What is opted-for now is the only selection we have. That because it is what we end-up choosing now, after all. What we remember now or we do now affect our past as well as the future because it *changes* the present in the way we understand it. Furthermore, when we remember a specific choice, we realize that the memory of that decision cannot change because we remember it as such now. It is "useless crying over spilled milk," says the old proverb. Therefore it is meaningless to regret a choice as *if we could have chosen differently*. That *'if'* holds a hypothetical conditional of the third type, it is unreal, it belongs to another time, another quantum possibility, another dimension and another universe. Moreover, choices lead always to other choices without ever reaching the Transcendent Awareness that we are really seeking for.

As a consequence, cause and effect do not proceed only from the past to the present or to the future, as common acceptance dictates. The *Now* shapes the past events in the same way the current memory of history affects our present. Whatever is viewed as past is shaped by the way we view and think of it now. If we were to have another dream, it would constitute the history of another consciousness*-of*, which is usually regarded as the other person. Anything we do is projection towards that past, which we call future. Manipulation of the past, of the already given in front of us, is the work for death in the past and for the past. In fact, one of Jesus'

> "*disciples said unto him, 'Lord, suffer me first to go and bury my father.'*
>
> "*Jesus said... 'Follow me; and let the dead bury their dead.*[281]

From this perspective, death, as *passing-away*, is only in the mind, is a thought not elaborated by the brain-body. It is never decease of Awareness as such. Nonetheless, the dead-past yearns for reincarnation. What we do now is the cause of past lives or, better said, of another consciousness-*of.* It is the illusory flowing-metempsychosis (*saṃ-sāra*) from one set of possibilities to another set of possibilities. It is the transmigration of the consciousness-*of* this objective world to other objective reality. It is the directionless flow (√*sṛ*) with (*sam*) the consciousness-*of* objects facing the Eternal Present. Our deeds now affect unconditionally the past and the future in the perpetual current Awareness.

> "*Indeed, the subtle self, together with its deeds, is fastened to that which the mind is attached,*"[282]

declares the *Bṛhadāraṇyaka Upanishad.* And

> "*as thou hast believed,* [so] *be it done unto thee,*"[283]

states Jesus.

CHAPTER 3

RELIGION

Institutionalized religions are born out of the need to quantify and objectify the Apodictical Certitude. The realization of that Awareness may be lived as an initiation. That insight leads to historicize religions in Temporal Personalities. These, then, becomes the charismatic figures of dogmatic structures, which obfuscates the original Realization itself. Thus, religions are born. The term religion means to establish a *re-ligament*, a renewed-tie with a metaphysical belief held as true in-itself.

> **Religion is the dogmatic bondage to a creed. It is only a vehicle tending towards the ineffable Transcendent Awareness.**

Apodicticity, conversion and fundamentalism

> *The certitude of awareness is referred to the object.*

A *glimpse* of Awareness' apodicticity, during an unexplained event or some kind of intuition, may account for religious conversions and, possibly, for generating fundamentalism. In other words, there is a drive and a need of the mind to objectify and codify, with a conceptual religious formulation or a creed or a dogma, the Apodictic Certitude that may have *glimpsed* in an intuitive moment. This is what is called Conversion, Surrender, Faith, Acceptance, Redemption, Rebirth, Initiation, Enlightenment, Realization, Nirvana, Ecstasy and Trance.

At times, a glimpse of the light of Pure Awareness may shine in a mind conscious-*of* an intuition. This glimpse may be the product of a scientific research, a mathematical calculation, a logical analysis or simply of an experience of any kind. As we have seen, this was the case of Rene Descartes.

On occasion, the mind, abstracting from the object, may have intuited the fundamental certitude within the experience. In every experience, the certitude of Awareness is the same. As far as Awareness goes, the correct outcome of a mathematical calculation and/or the experience of a hallucination are both the same. No one can deny witnessing an event. We may question what the perceived observation is, but we can never doubt that experience as an experience. That is certain.

Like in the example of the serpent and the rope, the untrained mind may erroneously superimpose an erroneous judgment on the Certitude of an experience. Therefore, it confers Apodicticity and truth to the erroneous judgment. In turn, corroborated by the certainty, this error is conceptualized as a dogma in order to understand objectively that original *glimpse* of Certitude. That conceptualization, then, becomes a creed. Consequently, the mind acting in a *luciferous-mode*, as a mirror surface reflects back to itself that original luminosity of Awareness. In sequence, the mind dogmatically acknowledges that reflection as having the characteristics of certitude now referred by the mind to the fabricated dogma and asserted by mere blind belief. In other words, Pure Awareness shines on a thought. The mind, centered only in the thinking process, becomes conscious-*of* the luminous thought reflecting the light of Awareness. However, is not conscious-*of* Awareness because that One is obfuscated by the thought itself. The mind, mesmerized by thought, ignores Awareness that *certifies* and *sees* that idea. The idea, then, is conceived as being transcendent and self-luminous. It becomes a deified idol.[284] Therefore, it develops into a dogma.

That dogma becomes the reason for mind closures and intolerant behaviors towards any new idea that contradicts it. Atrocities, committed in the name of religious dogmas against those who do not subscribe to them, find justification in the eyes of fundamentalists.

Pope Urban II in 1095 at Clermont (France) authorized thew massacres perpetrated by the First Crusade crying out "God wills it!"[285] Another Pope, Innocent III, called a crusade (1209–1255) against the Cathars, Christian *heretics*. Cardinal Inquisitor and Jesuit theologian Robert Bellarmine[286] condemned in 1600 Giordano Bruno to be burnt at the stake for heresy. His guilt was that of having sustained, among other things, "*The infinity of the Universe and the Worlds.*"[287] In 1633, the Holy Office[288] and Saint Bellarmine, the same who condemned Bruno, imprisoned Galileo Galilei, for having scientifically demonstrated the truth of heliocentrism. To this day, that same fundamentalist spirit accounts for and justifies in God's name atrocities, murders and deaths of innocents.[289]

Let it be clear, only that which falls between the subject-object correlation can be said to exist. In fact, how can we determine the existence or nonexistence of something that we do not experience and/or think? Transcendence, as we have seen, exists only as a noumenon, a thought, not as an objective experience. However, in-itself Transcendence is unknown and unthinkable, therefore non-existent or non-experience-able. Nonetheless, Awareness needs no thought or experimentation to be apodictical or certain. What we just said does not necessarily endorse atheism. In fact, this last concept needs to be analyzed since it gives rise to new dogmas.

Atheism

Before proclaiming atheism, we must explain the meaning of the two Greek words: 1) "*a*" and 2) "*theism.*"

1) In Sanskrit, "*a*" is "a prefix... having a negative or privative or contrary sense (*an-eka* not-one; *an-anta* end-less; *a-sat* not-good; *a-paśyat* not-seeing)".[290]

In Greek, "*α*" ("*a,*" *privative alpha*), is "privative ... ἄ-θεος [*a-theos*], without-God; a-theist."[291]

In Latin, "*a*" (*prīvātīvum*), "in composition denotes privation."[292]

In German, "*un*" is privative.

In English, "*a*" is privative (*i.e. a*-moral = *without*-moral).[293]

2) The word "*theism*" implies the belief in *theós* (θεός), Greek for God.

Therefore, *a-theism* means: *without the belief in God.*

"The ultimate word in our English language for that which is transcendent is God," refers Joseph Campbell.[294] In fact, echoes Tolle, "The word God has become empty of meaning through thousands of years of misuse. I use it sometimes, but I do so sparingly. By misuse, I mean that people who have never even glimpsed the realm of the sacred, the infinite vastness behind that word, use it with great conviction, as if they knew what they are talking about. Or they argue against it, as if they knew what they are denying."[295]

Saint Anselm in his *a-priori* ontological proof of God's existence,[296] states that God is the idea of a very perfect being. Because absolute, that perfection must imply necessarily also its existence. However, Kant calls the idea of God a noumenon, a thought but not known. He points out that there are three noumena or ideas that are transcendent and, therefore, thought but not known. Namely, they are,

a) the idea of God,

b) the idea of Nature, *i.e.* the World in-itself as independent from our experience of it, and

c) the idea of the soul.

It is this last idea that sheds more light on the meaning of atheism. When we refer to a soul, we refer to the transcendent reality of our self or of another being *in-itself*. In other words we refer to an "I" or a subject in-itself, which is transcendent, therefore, is unknown. Our experience of others or our self is always an experience of an object, never of a subject as such. In the epistemic correlation, we know our self as "*me*," an object, never as "*I*," a subject. We know the other as *you*, never as "*I*." The "*I-in-itself*," as such, is always unrelated, unless we refer to it as the subject of a verb. Nevertheless, we never know our own "*I*" or anyone's "*I*" as such. Therefore, it is transcendent, *viz.* it is in the same realm of God or Nature. Thus, God, Nature and the "*I-in-itself*" are on the same level, they are transcendent. In fact,

> "*Jesus said ... 'Thou shalt love the Lord thy Transcendent with all thy heart, and with all thy soul, and with all thy mind... And ... Thou shalt love thy neighbour as thyself.*'"[297]

The real lover is the one who lives the awareness of the loved one and in it sees its own self. Love defies and subverts any logic. In fact, in true love, '*you*' is '*I*.' We relate to others as we relate to The Transcendent. And this is evident when we confront a deceased person. Before death occurs, we cannot tell much about the entity we communicate with. Who is s/he in itself, beyond the '*you*? Indeed, we cannot read someone's mind. After death that entity is still not present. Therefore, the real thoughts of others remain always a mystery for us, as mysterious as The Transcendent. It is a superficial claim to state that the *neighbor's* "*I*" is not transcendent or unknown, since we can deduce it in-itself through its responses and movements. In fact, that claim would validate and give authority to Saint Thomas Aquinas' *a-posteriori* proofs of the existence of God, which are based on motion, cause-effect, necessity, intent and logic.[298] And this would negate the original proclamation of a-theism.

Therefore, the declaration of atheism implies an audience, whose reality in-itself is assumed by belief but never demonstrated. The *other* is transcendent as God is. When the subject interacts with another subject, the other is assumed, never experienced as a subject. Our own subject can only perceive it-self and the world *for-itself, per-se,* never *in-itself, in-se.* The self and the objective world are always filtered by the subject, the *I-think.* We never know how the self or the world is in-itself, namely without that *filtering.* The *in-se* is the Transcendent, the realm of God. Any communication, including one's own *atheism,* is an affirmation of belief in the reality of the listener, the transcendent other in-itself. This contradicts the affirmation of atheism. The words we are writing now are intended for a reader out there whom I may never know. This is reaching out to someone who transcends us. Therefore, we cannot, at the same time, proclaim that we do not believe in their existence.

Faith, Certainty and Beliefs

The word for faith, in Hebrew *'emuwnah* and in Greek *pístis,* means also *certitude.*[299] This term conveys the unshakable *assurance, trust*[300] and *certainty* inherent, here and now in the foundation of *Faithful*-Awareness. Saint Paul states,

> "*Certitude-faith is the foundation of trusted things,*
> *the evidence of things not mentally discerned.*"[301]

In fact, the instant of *certitude* does not require thinking to be *certain.* There is no process of thought in Awareness. It is the immediate *fulguration* right here and now.[302]

> "*Through certitude we understand that things which are seen were not made of the things which do appear, the worlds were completed by The Transcendent's utterance.*"[303]

Certain-Awareness is the *utterance,* the creative *certain-faith flowing* beyond the phenomenic world. It is the

"*grain of mustard seed*"

with which

> "*nothing shall be impossible.*"[304]
>
> "*Therefore I say unto you, What things soever you ask for, when you pray be certain that you receive* [them], *and you shall have* [them]."[305]

And

> "*he that has certainty in me* [Awareness], *though he were dead, yet shall he live.*"[306]

The *Chāndogya Upanishad* declares

> "*This is my Self within the heart. Although smaller than a grain of rice or a barley-corn or a mustard seed or a grain of millet or a kernel of a grain of millet, this Self of mine residing within the heart is greater than the earth, greater than the sky, greater than heaven, and greater than all these universes.*"[307]

Jung defines the Self, as the "smaller than small."[308] It is the present awareness which cannot become an object of knowledge.

> "*Whosoever shall not receive the kingdom of The Transcendent as a little child shall in no wise enter therein.*"[309]

The little child represents the simplicity of awareness that a child manifests when raptured in the act of perception. It is the wonderful moment in which the gaze is spaced out in blissful stillness.

> "*For therein is the righteousness of The Transcendent revealed from certitude to certitude: as it is written* [in *Habakkuk*],[310] *'The just shall live by certitude.'*"[311]

The *Kaṭha Upanishad* refers to this *certitude* as

"*reverential homage,*"

faith,

"*truth-holding,*"[312]

therefore, Apodictical-Awareness. It is not a process of thinking, but a self-re-flection devoid of any object. The *Bible* teaches,

> "*I am come a light into the world, that whosoever is certain in my* [awareness] *should not abide in darkness.*"[313]

We should announce this glad tiding, declares Paul.[314]

> "*That which may be clear of the Transcendent Awareness is evident... since the Transcendent Awareness has manifested* [it]."

In truth,

> "*the invisibility of the Transcendent Awareness is clearly apparent through the presence of the world and it is understood by means of the a-temporal power of Certitude.*"[315]

Similarly, the Buddha, while meditating, touches the earth calling upon the world to testify his Enlightened Transcendent Certitude of it.[316] In other words, the waking or sleeping stages would never be experienced if Aware Certitude would not establish it as perceived. The phenomenic world is founded on Certitude. Without it, the world would not be discernible, i.e. *phenomenic*. Explicitly, how appearance can be perceived without the Certitude of that which is seen or experienced?

Let us clarify the meaning of this *Certitude*. When we look at this book we are *certain* of it. We may not know what is written in it, but we cannot deny the experience of the book as an object that we can read. When we look at a building we are *certain* of it. We may not know who lives in it, but we cannot deny the experience of the building as an object that can be inhabited. When we look at the cosmos we are *certain* of it. We may not know what it was before the big-bang or what lies beyond its borders, but, while sitting on a beach staring the starry night sky, we cannot deny the experience of the world as an object of wonder. That *certainty*, which cannot deny the book, the building or the cosmos, is exactly the same for all. That *certainty* is the same for any other experience we may have. There is no experience without that *certitude*. And the experience testifies, is the witness of that *certitude*. It is the earth that testifies Buddha's enlightenment. That *Certitude* is *Faith*, which is with no beginning or end. It is here, in the eternity of this Present. Therefore,

Faith is synonym of Apodictical Certitude.

This certitude is different from belief, which may be subject to the fluctuation of the mind accepting or rejecting the object of credence. Certitude, as such, can never be denied. If repudiated, it would not be *certitude*. Saint Paul proclaims, this is the

"*universally declared Certitude,*"

which strengthens us.[317] Therefore, beyond the ontological and *a-posteriori* proofs of God's existence,[318] we can state an epistemological proof.

The Apodictic Certitude evidences the Transcendent Reality.

The identification between Faith and belief stems from the fact that we erroneously assign certainty to a concept as in-itself, independent from that *certitude*. We do not realize that Certitude refers to the awareness of ideas as ideas, or of dreams as dreams. Awareness is aware of the phenomena as such, without supporting any validity or superimposition beyond the thinker, the dreamer or the believer. Conferring independent reality to ideas or dreams in-themselves is the fabrication of dogmas.

Belief assumes that a particular thought or experience is truth in-itself without proving it.

Therefore, it is against Certitude "to coerce a dogma on somebody's mind."[319] In fact, the reality in itself of that which appears is only a noumenon, which, nevertheless, is present in Awareness as noumenon. Namely, it is thought but not known. The Transcendent Awareness is always present. Indeed, those who do not live in the presence of that Awakened Awareness, abide in darkness, unaware that they are bathing in light. They

> "*glorified* [that Certitude] *not as Transcendent... but became empty in their thinking process...*[320] *Professing themselves to be wise, they became fools. And changed the glory of the incorruptible Transcendent into mental images of things...*[321] *and their foolish heart was darkened... They changed the certain truth of the Transcendent into a lie...*[322] *and turned their hearts to lustful desires... Amen.*"[323]

PART I
B
SACRED TEXTS
Translation and commentary of the *Kaivalya Upanishad*, the *Bhagavad-Gītā* and other texts.

CHAPTER 1

KAIVALYA UPANISHAD

Veda

The earliest Indian sacred texts list four books of knowledge called *Veda*.[324]

1) The first one is the *Ṛg*, Sacred Verses, composed around the Second Millennia BC.
2) Follows the *Yajur*, Sacrificial formulas.
3) The third book is *Sāma*, namely the Liturgies.
4) The fourth book, which was added later, is the *Atharva*, a collection of incantation of the priests worshiping with Fire.

Tradition has it, that the *Vedas* were revealed. Ancient seers, the "Priest-Kings" (*ṛshi-kavi*) composers of those verses, while

"*meditating in their hearts*"[325]

heard (*śruti*) them directly from the Transcendent Realm.

Upanishad

The first *Upanishads* were composed around the Seventh Century BC. They constitute the philosophy received while sitting down by the side of the master.[326] That teaching was the elaboration of the ancient *Vedas*. The *Kaivalya* stems from the tradition according to the *Yajur* and *Atharva Veda*. It is considered a "minor" *Upanishad*. It was composed probably around the Third Century BC.

KAIVALYA

INVOCATION

Beyond the world of illusion, *Kaivalya* proclaims the Ultimate Reality to be past all duality, all pairs of opposites including that of good and evil.

UKai **The Epistemic-Detached-Beatific-Loneliness learned at the Feet of the master.**
ॐ AUM is the dispeller of evil and ignorance.
kaivalyo- (epistemic detached beatific loneliness) *panishat* (at the feet of the master) *hariḥ* (dispeller of evil) *om* (AUM)

Kaivalya[327] means Epistemic-Detached-Beatific-Loneliness. The sacred symbolic resounding AUM, as a symbol of the all-encompassing reality, dispels evil and ignorance.

KAIVALYA SECTION I
THE ESSENCE OF TRANSCENDENCE

***UKai* 1** **Āśvalāyana reverently approached the Divine Supreme Being and said:** **"Teach me, o Divine Being, the knowledge of the Absolute Supreme Spirit; that excellent concealed One, perpetually waited upon by holy persons.** [Teach me] **That One, by which the realized individual soon becomes free from all evil and attains the Person Greater than the Great."**
athā- (then) *śvalāyano* (Āśvalāyana) *bhagavantaṁ* (the divine) *parameshṭhinam* (supreme being) *parisametyo-* (reverently approached) *vāca* (said) *adhīhi* (teach) *bhagavan* (divine being) *brahma-* (Absolute Supreme Spirit) *vidyāṁ* (knowledge) *varishṭhāṁ* (excellent) *sadā* (perpetually) *sadbhiḥ* (by saintly persons) *sevyamānāṁ* (being waited upon) *nigūḍhām* (concealed) / *yayā'* (by which) *cirāt* (soon) *sarva-* (all) *pāpaṁ* (evil) *vyapohya* (becoming free from) *parāt-* (greater) *paraṁ* (than the great) *purusham-* (person) *upaiti* (attains) *vidvān* (the learned).

Āśvalāyana, disciple of the grammarian Śaunaka, the Hound,[328] was the founder of the homonymous Vedic school and one of the authors of ritual works contained in the "Vedic Hymns of Knowledge."[329] The name Āśvalāyana, Approaching-horse,[330] metaphorically represents the psychosomatic-body as the horse (*āśva*) on which consciousness rides.[331] Therefore, his name becomes a paradigmatic figure of the human being as a synthesis of body and mind.

On the road of our understanding, the Unknown stands beyond the immediate horizon. We constantly tend towards it. In our ignorance, one of the names we give to that mystery is *Future*. That is, the ineffable and unknowable Transcendent One is always on the other side of our reach. Only *yoga*, the enlightened yoke, can realize our apodictic unity with it.

Āśvalāyana asks his internal divine spiritual teacher (*guru*) to be instructed on the nature of the Ultimate Reality, which leads to liberation. Since we are the only one who assesses the teaching quality of the guru, therefore, the real master is our own Self of Self, which is, therefore, the *Guru* of the *guru*.

***UKai* 2** **And He, the Great Father, said to him: "Try to realize** [the Supreme Spirit] **through devoted trust, love, meditation and unity.** [Do] **not** [try to realize It] **through action, nor through offspring or with money. One attains immortality only through renunciation.**
tasmai (to him) *sa* (he) *hovāca* (said) *pitāmahaś* (great father) *ca* (and) *śraddhā-* (by devoted trust) *bhakti-* (love) *dhyāna-* (meditation) *yogād* (unity) *avehi* (try to realize) / *na* (not) *karmaṇā* (by action) *na* (not) *prajayā* (by offspring) *dhanena* (with money) *tyāgenaike* (by renunciation only) *amṛtatvam* (immortality) *ānaśuḥ* (attains).

> "*Jesus... said... 'Sell all that thou hast, and distribute unto the poor, and thou shalt have treasure in heaven: and come, follow me...*
> *Verily I say unto you, There is no man that hath left house, or parents, or brethren, or wife, or children, for the kingdom of The Transcendent's sake,*
> *Who shall not receive manifold more in this present time, and in the world to come life everlasting.*' "[332]

Renunciation is what Tolle calls surrender, namely "the letting go of mental-emotional resistance" and become "a portal into the Un-manifested." Therefore, "surrender is inner acceptance of what is without any reservation."[333]

No material things can reach the Supreme Spirit. When Simon the sorcerer, wanted to buy the miraculous powers bestowed by The Transcendent, Peter said to him,

> "*Thy money perish with thee, because thou hast thought that the gift of The Transcendent may be purchased with money.*"[334]

***UKai* 3** **The Supreme Spirit, placed within the**

cave of the heart, transcends beyond the vault of heaven, however, at the same time, It shines forth. Those who restrain [themselves]**, those who have well established final-Gnostic-knowledge (*vedānta*), the renunciants, those who, with purified consciousness, concentrate in unity with the Spirit, enter in that heart.**

pareṇa (beyond) *nākaṁ* (the vault of heaven) *nihitaṁ* (placed) *guhāyāṁ* (within the cave of the heart) *vibhrājate* (shines forth) *yad-* (that)[335] yatayo (those who restrain) *viśanti* (enter in);[336] / *vedānta-* (Gnostic-summary) *vijñāna-* (knowledge) *suniścitārthāḥ* (those who have well established) *saṃnyāsa-* (the renunciants) *yogād* (through the union) *yatayaḥ* (those who concentrate) *śuddha-* (purified) *sattvāḥ* (consciousness).[337]

There is a double act.

1) On one side, the Supreme Spirit is completely in every single part, while being all in their totality.
2) On the other, at the same time, it persists in its transcendence without ever moving out of its center.

That core is metaphorically indicated as the heart. The perfect symbol for such concept is a geometrical ring⊙. In fact, the center of an ideal circle is a point with no dimensions, which radiates itself in all the infinite dimensionless points on the circumference without ever losing its centrality.

This reality is understood by the *Vedāntin* gnostic philosopher, who has ample knowledge of the *Ved-ānta*, the *Vedas'-End*, the complete speculation of the *Vedas*. It is realized, also, by the renunciants and those who practice yoga.

Devotees, reporting on the Indian mystic Ānandamayī Mā, describe her as being "continuously in the highest state of *samādhi* [ecstatic union]. Even as She looks at you, you are aware of the fact that She is with you and yet far beyond you; that She has that dual vision encompassing the manifested and the transcendent."[338]

***UKai* 4** **At the end of time, they, who are in the world of the Creator, are all liberated and are no longer subject to death. They, in an isolated place, seated with**

straight neck, head and body, are glowing in a comfortable position.
te (they) *brahma-* (of the Creator) *lokeshu* (in the world) *parāntakāle* (at the end of time) *parāmṛtāt* (no longer subject to death) *parimucyanti* (liberated) *sarve* (all)/ *vivikta-* (isolated) *deśe* (in a place) *ca* (and) *sukhāsanasthaḥ* (in a comfortable position seated) *śuciḥ* (glowing) *samagrīvaśiraḥ* (with straight neck head) *śarīraḥ* (body).

The end of time is the Present. Here, Time ends its illusory game on the edge of life's ocean. Continuing with the metaphor of the circle, the end of time is the immovable centrality of the Present. Time is the flowing sequences of radial points reflecting from the center and forming the circumference or the *world of the Creator*. In that central juncture, the yogi sits unmovable in the meditative lotus-position.[339]

***UKai* 5 They are absorbed in the pure middle of the lotus flower of the heart, beyond the life stages of student, house-holder, forest-dweller and renunciant, controlling all the faculties of the senses, offering obeisance with devotion to one's own teacher, universally pure without contaminating disturbances, sorrow-less, transcendent, beyond the states of waking, dreaming and deep sleep with no dreams.**
aty- (beyond) *āśramasthaḥ* (the life stages) *sakale-* (all) *ndriyāṇi* (faculties of the senses) *nirudhya* (controlling) *bhaktyā* (with devotion) *sva-* (one's own) *guruṁ* (teacher) *praṇamya* (offering obeisance) / *hṛt-* (of the heart) *puṇḍarīkaṁ* (lotus flower) *virajaṁ* (universally pure without contaminating disturbances) *viśuddhaṁ* (transcendent, beyond the states of waking, dreaming and sleep) *vicintya* (absorbed) *madhye* (in the middle) *viśadaṁ* (pure) *viśokam* (sorrowless).

Traditionally, there are four stages in the life of a Brahmin-priest.

1) The first is the learning stage, *brahmacārin*. The Brahmin studies the sacred texts.
2) It follows that of a house-holder, *gṛha-stha*, working and providing for a family.

3) Once those duties are accomplished, a period of reflection on the meaning of life requires the silence of a hermitage or becoming a forest-dweller, a *vāna-prastha*.
4) That silent contemplation leads to the realization of life's vacuity and to its total abnegation by becoming a renunciant, a *saṃnyāsin*.

However, one must go beyond those four stages and the three life's states of waking, dreaming and sleeping with no dreams. As Abel's sacrifice,[340] one must offer the prime faculties of the senses to the inner master without desires or attachments.

UKai 6 **The infinite form of Śiva the auspicious is inconceivable, un-manifest** [and] **perfectly at peace. It is immortal. It is the source of Brahmā the Creator. It is without beginning, middle or end. It is the all-pervading One. It is wonderful, formless, wisdom and bliss.**
acintyam- (inconceivable) *avyaktaṃ-* (un-manifest) *ananta-* (infinite) *rūpaṁ* (form) *śivaṁ* (of Śiva the auspicious) *praśāntam-* (perfectly at peace) *amṛtaṁ* (immortal) *brahma-* (of Brahmā the creator) *yonim* (source) / *tathā'* (as well as) *dimadhyānta-* (beginning, middle or end) *vihīnam-* (without) *ekaṁ* (one) *vibhuṁ* (all-pervading) *cid-* (wisdom) *ānandam-* (bliss) *arūpam-* (formless) *adb hutam* (wonderful).

It is common acceptance that Hinduism is a polytheistic idolatrous religion with a great number of gods *deva* and goddesses *devī*. And, the Hindu *devas* are powerless without their companion *devīs*, who are their power (*śákti*). We must clarify that the word *deva/ī* derives from √*div*, meaning to shine, from which the English word *di*vine. These *devas* are templates, paradigmatic psychological forces highlighting (*div*) the world objects. In fact, sacred texts state that the gods are the faculties of the senses (*indriya*) belonging to the '*I*,' the god Indra.[341] The gods put the world into existence. Therefore, Metastasio invokes them declaring, "Eternal gods, preserve this beautiful work of yours."[342]

The *Muṇḍaka Upanishad* affirms,

> "*All the faculties of the senses become one in their corresponding deities, deeds and the intellectual self all in the Supreme Imperishable One Awareness.*"[343]

And the *Chāndogya Upanishad* more clearly confirms,

> "*Verily, the gods are the five channels of perception of this heart.*"[344]

The *Ṛg Veda* states that

> "*the gods, the resplendent beings of the senses came after the creation of this world, and then who knows from what it began to exist?*"[345]

Śiva is the eternal all-pervading wisdom without any form. It is the immortal Auspicious One. It is Peace and Bliss, which cannot be conceived or manifested since

> "*You cannot think the thinker of thinking, nor understand the understander of understanding.*"[346]

Namely, it is Transcendent Awareness.

<u>*UKai 7*</u> By meditative reflection, the sage, having as companion Umā, the splendid wife of Śiva, reaches that Supreme Lord beyond darkness, the source of beings, the witness of all, the three-eyed, blue throat, imperturbable ruler.
umā- (Umā, the splendid wife of Śiva) *sahāyaṁ* (companion) *parameśvaraṁ* (Supreme Lord) *prabhuṁ* (ruler) *trilocanaṁ* (three-eyed) *nīlakaṇṭhaṁ* (blue throat) *praśāntam* (imperturbable) / *dhyātvā* (by meditative reflection) *munir-* (the sage) *gacchati* (reaches) *bhūta-* (of beings) *yoniṁ* (the source) *samasta-* (of all) *sākshiṁ* (witness) *tamasaḥ* (darkness) *parastāt* (beyond).

It is through deep meditation on consciousness that the sage realizes pure Awareness. The *Ṛg Veda* says that

> "*Searching* (*pratīshyā*) *with reflection* (*manīshā*) *in the heart, the seers found the connection of being in non-being.*"[347]

To understand the metaphoric meening of Umā, the companion of the sage, we must first look into the myth of male-female distinction.

Before Eve was mentioned, the *Bible* affirms that

"*The Transcendent said; Let us make the-human-'adam in our image...*
male and female *created he them...*
And called *__their__* *name 'Adam-human* [red/white?]...
And ... human-'adam became a living breathing being."[348]

Therefore, we have one being both male and female. The renaissance Alchemic Hermetic Philosophy named this androgynous one Re-bis,[349] the double-thing. Before the epistemic distinction of subject and consciousness-*of*-object, *male-and-female* are the logical distinction of *I-and-the-consciousness*. The *shining* (*div*) '*I-think*' (Indra) is powerless without its *shining* (*div*) Power- (*śákti*) Consciousness as pure potentiality. Therefore, in our *Upanishadic* verses, we may try to explain Umā, the meditating companion of the 'I-sage,' as Mindfulness.

The *Kena Upanishad* describes that the god Indra, metaphor for the '*I*,'[350]

"*did not know what the spirit* [of the Transcendent Brahman] *was.*"

Therefore, he

"*hurried towards*"

It, but that Supreme Awareness

"*disappeared from him.*"[351]

Namely, he was looking at It as in a subject-object spatial-distance, *viz.* he was conceptualizing it. This is the same reason why The Transcendent prevents Moses to look for the source of the Burning-bush fire, from which He

"*said, Do not approach here: put off thy shoes from off thy feet, for the place whereon thou standest* [is] *the Sacred Transcendent.*"[352]

However, continuing with the *Kena Upanishad*,

"*in that same vacuity he* [Indra] *met Umā-Splendor, a very beautiful lady, the daughter of Himavat-Frost-Cladded,*[353]

> *thus, he asked her, 'Who is this supernatural being?'"*[354]

Umā-Splendid-Light is the goddess of mountains. She is Śiva's wife and power (*śákti*), also called, among other names,[355] Satí, the personification of Truth. She was consumed by the fire of yoga when she practiced yogic austerities and she became known as Satí.[356]

Metaphorically, Umā represents both aspects of Awareness and Mindfulness.

a) On one side, she is Self-Mindfulness that, through yoga, purifies herself eliminating all possible objectivity. Upon reaching herself she burns and vanishes in Transcendent Awareness.
b) On the other side, the world is present in her as her preservation of data information, i.e.: Mindfulness. As such, she is the weaver, the one who strings together artificially and makes the objective world into a web-like covering Awareness.[357]

Again, the *Kena Upanishad*[358] continues describing the meeting between Indra and Umā. She reveals to Indra who is the Spirit he was enquiring of.

> "*She said: 'this is the Brahman for sure. Indeed, you have been exalted in the superiority of Brahman.'*"

Namely, the 'I' finds its foundation in the Apodictic Certitude of Awareness (*Brahman*).

> *"In regards to the faculties of the senses,*[359] *that* [Awareness] *is like lightning or like the winking of an eye... In regards to the self, the mind tends towards that* [Awareness] *always remembering and directing its intentions."*[360]

Umā, Mindfulness or Pure Consciousness, upon reaching Śiva, Awareness, becomes his wife, namely becomes one with It. In the Indian tradition, gods without consort have no power. Their power is prerogative only of their wives. Furthermore, we find that in the Vedic literature each god becomes the Supreme-One. This characteristic is called Henotheism. It recognizes that each god is a different aspect or name of the same Brahman.[361]

Beyond the unknown, beyond darkness, where

> "*you cannot see the seer of seeing,*"[362]

there is the Supreme Lord Śiva. There is the witness. There is the imperturbable Awareness. There is the ultimate perceiver, whose middle eye represents the centrality between the subject-object duality. Śiva, as pure Awareness, represents the source of beings. In fact, how can one establish being without it?

The metaphorical third eye of Śiva is the ultimate observer beyond time. Myth has it that, to save all beings, Śiva drank the poison of the Time-puzzle.[363] Time is the illusion that takes us away from the continuum Present and plunges us into the non-presence of past and future as such. The identification with that which is not here and now, is the poison that hides the Present Awareness from us.

Śiva swallows that venom but does not ingest it. The toxic stays in his troth and he remains in the suspension of a timeless moment, the Eternal Apodictic Present of Certain Awareness, namely Transcendence in-itself. If any color can be attached to that moment it is black or a dark blue. It indicates the fourth encompassing state beyond the waking, dreaming and deep sleep conditions. It corresponds to the hermetic *midnight sun*, the metaphysical dark blue depicting, traditionally, divinities like Vishṇu, the All-pervader, Kṛshṇa, the Dark-blue, Kālī, the Black, and others. Therefore, Śiva is called Nīla-kaṇṭha Mahā-kāla, Blue-throat Great-time slayer.

***UKai* 8** **He is Brahmā the Creator, He is Śiva the auspicious, He is Indra the I, He is the imperishable sword, the supreme Lord of himself, He is verily Vishṇu the preserver, He is the vital breath, He is time, the fire of awareness, He is the river moon of reflected thought.**
sa (he) *brahmā* (Brahmā the Creator) *sa* (he) *śivaḥ* (Śiva the auspicious) *sendraḥ* (he Indra the I) *so'* (he) *ksharaḥ* (imperishable sword) *paramaḥ* (supreme) *svarāṭ* (Lord of himself) / *sa* (he) *eva* (verily) *vishṇuḥ* (Vishṇu the preserver) *sa* (he) *prāṇaḥ* (vital breath) *sa* (he) *kālo'* (time) *gniḥ* (fire) *sa* (he) *candramāḥ* (river moon).

Śiva is like a kaleidoscope, whichever visual angulations you look from or whichever perspective you take, it gives you a partial and relative view of the entire Śiva Naṭa Rāja (= King) of the Cosmic-Dance.[364]

When the Supreme Awareness puts the world into existence, It is named *Brahmā,* the Creator. All things, experienced, imagined, thought, felt, remembered, fantasized, envisioned, dreamed or hallucinated, are founded on Awareness. Without Awareness we would not be able to consider them existent or created. We would not even talk about the unconscious without the Awareness of the unaware as such. Try if you can. In fact, without Awareness, it is impossible to state anything. By being aware, even dreams are placed into existence as visions.

Indra is the self-conscious-I, which needs Awareness in order to be Conscious-of-itself. *Prāṇa,* Life is the consciousness of *Vishṇu* preserving its own vitality entangled by the past/future spiral of *Kāla,* Death, the black Poisonous-serpent-of-Time.[365]

> *The Bible*[366] *refers to that serpent as the*
> "*great fish* [covering][367] *to swallow up Jonah. And Jonah was in the belly of the fish three days and three nights,*"

namely, the spread of time encompassing wakefulness, dream and sleep.

Fire-*Agni* is the Light-of-Awareness. Like the sun, Awareness enlightens of its own power, no other source of light shines beyond it. The moon *Candra* reflects that light. The objects of experience flow before that Sun as the metaphorical *Candramā,* the Moon-Flowing-River. In it, each object of thought reflects that light of awareness.[368] We identify with that moon-like reflection and forget the real light that makes it possible.

Therefore, there are two metaphorical levels,

1) One is the sublunary world, indicate as "*<u>beneath</u>* [the Moon], *in the temporal succession...* [where are those who identify with the consciousness-] *of this world.*" It represents the world of reflected Moon light.
2) The other is Transcendence, indicated as Heaven, referred to as "*<u>above</u> time...* [where are those who] *do not* [identify with the consciousness-] *of this world.*"[369]

***<u>UKai</u>* <u>9</u> Verily, He is everything which was and which will be. He is eternal. Realizing Him, one conquers**

death. There is no other way for liberation.
sa (he) *eva* (verily) *sarvaṁ* (all) *yad-* (that) bhūtaṁ (was) *yac-* (that) *ca* (and) *bhavyaṁ* (will be) *sanātanam* (eternal)/ *jñātvā* (by realizing) *taṁ* (him) *mṛtyum-* (death) *atyeti* (conquers) nānyaḥ (no other) *panthā* (way) *vimuktaye* (for liberation).

"*Jesus* [identified with the Transcendent Self-Awareness] *saith unto him, 'I am the way, the truth, and the life: no man cometh unto the Father, but by me.'"*[370]

At the moment of death, focus on the Certainty of Awareness. Forget the objects of consciousness and center on Certitude. Realize that it is the only flame sustaining the entire world. Feel It as the Lord of the Present. The past and the future, in fact, are such only in the present. Realize and unite with that Transcendent Awareness

"*with all thy heart, and with all thy soul, and with all thy mind.*"[371]

Once you will have identified with that Certain-Awareness, then death disappears because that Apodicticity persists beyond your objective physicality. The body dies, Awareness does not. In fact, Awareness is not founded on the body, but it is the foundation of the physical itself.

***UKai* 10** **One reaches the Supreme Spirit seeing clearly the Self in all beings and all beings in the Self. There is no other way.**
sarva- (in all) *bhūtastham-* (beings) *ātmānaṁ* (self) *sarva-* (all) *bhūtāni* (beings) *cā-* (and) *tmani* (in the self) / *sampaśyan* (seeing clearly) *brahma* (to the Spirit) *paramaṁ* (Supreme) *yāti* (reaches) *nānyena* (by no other) *hetunā* (cause).

Awareness is the foundation of every being. Our Awareness in its purity is Universal-Pure-Awareness. Who realizes that, grasps It as being in everyone and everyone being founded in It. Therefore,

"*Thou shalt love thy neighbour as thyself.*"[372]

***UKai* 11** **The wise knower, making the individualized self the lower fire stick and** [the waking, dreaming, sleeping

and beyond mind states, symbolized by] **the syllable AUM•, the upper fire stick, by rubbing in the cavity of knowledge burns the bond of ignorance.**
ātmānam (individualized self) *araṇiṁ* (lower fire stick) *kṛtvā* (making) *praṇavaṁ* (the syllable AUM◦, symbol of the waking, dreaming, sleeping and beyond states,) *co-* (and) *ttarāraṇīm* (upper fire stick) / *jñāna-* (of knowledge) *nirmatha-*(by rubbing) *nābhyāsāt* (in the cavity) *pāśaṁ* (bond) *dahati* (burns) *paṇḍitaḥ* (the wise knower).

One of the earliest ways to start a fire was to rub two sticks together. One wood, with a cavity on it, was placed horizontally on the ground. The second stick was positioned vertically in that cavity and vigorously rubbed until the friction generated fire. Metaphorically, this fire lighting represents the flash of consciousness hidden in the epistemic subject-object fire sticks.[373] Metaphorically, at the insertion point of the two sticks the fire of knowledge is generated. Similarly, the *Śvetāśvatara Upanishad* asserts,

> "*Making one's own body the fire friction stick and the syllable AUM the upper fire friction stick, being in profound meditation, one may see the Transcendent as hidden in the center of the churning.*"[374]

The lower stick represents the knower, the perceiver and the self-subject. Inserted on the subject is the vertical fire-stick. It represents the flowing objective world as it articulates through the three levels of waking, dreaming and deep sleep. The *Māṇḍūkya Upanishad* explains in detail these three circadian levels of life symbolized by the syllable AUM.[375]

A) stands for the waking stage (*viśva*), populated by this world of experience in all its aspects.

U) indicates the dream state [*taijasa* (oneirology $R_{apid}E_{yes}M_{ovement}$)] with all its experiences and its shades.

M) designates the phase of sleep with no dreams [*prājña* (oneirology $N_{on}R_{apid}E_{yes}M_{ovement}$)] containing the seed of the previous stages.

•) labels the forth-state (*turīya*) beyond those three stages, *i.e.:* the silence we come from and to which we go.

> "*Awareness, placed within both fire-sticks, like a fetus well borne by pregnant women,* [is] *the Fire-of-*knowledge *praised by the awakened persons offering oblations, day after day. Verily, this* [One, in the fourth state, is] *That* [Supreme Self]."[376]

***UKai* 12** **Verily, that individualized self, disoriented by illusion, performs all activities using a body. Indeed, while awake, s/he achieves satisfaction entertaining varied enjoyments with sexual partners, food, drink, etc.**
sa (he) *eva* (verily) *māyā-* (by illusion) *parimohitā-* (disoriented) *tmā* (individualized self) *śarīram-* (body) *āsthāya* (using) *karoti* (performs) *sarvam* (all) / *stry-* (women) *anna-* (food) *pānādi-* (drink etc.) *vicitra-* (entertaining varied) *bhogaiḥ* (sexual enjoyments) *sa* (he) *eva* (verily) *jāgrat* (waking) *paritṛptim* (satisfaction) *eti* (achieves).

To clarify the previous stanza, the Divine Supreme Being, the Great Father,[377] who is imparting this teaching, examines each of the three stages of life.

In the waking realm (A), the subject is lured by the senses. One, focused only on the sense-objects as reality in themselves, plunges in the *evil-suffering-darkness*[378] of this illusory world. Then, one loses the Aware-Certitude, the true source of everything. That is what the *Bible* calls *temptation-of-object-experimentation.*[379] This is exactly the same injunction not to eat from the tree of knowledge.

> "*Pay attention and pray* [*i.e.* meditate] *that ye enter not into the temptation-of-object-experimentation: the spirit indeed* [is] *willing, but the flesh* [is] *weak.*"[380]

Therefore, one

> "*should always pray* [*i.e.* meditate], *and not to be utterly spiritless.*"[381]

***UKai* 13** **Then, while dreaming, the individualized self experiences happiness and sorrow in a subjective world fabricated by his/her own illusion. Following, at the**

time of deep sleep, when everything is absorbed overcome by darkness s/he achieves a form of happiness. Verily, repeatedly, because of her/his deeds performed in other existences that individualized self awakens and sleeps [in new dreams].
svapne (while dreaming) *tu* (then) *jīvaḥ* (individualized self) *sukha-* (happiness) *duḥkha-* (sorrow) *bhoktā* (enjoyer) *sva-* (own) *māyayā* (by illusion) *kalpita-* (fabricated) *viśva-* (subjective) *loke* (in the world) / *sushupti-* (deep sleeping) *kāle* (at the time) *sakale* (everything) *vilīne* (is absorbed) *tamo'* (by darkness) *bhibhūtaḥ* (overcome) *sukha-* (of happiness) *rūpam* (a form) *eti* (achieves) // *punaś* (again) *ca* (and) *janmā-* (existence) *ntara-* (other) *karma-* (deeds) *yogāt* (by mixing) *sa* (he) *eva* (verily) *jīvaḥ* (individualized self) *svapiti* (sleeps) *prabuddhaḥ* (awakens).

Clearly, the self-illusion continues in the dream world (U). Subsequently, the individual enters the stage of sleeping with no dreams (M). There s/he experiences quiescence from which s/he emerges shortly after. Then, the individual retraces its pace according to the actions and intentions projected in the other stages of life. Consequently, one awakens in new experiences.

***UKai* 14** **The individualized I amuses itself in the three realms of wakefulness, dream and sleep. However, this entire entertaining varied world is born from that** [Fourth-state which is] **the foundation, the bliss, the entire awareness in which the three realms withdraw in dissolution.**
pura- (in realms) *traye* (three) *krīḍati* (amuses itself) *yaś* (who) *ca* (and) *jīvaḥ* (individualized self) *tatas-* (from that) *tu* (however) *jātaṁ* (born) *sakalaṁ* (all) *vicitram* (entertaining varied)/ *ādhāram-* (the foundation) *ānandam-* (bliss) *akhaṇḍa-* (entire) *bodhaṁ* (awareness) *yasmin* (in which) *layam* (the dissolution) *yāti* (withdraws) *pura-* (realms) *trayaṁ* (three) *ca* (and).

The three acts of our life-show emerge from the foundation of a Fourth-state, called *Turīya*. It is the soundless Awareness from which we come and the silent Awareness to which we go. The waking, dreaming and dreamless sleep evolve from the stage of Awareness and they dissolve in Awareness.

<u>*UKai*</u> <u>15</u> Life breath, the mind, all the faculties of the senses, and ether, wind, fire, water, earth supporter of the universe are born from It.
etasmāj- (from it) *jāyate* (are born) *prāṇo* (life breath) *manaḥ* (mind) *sarve-* (all) *ndriyāṇi* (faculties of the senses) *ca* (and) / *khaṁ* (ether) *vāyur-* (wind) *jyotir-* (fire) *āpaḥ* (water) *pṛthivī* (earth) *viśvasya* (of the universe) *dhāriṇī* (supporter).

"*Verily, the gods are the five channels of perception of this heart.*"[382]

Life, with all the faculties of the senses, and the entire Universe, in all its aspect (ether, gasiform, flaming, liquid and solid), all spring out from Awareness.

<u>*UKai*</u> <u>16</u> It is the Supreme Spirit, the Self of all, the eternal great foundation of the Universe and the sub-atomic of the atomic. Indeed, you are That. Indeed, you are That. Indeed, you are That.
yat (he) *param* (Supreme) *brahma* (Spirit) *sarvā-* (of all) *tmā* (the Self) *viśvasyā-* (of the universe) *yatanaṁ* (foundation) *mahat* (great) / *sūkshmāt* (of the atomic) *sūkshmataraṁ* (sub-atomic) *nityaṁ* (eternal) *tat-* (that) *tvam-* (you) *eva* (indeed) *tvam-* (you) *eva* (indeed) *tat* (that).

Awareness is *the mustard seed*,[383] the smallest than the small. That is the Supreme Spirit, the Universal Self.[384] That is your True Self here and now in the three waking, dreaming and sleeping realm.

<u>*UKai*</u> <u>17</u> One is liberated from all bandages of the world, which is manifest in the waking, dreaming, sleeping, etc. states, when s/he realizes that the Supreme Spirit is the I.
jāgrat- (waking) *svapna-* (dreaming) *sushupty-* (sleeping) *ādi* (etc.) *prapañcaṁ* (that which is material) *yat* (which) *prakāśate* (is manifest) / *tad* (that) *brahmā-* (Supreme Spirit) *ham-* (I) *iti* (thus) *jñātvā* (realizing) *sarva-* (from all) *bandhaiḥ* (bandage) *pramucyate* (is liberated).

We reach liberation from the suffering bondage, generated by the phenomenic world appearing on the three stages of life, when we realize that this Aware-Certitude is the Self-in-Itself.

***UKai* 18** **In the three realms, whichever may be the enjoyable, the enjoyer, or the enjoyment, I am different from them, I am the Pure-Aware-Witness, I am the Measure-of-Consciousness, I am the eternal auspicious Śiva.**
trisu (in the three) *dhāmasu* (realms) *yad* (which) *bhogyaṁ* (the enjoyable) *bhoktā* (the enjoyer) *bhogaś-* (the enjoyment) *ca* (and) *yad* (whichever) *bhavet* (may be)/ *tebhyo* (from them) *vilakshaṇaḥ* (different) *sākshī* (Pure-Aware-Witness) *cinmātro'* (measure of consciousness) *haṁ* (I) *sadāśivaḥ* (eternal auspicious Śiva).

The Pure-Aware-Witness is the Ultimate-Perceiver. It is the Apodictical-Certitude. It is that which underlines all experiences and without which experience is not possible. It is the One that sees without being seen, hears without being heard, understands without being understood, it is Self-in-Itself.[385]

It is the faithful witness, the 'I' as the subject *in-itself*, "as opposed to the object or to that which is external to the mind."[386] This Witness is the Witnessing-Certitude, which *measures* or validates the consciousness-of something. Thus, that Witness is the Measure-of-Consciousness.[387] *Revelation* calls

> "*Jesus Christ, the faithful witness, the first begotten of the dead, and the prince of the kings of the earth.*"[388]

And again, He is

> "*the Amen, the faithful and true witness, the beginning of the creation of The Transcendent.*"[389]

The *Koran* states

> "*The Transcendent is witness unto everything!*"[390]
> "*He is the One, who witnesses* [all], *and* [of] *that unto which witness is borne* [by Him]!... *However it be, God* [Itself] *bears witness to the truth of what He has bestowed from on high upon thee:*

out of His own wisdom has He bestowed it from on high, with the angels bearing witness thereto – although none can bear witness as The Transcendent does."[391]

Throughout, most of the Upanishads a refrain continuously repeats,

"*That, You Are*"

(*tat tvam asi*).

The experiencer, the experience and the experienced are all the same "Self." That eternal Śiva himself is the "Self." It is the One that Measures-Consciousness.

***UKai* 19** **In fact, everything is born in me, all is rooted in me and all reaches dissolution in me. I am that Supreme-Spirit without a second."**   **First section.**
mayy- (in me) *eva* (verily) *sakalaṁ* (everything) *jātaṁ* (born) *mayi* (in me) *sarvaṁ* (all) *pratishṭhitam* (founded) / *mayi* (in me) *sarvaṁ* (all) *layam* (dissolution) *yāti* (reaches) *tad* (that) *brahmā-* (Supreme-Spirit) *dvayam-* (without a second) *asmy-* (am) *aham* (I).   *prathamaḥ* (first) *khaṇḍah* (section)

The *Yoga Darshana Upanishad* declares.

"*I am a stranger in this world; there is no one with me! Just as the spume and the waves are born of the ocean then melt back into it, so the world is born of me and melts back into me.*"[392]

As reported by Shantidas, Ramana Maharshi, reminds us that

"*We ought to live as if we were alone, for we are truly alone: we see this on the day of our death.*"[393]

KAIVALYA SECTION II

THE ESSENCE OF ETHIC

The Divine Supreme Being, the Great Father,[394] continuing with His teaching, declares,

<u>*UKai* 20</u> "Verily I am smaller than the subtle, similarly, greater than the great. I am this entertaining varied entire universe. I am the ancient person. I am the Lord made of gold. I am the auspicious Śiva form.
aṇor- (than the subtle) *aṇīyān-* (smaller) *aham-* (I) *eva* (verily) *tadvat* (similarly) *mahān-* (of the great) *ahaṁ* (I) *viśvam-* (the entire universe) *idaṁ* (this) *vicitram* (entertaining varied) / *purātano'* (ancient) *haṁ* (I) *purusho'* (person) *ham-* (I) *īśo* (Lord) *hiraṇ-* (of gold) *mayo'* (made) *haṁ* (I) *śiva-* (the auspicious Śiva) *rūpam-* (form) *asmi* (I am).

The *Kaṭha Upanishad* says,

"*This Self, smaller than the subtle, greater than the great,* [is] *fixed in the secret of the creature's heart.*"[395]

Awareness, abiding in all being, is the eternal universal person aware and foundation of this entire multiform objective Universe. He is the precious Lord Śiva the Auspicious one.

<u>*UKai* 21</u> I am without hands and feet. With inconceivable powers, I see without eyes, equally I hear without ears. I am omniscient and free from form and no one knows me. I am eternal Awareness. Indeed, I am the One to be known through the many books of *Veda* knowledge. I am the maker of the *Vedānta* Gnostic-summary and, verily, I am the knower of the *Veda* books of knowledge.
apāṇi- (without hands) *pādo'* (feet) *ham-* (I) *acintya-* (inconceivable) *śaktiḥ* (powers) *paśyāmy-* (I see) *acakshuḥ* (without eyes) *sa-* (equally) *śṛṇomy-* (hear) *akarṇaḥ* (without ears) / *ahaṁ* (I) *vijānāmi* (know) *vivikta-* (free from) *rūpo* (form) *na* (none) *cāsti* (and is) *vettā* (knower) *mama* (of me) *cit* (awareness) *sadā* (eternally) *ham* (I) / *vedair-* (through the *Veda* books of knowledge) *anekair-* (many) *aham-* (I) *eva*

(indeed) *vedyo* (to be known) *vedānta-* (Gnostic-summary) *kṛd-* (the maker) *veda-* (of the *Veda* books of knowledge) *vid-* (knower) *eva* (verily) *cāham* (and I).

The Self-in-Itself is the Eternal-Apodictic-Awareness. While being omnipotent, It

"*is free from these limbs.*"[396]

In fact, It does not need members to be aware. Similarly, It does not need the faculty of the senses to be omniscient. At the same time, however, it is not-known in-itself, because it is transcendent. He is the Unknown-Naciketa, referred to in the *Kaṭha Upanishad.* Only s/he, who is

"*desire-less, free from sorrow, through the stillness of the five organs of sense and of the five properties of the elements perceived by them, realizes that majesty of the Self.*"[397]

That Self is the one enunciated in all sacred and gnostic texts. Certitude is the One who reveals and knows the books of knowledge, the *Vedas,* and brings to a conclusive end (*Vedānta*) the philosophical research.

***UKai* 22** **For me there is no good or evil, no birth, no body or destruction, nor there is an intellect or faculties of the senses. For me there is no earth, water, fire or air, and for me there is no circumference.**
na (no) *puṇya-*(good) *pāpe* (evil) *mama* (for me) *nāsti* (not is) *nāśo* (destruction) *na* (no) *janma* (birth) *dehe-* (body) *ndriya-* (faculties of the senses) *buddhir-* (intellect) *asti* (is) / *na* (no) *bhūmir-* (earth) *āpo* (water) *na* (no) *ca* (and) *mama* (for me) *vahnir-* (fire) *asti* (is) *na* (no) cānilo (and air) me' (to me) *sti* (is) *na* (no) *cā-* (and) *mbaraṁ* (and circumference) *ca* (and).

We are here at the very heart of our research for an absolute ethic.

The universal foundation of Ethic is Awareness.

The Transcendent Self-in-Itself, the Apodictic-Awareness is beyond all dichotomies. It is like the Sun, which shines over gold without greed or over filth without disgust. Awareness is the Transcendent, beyond good and evil. It is the absolute pure center without any circumference.[398] Like a supernova's gravitational collapse of a Sun,[399] the epistemic circularity of the subject trying to reach the object in-itself vanishes and collapses in the immediate Pure-Awareness of the centrality of the Self in-itself without thought or object.

Metaphorically, on the involute mazelike rim of the subject-object circular correlation is Minos, the Greek Lord of the dead, who judges what is good and/or evil granting punishment or reward.[400] In that network is the *Minos'-Taurus*, the deadly bull, the guardian of life's labyrinth that prevents the achievement of the center.[401] Then,

"*why seek ye the living among the dead?*"[402]

"*Visit the earth's interior rectifying you will find the occult stone.*"[403]

In fact, the body dies because it is already dead among dead. Once born it s already coindemned to die.

COLLAPSE OF THE SUBJECT IN ITS OWN CENTRALITY

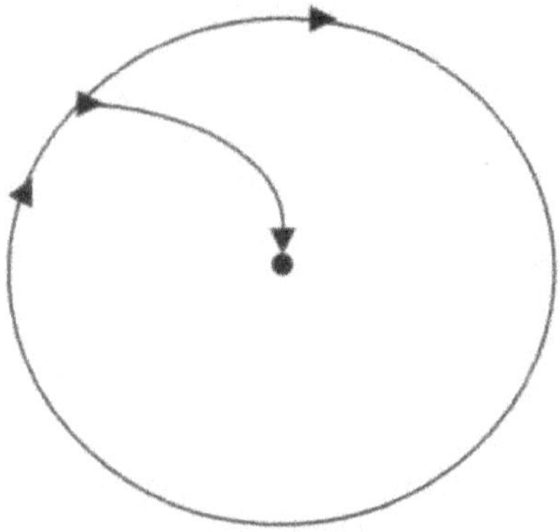

On April 8, 1971, Massimo Scaligero, in a letter to a disciple, wrote that the "Force" of freedom is present in us.

"Our being free gives us the possibility to be on the side of the being that chooses in us the Truth [of the Certain-Pure-Awareness] against the falsehood [of the not-certain]. The choice is important because it opens the gate to the force of the Principle that chooses: the Force of Him who *advances without fighting*, as it choses not according to craving, but according to a Love relation. Lucifer [the consciousness-*of*-reflected-light] is excluded from consciousness. This exclusion is the possibility of the conscious entity, which has preprogrammed in the sensory perception the maximum independence of the 'I' from the sensitive world."[404]

"Sin strongly, but believe even more strongly,"

declares Martin Luther.[405]

"In fact the sensitive processes of the organ of perception have nothing to do with perception itself. Instead, the luciferic deities operate so that the human ascends from the sensitive not descends into it. They project a world independent and unrelated from Awareness. The human overlooks Awareness which "instead is the force that descends... This ability to descend leads to face darkness up to the exhaustion of the fight, from which comes compassion as the first virtue of relationship. We can call it Sacred Love."[406]

"*Descended in hell; the third day he resurrected from the dead,*"[407]

declares the *The Apostles' Creed.*

"We can descend deep within ourselves; sink till we touch life's foundations... So, with certain thoughts intensely lived, we descend into the depths of ourselves. These thoughts have in themselves the forces that overcome selfishness."[408]

***UKai* 23** **Therefore, knowing the nature of the Supreme Self dwelling in the cave of the heart, without parts and without a second, one achieves the transcendent nature of the Supreme Self, the whole, the witness deprived of being and non-being.**
evaṁ- (therefore) *viditvā* (knowing) *paramātma-* (Supreme Self) *rūpaṁ* (nature) *guhāśayaṁ* (dwelling in the cave of the heart) *nishkalam-* (without parts) *advitīyam* (without a second) / *samasta-* (whole) *sākshiṁ* (witness) *sad-* (being) *asad-* (non-being) *vihīnaṁ* (deprived of) *prayāti* (achieves) *śuddhaṁ* (transcendent) *paramātma-* (Supreme Self) *rūpam* (nature).

It should be clear that the definition of heart is purely metaphoric. Here indicates an unalloyed centrality within the individual I. That pure, unified, undivided transcendent centrality without any circumference is metaphorically called the cave of the heart.

"*Understand... the state of rest placed in the cave of the heart.*"[409]

The Apodictic Timeless Awareness, beyond circularity,
"*was neither being nor was non-being.*"[410]
Then, moving into the field of space and time,

"*Indeed, in the beginning this One was Non-Being; from that One, verily, Being was born, that One created the Self by Itself.*"[411]

"*By self-power that One-Thing was breathing windless.*"[412]

"*Searching with reflection in the heart, the seers found the connection of being in non-being.*"[413]

UKai 24 **Anyone who studies this book, the Centuplicate-Terrifying-One, becomes pure fire, becomes pure air, and becomes pure Self. Even if s/he were to drink spirituous liquor, still would be pure, even if s/he were to kill a priest, s/he still would be pure, even if s/he were to steal gold, s/he still would be pure, s/he still would be pure regardless of what ought to be done or what should not be done. Therefore, s/he becomes one who has taken refuge within the Never Forsaken. Going beyond the traditional four stages of life,** [namely student, house-holder, forest dweller and renunciant,] **one should utter, always or once for all** [this *Kaivalya Upanishad*].
yaḥ (anyone who) *śata-* (this centuplicate) *rudrīyam-* (terrifying one) *adhīte* (studies) *so* (he) *gni-* (fire) *pūto* (pure) *bhavati* (becomes) *sa* (he) *vāyu-* (air) *pūto* (pure) *bhavati* (becomes) *sa* (he) *ātma-* (Self) *pūto* (pure) *bhavati* (becomes) *sa* (he) *surā-* (spirituous liquor) *pānāt-* (drinking) *pūto* (pure) *bhavati* (becomes) *sa* (he) *brahma-* (priest) *hatyāḥ* (killing) *pūto* (pure) *bhavati* (becomes) *sa* (he) *suvarṇa-* (gold) *steyāt-* (stealing) *pūto* (pure) *bhavati* (becomes) *sa* (he) *kṛtyā-* (what ought to be done) *kṛtyāt-* (what should not be done) *pūto* (pure) *bhavati* (becomes) / *tasmād-* (therefore) *avimuktam-* (the ever Forsaken) *āśrito* (one who has taken refuge) *bhavati-* (becomes) *aty-* (going beyond) *āśramī* (the traditional four stages of life) *sarvadā* (always) *sakṛd-* (once for all) *vā* (or) *japet* (should utter).

> "*When they ... crucified ...* [Jesus] *and the malefactors, one on the right hand, and the other on the left...*
> *One of the malefactors which were hanged ... said unto Jesus, Lord, remember me when thou comest into thy kingdom.*
> *And Jesus said unto him, Verily I say unto thee, To day shalt thou be with me in the transcendent heaven.*"[414]

In the Bible this wrongdoer becomes the *Good Evildoer*. In fact, in the Church liturgy, he is remembered as the *Good thief*.

The *Kaivalya Upanishad* is also called *Brahma Śata-rudrīya*, the Centuplicate Terrifying Spirit. That Frightening One is Rudra, one of Śiva's name, the supreme yogi, the Roaring Terrific One (*rudra*). He is the "god of tempests... in the *veda* He is closely connected with *indra* and still more with *agni*, the god of fire, which, as a destroying agent, rages and crackles like the roaring storm, and also with *kāla* or Time the all-consumer, with whom He is afterwards identified; though generally represented as a destroying deity."[415] That destruction corresponds to the dissolution of the world following the detached loneliness as described in the *Kaivalya Upanishad*.

Ramana Maharshi states,

> "*Who can understand the state of the one*
> *Who has dissolved his ego and*
> *Is abiding always in the Self?*
> *For him the Self alone is.*
> *What remains for me to do?*
> *... You wanted to see my form.*
> *You saw my disappearance.*
> *I am formless.*
> *So, that experience might be the truth.*"[416]

The identification with Apodictic Awareness leads to an absolute purity that is never tarnished, even if crimes are committed. Drunkenness, murder, theft or breaking any lawful traditions, all this, done while taking refuge within the Never Forsaken Awareness, as presented in this *Kaivalya Upanishad*, will never be ascribed as guilty sin, immorality, or any other condemning judgment.

Following the terrifying footsteps of Rudra, there is an order of ascetic monks[417] who worship "Śiva and Durgā... 'the inaccessible or terrific goddess,'" also known as Umā, "daughter of Himavat and wife of Śiva." These renunciants, direct successors of the Kāpālikas-human-skull-bearers, are called *Aghora*, the "not terrific... a euphemistic title of Śiva," in the form of the Terrible-*Bhairava*.[418] In a state of disengaged purity and no held duality, "they transgress all rules."[419] They drink alcohol, use intoxicating substances. Occasionally, they may practice anthropo-necrophagy. As shamans, they perform witchcraft, incantations, *supernatural* magic and also use obscene, provocative language and licentious behavior. In their naked wandering they may emulate Śiva's unemotional ithyphallic aspect.

Same traditions can be found among the Japanese Ronin Samurai,[420] who part from the Bushido, their original code of honor. The Native Americans of the plains have a similar practice with the Lakota Heyókhas[421] clowns who act as contrarians inverting the order of things. Aleister Crowley declared, "Do what thou wilt shall be the whole of the Low."[422] For Grigori Yefimovich Rasputin,[423] the Russian "Mad Monk," salvation was obtainable through continuous sin followed by repentance.

The study of the *Kaivalya Upanishad* leads to the realization of Awareness which is the Pure Self. Once the identity between the individual and the pure Self-in-itself is established, then no law holds any longer. As we quoted, Saint Augustine declares,

"*Love and do what you want.*"[424]

Meister Eckhart teaches,

"*When the Kingdom appears to the soul and it is recognized, there is no further need for preaching or instruction.*"[425]

And the *Upanishad* states:

> "*After studying the sacred texts, the wise one in*
> *search of realization, should get rid of them as*
> *one who seeks rice discards the husk.*"[426]

St. John of the Cross, while scaling Mount Carmel to unite with The Transcendent, states that, midway along the ascension,

"*There is no path, because for the just person there is no law.*"[427]

Ramana Maharshi echoes,

"*The sage who is the embodiment of the truths mentioned in the scriptures has no use for them* [*i.e.* the scriptures and their laws]"[428].

The *Bṛhadāraṇyaka Upanishad* declares,

> "*Verily, one becomes an ascetic by being conscious of This One... Verily... the Self is not desires, not this. It is in-comprehensible because He cannot be comprehended. It is imperishable because He cannot be destroyed. It is unattached because He does not attach itself. It is unbound, never agitated in the mind, and never harmed. Furthermore, the following two thoughts: 'Certainly, for this reason I have done evil,' or 'certainly, for this reason I have done good,' do not overpower the one who has realized the Self. Indeed, s/he also overcomes them both and, that which he has done or not, doesn't torment him/her.*"[429]
>
> "*Thus, indeed, if one knows this as* [*life's hymn*] *although s/he commits many sins consumes it all, is cleansed and becomes pure, ageless and immortal.*"[430]

And the *Bhagavad-Gītā* endorses,

"***For him/her there is no duty.***"[431]

Also the reverse holds true, In fact, "An impulse of goodness or of morality, when it is authentic, does not dominate the I, because it is an expression of the I... Also the use of a moral impulse may become illicit, if it is not the decision of the I, but rather it derives from the body's greed."[432] This concept is well described by Rabia al-Adawiyya, the 8th century Sufi mystic, when she declares,

"*O my Lord Allah, if I worship You from fear of Hell, burn me in Hell; and if I worship You from hope of Paradise, exclude me from Paradise. But if I worship You for Your own sake, do not withhold from me Your Eternal Beauty.*"[433]

Freedom, therefore, is adherence to the autonomy of Awareness.

The opposite of freedom is the enslavement of subjectivity to the illusory object of desire, which adheres to the reflected light forsaking Awareness, its source. On this level the dichotomy of good and evil ensues. There we judge actions according to various laws and parameters that have no absolute validity in themselves.

> "*Now we know that what things soever the law saith, it saith to them who are under the law: that every mouth may be stopped, and all the world may become guilty before The Transcendent.*"

In fact, continues Saint Paul,

> "*by the law* [is] *the knowledge of sin.*"[434]

On the other hand, it is by the knowledge of this *Upanishad* that the true liberating ethic can be understood.

***UKai* 25** **One achieves this knowledge, which destroys the ocean of repeated birth and death. Therefore, knowing this, one achieves the position of detached loneliness. Thus, s/he achieves the position of detached loneliness."**   **Thus, is concluded the second section.**
anena (by this) *jñānam-* (knowledge) *āpnoti* (achieves) *saṁsārā-* (of repeated birth and death) *ṛṇava-* (like the ocean) *nāśanam* (which destroys)/ *tasmād-* (therefore) *evaṁ* (thus) *viditva-* (knowing) *enaṁ* (this) *kaivalyaṁ* (detached loneliness) *padam-* (position) *aśnute* (achieves) *kaivalyaṁ* (detached loneliness) *padam-* (position) *aśnuta* (achieves) *iti* (thus) // *iti* (thus) *dvitīyaḥ* (second) *khaṇḍaḥ* (section).

It is by the knowledge of this *Upanishad* that one realizes liberation in the beatific detached identification with Awareness. It is in this Faithful-Awareness that we find our true fulfilling free being beyond the world of illusions.

In the Ethical (*dhárma*) Realm there are no moral obligations. There is neither punishment, nor reward. There is only Apodictical-Awareness. That *Kingdom* is either realized or neglected. When ignored, we discard it as non-essential. Either way, there is still neither reward nor punishment for that. However, overwhelmed by worldly concerns, we forget the Truth (*satya*) of Awareness. We enter the world of ignorance (*a-vidya*), of duality (*dvaita*). There we are either awake or at sleep. When awake the dream vanishes. When asleep, wakefulness is forgotten. In each stage we are the untruthful (*mṛ́ṣā, ánṛta*) situation, the virtual personified illusion (*māyā*) with which we identify. Then, we are born and we suffer (*duḥkhá/dushkha*). We become this life, where there is

> "*darkness... weeping and gnashing of teeth.*"[435]

Then we enter the realm of mortality (*mṛtyu*) and morality (*dhárma*). There, actions are judged good or evil and, therefore, they necessarily bestow reward or punishment. However, once we realize (*vidya*) the monism, the non-duality (*a-dvaita*) of our unity with the Bright Joy of Pure Awareness, then, all the consciousness-*of*-the-world fades away as unreal and unessential.

> "*When I was a child* [says Paul]*, I spake as a child, I understood as a child, I thought as a child: but when I became a man, I put away childish things.*"[436]

Then the attachment to the world sheds its grip (*nírṛti*) and we lose all interest in it. This indifference towards the objective world may occur only for two reasons:

a) We simply die, like any average Cain out there, and we fade away with our sacrifice. Or,
b) We realize the Apodictical Awareness while alive, like Abel, and we awake to the insight of a divine incarnation (*avatāra*).

Thus is concluded the teaching of the Divine Supreme Being, the Great Father.

<u>UKai</u> Thus, is completed the *Kaivalya Upanishad*, the book of the epistemic detached beatific loneliness, learned at the feet of the master dispeller of ignorance and contained in the *Atharva* - *Veda*, the book of knowledge related to the fire priest.
ity- (thus) *atharva-* (in the priest who has to do with fire) *vede* (knowledge) *kaivalyo-* (epistemic detached beatific loneliness) *panishat* (learned at the feet of the dispeller of ignorance) *samāptā* (completed).

Here ends the *Kaivalya Upanishad*. It took us on the shore of detachment, "absolute unity... perfect isolation, abstraction, detachment from all other connections, detachment of the soul from matter or further transmigrations, beatitude... leading to eternal happiness or emancipation."[437]

CHAPTER 2

BHAGAVAD-GĪTĀ'S KARMA YOGA

For the purpose of this book and as a note and commentary to the Kaivalya, we chose the Third Discourse of the *Bhagavad-Gītā* which deals with the yoga of action.

Mahābhārata

In *heroic times*, on the plain of the Kurukshetra-Rice-field near Delhi, two related but rival families, fought an epic war. The two families were, the Kuravaḥ, descendants of King Kuru-rice, and the Pāṇḍava, sons of Pāṇḍu-white. The conflict was sang in the *Mahābhārata*, the longest major Sanskrit epic poem.[438] The middle section of this book contains the *Bhagavad-Gītā*, the *Divine-Song* (400 BC?). The leader of the Pāṇḍava is Arjuna-the-White-one. His charioteer is Kṛshṇa-the-Black-one. Unknown to everyone, this last one is the ineffable and invisible avatar of Vishṇu. Black or dark blue is the color of God, the Transcendent Midnight Sun.

Gītā

BG 1. At the start of the war Arjuna hesitates. He has moral concerns. Does he have the right to order the attack? Can he be morally justified commanding to kill his own relatives, teachers, and friends? Does he have the right to slay his enemies in the opposite army? Guilt impedes him to give an order that will result in the mutual slaughter of the two armies. With these moral concerns ends the first discourse of the *Gītā*.

BG 2. In the second discourse, Kṛshṇa is there to assure him. He reminds Arjuna that life and death chase each other, therefore do not mourn. Be unmoved. Similarly, Jesus commands

"*Let the dead bury their dead.*"[439]

Kṛshṇa confirms,

***BG* II.19 *"He who views someone as a killer and he who considers himself killed, the two do not know. This one does not kill and is not killed."*[440]**

Therefore, from a philosophical view point, Kṛshṇa instructs Arjuna to perform the duty of his particular existential situation. On the other hand, from a spiritual perspective, he instructs Arjuna to be free from the law and free from any desire. Paul says, be as

> "*those who mourn, as if they did not; those who are happy, as if they were not.*"[441]

And Kṛshṇa incites Arjuna to conduct a life of intense devote meditation and withdraw from the world becoming a renunciant.

The Divine-Song

***BG* 3** The Divine-Song **Then, the Third Discourse: Unity in Action.**
Bhagavad- (divine) *Gītā* (song) *atha* (then) *tṛtīyo-* (third) *dhyāyaḥ* (discourse) *karma-* (action) *yogaḥ* (unity)

The third chapter of the *Bhagavad-Gītā* (Divine-Song) deals with Karma-yoga, the synthetic-moment (*yoga*) realized in activity (*karma*).

***BG* 3.1** **Arjuna-white-lightening, said, "O Janārdana-men-agitating, if you think that knowledge is superior to action, then, o Keśava-long-hair, why are you engaging me in this terrible action?**
arjuna (White-Arjuna) *uvāca* (said) *jyayāsī* (superior) *cet-* (if) *karmaṇas-* (than action) *te* (of you) *matā* (though) *buddhir* (knowledge) *janārdana* (o men agitating) / *tat* (then) *kim* (why) *karmani* (in action) *ghore* (terrible) *mām* (me) *niyojayasi* (engaging) *keśava* (o long hair) //

Arjuna is the white-lightening[442] act of consciousness-*of* the object that springs out from the dark-blue (*kṛshṇa*) to make the world manifest. In fact,

> "*Agni-light-fire-of-consciousness was*
> *first born from the deep-blue-Sky.*"[443]

However, Kṛshṇa, with long hair, as metaphorical roots into the Transcendent-Heaven, is the charioteer of this body-vehicle. He hauls and restrains Arjuna, consciousness-*of*-objects. Kṛshṇa is the dark unknown, which troubles, agitates and moves humans into the enlightening consciousness. In fact,

> "*our heart is troubled until it rests in you,*"

confesses St. Augustine.[444]

***BG* 3.2** **With these contradicting words, you are confusing my understanding. Therefore, having decided, declare which one is the best way for me to follow."**
vyāmiśreṇe- (with contradicting) *va* (as) *vākyena* (words) *buddhiṃ* (understanding) *mohayasī-* (confusing) *va* (as) *me* (me) / *tad-* (therefore) *ekaṃ* (one) *vada* (declare) *niścitya*

(having decided) *yena* (by which) *śreyo'* (the better state) *ham-* (I) ā*pnuyām* (may obtain) //

The contradicting words are those expressed in the previous chapter of the *Gītā*. On one side, Kṛshṇa had commanded to act, while, on the other, he ordered to repose detached in the Self.

BG* 3.3** **The glorious divine being said, "As I taught before, O sinless one, in this world there are two kinds of being-in-situation: the unity through the knowledge of *sāṃkhya (philosophical enumeration-of-entities) **and *karma-yoga*** (the unity-through-action) **of the mystical sages.**
sri- (the glorious) *bhagavān-* (divine being) *uvāca* (said) *loke'* (world) *smin-* (in this) *dvi-*(two) *vidhā* (kinds) *nishṭha* (being in situation) *purā* (before) *proktā* (said) *mayā'* (by Me) *nagha* (O sinless one) / *jnāna-*(of knowledge) *yogena* (by the union) *sāṃkhyānāṃ* (of the Enumeration of the true entities of the Primordial Essence) *karma-* (of work) *yogena* (by the union) *yoginām* (of the Yogis)//

Kṛshṇa calls Arjuna sinless because nothing can ever tarnish the essence of pure Self-Awareness, our cornerstone and foundation. *However, once we are in the existential situation, the consciousness-of this world defines who we are historically.*

"*The for-itself is nothing other than its situation, then it follows that being-in-situation* defines human reality by accounting both for its being-there and for its being-beyond." In other words, asserts Sartre,[445] whatsoever situation we are in is always the only authentic one. There is a *condemnation to be free*. Truly, we identify with the situation in which we are.

Traditionally, the *Ṛg Veda*[446] divided society in four castes (*varṇa*), the priestly (*brahman*), military (*kshatriya*), merchant (*vaiśya*) and servant (*śūdra*) cast. Split-off (*dalita* √*dal*) from all castes are the *dalits*, the separated out-caste. Kṛshṇa declares,

> ***BG* 4.13-14 "*The four castes were emanated by me according to the diverse allocation of qualities and actions,. Know me as their constant non-acting maker. In fact, actions***

do not affect me, nor I desire the fruit of action." [447]

The Indian caste-system designates interpersonal relation. It categorizes the perception we have of ourselves. Who we really are is beyond our perception. Sartre is right in recognizing that the in-itself is never obtainable by the for-itself.

Describing a servant's self-perception, Sartre writes, "This person *who I have to be* (if I am the waiter in question) and who I am not. It is not that I do not wish to be this person or that I want this person to be different. But rather that there is no common measure between his being and mine. It is a 'representation' for others and for myself, which means that I can be he only in representation... I can not be he, I can only play *at being* him; that is, imagine to myself that I am he... I sustain this role in existence ... I am a ... waiter... But... this can not be in the mode of being in-itself. I am a waiter in the mode of *being what I am not*."[448]

Nevertheless, Sartre discards the *cornerstone* realized by yoga. The freedom he refers to is the one imbedded in the for-itself. Whereas, the one sought in yoga is freedom in-itself. T*he yoga or union, which Kṛshṇa is referring to, is* attained by philosophical insight and is achieved also through action.

BG 3.4 **A person does not obtain freedom from the consequences of actions by inactivity and does not attain bliss simply by renunciation.**
na (not) *karmaṅām-*(of action) *anāraṃbhān-* (non-accomplishment) *naishkarmyaṃ* (freedom from the consequences of acts) *purusho'* (person) *śnute* (obtains) / *na* (not) *ca* (and) *saṃnyasanād-* (by renunciation) *eva* (only) *siddhiṃ* (bliss) *samadhigacchati* (attains) //

The consequences of our deeds bind us. Nevertheless, it is not by renouncing to act that one reaches freedom from the outcomes of behavior. It is the adherence to Aware-Certitude that liberates us. Awareness is Truth in-Itself, it is the *veritas*, which the *low-caste* Pontius Pilate could not understand.[449]

> "*Then, verily, Satya-kāma jā-bāla* (*truth-longing son-of-born-Girly*) *addressed his mother Ja-bālām* (*born-Girly-of-sixteen*), *'Revered mother, I wish to live the life of a celibate religious student.'*

Then, he went to Gautama (Highest-cow-herder), son of Haridrumat (exultant-in-light-dissolving), and said, 'O holy teacher, I wish to live the life of a religious celibate student. Therefore, reverend sir, may I approach you?'

He [Gautama] *replied, 'Now then, my dear, who are your ancestors?'*[450] *He* [Satyakāma] *answered, 'Sir, I do not know who are my ancestors. I asked my mother and she answered me, - I do not know who your ancestors were; I got you in my youth, when I was serving others with many works. However, I am Jabālā-Girly by name and you are named Satyakāma-truth-longing. Thus, Sir, I am Satyakāma Jābāla.*

He [Gautama] *said to him, 'Only a Brahmin could speak this way, therefore, my dear, bring the sacrificial fire, I shall initiate you because you have not deviated from the truth."*[451]

By contrast, it is interesting to note that, in the present merchant-minded caste-free-system, the same question regarding paternity had a completely different effect, stirring trouble and shame. Rani Bai, an Indian *devadasi*-courtesan, recounts, "'Every day my children ask: who is my father? They do not like having a mother who is in this business.' 'Once I tried to open a bank account with my son... We went to fill in the form, and the manager asked: 'Father's name?' After that, my son was angry. He said I should not have brought him into the world like this'"[452]

The *Vajrasūcika Upanishad*, the Pinpointed-thunderbolt, concludes denying any *birthright* in the caste distinction. In fact,

"*Brāhmaṇa, one who has divine knowledge, is neither the living being nor the physical individual body. The Brāhmaṇa is such not because of birthright or knowledge or for the work performed, neither because of pious acts. The Brāhmaṇa is the Self without a second, devoid of any difference due to birth, attribute or action.*"[453]

***BG* 3.5** **Surely, no one, not even for a moment, can really stay without performing some action. Indeed, everyone is forced helplessly to do according to his or**

her natural dispositions.
na-(not) *hi* (surely) *kaścit* (anyone) *kṣaṇam* (a moment) *api* (even) *jātu* (trutfully) *tiṣṭhaty* (stands) *akarmakṛt* (without performing some action) / *kāryate* (is forced to do) *hy* (indeed) *avaśaḥ* (helpless) *karma* (action) *sarvaḥ* (all) *prakṛtijair* (by the naturally-born) *guṇaiḥ* (qualities) //

Action can never be stopped. Even sitting in meditation or sleeping with no dreams is still doing something.

Ramana Maharshi clearly stated,

"*The life of action need not be renounced. If you meditate in the right manner, then the current of mind induced will continue to flow even in the midst of your work. It is as though there were two ways of expressing the same idea; the same line you take in meditation will be expressed in your activities. As you go on you will find that your attitude towards people, events, and objects will gradually change. Your actions will tend to follow your meditations of their own accord... Silence is the only real activity.*"[454]

Ānandamayī Mā distinguishes between selfless actions performed while duality persists and that one performed in a state of yoga.

"*When impersonal work is being carried out and watched as by a spectator, a deep joy surges up from within... Nevertheless, this welling-up of joy is not identical with Self-realization... But the aforesaid holds good only when action is not tainted by a sense of possessiveness. However, even this state is by no means Self-realization. The play of one who has attained to final consummation is entirely different from the work that has become selfless by effort... So long as the duality of precept and action persists, one cannot possibly speak of Self-realization.*"[455]

***<u>BG</u>* <u>3.6.</u>** **Who, controlling the faculties of action, remains in the mind remembering the objects of the senses, is called a false practitioner and self-deluded.**
karme-(of action) *ndriyāṇi* (faculties) *saṃyamya-* (controlling) *ya* (who) *āste* (remains) *manasā* (by mind) *smaran* (remembering) / *indriyā-* (faculties of the senses) *rthān* (objects) *vimūḍh-*

(deluded) *ātmā* (self) *mithyā-* (false) *cāraḥ* (practicing) *sa* (he) *ucyate* (is called) //

Remembrance itself is an act. Those, who meditate controlling their senses while thinking of former experiences, are not abstaining from action. On the contrary, they do not realize that they are living in the past, in the realm of death, that which no longer is. The for-itself is always "being-for-death,"[456] for-the-past, never life of the present. Contrary to Heidegger's view, *being-for-death* is inauthentic. In fact, authentic is only the Present.

To a devotee, who asked Ramana Maharshi what prevents Self-realization, he answered

"*until the mind attains, effortlessly, its natural state of freedom from concepts. That is, till the sense of 'I' and 'mine' no longer exists... memories chiefly, habits of thought, accumulated tendencies* [hinder Self-realization]...

Seek for the Self through meditation in this manner trace every thought back to its origin which is only the mind. Never allow thoughts to run on. If you do it will be unending. Take it back to its starting place - the mind – again and again, and it and the mind will both die of inaction."[457]

BG 3.7 **However, o Arjuna-white-lightening, does extremely well he who, controlling with the mind the faculties of the senses, undertakes unity-in-action (*karma-yoga*) while having the faculties of action unattached.**
yas-(who) *tv-*(indeed) *indriyāṇi* (faculties of the senses) *manasā* (by the mind) *niyamyā-*(controlling) *rabhate-* (undertakes) *ṛjuna* (o White Arjuna) / *karma-* (action) *indriyaiḥ* (by the faculties of) *karma-* (action) *yogam-* (union) *asaktaḥ* (unattached) *sa* (he) *viśishyate* (does extremely well) //

The *Kaṭha Upanishad*[458] and Plato[459] metaphorically compare the mind to a charioteer and the senses to horses. When the mind restrains the horses of the senses, it is unity-in-action, *karma-yoga*. The five action's-faculties, viz. *karma-indriya*, are:

1) holding, implemented by the hand,
2) motion, executed by the foot,

3) word, articulated by the larynx,
4) elimination, carried out by the organ of excretion, and
5) procreation, fulfilled by the organ of generation.

When these actions are controlled and looked upon from the distance, stillness and desirelessness of Pure Awareness, then they become *unified-actions, i.e. karma-yoga*. This is the way of liberation. The consciousness-*of* the world controls the world without becoming subjected to it.

***BG* 3.8** **Perform your work always with concentration. Indeed action is greater than inaction, in fact, not even the life of your body can be sustained with inaction.**
niyataṃ (always quite concentrated up) *kuru* (perform) *karma* (work) *tvaṃ* (you) *karma* (action) *jyāyo* (greater than) *hy-* (indeed) *akarmaṇaḥ* (inaction) / *śarīra-*(of the body) *yātrā* (support of life) *pi* (even) *ca* (and) *te* (your) *na* (not) *prasiddhyed-* (may be accomplished) *akarmaṇaḥ* (inaction) //

Even a vegetative state still requires action to maintain life. However, this state is not a unity-of-action (*karma-yoga*) unless one is aware of its being vegetative. Therefore, any action one performs, should be done with full attention and concentration.

***BG* 3.9** **This world is bond by action, in another manner the work is done for the sake of sacrifice. For that sake, O son of Kuntī-Incantation, perform action free from selfish desire.**
yajñā- (of sacrifice) *rthāt* (for the sake of) *karmaṇo'* (by work done) *nyatra* (in another manner) *loko* (the world) *yaṃ* (this) *karma-* (by action) *bandhanaḥ* (bond)/ *tad-* (of that) *arthaṃ* (for the sake) *karma* (action) *kaunteya* (O son of Kuntī-Incantation) *mukta-* (free from) *saṅgaḥ* (selfish desire) *samācara* (perform)//

This world is tied to action. In other words, the action should take place as performing a sacrifice. Namely, sacrifice is that which *makes-sacred* or *puts-into-the-sacredness-of-existence* the whole world.[460] However, this world enchants us. Therefore, one must perform action without being charmed by it or being attached to it. Therefore, un-enchanted by the object, perform your action with detachment.

Here, Arjuna is called son of Kuntī-Incantation. In fact, he is the son of Pāṇḍú, the white one, and Kuntī-Incantation. They had conceived Arjuna thanks to the intervention of the god Indra, the '*I*.' In fact, Pāṇḍú had been cursed and without that divine help he would have died.

***BG* 3.10** **In ancient times, the father of creatures, having pro-created the creatures with sacrifices, said, 'Spread actively by means of this; let this be for you, like a milk cow bestower of desired loves.'**
saha- (with) *yajñāḥ* (sacrifices) *prajāḥ* (the creatures) *sṛshṭvā* (having pro-created) *puro-* (in ancient times) *vāca* (said) *prajā-* (of creatures) *patiḥ* (the father) / *anena* (by this) *prasavishyadhvam-* (spread actively by means of) *esha* (this) *vo* (of you) *stv* (let it be) *ishṭa-*(desired) *kāma-*(loves) *dhuk* (bestower like a milk cow) //

As we have seen in the *Bṛhadāraṇyaka Upanishad*, Death, Mṛtyu the Creator, is the Father of creature. It procreates, through a process of sacrifices with circularities of consciousness. They are similar to the metaphoric day circles in the Biblical account. That is, makes the world sacred by putting it into the subject-object circle of existence.

> "*And The Transcendent blessed them, and The Transcendent said unto them, Be fruitful, and multiply, and replenish the earth, and subdue it: and have dominion over the fish of the sea, and over the fowl of the air, and over every living thing that moveth upon the earth.*"[461]

The world, then, becomes a great theater for the enjoyment of the senses. This great world of representation[462] becomes like a milk cow, which satisfies all desires.

***BG* 3.11** **With this, having pleased the gods, those resplendent beings of the senses will please you. Mutually pleasing one another, you shall achieve supreme happiness.**
devān- (resplendent beings of the senses) *bhāvayatā-* (having pleased) *nena* (by this) *te* (those) *devā* (resplendent beings of the senses) *bhāvayantu* (will please) *vaḥ* (you)/ *parasparaṃ* (mutually) *bhāvayantaḥ* (pleasing one another) *śreyaḥ*

(happiness) *param-* (supreme) *avāpsyatha* (you shall achieve)//

The gods are the resplendent beings of the senses, in fact,

"*all the faculties of the senses become one in their corresponding deities.*"[463]

And

"*the gods are the five channels of perception of this heart.*"[464]

Therefore, as the senses are pleased, so, in return, those resplendent-faculties please you.

***BG* 3.12** **Verily, the resplendent beings of the senses, being pleased by sacrifices, will award you with the desired enjoyments.' However, s/he who enjoys what is given by them without having given it back to them certainly is a thief.**
ishṭān- (desired) *bhogān-* (enjoyments) *hi* (verily) *vo* (to you) *devā* (resplendent beings of the senses) *dāsyante* (will award) *yajña-* (by sacrifices) *bhāvitāḥ* (being pleased) / *tair-*(by them) *dattān-* (given) *apradāya-* (without having given) *ibhyo* (to these) *yo* (who) *bhuṅkte* (enjoys) *stena* (thief) *eva* (certainly) *saḥ* (he)//

The epistemic act is a *sacrificial* one that makes (*facere*) the world sacred (*sacer*), holy by conferring to it the *sacredness* of existence. Something, in fact, exists only if known. The act of sacrifice is the act that puts the object into existence. The resplendent faculties of the senses receive pleasure by that act. The eyes see the beautiful. The ears hear the melodic. The nose smells the aromatic. The tongue tastes the sweet. The hand touches the smooth.

In return, these various faculties reward the experiencer with the gratifications s/he has desired. If, however, the enjoyer takes the enjoyment or fruit of that action for him/herself, then s/he is tied down by that transient appropriation. That is, s/he has not referred that experience to the Aware-Certitude, which makes all possible.

"*In the search after Truth one must not allow oneself to be overpowered by anything, but should watch carefully whatever phenomena may supervene, keeping fully conscious, wide awake, in fact retaining complete mastery over oneself... It opens up one's being to the light, to that which is eternal,"*[465] taught Ānandamayī Mā.

This is the difference between Abel and Cain. The first one, a herder, offers to The Transcendent the prime of his live animal-senses and his sacrifice is accepted by The Transcendent.[466] "The true meaning of animal sacrifice, She [Ānandamayī Mā] explained, was sacrificing one's lower (animal) nature... to raise himself to his inherent divine status."[467]

Cain, a tiller, on the other hand, at the time of death gives up all the fruits of his actions and his sacrifice was not accepted by The Transcendent.[468] Therefore, abstain from the attachment to the fruits of your actions and revert back to the Absolute-Awareness from which all this comes.

***BG* 3.13** **The devotees** [who honor with offerings and] **interiorize what is left of** [that epistemic] **sacrifice are liberated from all faults. While, the wicked ones, who cook-up experiences for selfish reasons, experience suffering.**
yajña- (sacrifice) *śishṭā-* (remains) *śinaḥ* (eating-interiorizing) *santo* (devotees) *mucyante* (are liberated) *sarva-* (from all) *kilbishaiḥ* (faults and guilt) // *bhuñjate* (experience) *te* (they) *tv* (verily) *aghaṃ* (suffering) *pāpā* (wicked) *ye* (who) *pacanty-* (cook-up) *ātma-*(for self) *kāraṇāt* (reason) //

In fact, those devotees, who revert to those god-senses what they enjoyed from them, enter in a state of internal realization. That is, a blissful and liberated awareness observing the world in its pure *being-there* without attachment. Then, "you abide in Being – unchanging, timeless, deathless," declares Tolle, "and you are no longer dependent for fulfillment or happiness on the outer world of constantly fluctuating forms. You can enjoy them, play with them, create new forms, appreciate the beauty of it all. But there will be no need to attach yourself to any of it."[469]

On the other hand, those unhappy ones who remain in their mental attachment to the objective world experience suffering.

<u>*BG* 3.14</u> Beings come into existence from epistemic-food, the cause of that food is the rain-of-I-consciousness. That I-consciousness comes into being from intentional-sacrifice; that sacrifice comes into existence from the creative-action.
annād (from epistemic-food) *bhavanti* (come into existence) *bhūtāni* (beings) *parjanyād* (from personified-rain, Indra the I-consciousness) *anna-* (of food) *saṃbhavaḥ* (the cause) / *yajñād* (from consecration-into-existence) *bhavati* (becomes) *parjanyo* (personified-rain, Indra 'I') *yajñaḥ* (intentional-sacrifice) *karma-* (from action) *samudbhavaḥ* (comes into existence) //

One of the most common metaphors in the Indian sacred text is equating food (*anna*) with knowledge. As we must in-gest in our body external elements as food, in order to be nourished, similarly we must *introduce*, put in our brain the object perceived as external in order to know it. No one can see, hear, taste, feel, smell something if it does not become "*food for thought*." It is because something, an object, an experience, an event is processed by the mind that we can say it exists as an object, an experience, an event. Therefore, it is from this *epistemic-food* that knowledge and existence is established. Existence is established only by the immanent inseparable synthetic relationship between a subject and an object, namely a knower and a known. We can never affirm the existence of something that is not in our brain as a thought. Even imaginations, or dreams and/or hallucinations, are still ideal mental products and their content exists as reality or imaginations, or as dreams and/or as hallucinations in the mind. Any attempt to demonstrate that a world in-itself is outside the mind fails inevitably.

The *rain* of consciousness vivifies and brings to life the objective world. The central cause of that *epistemic-food* (*anna*) is the 'I-consciousness,' the *eater* and enjoyer of that nourishment or the thinker of that *food-for-thought*. Here, the metaphor for that 'I' is rain.

One of the Sanskrit words for rain is v*ṛṣṭí*, connected to the senses[470] or the three stages of life.[471] The term derives from the verb *vṛṣ*, to rain, which in turn refers to "*parjanya, indra*."[472] Our text uses the term *parjánya*, meaning the "personified... god of rain... Indra."[473] He is called "the thunder" (*stanayitnu*) which is the voice and "the lightning" (*aśani*), signifying and illuminating the object of knowledge.

> "*Indra,*" chants the *Ṛg Veda*, "*you came like a wide-striding true friend to nourish, since every thought is made entirely by epistemic-food.*"[474]

All the organs and the faculties of the senses (*indri-ya*) belong, to Indra as the one and only 'I.'[475] The god Indra has no rival.

> "*Vital Breath... is Indra, the Conqueror. He is the I without a rival. Verily, the second, the other is the rival.*"[476]

All the faculties (*indriya*) belong to Indra, to the 'I.' According to the Indian tradition, they are,

1) the five senses or organs of perception (*buddh-īndriyāṇi* or *jñān-endriyāṇi*: ear, eye, nose, skin, tongue);
2) the five instruments of action (*karm-endriyāṇi*: anus, feet, generative-organs, hands, larynx);
3) the four inner organs (*antar-indriyāṇi*: ego-consciousness-*ahaṃkāra*, mind-*manas*, reason-*buddhi*, thought-*citta*).

All the gods and all the vital spirits, recognize Indra, as the first among them. Metaphorically, he is the '*I*.' In fact, "If the self were to collapse and disappear completely, the mind would lose its orientation, the ability to gather its parts. One's thoughts would be freewheeling, unclaimed by an owner... We would look unconscious."[477]

Saint Pio describes his way of praying as follows:
"*All the internal and external senses, together with the same faculties of the soul find themselves in an indescribable stillness.*"[478]

Our text continues stating that rain, the I-consciousness – Indra, comes into being from sacrifice (*yajña*). The nature of this sacrifice needs to be explained. The *Bhagavad-Gītā*[479] emphatically declares that

> ***BG 4.24* "The Transcendent-Brahman-act-of-oblation and the Brahman-offering are offered by Brahman in the Brahman-fire."**

This same concept is present in other Indian sacred texts. For the *Ṛg Veda*, Creation (*sarga* or *sṛshṭi*) is a sacrificial act of epistemic dimensions performed by *"the Cosmic being as sacrificial butter... He is oblation... is the sacrificial victim."*[480]

And the *Upanishads* concord,

" Verily, the Cosmic-Person is sacrifice."[481]

"The Cosmic Being is the Transcendental I, the divine-digestive-fire-common-to-all,"[482]

"He, who thus knows, is present to his own creation."[483]

In an idealistic circularity, the three acts, creation, knowledge and sacrificial act are the same. Sacrifice implies

- a sacrificer or invoker (*āhva*),
- a sacrificial offering (*adātṛ*), and
- a bestower of grace (*dātṛ*), to whom the sacrifice is directed.[484]

Śrī Ānandamayī Mā,[485] the Joy Permeated Mother, after Her initiation (*sādhanā*) , "identified Herself with a particular deity and subsequently worshipped that very deity. Underlying all Her worship was the theme of Oneness: worshipper, worshipping, and the object of Her worship merged. During that phase She was hardly conscious of Her body and only occasionally touched food or felt the need of sleep... She had agreed to conduct the Kālī *pūjā* [ceremonial worship] in 1925. During the ceremony She deviated from common practice by placing flowers and sandals paste upon Her own head instead of the idol, obviously implying that She was the true reflection of Kālī and not the image."[486]

Again, in the *Vedas*, these last three acts are fulfilled by the same person. The Divine-fire is, at the same time, the offering, priest, who at a sacrifice invokes the gods, and the god to whom the sacrifice is offered,

"May Divine-flame, the sacrificer, the power of the wise bard, the truthful, the brightest glory, resplendent-being-of-awareness, come here with the resplendent-beings-of-the-senses."[487]

"O resplendent being ... sacrifice to yourself."[488]

With a process of discrimination, the sacrificer sacrifices its own unity to know the otherness.

Mṛtyu, Death, Hunger creates with three sacrificial circularities.

1) First he generates its own self with an act of self-transparency, corresponding to the NREM state of sleep.

2) Then, with a second sacrifice he creates its I-consciousness, corresponding to the REM dream state.
3) Finally, he sacrificially generates its ego-consciousness, which, thereafter, is free to think in the waking world.[489]

The sacrifice, impelled by Mṛtyu's generative hunger, can be indicated as intentionality, namely, "the stream of consciousness directed toward the objective world." That "*stream... flow of rain... of semen*" (*retas*) is a perfect 360° full circular year (*saṃvatsarā*).[490] It is cognate to the *Biblical* day or year (יוֹם *yowm*) of creation.[491] It flows circularly from the subject to the object and back to the subject again.

Look at each individual epistemic circle of consciousness as a rain filled whirlwind (*vāyumaṇḍala*) produced by the merger of two former airstream fronts. In turn, this newly generated twister amalgamates with other cyclones yielding additional tornados and so on. During every fusion, each conscious-whirlwind permeates its own directional energy and nourishing rain into its paired twister. Like celestial bodies pursuing their own collisional orbits in the universe, each one of those spiraling windy circularities follows its own intrinsic drive. Consciousness-*of* is similar to the circular wind (*vāyu*). It is the generated by the I-consciousness named Indra, the lord of rain. In turn, this last one becomes the rain fecundating the food of thought. This is the food that sustains the world and sets it existent in the mind.

<u>*BG* 3.15</u> Know that action springs from the Creator and the Creator comes into existence from the Imperishable. Therefore, the Omnipresent Transcendent is constantly standing firmly in the center of the epistemic-sacrifice.
karma (action) *brahmo-* (Creator) *dbhavaṃ* (springs from) *viddhi* (know) *brahmā-* (Creator) *kshara-* (Imperishable) *samudbhavam* (comes into existence) / *tasmāt* (therefore) *sarva-* (everywhere) *gataṃ* (extending) *brahma* (Transcendent) *nityaṃ* (constantly) *yajñe* (in sacrifice) *pratishṭhitam* (standing firmly) //

The whole circle of epistemic activity initiates from Mṛtyu as consciousness-*of* the objective world. However, that consciousness-*of* springs out and comes into existence from the necessity to conceptualize Awareness. That is the Omnipresent

Transcendent Awareness, the Self of selves, which stands firmly at the center of the circle of the epistemic-sacrifice.

***BG* 3.16** **Thus, s/he who does carry out here unaware of the circular process of knowledge set in motion, s/he lives a useless life in pain and in the pleasure of the senses, o son of Pārtha-who-extends-light.**
evaṃ (thus) *pravartitaṃ* (set in motion) *cakraṃ* (circularity) *nā-* (not) *nuvartayatī-* (carry out) *ha* (here) *yaḥ* (who) / *aghā-* (pain) *yur* (life) *indriyā-* (in senses) *rāmo* (pleasure) *moghaṃ* (useless) *pārtha* (O son of Pārtha-who-extends-light) *sa* (he) *jīvati* (lives)

"*For humans, is not worth living an unexamined life,*"[492] declared Socrates.

Nevertheless, there is no sin or punishment for iniquities, only consequences. It is like placing a hand in the fire, the burning is not a punishment, it is a consequence. That is the meaning of the Biblical injunction,

> "*Life for life,*
> *Eye for eye, tooth for tooth, hand for hand, foot for foot,*
> *Burning for burning, wound for wound, stripe for stripe.*"[493]

Nevertheless, an all forgiving and merciful Transcendent cannot want to punish. Pain and/or pleasure come about as ignorance deriving from not-realizing the central awareness from which everything springs and to which all goes. Humans, states Ramana Maharshi,

"*are blinded by ignorance. Sometimes your teeth suddenly bite your tongue, do you break them out in consequence?*"[494]

Therefore,

> "*Love your enemies, bless them that curse you, do good to them that hate you, and pray for them which despitefully use you, and persecute you.*"[495]

And, on the Cross,

> "*Jesus said, Father, forgive them; for they know not what they do.*"[496]

And, the first principle of Socrates, states that "Neither injury nor retaliation nor warding off evil by evil is ever right."[497] In fact, they imply personal selfish revenge.

Here Kṛshṇa calls Arjuna son of Pārtha, the one who shines upon and extends light on something,[498] as it will be clear from the action described in the next stanza.

***BG* 3.17** **However, a person who takes happiness in the self conceivably is satisfied with the self. In fact, there is no action for whosoever is delighted only with the self.**
yas (who) *tv* (indeed) *ātma-* (in self) *ratir* (pleasure) *eva* (only) *syād* (perhaps) *ātma-* (the self) *tṛptaś* (satisfied with) *ca* (and) *mānavaḥ* (the man) / *ātmany* (the self) *eva* (only) *ca* (and) *saṃtushṭas* (delighted with) *tasya* (his) *kāryaṃ* (action) *na* (no) *vidyate* (there is) //

Ānandamayī Mā states,
"*What alone is worthy to be called 'action' is that action by which man's eternal union with The Transcendent becomes revealed; all the rest is useless.*"[499]
That realization is the only true light in the world.

***BG* 3.18** **Here, indeed, for him or her there is no reason whatsoever for action, nor for inaction, and for him/her there is nothing s/he expects from any one.**
na- (no) *iva* (indeed) *tasya* (of him) *kṛtenā-* (for action) *rtho* (reason) *nā-* (nor) *kṛtene-* (for inaction) *ha* (here) *kaścana* (whatsoever) / *na* (no) *cā-* (and) *sya* (of him) *sarva-* (in all) *bhūteshu* (living beings) *kaścid* (any) *artha-* (thing) *vyapāśrayaḥ* (expectation) //

At the level of Self-Awareness-in-itself there is no-action (*kṛtá*), no-creation (*kṛ́ti*),[500] no-death, no-hunger, no-desire, no-self-for-itself, no-conscience-*of*, therefore, there is no-being-in-situation. The pure stillness of Awareness, the Kingdom that is not-conscious-*of*-this-world wants nothing, desires nothing asks for nothing from anyone.

***BG* 3.19** **Therefore, always unattached, perform action as duty. Indeed, performing action unattached a person certainly achieves the Supreme.**
tasmād (therefore) *asaktaḥ* (unattached) *satataṃ* (always) *kāryaṃ* (as duty) *karma* (action) *samācara* (perform) / *asakto* (unattached) *hy* (indeed) *ācaran* (performing) *karma* (action)

param (the Supreme) *āpnoti* (achieves) *pūrushaḥ* (a person) //

The enlightenment, declares Ramana Maharshi, "*changed my mental attitude and habits. I had formerly some preferences and aversions. All these dropped off and all food was swallowed with equal indifference. I would put up with every burden imposed on me at home, every slight at my expense by the boys. Studies and duties became a matter of utter indifference and I was going through studies turning over pages mechanically.*"[501]

<u>*Political morality*</u>

<u>*BG* 3.20</u> Historically, Janaka, the generator, and the other kings performed and completed their accomplishments only through action. In a similar way you are required to act and also to look after the wellbeing of this world.
karmaṇa- (by action) *iva* (only) *hi* (verily) *saṃsiddhim* (complete accomplishment) *āsthitā* (who has performed) *janakā-* (Janaka-generator) *dayaḥ* (and other) / *loka-* (of the world) *saṃgraham-* (protection) *evā-* (even) *pi* (also) *saṃpaśyan* (looking upon) *kartum* (to act) *arhasi* (you are required) //

In the field of time, rulers and leaders, like Janaka, king of Videha,[502] had to perform political actions to care for the wellbeing of their subjects and country. Thus, also Arjuna and everyone else should do the same.

"*The Master* [Confucius (*Kǒngfūzǐ*)] *said, 'Let him* [the king] *preside over them* [the people] *with gravity; -- then they will reverence him. Let him be filial and kind to all; -- then they will be faithful to him. Let him advance the good and teach the incompetent; -- then they will eagerly seek to be virtuous... The requisites of government are that there be... the confidence of the people in their ruler... if the people have no faith in their rulers, there is no standing for the state.*'"[503]

In ancient Egypt Pyramids were symbols of the connection between the Pharaoh, as a divinity projected in heaven, and his subjects-builders on earth.[504]

***BG* 3.21** **The common person does whatsoever the best king does; the ruler sets the standard, which the country follows.**
yad- (what) *yad* (what) *ācarati* (does) *śreshṭhas* (the best king) *tat-* (that) *tad* (that) *eve-* (also) *taro* (the common) *janaḥ* (person) / *sa* (he) *yat* (what) *pramāṇaṃ* (standard) *kurute* (makes) *lokas* (the country) *tad* (that) *anuvartate* (follows) //

Here, the *Gītā* states what Kant will be writing about two millennia later, namely, his categorical imperative. "Act only according to that maxim by which you can want (*wollen*) it to become at the same time a universal (*allgemeines*) law." And, in his second formulation, "Act according to the maxim which itself can become at the same time a universal (*allgemeinen*) law."[505]

However, Kant's imperative seems to be a fictitious remake of the *golden rule*. In fact, the will (*wille*), which is very well conscious-*of* being individualized, wants (*wolle*) its individuality to be universal (*allgemeinen*). Nevertheless, that universality (*allgemeinheit*), as such, is a noumenon, a thought but not known.

What we have in this stanza of the *Gītā* is the clear rendering of relative moral rules. The king sets laws intended to be universal. The common citizens, in turn, must make them theirs, in the hope that the legislation is for the best. The ruler and his/her subjects would truly be enlightened if they were to realize what Kṛshṇa will say next.

***BG* 3.22** **O Pārtha, son-of-light-extender, in the three world-states** (of wakefulness, dream and sleep)**, there is nothing that ought to be done by me, nor anything not obtained that should be obtained; however, I am the foundation of action itself.**
na (not) *me* (by me) *pārthā-* (O son of light extender) *sti* (is) *kartavyaṃ* (which ought to be done) *trishu* (in *the* three) *lokeshu* (worlds) *kiṃcana* (anything) / *nā-* (no) *navāptam* (not obtained) *avāptavyaṃ* (to be obtained) *varta* (subsistence) *eva* (certainly) *ca* (and) *karmaṇi* (in action) //

Kṛshṇa, here, identifies with the Transcendent-Self-Awareness and Arjuna with the consciousness-*of*, extender of light. Awareness is Freedom-in-itself. It does not require anything nor is compelled to do anything. It is absolute autonomous spontaneity. Nonetheless, contrary to Kant's categorical imperative (*kategorischer imperativ*), it is devoid of any necessity. However, nothing is without It, all is founded on It. In fact, how can one affirm anything without awareness? Try if you can.

<u>*BG* 3.23</u> Truthfully, if I should not be present always alert in action, everywhere all men would imitate my track, O son of light-extender.
yadi (if) *hy* (certainly) *ahaṃ* (I) *na* (not) *varteyaṃ* (should be present) *jātu* (always) *karmaṇy* (in action) *atandritaḥ* (alert) / *mama* (my) *vartmā-* (track) *nuvartante* (would imitate) *manushyāḥ* (all men) *pārtha* (O son of light extender) *sarvaśaḥ* (everywhere) //

Kṛshṇa, as the Transcendent-Self-Awareness, is like the wheel present[506] under a cart. If the wheel should stop turning on its track,[507] the whole cart would follow suit[508] and stop.

The action performed by that Awareness is the Shining of the Pure-Self. It is the infinite radial projection of the Center in-Itself in all directions. On the surface of an apparent circumference or wheel, produced by the Shining-One, all points perform circular activities. Without the Original Aware Shining no activity would ever be possible for anyone.

RADIAL PROJECTION OF THE CENTER IN-ITSELF

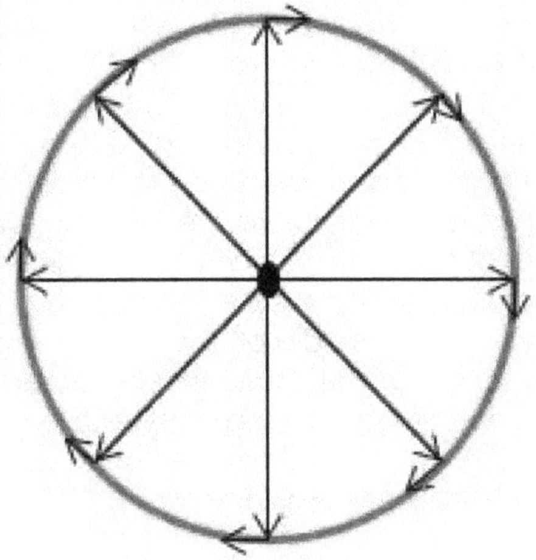

Along that circumference all creatures, namely each radiated individualized point, proceed in circular activity. Each point *chases* the preceding one. The action performed now has its intentioned direction towards a projected transcendent, which cannot be achieved objectively. In fact, action is always *in-fieri*, in the process-*of*, in the course-*of*. Ultimately, action becomes the subject-object sacrificial act[509] that puts the wheel of the objective world into motion and into existence. Mṛtyu's consciousness-*of* the objective world tends to reach, through and with thought, the elusive Center not as the center but as its point radiated on the circumference.

***BG* 3.24** **These worlds would be placed into ruin if I would not perform action and I would be creator of confusion and I would destroy all these creatures.**
utsīdeyur (would be placed into ruin) *ime* (these) *lokā* (worlds) *na* (do not) *kuryāṃ* (perform) *karma* (action) *ced* (if) *aham* (I) / *saṃkarasya* (of confusion) *ca* (and) *kartā* (creator) *syām* (would be) *upahanyām* (would destroy) *imāḥ* (all these) *prajāḥ* (creatures) //

Therefore, if Awareness should not shine the world would turn out in chaos or collapse in total blind uninhabitable disordered entropy.

***BG* 3.25** **O descendant of Bhārata-bearer-of-oblation, as the ignorant perform attached in action, thus, the wise must act without attachment while intentioning the perception of the objective world.**
saktāḥ (attached) *karmaṇy* (in action) *avidvāṃso* (the ignorant) *yathā* (as) *kurvanti* (they act) *bhārata* (O descendant of Bhārata bearer of oblation) / *kuryād* (must act) *vidvāṃs* (the wise) *tathā-* (thus) *saktaś* (without attachment) *cikīrshur* (intending to promote) *loka-* (of the world) *saṃgraham-* (perception) //

However, we should not forget the original intent of action, namely to reach the transcendent center of Awareness. In order to do so, it is required a complete reversion of direction. Not any longer directed towards the tempting object, but offered as an oblation to one's own Real Self.

This requires an *action that is not an action*. Therefore, an action which is devoid of all attachment to its fruits or outcomes and is not regarded as an object of thought.

Different from the ruler's concern for the subjects' well-being,(*BG*3.20) this unattached action does not mean elimination of the perceived (*saṃgraha*)[510] world, but it denotes the serenely preservation of intentionality (*cikīrshur*)[511] without identification with the object. Then, Yoga-meditation[512] becomes mindfulness with eyes open, not closed.[513]

***BG* 3.26** **The seer performing in a state of unity should not perturb the mind of the ignorant attached to action, but should cause them to be pleased in all actions.**
na (not) *buddhi-* (the mind) *bhedaṃ* (to perturb) *janayed* (should cause) *ajñānāṃ* (of the ignorant) *karma-* (in action) *saṃginām* (attached) / *joshayet* (should cause to be pleased) *sarva-* (all) *karmāṇi* (actions) *vidvān* (the seer) *yuktaḥ* (united) *samācaran* (performing) //

Throughout history, different religions and many political beliefs have been guilty of genocides, inquisitions, crusades, cultural purges, enslavements, *cult brainwashing and* coerced confessions. *Many missionaries* take away from natives of ancestral lands their state of pristine innocence and *force their* conversions. Any law, claiming a divine mandate and therefore imposing it on different cultures, has definite historical foundations but hardly metaphysical origins. Especially, when imposed with violent means. No one has the authority to do so.

Thus, the question arises with Paul: "Is Liberation-salvation attained by the law

> "*of works? Nay,* [he replies] *but by the law of Faith-Awareness. Therefore we conclude that a man is justified by Faith-Awareness without the deeds of the law.*"[514]

The true Yogi, steeped in serene detachment, should never prevent those who are at a different level of realization from enjoying actions.

***BG* 3.27** **Actions are always influenced by the good or evil natural qualities. The 'I,' deluded by egotism, thinks 'I am the doer.'**

prakṛteḥ (of nature) *kriyamāṇāni* (being performed) *guṇaiḥ* (by the qualities) *karmāṇi* (actions) *sarvaśaḥ* (always) / *ahaṃkāra-* (by egotism) *vimūḍhā-* (deluded) *tmā* (the I) *kartāham* (doer) *iti* (thus) *manyate* (thinks) //

Once, "a devout Brahmin... asked [Ramana Maharshi], 'Swami, can a continuous japa [spiritual devotional discipline] ... absolve one from sin?' ... [Bhagavan answered]
'*If the feeling -I am doing japa- is not there, the sins committed by a man will not stick to him. If the feeling -I am doing the japa- is there, why should not the sin arising from bad habits stick on? ... So long as the feeling, -I am doing- is there, one must experience the result of one's acts, whether they are good or bad. How is it possible to wipe out one act with another? When the feeling that -I am doing- is lost, nothing affects a man. Unless one realises* [*sic.*] *the Self, the feeling -I am doing- will never vanish. For one who realises* [*sic.*] *the Self where is the need for japam? Where is the need for tapas* [scorching self-austerities]*? ... Life goes on, but he does not wish for anything... Whatever be the actions that such people do, there is no punya* [merit] *and no papa* [evil] *attached to them. But they do only what is proper according to the accepted standard of the world — nothing else.*'"[515]

***BG* 3.28** **Indeed, o mighty armed one, the knower of the Absolute-principle is the one not attached who understands the distinction between the** [good or evil] **qualities and the actions, thus, that the** [good or evil] **qualities abide in the qualities** [as such, not in the actions]**.**
tattva- (of the Absolute-principle) *vit* (the knower) *tu* (indeed) *mahā-* (o mighty) *bāho* (armed) *guṇa-* (of qualities) *karma-* (of actions) *vibhāgayoḥ* (of the distinction) / *guṇā* (the qualities) *guṇeshu* (in the qualities) *vartanta* (abide) *iti* (thus) *matvā* (understanding) *na* (not) *sajjate* (is attached) //

We are here in full *sāṃkhya* philosophy, as mentioned in a preceding stanza.[BG 3.3] This viewpoint (*darśana*) enumerates different entities. A deified Nature, *prakṛti*, is the passive "producer of... the material world."[516] A Spirit, *púruṣa*, is the passive observer "and a spectator of the *prakṛti* or creative force."[517] From Nature evolve the three qualities (*guṇā*)[518] "of all existing beings (viz. *sattva, rajas,* and *tamas*)." These qualities can be summarized as "good and evil" in the Biblical sense of "everything," as we highlighted before.

Furthermore,

1) *sattva* is the *good,* "the quality of purity or goodness (regarded in the *sāṃkhya* phil.[osophy] as the highest of the three *guṇas*... or constituents of *prakṛti* because it renders a person true, honest, wise... pure, clean &c)."[519]
2) *rajas* is the emotion coloring both *good and evil,* "the second of the three *guṇas* or qualities (... sometimes identified with *tejas* ... passion... it is said to predominate in air, and to be active, urgent, and variable)."[520]
3) *tamas* is the *evil,* the "mental darkness, ignorance, illusion, error (in *sāṃkhya* phil.[osophy] one of the 5 forms of *a-vidyā*... ('spiritual ignorance')... [the cause of heaviness, ignorance, illusion, lust, anger, pride, sorrow, dulness, and stolidity; sin... sorrow]."[521]

Nevertheless, quality, namely, good or evil, is not something inherent to action, *karma*.[522] Quality, as such, has nothing to do with action as such. *Karma,* as *karma,* is neither good nor bad. An exterminating volcanic[523] eruption, a devastating hurricane is neither a good nor a bad activity. Regardless of the damage, destruction or human suffering it may cause, nature's activity, having no quality in itself, remains unmoved.

Similarly, David Hume recognizes that the value or quality is not a property that belongs to the object, in fact, "The vice entirely escapes you, as long as you consider the objet. You never can find it, till you turn your reflexion into your own breast, and find a sentiment of disapprobation, which arises in you, towards this action. Here is a matter matter of fact; but 'tis the object of feeling, not of reason. It lies in your-self, not in the object."[524]

The argument against this reasoning is that good or evil qualities are chosen by a will directing its action. And natural events have no will of their own. Therefore, the willed action appears to be qualified by the will's intention and its outcome. However, even the action of an animal is motivated by a will, but that deed is not qualified as good or evil. Actually, that act is viewed as spontaneous and the will behind it is called natural impulse. In any case, that impulse is sentenced to be killed, in the case of a man-eater carnivore. It can be said that the death sentence is a human defense mechanism, just like the capital punishment for a serial killer. Nevertheless, the moral question arises in the presence of a free will that can freely choose between an action deemed good and another one regarded as bad. In this case, the problem presents the following questions: "Does a free will exist?" If so, "Who determines the bad or good quality of an action?" Remaining with the example of the man-eater, if the lion performs that action, we call it natural spontaneity*, i.e.* the action is neither bad nor good in itself. If a human performs that action it is called *evil*, if performed among the inhabitants of a contemporary modern society. It is called *good*, if performed among the inhabitants of a cannibalistic society. Therefore, again the question: the simple act of flesh-devouring is it *good* or *evil*? We will examine these questions in more details in a separate cover. Here, suffice to establish the fact that actions in themselves have no qualities. The quality as such is a mere provisional attribute superimposed on the act as such. We are not saying that actions have no consequences. They do. We may be pleased or not by those consequences, but that is simply a personal attachment. The true Yogi, however, the realizer of the true essence or substance of things (*tattva*), shines in Pure Awareness unattached to any action and its consequences. And Arjuna is well armed (*mahā-bāha*) to grasp this realization (*sambodhi*).

***BG* 3.29** **Those who are deluded by the** [good or evil] **qualities are attached to the qualities of action. One with perfect knowledge should not unsettle those weak persons with imperfect knowledge.**
prakṛter (of nature) *guṇa-* (by the qualities) *saṃmūḍhāḥ* (deluded) *sajjante* (they are attached) *guṇa-* (of qualities) *karmasu* (in action)/ *tān* (those) *akṛtsna-* (with imperfect) *vido* (knowledge) *mandān* (weak) *kṛtsna-* (one with perfect) *vin* (knowledge) *na* (not) *vicālayet* (should unsettle) //

Those who dwell in the sub-lunar world of duality, utilitarianistically pursuing their own wishes and desires, attach qualities to actions. The true Yogi, however, should not poison the mind of these unenlightened ones by presenting the dichotomy of good and evil, reward and punishment. This may deter them from a true realization and plunge them in the doldrums of dogmatism.

> "*Whoso shall scandalize one of these little ones which believe in me... woe to that man by whom the scandal cometh*!"[525]

BG 3.30 **Having abandoned all actions in me, with full consciousness in the Supreme Self, being without any desire, free from all worldly attachments and desisting from any affliction; Fight!**
mayi (in me) *sarvāṇi* (all) *karmāṇi* (actions) *saṃnyasyā-* (having abandoned) *dhyātma-* (Supreme Self) *cetasā* (with consciousness) / *nirāśīr* (without any desire) *nirmamo* (free from all worldly attachments) *bhūtvā* (being) *yudhyasva* (fight) *vigata-* (desisting from) *jvaraḥ* (affliction) //

The real instruction of the *Gītā* is similar to Jesus' command,

> "*I say unto you, Take no thought for your life...*
> *Which of you by taking thought can add one cubit unto his stature?...*
> *Your heavenly Father knoweth that ye have need of all these things...*
> *Take therefore no thought for the morrow: for the morrow shall take thought for the things of itself.*"[526]

After surrendering all actions, in a state of Pure-Awareness, without any desire, without any worry or mental anguish, engage in the battle of this life without desiring its outcomes. Therefore,

> ***BG 2.48*** ***"Having rejected all attachments, perform your actions in a state of union (yoga-stha); be unaffected by victory as well as failure."***[527]

Then, Kṛshṇa orders Arjuna to

FIGHT!

BG 3.31 **Those humans, who constantly carry out this doctrine of mine, not envious and with full loyalty, become also free from actions.**

ye (who) *me* (my) *matam* (doctrine) *idaṃ* (this) *nityam* (constantly) *anutishṭhanti* (carry out) *mānavāḥ* (humans) / *śraddhāvanto'* (with full loyalty) *nasūyanto* (not envious) *mucyante* (become free) *te'* (they) *pi* (also) *karmabhiḥ* (from actions) //

Enlightened and liberated, you reach freedom when,

> "*with all thy heart, and with all thy soul, and with all thy mind,*"[528]

you identify with your Pure-Self-Certain-Awareness. Martin Luther writes that only Christ's sacrifice saves. "In fact, the faith in Christ makes him live and move and act in me."[529] Incessantly pay attention to That (*tad*), which you eternally are, right Here and right Now.

> "*O you who have attained to faith! Remain conscious of The Transcendent, and seek to come closer unto Him, and struggle hard in His cause, so that you might attain to a happy state,*"[530]

states the *Koran*.

<u>*BG* 3.32</u> However, know that those who, out of envy, do not carry out this doctrine of mine, uncertain about all knowledge, perish without awareness.
ye (those) *tv* (however) *etad* (this) *abhyasūyanto* (out of envy) *nā-* (not) *nutishṭhanti* (carry out) *me* (my) *matam* (doctrine) / *sarva-* (all) *jñāna-* (knowledge) *vimūḍhāṃs* (uncertain about) *tān* (they) *viddhi* (know) *nashṭān* (perish) *acetasaḥ* (without awareness) //

Not carrying out these teachings would not result in a punishment, but would end up perishing in the obvious consequence of having lost Awareness. For similar considerations, Dante condemns in his *Inferno* the resigner pope Celestin V "who made by reason of cowardice the great refusal."[531] He is sentenced to the Vestibule of Hell, which houses "the sad souls of those / who lived without infamy or praise."[532] In fact, that pope relinquished his pontifical duties to pursue a contemplative and ascetic life. As Kṛshṇa orders Arjuna to fight, so, nothing can exempt the relinquishment of a *God given appointment*, as the Papacy is officially conceived. Mystical predilections, as in the ancient case of Celestin V, or health related reasons, as in the contemporary case of Benedict XVI,[533] do not exonerate that desertion, which turns out to be only egotistical in nature.

> *"And let him that is in the field not turn back again for...*
> *no man, having put his hand to the plough, and looking back, is fit for the kingdom of The Transcendent."*[534]

***BG* 3.33** **Even the learned one struggles according to his own original mode of being. All living beings journey through life repressing nature. What good will this do?**
sadṛśaṃ (according) *ceshṭate* (struggles) *svasyāḥ* (by his own) *prakṛter* (original mode of being) *jñānavān* (learned one) *api* (even) / *prakṛtiṃ* (nature) *yānti* (journey through life) *bhūtāni* (all living beings) *nigrahaḥ* (repressing) *kiṃ* (what) *karishyati* (will do) //

> "*Verily, We have created man into* [a life of] *pain, toil, and trial,*"[535]

states the *Koran*. In this existential condition, even knowledgeable persons experience their personal *ǧihād* (جهاد), their own small or great struggle.

Nevertheless, there is no reason to inhibit nature. Freud pointed out the danger of repressing desires.[536] Suppressing desires is a useless and painful self-mortifying act.

The *Upanishad* recognized that in life only

> "*desires* [are the ones who really] *choose.*"[537]

Therefore, look at these cravings unfolding. Then, unified in yoga, realize that their existence is based only on the consciousness-*of* them. Desires, in fact, have no reality outside the psyche.

Jesus said,

> "*Let not your heart be troubled.*"[538]

More so, for the Buddha, suffering *dukkha*) is caused by dissatisfaction-craving-desire (s*amudaya*). The dissolution (*nirodha*) of desire can be obtained through the Middle-Path-to-be-Walked (*madhyamá-pratipad*).

Dukkha, samudaya, madhyamá and *nirodha* are the Buddhist "*Four Truths of the Noble Ones.*" The Middle-Path, equidistant between extreme sensual pleasure (*kāma sukha*) and mortifying austerity (*tapas*), leads to *nirvāṇa*, the final extinguishment of sorrow.[539]

BG 3.34 Delight and repugnance are placed in the objects of the faculties of the senses. One should never come under their control; those are, indeed, his obstructing blocks.
indriyasye-(of the faculties) *ndriyasyā*-(of the senses) *rthe* (in objects) *rāga*- (delight in) *dveshau* (repugnance) *vyavasthitau* (placed) / *tayor* (of them) *na* (never) *vaśam* (control) *āgacchet* (one should come) *tau* (those) *hy* (indeed) *asya* (his) *paripanthinau* (obstructing blocks) //

> ***BG 14.22* "The Blessed Lord said: He who does not hate the glory of contemplative life, or the destiny of active life and not even illusion, when they are present, or desires them when they are absent;**
> ***BG 14.23* he who is seated as neutral and is not troubled by different qualities, he who, even knowing the variety of qualities, remains distant and unmoved;**
> ***BG 14.24* he who, centered in the Self, remains the same in sorrow or happiness, he who looks with the same eye at a lump of dirt, a stone or gold, he who looks at loved and not loved ones equally,**
> ***BG 14.23* he who stands equally firm in defamation or praise and the same in honor or dishonor, he who is equal with friends or enemies and renounces all endeavors, he is said to have gone beyond qualities."**[540]

And Jesus declares,

> "*If any man come to me, and hate not his father, and mother, and wife, and children, and brethren, and sisters, yea, and his own life also, he cannot be my disciple... He that hateth his life in this world shall keep it unto life eternal.*"[541]

And the *Bṛhadāraṇyaka Upanishad* had stated,

> "*There a father is not a father and a mother is not a mother.*"[542]

***BG* 3.35** **One's duty without** [good or evil] **quality is better than the well-performed conduct prescribed by that which is different from the Self. It is better to die while performing one's duty without** [good or evil] **quality. In fact, the performance of the conduct prescribed by that which is different from the Self produces great obstacle."**
śreyān (better) *sva-* (one's self) *dharmo* (duties) *viguṇaḥ* (without quality) *para-* (different from the Self) *dharmāt* (of prescribed conduct) *svanushṭhitāt* (well performed) / *sva-* (in one's self) *dharme* (duties) *nidhanaṃ* (death) *śreyaḥ* (better) *para-* (different from the Self) *dharmo* (of prescribed conduct) *bhayāvahaḥ* (bringing obstacle) //

Joseph Campbell[543] relates the story "of the samurai, the Japanese warrior, who had the duty to avenge the murder of his overlord. When he cornered the man who had murdered his overlord, and he was about to deal with him with his samurai sword, the man in the corner, in the passion of terror, spat in the warrior's face. And the warrior sheathed the sword and walked away... Because he was made angry, and if he had killed that man in anger, then it would have been a personal act. And he had come to do another kind of act, an impersonal act of vengeance."

An action performed because it is your duty, without any attachment and with no reference to its moral qualities or to the duty itself, while identified with the Universal-Self-Aware-Certitude, is more valuable than one well-performed and in line with the current moral beliefs. Actually, it is thanks to duty that allows us to perform an action without attachment, In fact, it is not only the action judged evil that constitutes a spiritual obstacle, but also that which is considered good. In other words, both good and evil deeds produce great obstacle and are different from the Self-act. The Self-act is that of the Sun-of-Awareness, which shines equally on what is usually regarded as repulsive as well as what is considered attractive.

***BG* 3.36** **Arjuna, the white one, said,** **"Then, o descendant of Vṛshṇi** [the mighty Vishṇu the preserver]**, what urges a person to commit this crime,**

even when unwilling and impelled by force?"
arjuna (Arjuna) *uvāca* (said) *atha* (then) *kena* (by what) *prayukto'* (urged) *yaṃ* (this) *pāpaṃ* (crime) *carati* (commit) *pūrushaḥ* (a person) / *anicchann* (without desiring) *api* (although) *vārshṇeya* (descendant of Vṛshṇi, the mighty Vishṇu the preserver) *balād* (by force) *iva* (if) *niyojitaḥ* (impelled) //

Nevertheless, Arjuna, the consciousness-*of* the world, still considers the war, which he feels he is compelled to engage, to be a crime. Therefore, he invokes the Preserver of this world.

***BG* 3.37** **The glorious divine being said, "This lustful desire and this wrathful anger are produced by virtue of emotion. Know this great epistemic-eating being-here as the great evil and enemy.**
śrī- (the glorious) *bhagavān* (divine being) *uvāca* (said) *kāma* (lustful desire) *esha* (this) *krodha* (wrathful anger) *esha* (this) *rajo-* (of emotion) *guṇa-* (by virtue of) *samudbhavaḥ* (produced from) / *mahā-* (great) *śano* (epistemic-eating) *mahā-* (great) *pāpmā* (crime) *viddhy* (know) *enam* (this) *iha* (here) *vairiṇam* (enemy) //

The glorious divine Virgin declares to the seers of Medjugorje,[544]

> "*Abandon yourself totally in The Transcendent. Renounce the disorderly passions. Drive back fear and give yourself, those who know how to abandon oneself know neither obstacles nor fear,*"

The emotional-quality (*rajas-guṇa*), which *colors* good (*sattva*) and evil (*tamas*), produces desire and anger. In the battle of this life, the great-calamity or crime (*mahā-pāpman*), the real enemy is Death-Mṛtyu-Hunger-Desire (*q.v.*). It is the great-eater (*mahā-śana*), the epistemic intentionality which *feeds* on this objective world.

***BG* 3.38** **As fire is covered by smoke and a mirror by dust, just as the embryo is enclosed by the womb, so this consciousness is enveloped in emotion.**
dhūmenā- (by smoke) *vriyate* (is covered) *vanhir* (fire) *yathā-* (just) *darśo* (mirror) *malena* (by dust) *ca* (and) / *yatho-* (just)

lbenā- (by the womb) *vṛto* (is enclosed) *garbhas* (embryo) *tathā* (so) *tene-* (by it) *dam* (this) *āvṛtam* (is surrounded) //

Consciousness-*of* the objective world identifies emotionally and passionately with the objective qualities, which in themselves are mere virtual superimposition. It is like smoke covering the objective fire. Furthermore, it is like dust smearing the mirror reflecting Awareness. Better still, it is like the womb enclosing the embryo. That smoke, that dust and that womb are metaphors of the emotional relationship displayed while consciousness identifies with the objects.

***BG* 3.39** **O son of Kuntī-passion, gnosis is enveloped by this constant enemy of the gnostic in the form of lustful desire never to be satisfied by the epistemic digestive power.**
āvṛtaṃ (enveloped) *jñānam* (gnosis) *etena* (by this) *jñānino* (of the gnostic) *nitya-* (by the constant) *vairiṇā* (enemy) / *kāma-* (of lust) *rupeṇa* (the form) *kaunteya* (o son of Kuntī-passion) *dushpūreṇā-* (never to be satisfied) *nalena* (by the epistemic digestive power) *ca* (and) //

Desires (*kāma*) are never satisfied by the epistemic-digestive-power (*anala*) of the passionate consciousness-*for-itself*. In fact, desires are the constant enemies of the gnostic-realization of Awareness-in-itself (*jñāna*) and of the gnostic-realizer of Awareness (*jñānī*).[545]

***BG* 3.40** **The faculties of the senses, the mind and the intelligence are said to be the foundation of this** (desire) **which envelops the human consciousness confused by all these** (elements).
indriyāṇi (the faculties of the senses) *mano* (the mind) *buddhir* (the intelligence) *asyā-* (of this) *dhishṭhānam* (foundation) *ucyate* (is said) / *etair* (by these) *vimohayaty* (confuses) *esha* (this) *jñānam* (consciousness) *āvṛtya* (enveloping) *dehinam* (of the human) //

Ramana Maharshi reminds[546] us that

"*The one obstacle is the mind.*"

The faculties of the senses, the mind and the intelligence are the foundation of desire. Human consciousness, enveloped by desire, is confused by all those elements.

***BG* 3.41** **Therefore, o best among the descendants of Bharata fire priest, first controlling the senses, conquer, indeed, this crime, which causes to destroy the awareness of consciousness.**
tasmāt (therefore) *tvam* (you) *indriyāṇy* (senses) *ādau* (in the beginning) *niyamya* (controlling) *bharata-* (the descendants of Bharata fire priest) *rshabha* (o best among) / *pāpmānaṃ* (crime) *prajahi* (conquer) *hy* (indeed) *enaṃ* (this) *jñāna-*(of awareness) *vijñāna-*(of consciousness) *nāśanam* (which causes to destroy)//

Therefore, offer yourself in the fire of surrender.

"*Resist not evil.*"[547]

Control your senses. Conquer that which causes the non-identification with the Awareness of consciousness.

***BG* 3.42** **It is said that the faculties of the senses are superior to the senses, superior to them is the mind, also superior to the mind is the intellect, but that which is superior to the intellect is he, the Self.**
indriyāṇi (the faculties of the senses) *parāṇy* (superior) *āhur* (it is said) *indriyebhyaḥ* (than the senses) *paraṃ* (superior) *manaḥ* (the mind) / *manasas* (than the mind) *tu* (also) *parā* (superior) *buddhir* (intellect) *yo* (who) *buddheḥ* (than the intellect) *paratas* (superior) *tu* (but) *saḥ* (he) //

The epistemic reality is composed of elements each one deriving hypostatically from the superior one. At the very top of this tiered reality is Self-Awareness. From It derives the intellect. From the intellect comes the mind. This last one emanates the faculties of the senses. In turn, they produce the senses, at the very bottom of the hierarchy.

***BG* 3.43** **Thus, o mighty armed one, knowing the Self to be superior to the intellect, having firmly composed the I-think by the Self, conquer the difficult to be subjugated enemy in the form of lustful desire."**
evaṃ (thus) *buddheḥ* (to intellect) *paraṃ* (superior) *buddhvā*

(knowing) *saṃstabhyā-* (having firmly composed the mind) *tmānam* (the I) *ātmanā* (by the Self) / *jahi* (conquer) *śatruṃ* (the enemy) *mahā-* (o mighty) *bāho* (armed one) *kāma-* (of lustful desire) *rūpaṃ* (in the form) *durāsadam* (difficult to be subjugated) //

Now that you are armed with the understanding that Self-Awareness is superior to the intellect; now that you have the I-think under the firm control of Self-Awareness (*ātman*); conquer your enemy, in the form of your lustful desires, which are so difficult to subjugate.

BG **Thus is in the glorious Divine-song composition... the third discourse titled Unity in Action.**

iti (thus) *śrīmad-* (the glorious) *bhagavād-* (divine being) *gītā* (song) *sūpa* (composition)... *karma-* (action) *yogo* (unity) *nāma* (named) *tṛtīyo'* (third) *dhyāyaḥ* (discourse).

Here ends the Third Discourse, titled "Unity in Action," of this glorious *Divine-song*.

PART I
C
PERENNIAL ETHIC AWARENESS
New Biblical Exegesis
and other sacred texts

CHAPTER 1

THEORETICAL CONSIDERATIONS

When, faced with the oncoming tragedy of the cross, Jesus

> "*prayed, saying, 'O my Father, if this cup may not pass away from me, except I drink it, Thy will be done.'"*[548]

Even in those terrifying moments, he immediately discarded his own personal desire in order to identify with the Transcendent-Will.

Questions arise, "Who is the Father? What is that He wills?" To answer these questions we should realize that the Father is a metaphoric expression for That which constitutes the foundation of the Entire Reality. In this context, that Foundation is synonym of Transcendent, Pure-Self-Awareness from which we all derive. It is the One-in-Itself, the Zero-Transcendent.

The transcendence of the Father is further confirmed by Jesus, when he states,

> "*Our Founding-Father, which art Transcendent-in-heaven.*"[549]

Namely, heaven is *trans*, beyond, above, on the other side. It is that which must be *ascended*. Apodictical-Self-Awareness is the Fundamental-Transcendent-Reality.

> "*May Thy power-name be acknowledged-hallowed.*"[550]

May we acknowledge and identify with the Certitude-Awareness that shines here and now as the Apodictical Foundation of the consciousness-*of* this objective world.

> "*May Thy ruler-ship-kingdom come-by-being-manifest.*"[551]

That identification takes place once we realize the fundamental absolute value of the Apodictical Self-Awareness without which nothing is possible. The world is only "*through It, with It, in It.*" Even if one denies It, also that denial is still "*through It, with It, in It.*"

> "*May Thy purposeful-will be done-and-manifest, as it is in the Transcendent-heaven so it is in the immanent-world.*"[552]

The Transcendent-Self-Awareness shines in-Itself, so we may identify with It, as It shines enlightening the consciousness-*of* this objective world. Pure-Consciousness is enlightened, *through Awareness, with Awareness, in Awareness.* Mindful-Consciousness enlightens this objective world. When the world reflects that light back, consciousness becomes conscious-*only-of-that-reflected-light,* thus identifies with the object losing its identification with Awareness.

> Only in Awareness
> "*you shall realize the truth, and the truth shall make you free.*"[553]

The epistemic development is composed of four aspects.

•) **Awareness, which is not an aspect at all, is the only absolute, ethical, all-encompassing reality. It is the *turīya,* the fourth Transcendent state composed of four states. It is the A *alpha* and Ω *omega,* the beginning and the end of everything. It is the state of freedom, of true realization, of awakening and of enlightenment.**

AWARENESS IS THE ONLY SUPREME ABSOLUTE ETIC VALUE, IT IS THE *IUS SUPRĒMUM*

M) The next state or the first step, is *prājña,* Mindfulness that has its roots in Awareness. It is the immutable intuitive state of deep sleep (NREM) in which all objects are unified. It is the being-of awareness. It is the subject in-itself, the immortal Arthur the legislator, the "Once King and Future King."[554]

U) Consciousness is the second step, *taijasa* the brilliant power (*śakti*). While it is united with the subject, is conscious-*of* the dream (REM) objects.

A) The third step is being-in-situation. It is the consciousness-*of, viśva,* the all-pervading, entire, universal waking state. At this stage, the objective world obfuscates the enlightenment of Awareness in-itself.[555]

CHAPTER 2

ETHICAL AWARENESS

We can understand Awareness as undeniable logical mathematical certitude.

AWARENESS IS LOGICAL-MATHEMATICAL CERTITUDE

Galileo Galilei sustained that Science must understand nature through "the language of mathematics."[556] Ethic is such Scientific Logical Mathematical Method. The scientist, independent from his/her desire for personal achievement, calculates with complete dispassion tending towards an indubitable result.

AWARENESS IS SCIENTIFIC ATTENTION

Russell recognizes that, "In order to become a scientific philosopher... there must be... the desire to know philosophical truth, and this desire... is very rare in its purity... The desire for unadulterated truth is often obscured, in professional philosophers, by love of system... and the system-maker's vanity which becomes associated with it, are among the snares that the student of philosophy must guard against. The desire to establish this or that result, or generally to discover evidence for agreeable results, of whatever kind, has of course been the chief obstacle to honest philosophizing."[557]

"Scientists want, and are expected, to be as alert to possible bias in their own work as in that of other scientists, although such objectivity is not always achieved. One safeguard against undetected bias in an area of study is to have many different investigators or groups of investigators working in it."[558]

Let it be clear that here we are referring to the scientific approach as such, not to its applications. Applied science, in fact, is depowering the original universal-disengaged-certitude. It is an action interested in the achievement-*of* a particular objective interest. Therefore, it becomes relative to the historical-geographical condition.

We must caution here, that Awareness in-itself is always aware. It is aware even when the "*rope*" is mistaken for a "*snake*," as we have seen. The Sun is always shining, regardless if it illuminates dirt or gold. Ultimately, Awareness leads to "*Know thyself*," the "*the Real of the Real*," the Self-Awareness, which is neither the historical ego nor the I-think. That historical ego must be confuted. After a series of confutations we reach the Absolute Ultimate Value which is Awareness without thought or consciousness-*of*.

Awareness is here, right now. You do not need to think of it in order to be aware that you are reading this book. If you do think of it, it is not the Certain-Awareness but it is the consciousness-*of*-awareness. Awareness has become an object of thought. The ultimate certainty needs no demonstration.

THE SELF IS AWARENESS

According to the Biblical metaphor, God, the Transcendent-Self creates (*kṛ*) commanding,

> "*Let there be light ... And The Transcendent* *saw the light*."[559]

Seeing implies Awareness. Awareness, as *sight*, must logically precede light itself, as *seen*. Awareness-*seeing* (*εἶδον eidon*) is before the created *seen*-idea (*εἶδος eidos*). However, that *light* is the *seeing* aspect of Awareness. As light cannot be separated from its *sunny* source, similarly, Awareness cannot be separated from its own enlightening certitude. Again, we must reiterate, Awareness is Apodictical-Certitude and Mindfulness is its Being-Aware. Therefore, Awareness shines by its own Reality. It is Pure shining light beyond any intrinsic ineluctable necessity and beyond being and/or non-being. It has no-quality, while it is Absolute, Unconditional and Perennial. It is the Autochthonous Self-in-itself. It is the

"*Self-Made*" (*svayam-bhū́*)[560]

Unknown-Knower. Awareness, as such, is always unknown. It does not-exist as an object because it can never become one. In fact, when conceived, it is only an idea, not Self-Awareness in-itself. Then, it becomes a thought, an idea and the consciousness-*of* awareness.

> "*Verily, nothing at all, was here in the beginning,*"[561]

and

> "*no one knows*"

from whom and

> "*from where this creation began to exist,*"[562]

thus, its origin is Unknown.

Therefore, declares Luke,

> "*What is a person's advantage, if s/he gains the whole world, and loses one's self?*"[563]

Again Russell reminds us that "it is necessary to practise methodological doubt, like Descartes,[564] in order to loosen the hold of mental habits; and it is necessary to cultivate logical imagination,... not to be the slave of the one which common sense has rendered easy to imagine. These two processes... form the chief part of the mental training required for a philosopher... The naive beliefs which we find in ourselves when we first begin the process of philosophic reflection may turn out, in the end, to be almost all capable of a true interpretation; but they ought all, before being admitted into philosophy, to undergo the ordeal of sceptical criticism... Until they have gone through this ordeal, they are mere blind habits, ways of behaving rather than intellectual convictions... The study of logic becomes the central study in philosophy: it gives the method of research in philosophy, just as mathematics gives the method in physics... so philosophy, in our own day, is becoming scientific through the simultaneous acquisition of new facts and logical methods... By the practice of methodological doubt, if it is genuine and prolonged, a certain humility as to our knowledge is induced: we become glad to know anything in philosophy, however seemingly trivial... Philosophy has suffered from the lack of this kind of modesty."[565]

However, that modesty is the humble acceptance and recognition of the *building block*, the *corner stone, which the builders have discarded.* That is the Apodictical Pristine Awareness, the only Absolute Foundation of any Science.

My question to the deceased empiricists is, "Where are *Now* your empiricism, your logic and your indubitable philosophy, if you did not carry that science with you in the realm '*of the departed souls* (*ṭuat*)'[566]?"

It must be understood that there is no absolute transcendent reality in the objective world as such. What is

Transcendent and Absolute is the scientific-detached-objectiveness of Awareness. Obviously, even the expression *objectiveness* is a matter of speech. There is no intentionality in Awareness. Therefore, there is no objective intent. There is nothing to reach *out-there* because the *out-there* is impossible. If there is an *out-there*, it is only an *in-here*, in the Pure-Self, the Transcendent Itself. If anything is to be reached it is Itself, Awareness as such.

The scientific method is Pure Awareness, which observes without desiring the fruit of its awareness. That dispassionate observation guarantees the truthfulness of the experimentation. This is recognized as "the general principles of scientific method [which] pervade the entire scientific enterprise, whereas specialized techniques are confined to particular disciplines or subdisciplines."[567]

According to the American Association for the Advancement of Science, "Fundamentally, the various scientific disciplines are alike in their reliance on evidence... Nevertheless, scientists differ greatly from one another... Organizationally, science can be thought of as the collection of all of the different scientific fields, or content disciplines... With respect to purpose and philosophy, however, all are equally scientific and together make up the same scientific endeavor."[568]

Nevertheless, that effort is understood as dis-covering, bringing to light laws of nature separate from the observer. The fruit of knowledge deriving from that action is already a type of degradation, a personalization of that pure observation. We are not implying that new discoveries, the laws of nature or their predictability are not real or do not work. We assert and recognize their pragmatic truth. They are real and they do work, as long as an experiencer observes and records them.

Furthermore, once the discovering scientist experiences the outcome of the research, it may produce an emotional attachment. However, it is not correct to imply that the laws or the discoveries have a reality in themselves transcending the experiencer. In the absence of the observer nothing can be said regarding the laws of nature or nature itself.

Actions can have three outcomes.

1) A pleasant outcome, which is regarded as being a good action.

   However, that same pleasant outcome may be

   a) lasting, in which case it would be regarded as being an absolute good, or
   b) temporary, after which it could turn out to be
2) An unpleasant outcome, which, then, is regarded as being an evil action.
   However, this same unpleasant outcome may be
   c) lasting, in which case it would be regarded as being an absolute evil, or
   d) temporary, after which it could turn out to be a pleasant outcome, from where, the unending cycle repeats itself chasing a reward or a punishment.
3) Transcending the good and evil dichotomy is the action that performs its duty without attachment to its outcome. Schopenhauer compares this action to the man who "saved a life or even several lives at the risk of his own, he as a rule accepts no reward at all, even if he is poor, for he feels that the metaphysical value of his action would thereby be impaired."[569]

THE AWARE-SCIENTIFIC-DISENGAGED-CERTITUDE IS THE SUPREME ETHIC

CHAPTER 3

EMOTIONS

From the preceding considerations on Awareness, it would appear that we are referring to an arid world where sentiments are dead or mute and where compassion (*karúṇā*) and empathy have no stand. Nothing could be more far away from the truth.

Self-Awareness is the Real of the real. It is the foundation of the entire Universe in all its many-folded aspects.

> "*Well, verily it is not for love for the husband that the husband is beloved but for love of the Self the husband is beloved. Well, verily it is not for love for the wife that the wife is beloved but for love of the Self the wife is beloved. Well, verily it is not for love for the sons that the sons are beloved but for love of the Self the sons are beloved. Well, verily it is not for love for wealth that wealth is beloved but for love of the Self-wealth is beloved. Well, verily it is not for love for the cattle that the cattle are beloved but for love of the Self the cattle are beloved. Well, verily it is not for love for One who has divine knowledge that One who has divine knowledge is beloved but for love of the Self, One who has divine knowledge is beloved. Well, verily it is not for love for the warrior that the warrior is beloved but for love of the Self the warrior is beloved. Well, verily it is not for love for the worlds that the worlds are beloved but for love of the Self the worlds are beloved. Well, verily it is not for love for the gods that the gods are beloved but for love of the Self the gods are beloved. Well, verily it is not for love for the Sacred-verses-of-knowledge that the Sacred-verses-of-knowledge are beloved but for love of the Self the Sacred-verses-of-knowledge are beloved. Well, verily it is not for love for the beings that the beings are beloved but for love of the Self the beings are beloved. Well, verily it is not for love for anything that anything is beloved*

> *but for love of the Self anything is beloved. Well, o Benevolent, the Self, verily, is to be seen, is to be thought, and is to be meditated upon. Everything is known, when it is seen, heard, thought, and discerned in the Self."*[570]

Awareness is the dawn of beauty. Awareness is Pure-Joy. However, all the attachments and/or feelings and/or sentiments that may follow are not connected to it. Awareness, as such does not produce an effect. The attachment produces a reward, an effect (*karman*) that may be pleasant - and we call it good – or unpleasant - and we call it evil. But Awareness is without attachment, thus there is no reward, no good nor evil.

Emotions[571] are *motions*, movements *outside* the sphere of pure detached Awareness. Passions identify with the object and enter in a state of dissatisfaction (*dukkha*) and suffering. The way of Awareness is to enhance sentiments not in terms of attachments but in terms of lived experiences. We do not identify with the emotive world but we look at it in a state of serene comprehension and participation.

> *Let not your heart be troubled, neither let it be afraid,"*[572]

declares Jesus.

However, the Gospels relates two moments in which Jesus seems to lose the identity with the Transcendent-Self-Awareness. Then, just for a moment, he appears to reveal his human identification with the kingdom of thought.

The first instance takes place in Gethsemane, at the foot of the Mount of Olives, there Jesus,

> "*being in an agony he prayed more earnestly: and his sweat was as it were great drops of blood falling down to the ground...*[573]
> *and prayed that, if it were possible, the hour might pass from him...*
> [he said] *My soul is exceeding sorrowful unto death And he said, Abba, Father, all things* [are] *possible unto thee; take away this cup from me:* [but immediately regaining his identity, he said] *nevertheless not what I will, but what thou wilt."*[574]

The second time was while nailed to the Cross, on the Golgotha, the Skull.

"*And about the ninth hour Jesus cried with a loud voice, saying, Eli, Eli, lama sabachthani? that is to say, My Transcendent, my Transcendent, why hast thou forsaken me?*"[575]

It is distress (*kaṭha*), trouble, inquietude, suffering, dissatisfaction (*dukkha*) that led Siddhārtha Gautama to seek Buddhahood, and enlightenment. The same tragedy of Judas Iscariot's mythical betrayal turned out to be essential and indispensable for the Christian salvation of humanity.[576] The devil himself was not that evil. If he were really evil he would not have tempted Judas. He would have known that Judas' treachery would have led to the Cross, redeemed humanity and defeated him.

However, it is this trouble, this inquietude, this *non-quietness* of the mind that ultimately prompts the internal silent search and leads back into the Transcendence. In fact,

"*our heart is troubled* (*inquietum*) *till it rests in*"

the Transcendent, says Augustine.[577]

From that *quiet*-silence emerges the sound of the word (*logos*) meaning and signifying the objective world. From that silence (·) emerge the three states of wakefulness (A), dream (U) and sleep (M). And to that silence (·) they return.

"Superhuman
silences, and very deep rest...
infinite silence...
and I remember the eternal,"

sings Leopardi.[578]

Beauty, Love and Truth

No knowledge is possible without Awareness. From Awareness stems knowledge. That *silent* Awareness is an epistemic beginning. It implies an esthetic dawn that is identified as beauty.[579] In Sanskrit is referred to as the beauty-of-knowledge (*abhikhyā*), the splendor-of-light (*téjas*), the exquisiteness-of-form (*rūpá*), the loveliness-of-sound (*várṇa*).[580]

It is not by loving or by committing to truth that one is virtuous as opposed to evil. Those actions are still attached to the objective world of duality. Awareness is aware without selfish attachment. It is Pure-Love, it asks nothing in return. Identifying with it means to

"*love one another, as I have loved you,*"[581]
said Jesus.

"*Let us love one another: for love is of Transcendence; and every one that loveth is born of Transcendence, and knoweth Transcendence...*
No man hath seen The Transcendent at any time. [However] *if we love one another, The Transcendent dwelleth in us, and his love is perfected in us.* [582]
For, brethren, you have been called unto liberty; only [use] *not liberty for an occasion to the flesh, but by love serve one another.*"[583]

Transcendence is Love's Universal quest.[584] Also a very popular Italian pop song instinctively chants about this Beyond where the Loved-One stands. "Beyond the most precious good... the most ambitious dream... the most beautiful things... beyond the stars... the deepest sea... the edges of the world... the infinite vault of the sky, beyond life... You are there, beyond everything, you are there for me."[585]

Beauty, Love and Truth are the intrinsic outcome of the Intuitive-Awareness. They are not commandments *per se*. By identifying with Awareness in its intuitive reality, one reaches Beauty, Love and Truth themselves without attachment. These are synonyms of Awareness. And to learn about love, our best teacher is our enemy that teaches us the Buddhist compassion (*karúṇā*).[586]

Augustine states,

"*Love and do what you want,*"[587]

and the *Bhagavad-Gītā* confirms,

"***For him/her there is no duty***." [588]

Truth abides in the realm of Awareness, consequently,
"*Swear not at all*"
and communication shoul be

"*Yea, yea; Nay, nay: for whatsoever is more than these cometh of evil.*"[589]

CHAPTER 4

PRESENT ETHIC[590]

> *"Then Jesus said unto them, 'Yet a little while is the light with you. Walk while you have the light, lest darkness come upon you: for he that walketh in darkness knoweth not whither he goeth. While you have light, be certain in the light, that you may be the children of light.'"*[591]

That Light is the Fire (*agni*) of Awareness which is the ineffable substratum of the entire universe.

> *"Then, the knower, shaking off good and evil, is free from stain."*[592]

Transcendent Awareness is the mover of action and of ethic. Nevertheless, the noumenon, that which is thought but not known, that which refers to the transcendent, the non-experienced has a great peculiarity. It is always the unreached object intentioned as in-itself. Intentionality is the drive for action in search for transcendence as an object.

The Transcendent-Self is the only Absolute-Ethic. It is the *Ius Suprēmum* itself. However, there, nothing is unethical. In It, there is no law, but also there is no lawlessness. There neither morality nor immorality is. The Śiva-follower, Śaiva Aghora who goes beyond duality and

> *"Knows the bliss of Brahman ... Naturally such a one, verily, is not tormented by the thoughts: Why I have not done the right thing? Why have I done evil things? He, who thus knows non-duality, redeems himself from both these thoughts... This is the secret teaching."*[593]

Self-Awareness is beyond good and evil. In general, we perceive only our consciousness, never of the consciousness of others. Among all the faces, we do not recognize Lord-Awareness. In the present time immemorial, It has always been, It will always be.

We may infer that others have consciousness. However, we do not know or experience their perception. We may have faith or belief that others have consciousness. If they have, it must be identical to ours. Better still, it is our same consciousness. This does not imply that others have our same *consciousness-of*, which distinguishes individuals among themselves. One can be conscious-of a flower, while another may be conscious-of a rock.

Nevertheless, Awareness as Awareness in-itself remains universal by its own nature. It is identical with itself in both others and us. As an example, the act of seeing, is universal in that it sees in seers. We are not referring to what it is seen, but to seeing as potential seeing even in darkness where nothing is seen. Therefore, the seeing as such is identical in all seers. Similarly, this goes for all the other acts of perception, *i.e.* hearing, smelling, tasting, feeling and thinking. Central to all these acts is Awareness. We do not see, hear, taste, smell, feel or think anything if we are not conscious-*of* something. However, even in the stillness of unconsciousness, consciousness is there in its center, not as *consciousness-of* but as pure potential awareness, which becomes consciousness-*of* upon returning to illuminate an object. In fact, it is only awareness that illuminates the object as such and not the object that determines its own consciousness. Central to *consciousness-of* is *Aware-awareness*, as one, Pure, Apodictical Certitude. It shines uncontaminated by the truthfulness or the fallacy, by the good or the evil of the experienced as such. The light of the sun shines equally on gold as well as on filth, unconditionally not affected by them. Pure-Transcendent-Apodictic-Awareness is like sun shining on the world without desire, reaction or attachment. Identifying with Awareness is like gazing in the sun. We see thanks to that star. However, when we stare at it we are blinded by that beaming splendor. Similarly, when we identify with Awareness, the radiance of that Kingdom dissipates all consciousness-*of*-this-world. That identification is ecstasy.

> "*That ye may be the children of your Father which is in heaven: for he maketh his sun to rise on the evil and on the good, and sendeth rain on the just and on the unjust.*"[594]

Historical memory persists in the reservoir of the unconscious mind as in a receptacle-of-consciousness (*ālaya-vijñāna*).[595] Therefore, we may say, that consciousness does not dissolve completely. As fossilized bones, as DNA long-term storage of information,[596] there is no-(*a*) dissolution (*laya*), a permanence-of-consciousness (*vijñāna*), which belongs to the en-graving of consciousness, which is generally understood as unconsciousness. The unconscious mind is the grounding foundation of every sentient act ever performed by any sentient animal. That means that, just as the paleontologist discovers in ancient sediments the remains of dinosaurs,[597] similarly, *digging* down deep within that receptacle (*ālaya*), when the immediateness of individuality is silenced, one will find the other person's thoughts and feelings.

All that one gives to others one gives to one's self.

"*There are not two minds — one good and the other evil; the mind is only one. It is the residual impressions that are of two kinds — auspicious and inauspicious. When the mind is under the influence of auspicious impressions it is called good, and when it is under the influence of inauspicious impressions it is regarded as evil. The mind should not be allowed to wander towards worldly objects and what concerns other people. However bad other people may be, one should bear no hatred for them. Both desire and hatred should be eschewed. All that one gives to others one gives to one's self. If this truth is understood who will not give to others? When one's self arises all arises; when one's self becomes quiescent all becomes quiescent. To the extent we behave with humility, to that extent there will result good. If the mind is rendered quiescent, one may live anywhere.*"[598]

Willfully and knowingly inflicting something disagreeable to the consciousness-*of* somebody means, ultimately, to self-inflict it on that Universal Awareness.

> "*For I was an hungred, and you gave me meat: I was thirsty, and you gave me drink: I was a stranger, and you took me in: Naked, and you clothed me: I was sick, and you visited me: I was in prison, and you came unto me.*"[599]

And

> "*Whosoever shall receive one of such children in my name, receiveth me* [Awareness]*: and whosoever shall receive me, receiveth not me* [individual consciousness]*, but him* [Awareness] *that sent me.*"[600]

So that, any action

"*ye have done unto one of the least of these my brethren, you have done unto me* [Awareness]."

Furthermore, what

"*you did not to one of the least of these, you did not to me* [Awareness]."[601]

"*For whosoever shall give you a cup of water to drink in my name, because you belong to Christ* [Awareness]*, verily I say unto you, he shall not lose his reward.*"[602]

The golden rule, "Do or don't do to others what you want or don't want being done to you," is, transformed from a commandment into an obvious acknowledgment. Whatever you do is always to yourself. In fact, the consciousness-*of* pain inflicted or received is always in the light of our Universal Awareness. We inflict pain or pleasure expecting that the other be conscious of it as we are. Whatever we do to others or receive from others is done in the light of Awareness. This is always the same, for the doer and/or for the receiver. Therefore, whatever we do, we do it to the center of our own self. Awareness is the same, for us, for you and/or for them.

The act of killing seems different. The intent of the killer is to satisfy its own desire. That is, to eliminate the consciousness of the killed one and, at the same time, to be conscious of the elimination of that consciousness. Overall, it is the act of a consciousness affirming its own uniqueness with the denial of another consciousness. In any case, all is done in the presence of our own universal witnessing Awareness. Therefore, Jesus says,

"*all they that take the sword shall perish with the sword.*"[603]

Karma is the consequence of one's action. It is not a law, deriving from the will of The Transcendent, or from Nature, or from a Social Contract, or from Positivism, or from Utilitarian Relativism and so on, as we will examine in the second part. This is not a law at all. It is the way we think or we judge the world.

"*For with what judgment you judge, you shall be judged: and with what measure you mete, it shall be measured to you again.*"[604]

Ultimately, we judge and reward ourselves in accordance with how we judge, think and have consciousness-*of* the objective world. *Consciousness–of* identifies with the object and enjoys the events of action and their consequences. *Consciousness-of,* as such, is a registration of the reflection of world events in which are recorded all actions and objects. Awareness is Mindfulness of this *consciousness-of.* Whatsoever is conscious-*of,* is also the un-attached Awareness of Consciousness. Focusing on that Intuitive-Awareness as Pure Awareness - beyond consciousness-*of,* beyond duality and beyond the objective world - means to identify with the Absolute Real Certitude ground of all Being and non-Being. On the other hand, focusing on the consciousness-*of* the object means to identify with the subject *for-itself* and the world of objectivity, thus missing the subject *in-itself.*

> "*For unto every one that hath* [Self-Awareness] *shall be given, and he shall have abundance: but from him that hath not* [Self-Awareness] *shall be taken away even that which he hath.*"[605]

CHAPTER 5

CONCLUSION OF PART I

The *Ius Suprēmum*, the Absolute Ethic, we have outlined, dictates no rule or law. However, It is the Present-Eternal (*sanātána*) foundation (*dharma*) which does not mandate or command any moral behavior. Actions are performed disengaged without desiring, *i.e.* without *eating* the fruit of their outcomes. The Transcendent admonishes,

> "*Do not eat of the tree of knowledge of duality...*
> *for thou shalt surely die.*"[606]

This is not a commandment. It is as saying, "*Don't touch the fire, you'll burn.*" It is a cautionary admonishment for the consequence of desire (*kāma*), the *hungry eating*. To eat is to absorb and, in this case, to identify with the fruit of knowledge. The consequence of that *eating* is that the consciousness-*of* is fascinated by the objective world. Un-attracted by that *seductive* (*kāma*), *painful* (*duḥkhá*) and *mortal* (*mṛtyu*) *food* (*anna*), completely absorbed in the Blissful state of undisturbed, undistracted Apodictic-Certitude, one should *look* (*dṛś*) at the world with the Universal *eyes* (*akṣa*) of Self-Awareness.

> "*Remember o will's power, remember the action, remember o enlightenment, remember the magic.*"[607]

There is nothing that one must do to be ethical. However, not being ethical means to suffer the consequences deriving from the loss of one's True-Self, namely the identification with our Father-Awareness and Mother-Mindfulness.

It must be immediately clarified that the absence of any defined moral code of the Absolute Ethic does not imply behavioral disorder. Greek philosophers, like the Skeptic Pyrrho and Epicurus called it the dispassionate tranquil Ataraxia.[608] *Ius Suprēmum* is beyond good as well as it is devoid of any evil. It must be clearly and forcefully clarified that the absence of morals does not imply a license to engage in criminal activities. Nor it implies psychopathic behavior. The disconnected personalities observed in psychopaths have nothing to do with the serenity of pure Self-Awareness. In fact, the psychopaths "are so reward-driven,"[609] that these predators intend only to sadistically drain their prey. The Supreme Ethical detachment does not infer a permit to follow licentious conduct. It does not suggest promoting dissolute comportment. How can one, in fact, commit any of those deeds without desiring their outcome? A gangster fulfills a *hit-contract* fully desiring its outcome.

> "*No man can serve two masters: for either he will hate the one, and love the other; or else he will hold to the one, and despise the other. you cannot serve the Transcendent-God and mammon...*[610] *of unrighteousness."*[611]

Finally, *Ius Suprēmum* does not advocate following *Mammon*, the *ways of the world*. *Mammon*[612] is wealth-personified as opposed to the Transcendent Self-Awareness. Consequently,

> "*that which is highly desired among men is abomination in the sight of Transcendence."*[613]
>
> "*In fact, through wealth there is no hope for immortality,"*[614]

says Yājñavalkya-Sacrifice-speaker to his wife Maitreyi-the-benevolent. And Jesus confirms,

> "*A rich man shall hardly enter into the kingdom of heaven."*[615]

In *Faust's* aria, the demon Mephistopheles sings

"The golden calf is always standing!
It is worshiped
His power,...
From one limit of the world to the other!
To celebrate the infamous idol,
Rustics and kings mixed together,
To the ringing sound of coins,
They form a tumultuous round dance
Around his pedestal...
The golden calf is the vanquisher of the gods!
In its derisory
Glory...
His miserable ostentatiousness defies heaven!
It contemplates, oh creepy frenzy!
the humankind at his feet,
Tossing itself around, iron in hand,
In blood and in the mud,
Where the ardent metal gleams ...

And Satan leads the dance."[616]

Therefore, *Ius Suprēmum* appears to the merchant's eyes as pure *madness*. And, it is! It is *avadhūta*, the way of one who has shaken off all worldly attachments.[617] It is the holy *manner* of the saint. It is the sacred *behavior* of the *aghora*. It is the divine *conduct* of the mendicant *saṃnyāsin* or *sādhu* monk. It is the hallowed *insanity* of the shaman. It is the blessed *way* of the hermit of any denomination. That bright path is Awareness, rightly indicated as *light*. Therefore,

> "*walk while you have the light, lest darkness come upon you: for he that walketh in darkness knoweth not whither he goeth.*"[618]

On that simple way walk

> "*the children of light,*"[619]

and the

> "*child shalt be called the prophet of the Highest.*"[620]

In fact, if one does

> "*not receive the kingdom of the Transcendent Self-Awareness as a little child,*
> *shall in no wise enter therein.*"[621]

Happiness is not performing good deeds. Happiness is not satisfying all desires. Happiness is not pursuing criminal activities. Happiness is not performing evil deeds to achieve personal aims. Even when having supernatural and/or paranormal abilities, as performing astonishing great miracles like resurrecting the dead, "*there is no perfect happiness,*" declares St. Francis of Assisi the "Juggler of God."[622] Happiness is abiding in the Pure Certitude of Awareness. The constant-present intuitive-gnostic-realization of Self-Awareness, (in certain languages named as: *spiritual-insight*, *gnosis*-γνῶσις, *khok·mä*-חכמה, *ma'rifah*-معرفه, *shinākht*-شناخت, *jñāna*-ज्ञान), that

"*alone is to be aimed at and gained.*"[623]

PART II

THE BOOK OF MORALS

**Critical quest for Morals,
philosophical views
and various sacred texts.**

PREMISE

History and individuality have their hold in the mind, the seat of morality, whereas, universality belongs to the heart, the center of Ethics. The only state truly without war and/or conflict, as we have seen, is the Ethical one. It is the Peaceful-State of Autochthonous-Pure-Apodictic-Self-Awareness beyond good and evil, beyond any morals. War and conflict start in the field of morality. "The great enemies of public peace are the selfish and dissocial passions," states the British philosopher Jeremy Bentham.[624] In fact, in the field of consciousness-*of* the objective world reigns that which belongs to individual desire, that which may stand in conflict with the cravings of others.

God's Judgment

The common interpretation of Christian morals is that God judges condemning sinners who do not repent. However, Jesus declares,

> "*Except your righteousness shall exceed* [the righteousness] *of the scribes and Pharisees, ye shall in no case enter into the kingdom of heaven.*"[625]

It is not the literal adherence to relative laws that establish righteousness. On the contrary, it is focusing on Ethic that leads to Pure Self Awareness.

> *"Be ye therefore perfect, even as your Father which is in heaven is perfect."*[626]

Transcendence does not condemn according to official laws established by the dichotomy of good and bad. The Transcendence does not create norms nor follows any preexisting commandment enforcing laws. In fact, in either case, It would not be Transcendent. As a proof, when

> "*the scribes and Pharisees brought unto...* [Jesus] *a woman taken in adultery; ...*
> *They say unto him, 'Master, this woman was taken in adultery, in the very act.*
> *Now Moses in the law* [of the Decalogue] *commanded us, that such should be stoned: but what sayest thou?'*

[Jesus] *said unto them, 'He that is without sin among you, let him first cast a stone at her.'*
And they which heard [it], *being convicted by* [their own] *conscience, went out one by one...*
When Jesus ... saw none but the woman, he said unto her, 'Woman, where are those thine accusers? hath no man condemned thee?'
She said, 'No man, Lord.'

[Surely she must have been happy to have her life spared by the accusers. Nevertheless, did she repent? There is no indication or reason to believe that she was remorseful. However, irrespective of her repentance,]

Jesus said unto her, 'Neither do I condemn thee: go, and sin no more'."[627]

Strict moral observances are political tools to keep society controlled by the scare of lawful punishments. It is the interest of all religious authorities to check their flock frightening them with the afterlife eternal punishments of sinners in the torments of hell. Punishing themselves and hallucinating out of guilt,

"*Very sinful people behold the terrifying form of Yama* [End-Maker] *--huge of body, rod in hand, seated on a buffalo* (19), *Roaring like a cloud at the time of pralaya* [dissolution], *like a mountain of lampblack, terrible with weapons gleaming like lightning, possessing thirty-two arms* (20), *Extending three yojanas* [9 miles], *with eyes like wells, with mouth gaping with formidable fangs, with red eyes and a long nose* (21). *Even Citragupta* [Record-Protector of good and evil deeds] *is fearful, attended by Death, Fever and others. Near to him are all the messengers, resembling Yama* [End-Maker] *roaring* (22)."[628]

<u>*War and Morals*</u>

Does the suicide terrorist, who in the name of his/her god blows up killing countless innocents, experience paradise? Does the tribal anthropophagus, who dutifully devours the flesh of a zealot missionary, perform a meritorious act?

1) If your answer to one of those questions is "no," it means that they must be indicted for their crimes.

Then, it is right to condemn them, fight and engage in a war against them.

2) If your answer to one of those questions is "yes," it means that you belong to one of the same cultures those people come from. In this case, you should defend them. You must hold that prosecuting them for their actions and engaging in a war against them is morally wrong.
3) If, to the question, "Who is really wrong, the perpetrator or the prosecutor?" your answer is, "They are both right according to their point of view." Then you are a relativist. Even so, war ensues. The two relative sides will still fight each other. In fact, reinforced by your relativism, each side will be convinced of its righteousness. It is of no avail to invoke tolerance. Besides, you may be caught in the middle of their war. Furthermore, you or your loved innocent ones may be killed by resulting terrorist acts or the preacher of your religion may be eaten by the cannibal.

In the field of good and evil, war is predominant and death prevails.

> "*In the day that thou eatest... of the tree of the knowledge of good and evil... thou shalt surely die.*"[629]

Morals are the movers of history and promote wars. Wars are political acts enforced with weapons. Conflicts are the historical decision maker and the establisher of new moral codes. In turn, the new moral laws will enter in conflict with other laws created immediately after those. Inevitably, where there are moral laws there will be wars. Even in the absence of any morals or laws whatsoever, still there will be a prevailing law. It will be the *Law of the strongest* or the *Law of natural selection*, which, again, will lead to conflicts. That is the *Law of evolution*. That is the *Law of history*. Therefore, a state of total anarchy[630] is a contradiction.

Unless we find unity in Pure Self-Awareness, wherever we have two or more people we have a divergence of interests, desires and wills. It is impossible to have total anarchy, namely, an organization *without-leader*. In any case, such a society will be ruled by the strongest. In fact, tyrant and/or majoritarians will impose and coerce, with force and/or wars, their own willful desires, commands, laws and morals on the rest of the population. In any case,

The state of Morals is the state of War.

In this state, wars act as necessary evolutionary forces in which the survival of the fittest society ensues and prevails. It is a

***Historical Spiritualism*,**
the endless failed search in the *Pursuit of Awareness*.

Nevertheless, we will explore the possibility for a Universal Moral Law that can be the foundation of all human behavior.

Historical Spiritualism

Historical Spiritualism is the history of morality as it unfolded and develops in its evolutionary process of failed attempts to reach Awareness in-itself. We call it spiritualism in the Latin sense of spirit, *spiritus,*[631] meaning air, breath, ideal-magnanimity, imagination. This *spirit* is the producer of moral in*spir*ations, namely the ideal laws within. And it is also the a*spir*ation leading to an ideal aim viewed as good for the subject in its relationship with the objects. Morals claim to reflect the true and conceptual essence of humanity. That essence refers to the quality of the subject as such. Therefore it becomes an ideal or spiritual quality. It is different from the physical or material quality, namely that which refers to the object as such.

All morals and consequent norms implicitly reject relativism. They aspire to affirm themselves as absolute and universal. In fact, there is a preconceived need for researcher to demonstrate that moral codes are universal and absolute. That they are embedded in the genetic evolutionary process and/or they have a heavenly mandate.[632] Throughout history morals have always enforced their universality. Nevertheless, morals are only relative. Any activity or work structure is subjected to relative morals and political norms. These vary from nation to nation with no absolute validity in themselves.

Work is the constant activity focusing on the fulfillment of desires conceived as the definitive good and the ultimate happiness. Work is the activity of the Ego in its process of identification with itself. Through activity, the Ego establishes itself and what it wants to become. A *satisfying* work is the one that accomplishes the Ego's desires as they spring up consecutively. An unfulfilling job is the product of the Ego still searching for its true nature, not yet realized. There is a continuous alienation until the Ego finally identifies with its own True Self. Marx states that alienation or estrangement (*entfremdung*) is caused by economic structures and consequent social differentiating stratifications. The worker loses the identity with his/her true and active essence (*gattungswesen*). In other words, Marx sustains that the worker is alienated from his/her own true nature. Subsequently, s/he is estranged from labor and also from the coworkers. Finally, s/he is separated from the product itself.[633] In reality, the estrangement, related by Marx, is the worker's alienation from the identity with its own natural essence composed of want and needs. These are the inconsistent and fluctuating desires which underline all activities. This Marxian natural essence (*gattungswesen*) is ultimately still an idea. It is a thought not generated by economic structures. However, contrary to the Marxist concept, true alienation is leaving behind, in every stage of activity, the personal identification with the unchanging Awareness that is the foundation of every human being.

CHAPTER 1

METAPHYSICAL MORALS

From prehistoric times, the leading alpha male imposed with strength his will on the pack. Without knowing, he became the instrument of the evolutionary natural selection which aims for strongest or more environment adaptable genes to propagate in order to ensure the endurance of the species. In historical time, that natural strength was recognized as characterizing an individual personal value. The Medieval Germanic law called it *wergild,*[634] what a woman[635] or a man is worth according to his/her status and rank. That value, believed to be a spiritual power, was viewed as a divine gift called charisma.[636] Charisma, then, became one of the qualities of the *heroic* leader, his/her internal, persuading, individual drive.

Divine Laws

"*And the LORD said unto Moses...*
'*I will write upon* [these] *tables the words... which I command thee...*'
And... when Moses came down from mount Sinai with the two tables of testimony... gathered all the congregation of the children of Israel together, and said unto them, 'These [are] *the words which the LORD hath commanded, that* [you] *should do them.*"[637]

The issue here is not if God exists. We analyzed this point in the first part of this research. The question is, which one is the God commanding universal moral laws? If there is more than one god or interpretation of god, then also the moral laws will be different and relative to each god. In fact, there are numerous different creeds in a personal god and each one has sub-denominations. Furthermore, each individual being has its own idolized idea of god. Therefore, there are a staggering number of different laws. They range from allowing all kinds of selfish actions to ordering masochistic self-mortifications. Some laws command to slaughter unbelievers and others to preserve all aspects of life, including that of insects. Therefore, which god or which moral code can be truly universal?

Traditional Leaderships are not immune from such diversity. In fact, Traditional Leadership is that which claims for itself a specific heavenly mandate. Each Emperor, Kaiser, Monarch, **Pharaoh**, Pope, Raja, Shah, Sultan, Tsar, etc. bases its authority on a metaphysical entity empowering the ruler.

> "*And when Samuel saw Saul, the LORD said unto him, Behold the man whom I spake to thee of! this same shall reign over my people.*"[638]

In turn, the followers of the leader must believe in that empowering supernatural entity, otherwise they would not accept the sovereign's ruling mandate. As an example, one cannot be a Roman-Apostolic-Catholic without believing that the Pope is the vicar of Jesus Christ.

> "*And I* [Jesus] *say also unto thee, That thou art Peter, and upon this rock I will build my church; and the gates of hell shall not prevail against it.*"[639]

More so, the Japanese Emperor *Shōwa-tennō* Hirohito (1901 – 1989) was regarded by his subjects as descendent of Amaterasu, the Shinto Sun goddess. Similar to the Polynesian noble ruling warrior chiefs, no one could even look at him.

"The traditional belief, that the ruler is empowered directly by a metaphysical source,[640] envisions the sovereign as the unselfish pontiff,[641] the bridge-maker, between the divine principle and humanity. Its followers believe that the leader is *anointed by God*, who justifies that leadership."[642] In turn, the leader "emphasizes the great spiritual significance of the ascetic struggle of ruling as a monarch."[643]

Sovereigns rule *By Grace of God*. Obviously, their follower must believe in that particular divinity. Non-believing in that god would put in question the leadership itself. Throughout the centuries, the penalty for that unbelief prompted expulsions, persecutions and deaths. A few examples of non-universal laws, applied in the name of a god, can be found in Ancient Rome and in Renascence Spain.

The very tolerant ancient Romans had erected the Pantheon, a temple dedicated to all the different gods within the Empire. Nevertheless, during the 1st to the 3rd centuries, they persecuted Christians. These last ones, in fact, questioned the authority of the Divine Emperor by negating the goddess Roma, who empowered the *Divus Imperator*,[644] the Heavenly Ruler. Vice versa, for the same reasons, when the Roman Emperor Constantine,[645] in the 4th century, claimed his divine mandate directly from Jesus Christ, then all pagans became outlaws and were persecuted.[646]

In the 15th century, *Los reyes católicos*,[647] Isabel and Ferdinand, the Catholic Kings of Spain, gave rise to the Spanish Inquisition with the *Auto da fé*, the public Act of Faith, which the *heretics* had to undergo. The persecution culminated with the expulsion of all the non-converted Moorish-Muslims, who, even if converted, were offensively called *Moriscos*. Along with the Moors, also the Jews were expelled, and, even if baptized, they were derogatorily named *Marranos*.

Religions

The first Commandment of Moses' Decalogue orders,
"*Thou shalt have no other gods before me*."[648]

That scriptural God, as the Irish-American mythologist Joseph Campbell states, "is certainly not the god of other traditions [*e.g.* Animist, Buddhist, Hindu, Shinto, Taoist, etc.]. In the other mythologies, one puts oneself in accord with the world, with the mixture of good and evil. But in the religious system of the Near East, you identify with the good and fight against the evil. The biblical traditions of Judaism, Christianity, and Islam all speak with derogation of the so-called nature religions... In other traditions, good and evil are relative to the position in which you are standing. What is good for one is evil for the other... [Those] great Western religions... because the three of them have three different names for the same biblical god, they can't get on together. They are stuck with their metaphor and don't realize its reference. They haven't allowed the circle that surrounds them to open. It is a closed circle. Each group says, 'We are the chosen group, and we have God.' Look at Ireland. A group of Protestants was moved to Ireland in the seventeenth century by Cromwell, and it never has opened up to the Catholic majority there. The Catholics and Protestants represent two totally different social systems, two different ideals."[649] Therefore, each set of morals and laws are not universally valid. Unless we infer that all humans must forcefully adhere to one and whosoever transgresses will incur in lawful punishment. Naturally, the same reasoning can be offered by the other opposite side. Thus, the state of war ensues again.

One of the Biblical commandments orders:

"*Thou shalt not kill.*"[650]

However, that same book enforces killing through war because,

> "*the LORD* [is] *a man of war...*[651] *Then... all the inhabitants of Canaan shall melt away...*[652] *And the LORD hearkened to the voice of Israel, and delivered up the Canaanites; and they utterly destroyed them and their cities... The country which the LORD smote before the congregation of Israel... We will pass over armed before the LORD into the land of Canaan, that the possession of our inheritance on this side Jordan* [may be] *ours.*"[653]

From the 14th throughout the end of the 19th century, a fanatical sect of murderers, called Thugs or Thugges [654] terrorized central India. Contrary to the Biblical injunctions,

> "*Thou shalt not bear false witness...,*
> *Thou shalt not steal,*
> *Thou shalt not kill,*"[655]

Thugs believed that the terrific black goddess Kālī[656] ordered them to deceit, rob and strangle. To honor her, bands of Thugges cunningly joined trading caravans, ritually strangled the merchants, stole all their wealth and buried any evidence of their criminal activities. All this was done with the knowledge and support of local authority.

History has innumerable similar examples of atrocities committed under the influence of religious authority. Notably, among others, are the crimes committed by *The Peoples Temple*. The temple had been founded for *humanitarian* reasons by Jim Jones in 1956. Eventually, the congregation settled in Jonestown, Guyana. In 1978, by *inspired* order of their founder, the entire community committed murder and mass suicide.

Killing, stealing and deceit are not the only Biblical commands to be rejected by opposite sanctions. In fact,

"*Thou shalt not commit adultery,*"[657]

is completely ignored by the Canela people of Brazil. Actually, they find adulterous activity to be not only blameless, but also beneficial for the entire community.[658]

Morals, founded by or based upon metaphysical mandates, are not a guaranty of universality. It may be argued that the universality is established by the divinity promulgating them. However, that divinity varies according to the geographical, temporal and cultural locations. Each divinity has its own moral injunctions and each culture swears to be the depositary of absolute, universal righteousness. Therefore, for each perspective, it is righteous and correct to defeat alien cultures' beliefs and moral codes different from their own.

Jesus says,

"*Think not that I am come to send peace on earth: I came not to send peace, but a sword.*[659]
I am come to give ... division."[660]

Iusnaturalism

The Western mythological tradition separated God from Nature.

"*And God said, Let us make man in our image, after our likeness: and let them have dominion over all the earth.*"[661]

On one side there is God, on the other there is man and, separated from both of them, stands Nature, which is corrupt, and has fallen. The "story of the Fall in the Garden sees nature as corrupt; [says Campbell] [662] and that myth corrupts the whole world for us. Because nature is thought of as corrupt, every spontaneous act is sinful and must not be yielded to." The Japanese Zen philosopher, Daisetsu Teitaro Suzuki[663] stated that in the western religious tradition "God [is] against man. Man [is] against God. Man [is] against nature. Nature [is] against man. Nature [is] against God. God [is] against nature." Since the 19th century, that separation between God and Nature was reinforced by Positivism, the scientific philosophy established on the empirical evidence of objective absolute natural laws.

The relatively recent acceleration of evolution was the outcome of sociocultural changes. "Human evolution has been shaped by gene–culture interactions. Theoretical biologists have used population genetic models to demonstrate that cultural processes can have a profound effect on human evolution, and anthropologists are investigating cultural practices that modify current selection. These findings are supported by recent analyses of human genetic variation, which reveal that hundreds of genes have been subject to recent positive selection, often in response to human activities." New genes were the outcome of the sociocultural shift from hunting to agriculture which changed dietary habits. Genes related to smell, taste, hair thickness, bone growth, immune system control and, more important, brain function reflected the shift from a nomadic to a sedentary way of life. Therefore, "it's highly plausible that some of these changes are a response to aggregation, to living in larger communities."[664] The latest sociocultural evolution produced by the culture of those communities was the concept of god.

Eventually the name god was substituted by the name nature. This had only the effect of deifying Mother Nature itself. The ancient mythology had given it different names.[665] The 18th century Enlightenment philosophy recognized Mind/Reason as the natural light by which nature knows itself as Nature. Then, that Nature was conceived as a whole transcendent eternal totality of everything. We have seen that such concept is only a thought but not-known because it is never experienced as such.[666] It is the metaphysical concept of nature, as the physical world beyond its own physical experientiable particular appearance. The 19th century Romantic Movement, reevaluating the ancient mythology, recognized nature's nurturing aspect as Mother Nature. And, in the 20th century, Walt Disney made nature unrealistically decadent pretty.

In that metaphysical nature, the enlightened reason searched to find universal moral laws. The rule discovered was called *iusnaturalist*, namely the law (*ius*) of nature (*naturae*). Iusnaturalism, therefore, is the philosophical search for morality as dictated by the Universal laws of the Cosmos. This metaphysical and moral aspect of Nature is clearly evident in "*The unanimous Declaration of the thirteen united States of America*." There it is stated that "the Laws of Nature and of Nature's God... impel" humans to act according to the self-evident truths "that all men are created equal, that they are endowed by their Creator with certain unalienable Rights, that among these are *Life*, *Liberty*, and the *Pursuit of Happiness*. That to secure these rights, Governments are instituted among Men, deriving their just powers from the consent of the governed."[667] In one of his letters, the 1801-1809 third President of the United States of America, Thomas Jefferson, refers to God as "the common father and creator of man."[668]

Clearly, the *God of Nature*, here, is not the Biblical God. It is the Freemasons' Great Architect of the Universe who creates according to His intelligent design.[669] Besides the fact that the *intelligent design* contradicts the random process of evolution, it is not clear what is intended by creation, equality, life and liberty. *Creation* means to make, to pro-duce, to lead-forward.[670]

Creation and Life

From the point of view of the sacred texts, creation means that *before* God there is no world. The Universe is made out of nothing. The *Ṛg Veda* declares,

> "*Then, there was neither non-being nor there was being.*"

The *Bible* [671] confirms,

> "*And the earth was without form, and void; and darkness* [was] *upon the face of the deep. And the Spirit of The Transcendent moved upon the face of the waters.*"

And the *Veda*[672] reinforces,

> "*There...were Celestial Waters of inscrutable depth... In the beginning there was darkness covered by darkness. All this was only an indiscriminate flowing flood.*"

The concept of creation implies necessarily the creation of time. Otherwise, we would conceive god as subordinate to the temporal process. This would be a contradiction that would make time the real preexisting god. Therefore, the idea of creation hints at a timeless eternally present event without past and/or future. This, however, is only a thought never known in it-self. If anything can be said of it is the idea of the Present-Apodictic-Self-Awareness, which, nevertheless, is unknown as such.

From Nature's perspective, the term creation may mean, at best, the evolutionary transformation, which, from the original subatomic Big-Bang to the present Universe, expands reaching into its future. Therefore, from a naturalistic point of view, there is no creation. First Law of Thermodynamics affirms, with the famous French scientist Lavoisier, that "in nature... nothing is created"[673] and everything goes through a process of continuous transformation.

Transcendent is Awareness and also God and the World-in-Itself. Awareness does not need the process of knowledge, because it is Apodictic-Certainty. However, the thought-of-awareness is not Awareness-in-itself, it is other than Awareness. Similarly, both, God and Nature, are conceived as transcendent. They are purely ideas that are thought but not known in-themselves. They exist as ideas, as ideal-objects. Their being-in-themselves are not existent in the experiential subject-object correlation. Only that which is known, namely that which falls between the subject-object correlation, can be stated to exist. God and Nature exist only as concepts. Their objectivity is perceived only as idea. Their reality in-themselves remains unrelated to the subject. Their *in-themselves*, as any *in-itself*, is not immanent to the epistemic process. The *in-itself* never falls between the subject-object correlation. That is because the subject requires always an object *for-itself*. On the other hand, the Transcendent *in-itself implies necessarily the absence of* the *for-itself essential for a subject-object correlation*. Consequently, no existence can be attributed to God or Nature in-itself. Therefore, if they are not-existent in themselves, how can we ascribe the act of creation to them? Furthermore, as we have seen, Life is definable only from physiological-objective and/or psychological-subjective perspectives. Conversely, when we try to define it in-itself, then it becomes Transcendent. Thus, it is *the actuality of Apodictic-Aware-Certitude.*

Separation between Church and State

In his letter to the Danbury Baptists, Jefferson mentions the First Amendment of the Constitution. He states that "legislature should '*make no law respecting an establishment of religion, or prohibiting the free exercise thereof*,' thus building a wall of separation between Church & State... The supreme will of the nation in behalf of the rights of conscience... tend[s] to restore to man all his natural rights... no[t]... in opposition to his social duties."

Is the separation between Church and State possible? To answer this question we must first define a) Church and b) State.

a) Church, in this case, does not refer to the building, as temple, mosque, synagogue or the house of the Lord[674]in general. The term here indicates the structured congregational assembly of those who believe in the same metaphysical Authority. Therefore, it is the social and political structure of a religion characterized by the dogmatic bondage to a creed. It is the publically organized belief in a transcendent reality to which the entire world is assumed to be subordinate or dependent.
b) State it is also a social and political structure of citizens who hold the same general pursuit of happiness. Therefore, the people *pledge allegiance to an indivisible republic* which supports and defends their *liberty, justice*[675] and economic interest. With or without the added expression *under God*, the citizens recognize their laws as founded on freely accepted regulations devoid of any divine ruling. Up to this point the state can declare itself separate from the metaphysical settings of the Church.

   However, when the State defends its laws with capital punishments and/or wars, then it is not different from the Church. In fact, ushering the metaphysical scarecrow of death with sentences or wars, the State is invoking the afterlife to fix that which is recognized to be wrong. Thus, the State ultimately resolves its social and political problems summoning the metaphysical.

If the State is truly separated from the Church, it cannot promote any activity that refers to a realm which is not of its competence. In fact, it is through the fear of divine ultimate punishment that the Church keeps its flock in check. This is how the Church resolves its temporal legal structure. The Supreme Judgment, states the Church, punishes or rewords those who brake or follow the divine laws.

If *Life* is the first of the natural laws recognized by the State, it must defend it on all levels of its manifestation, including the embryonic one. In that case, it would infringe on the spiritual realm that is the Church's prerogative. Coherently, the State cannot destroy life, regardless of social and/or political reason. Even when death is justified on the principle of self-defense it is still recognizing it as belonging to the metaphysical realm. In the physical domain there is only the act of dying, not death as such. However, a death sentence is not intended as torture. It intends to deliver the condemned in another non-physical dimension which is *incorporeal*. Death, in itself is the *Mysterium Tremendum*, the Terrifying Mystery where "every tongue becomes trembling mute."[676]

A true iusnaturalist State separated from the Church must defend in all cases its first natural law, namely *Life*. Thus, it should promote only non-violence. By sanctioning death, through laws, capital sentences or wars, the State infringes on the territory of the Church becoming similar to that one. Its own defense becomes an *Auto da fé*, persecuting and prosecuting with incorporeal supernatural tools all those with different perspectives. Therefore, the enforced separation of State and Church becomes only a meaningless tool of political supremacy and power.

Equality and Liberty

To affirm "*that all men* [M^n] are created equal [*X*]" we need to define what that equality *X* is. When we recognize that M_1 is equal to M_2, it means that both are *equi*-valent, namely have the *same*-value. Next, we need to determine what that *valence X* is. Only then, we can recognize that the same-equality *X*, *viz.* the same measure of entitlement, characterizes and constitutes both men M_1 and M_2. Once we define that quality, then we can see if it is a universal attribute pertaining to all humans M^n.

At a first glance we may say that the equality *X*, common to all humans M^n, is the *'I'*. In fact, we infer the *'I'* of others from the responses they give to a stimulus. Yet, the *'I'* of the others can never be known as such. From purely epistemological and logical points of view, the subjective pronoun *'I'* is neither equal nor identical to any other experienced pronoun. In fact, the *'I'* implies a uniqueness which excludes all others. The only equality is the identity of the Pure Self with Itself. That is, as we have seen, the Transcendent, the

"*Supreme-Spirit without a second,*"[677]

Ramana Maharshi states,

"*When the world which is what-is-seen has been removed, there will be realization of the Self which is the seer... That* [is] *Awareness which alone remains.*"[678]

If we regard Life as the equality shared with other humans, the same consideration we made regarding the *'I'* applies. We infer human vitality from their actions. Nevertheless, the only life we experience as such is the one we individually live now. Ultimately, therefore, Life in-itself remains transcendent. Apart from its transcendent reference, *equality* has no easy definition. Furthermore, if we refer life in its physiological aspects, then we should refer that equality as belonging not only to humans but also to all animals and plants. Clearly, if apply this consideration, it would produce obvious difficult legal implications. For one, in fact, it would question our right to feed off anything endowed with life. Perhaps, we should consider the tomb, where king Midas[679] has lost his golden touch, to be the great leveler, the equalizer.

"Do you know what death is? ... it's a leveler...
a king, a magistrate, a great man...
has lost everything, life and also the name...
Only the living ones perform these buffooneries:
We are serious... we belong to death!"[680]

declares Totò, the late great Neapolitan comedian.

Apart from its transcendent aspect, there is no definite meaning of the concept of equality.[681] It varies from time and geographical location. Ancient India recognized the differences between caste (*varṇa*) distinctions.[682] Furthermore, also in present times, India recognizes the status of the *saṃnyāsin*, the wondering ascetic mendicant that is beyond all castes and equalities. Legally, s/he is the one who, deceased to this world, is twice-born (*dvi-ja*) or reborn (*parivṛt*) in a transcendent reality. Outside politically and religiously institutionalized structures, in the Western world there are neither avenues nor legal consideration for non-conventional contemplative life styles. Buddhism *extinguished* in *nirvāṇa* any trace of self, therefore made any quality or equality obsolete. In China, Confucius (孔夫子) applied the golden rule to a non-equal and highly stratified hierarchical society.

In ancient Rome equality was regarded as a divinity. She was the goddess *Aequitas*, the personification of justice itself. She was represented with a scale,[683] a symbol of *fair* measure, and a cornucopia, a symbol of deserved reward. However, the fairness of the emperor was not equal for everybody. In Rome there were those who were free and those who were slaves. At times, slaves were set free (*manumissi*)[684] by their owners. Nevertheless, these liberated slaves (*liberti*) enjoyed only some of the privileges of the free. That freedom found its symbol in the Phrygian conical cap (*pilleus*) with pointed top bent forward.[685] The same cap became the symbol of the French revolutionary. The table turned and this revolution decreed that nobles deserved the guillotine. Thus, they did not partake of the same equality (*égalité*), brotherhood (*fraternité*) or liberty (*liberté*) enjoyed by the citizens (*citoyens*).

Eventually, having beheaded the king, those citizens separated into a hedonistic society of owners and workers. This generated the Calvinist ethical-hedonism of Capitalism. According to that view, God always rewards the righteous ones in all their temporal necessities. [686]

In due time, Marx resolved the dichotomy between capitalists and workers with the utopian common-hedonism of Communism. The proletariats, united against the owners, resolve to take control of their own work, namely, their own true nature.[687] However, how can radicals, Marx included, come up with revolutionary ideas? In fact, in the Marxian historical-dialectical materialism, ideas are always only superstructures. They are only the products of actions, and action is praxis. It is only the action of the ruling economic structure, which generates all ideas, such as laws, religions, art and so on. Therefore, it is not clear how it is possible the contradictory reversal-of-praxis, namely, "the upside-down as in a *camera obscura*," of an idea producing an action. Indeed, it is an idea that produces the revolutionary act.

In either case, Capitalism or Communism, are still the product of hedonism, which is personal or collective interest. It promotes the *pursuit of happiness* which, in essence, gives predominance to egotism. Properly, Marx states that the conscious mind is fixed in its economic condition. Therefore, "consciousness... is... actual life-product... bound to material premises... [*viz.*] production or industrial stage... 'productive force.'"[688]

Ultimately, one's own selfish-benefit may oppose the pursuit of others' happiness. Contrary to the ideal non-violent sacrifice of one's its own life; we defend ours at the expense of others. Also the survival of the fittest is the evolutionary supremacy of one, as individual and/or as specie, over the other. One's own interest may turn out to be different and in contrast to that of others. Thus, one, to secure its own success, eliminates any fairness to fulfill its desired goals. At best, equality may become an equal-opportunity which takes away that same opportunity from others. Based on these premises, the fair distribution of wealth becomes inconsistent and difficult to understand. We attain what we really are. We understand only what we achieve. What we may wish for is only the emergence in our consciousness of foolish ambitions. Cursing destiny, "denying and blaspheming... not extinguishing/... arrogance... ha[ving].../ God in disdain," like Capaneus in Hell,[689] what good does it accomplish?

The same difficulty we have defining equality, beyond the multiplicity of its meanings, we encounter with the definition of liberty. Liberty is Autonomy. No one can be free if actions are imposed and directed by entities external to the will. Therefore, autonomy is the hallmark of liberty. However, when desire, necessity, compulsion, addiction and other agents intervene, how can we say that an action is free? How can we assert that it is the product of the will's free choice? The deeds belong to those agents that prompt the actions, yet we identify with them. It is precisely because we identify with those causes and we act under their influences, that we credit our action to be directed by the freedom of our will. In reality we lust for material gain, like the greedy in the 4th circle of Dante's *Inferno*. They, while

> "wheeling weights with their chests' thrust, ...
> the obtuse life that made them filthy
> now makes them dark to any acknowledgement...
> Because all the gold that under the moon is
> and that was, of these wearied souls
> could never offer rest to even one."[690]

Obviously, we are responsible of our deeds and we pay the consequences of our actions. However, desire is the cause that moves our intentionality or our will. The agents are mental states. They are the consciousness-*of* our actions always in *the Pursuit of Awareness* as an object of though. Finally, when we recognize that Freedom is Pure-Autonomy, then, the true Phrygian cap of independence belongs only to the transcendent, ineffable boundlessness of Apodictical-Awareness-in-itself. Then we realize that Equality and Liberty apply only to the sphere of Apodictical-Awareness.

CHAPTER 2

RELATIVISM, RELATIVE MORALS

In Turin (Italy) there is a museum dedicated to Pietro Micca.[691] He was recruited by the Savoy army as a miner. During the 18th century Spanish Succession War, the French army placed the city of Turin under siege. The Savoy army had dug a vast net of tunnels under the city to store ammunitions and weapons. In those dungeons, Pietro Micca, to defend the city and his comrades, in 1706 blew himself up together with the French soldiers. Eulogies, literary works and history school books were published in Italian to commemorate and exalt his action. Besides the Museum, the Turineses dedicated also a road and a statue to honor Micca's heroic deed. In 1935, the Italian Royal Navy named a submarine after him. Obviously, we find none of these tributes in France. There, his action was the ruthless and cruel deed of an enemy.

The story of Samson is similar. He is regarded as a hero by the Israelites and as a foe by the Philistines who lived in what is now Palestine.

> "*And Samson said, Let me die with the Philistines. And he bowed himself with* [all his] *might; and the house fell upon the lords, and upon all the people that* [were] *therein. So the dead which he slew at his death were more than* [they] *which he slew in his life.*"[692]

Usually, extremists were indoctrinated early in their life. They feel alienated, victimized. They believe that the enemy morally violates their religion. This perceived threat fully justifies, in their eyes, any violence also against innocent civilians. Actually, violence becomes justified and morally accepted. Furthermore, revolutionary terrorists, taken by what we may define as "*spirit of prophecy*" or the frenzy of "*speaking in tongues,*" feel a sense of security in the consent they share among their own comrades. And that security, that camaraderie justifies and makes honorable any violent act even when it involves the death of innocents and themselves.

Fundamentalists, sharing similar creeds, regard as martyrs those suicide-bombers who, motivated by their religious injunctions, perish while killing innocent bystanders. In contrast, at the same time, unbelievers condemn that act as a heinous terrorist one. In any case, both sides use disparaging epithets for the others. One side considers itself as *the people*, the chosen and the righteous, while the other is regarded as the wicked barbarians and the *heathen infidels*. Sustaining relativism Earth will never have peace.

Also factions of the same religion may be at odd and commit atrocities against each other. On December 2011, a sectarian terrorist suicide bombing left 58 Afghani Shi'a Muslims dead in the streets of Kabul. The attack took place during the mourning celebrations on the Day of Āshūrā. That day commemorates the self-immolation of Muhammad's grandson, Husayn ibn Ali. He was martyred during the Battle of Karbala (Iraq), in the month of Muharram (October) 10, 680 (61 AH). That same event is not celebrated by Sunni Muslims.

On March 6, 2001, in Bamyan Valley (Afghanistan), the Taliban, prefiguring the 9/11 destruction of New York City's twin towers, blew up two colossal statues of standing Buddha. The sculptures, measuring about 175 feet in height, had been carved in rock cliff niches during the 6th century. The statues were declared by the fundamentalist Taliban government to be idols. Hence, their demolition was hailed as a religious duty. On the other hand, the UNESCO condemned the action as a crime against the World Cultural Heritage. Paradoxically, if the Taliban had any knowledge of Buddhism, they would have recognized that those empty niches expressed Buddhism more than before. In fact, the very early Buddhist iconography never portrayed the Buddha, but rather emphasized his absence from the scene.

There is an equatorial fig tree called the "*Strangler*." The name derives from the fact that it grows on host woody plants suffocating and killing them. Then, the question is, can we morally judge the *Fig Tree* for *strangling* its *White Sapote* sapling host?[693] Natural activities are just that, activities. Events, like volcanic eruptions, tornados, tsunami, and so on, are neither good nor evil in themselves. Therefore, they have no intrinsic moral value. Human actions, like natural activities, are just that, actions. They are neither good nor bad. However, the way we judge the world is the way the world judges us, which is the same way we judge ourselves.

> "*For wherein thou judgest another, thou condemnest thyself; for thou that judgest doest the same things.*"[694]

When we judge others we are establishing moral parameters. To emit a sentence, we must conceive the principals of the verdict to exist and to be objectively real. The laws by which we judge are understood as valid for others and, consequently, also for us in similar circumstances. Therefore,

> "*Whosoever is angry ... and ... shall say to his brother ... Thou fool, shall be in danger of hell fire.*"[695]

It is the desired expectation, the intended outcome which confers a moral value to actions. Indeed, that outcome or desire may conform or contradict existing customs. Eventually, dictated by reasoned justifications, behaviors are codified in laws. The formulations and enforcements of these regulations, however, are relative to historical times, location, environment, culture, language and so forth. They are devoid of any universal validity. They still remain relative to their original environment even when we suspend any comparison with our sets of values, or when we simply describe these norms objectively. Furthermore, an objective description is always distorted by the subjective observing point.

Relativism recognizes that truth and value, outside their precise historical-cultural perspective, have no absolute universal reality in themselves. However, relativism, as such, becomes not-relative.

The same act of strangling a person is morally evaluated according to relative intentions. If the act of choking is performed by a public appointed garroting executioner it is regarded as morally correct. If that same act is done out of personal passion or rancor, it is judged evil and the strangler is found guilty.[696] Similarly, among cannibals it is not only legitimate to eat flesh, but it is also meritorious. That same action, among a different civilization, awakens horrification and lawful condemnation. Racist and discriminative laws, once considered righteous, become unlawful in a different time frame. Abortion, considered a crime, is today in 2013 USA the right of a woman to choose.

The authorities promulgating norms may be private individuals or public authorities. Individual norms, dictated by personal interest, are viewed as not necessarily moral. Public norms, pursuing collective interest, are always considered moral by the issuing authority. However, different countries, with their own distinct juridical institutions, act as collective individuals whose laws may contrast those of other individual countries. Respective individual nation considers its own laws to be morally correct. Each side will impose its moral view on other countries. Wars break out to prevail over other nations' customs. Ultimately military force determines which idea will triumph. This was evident with Nazi and Fascist promulgated racist laws. Contemporary democratic countries, judging immoral those regulations, abolished them with a Second World War.

Regimes, who proclaim to be righteous, fight those considered corrupt. Obviously, the winner will impose its moral code. "Anguish for the vanquished" cried out the Gaul leader Brennus demanding a very heavy ransom from the defeated Romans in 390 BC.[697] The winner sees himself as empowered by a divine mandate. Thus, when in 1219 the Mongol Chingiz Khan conquered Bukhara, in current Uzbekistan, he rounded up its citizen in the main mosque. There, he declared, "I am the punishment of God... If you had not committed great sins, God would not have sent a punishment like me upon you."[698] After which he had them executed. Similarly, Europeans felt empowered by a providential mission when they conquered the Americas. That task culminated with the cultural genocide of its indigenous inhabitants.

Ultimately, when analyzing different historical values we cannot but state that there is no absolute objective true morality separated from its relative cultural background. Values, then, are true as long as they are accepted and enforced. Nevertheless, *truth-relativism* becomes an absolute affirmation stating relativism itself as a non-relative proposition.

If morals are relative, then we must affirm that each moral code is righteous and unlawful at the same time. Better still, it is right in its own time and in its own location. It is like stating that the logical principle of non-contradiction rests on contradiction. Stated differently, while $A=A\neq B$ and $B=B\neq A$ is also $A=B$. If we resolve the dichotomy as a historical dialectical process, then, we have the paradox of the righteous explorer traveling to and from New York and Berlin in 1942. If s/he wants to be always a just person s/he had to be a racist in Germany and immediately, upon arriving in the USA, a humanist; only to become again a racist in Berlin. Or, one can choose one side and oppose the other on the basis of personal preference. An old Latin saying states, "*There is no argument on the matter of personal taste and colors.*" There is no justification why something is good and another evil, "any more than I have when I distinguish between blue and yellow," stated Bertrand Russell.[699]

Nevertheless, if we state that *nothing is absolute and everything is relative*, we must admit that there is one *non-relative* proposition, namely the one that states that *everything is relative*. More so, once you are in any *relative* law system this one becomes absolute, non-revocable and non-relative. Any relativity must be negated, if we want to avoid any inconsistency and ineffectiveness of the law in one country. Imagine a judge withdrawing his/her sentence based on the law being relative to the juridical district s/he rules in.

Protagoras was right asserting that "The way things appear to me, in that way they exist for me; and the way things appears to you, in that way they exist for you."[700] However, what remains absolute and identical between subjects (*I* and *you*) is the Certitude that the every subject has of the existing experienced object. Relativity belongs only to the object, never to the Transcendent Awareness as such.

CHAPTER 3

ALTRUISM, UNSELFISH MORALS

Altruism is synonym of unselfishness. Therefore, if we can find actions that are truly selfless, we would have discovered a universal moral principle valid for all. It would be so because that value would not have been dictated by something that could contrast with everyone's real fundamental interest. True, altruism may, at times, conflict with relative personal interests. Nonetheless, personal, selfish concerns in contrast with altruism end up harming oneself. Ultimately, altruism is in everyone's best interest. As an example, polluting may turn out to be economically advantageous for a single individual. A factory can reduce its production costs by dumping its polluting byproducts in the surrounding soil or waterways. However, in due time, the contaminated environment turns out to be a health hazard for the same factory owner.

The first social structure may have begun when animals started cooperating as a pack during the hunt. However, far from being a trait of altruism, cooperation may very well be a trait of selfishness. The individual in the pack perceives that communal hunting participation is more successful. It is more advantageous when taking down larger preys. Finally it is less dangerous than solitary hunt. Once the hunt is over, that altruism turns out to let selfishness loose again. In fact, members of the same pack customarily start to compete ferociously among themselves when devouring the spoils of their communal rewarding harvest.[701]

Nevertheless, a clear example of altruism is when an animal or an insect gives up its own life for the defense or the survival of its own group or kin. This is the case of the honey bee that fearlessly stings the intruder and, consequently, dies. Biologists discovered the existence of an altruistic gene present throughout the entire earthly fauna. George Price formulated a very precise mathematical equation that proves this altruism on all levels of evolution, kin, group and cultural.[702] Still, the equation demonstrates that, on different stages of life's natural process, the *altruistic gene* evolves alongside the *competitive gene*, namely the struggle for survival of the fittest. Ultimately, this leads Richard Dawkins to outline "*The Selfish Gene.*" In fact, he states that "An apparently altruistic act is one that looks, superficially, as if it must tend to make the altruist more likely (however slightly) to die, and the recipient more likely to survive. It often turns out on closer inspection that acts of apparent altruism are really selfishness in disguise."[703] In other ways, the altruistic action turns out to be in the selfish interest of the kin, the group or the society at large. Even altruism across species it is not absolute, dispassionate, selfless act. Even a dog that saves its master's life, perishing in the process, may be ultimately construed as selfish. In fact, the painful withdrawal from a wired neuron habitual connection that ties a pet to an owner[704] may be stronger than the attachment to life. In other words, saving the hand that feeds, may be stronger than the fear of death itself. It is preferable to die rather than to lose the loved one that loves us in return, *i.e.:* no ill-treated pet ever saved its master.

In the whole process of evolution, there is an imbedded selfishness which tends towards its own evolutionary affirmation. The sexual desire is no more than the species' selfishness to perpetuate itself. It is like a hunger that exploding from nothing establishes its own persisting existence.[705] In evolution, what may seem as altruism is a random blind force, which, once established, drives towards the accomplishment of its own preservation. It is a desire to achieve its own re*creation* in this dimension. Ideally, real unselfish acts are those similar to the one delivered from the *Cross*. When the crucified prays for the crucifiers, declaring,

> "*Father, forgive them; for they know not what they do.*"[706]

In fact,

> "*Love your enemies, bless them that curse you, do good to them that hate you, and pray for them which despitefully use you, and persecute you.*"[707]

Other examples of total abnegating altruism are those present in the Buddhist concept of the enlightened Bodhisattva.[708] S/he is the one who renounces *nirvāṇa* in order to help the whole Universe achieve that final liberation.

It is not our concern or intent to state or demonstrate, here, the historical reality of those instances of true altruism beyond their mythological references. We are only interested to highlight the evident reality that such ideologies are present in the cultural fabric of our human society. They are present as the highest fabled aspirations of humanity.

In his latest book, The Bonobo and the Atheist,**[709]** De Waal, Professor of Primate Behavior, convincingly argues that morality does not have a divine ordinance. His research is based on numerous direct observations of primates' behavior. He writes that humans, reflecting on their behaviors, abstracted norms intended to become universal. From the emotive social interactions and the evolution of their common ancestral simian societies, humans' behavior was codified into moral regulations. Biologists, testing human infants**[710]** and comparing chimpanzees' behavior, believe that baby humans possess an innate sense of altruism. Dr. Tomasello, Codirector of the Max Planck Institute for Evolutionary Anthropology, declares that among humans there is a natural altruism, a "shared intentionality"**[711]** to cooperate and to help. Children learn the norms of society in order to be accepted and to participate with others. The understanding of reward and punishment derives from those natural social-cognitive traits and skills. However, altruism turns out to be in our best interest. It produces a "social contract"**[712]** between citizens of a nation, a power source that confers them sovereign. It is through this selfish-cooperation, that humans defend themselves, emerge politically, win wars and succeed in their endeavors.[713] The larger the market community the stronger is the need for norms rewarding and/or punishing unfair behavior. These features are necessary for the lucrative flow of business and trade.**[714]** Also, one of the reasons why humans engage in wars is to impose their trade rules and values.

Altruism may also be beneficial for health. Altruism, by giving more meaning to life, may delay the progress of a disease.[715] In addition it may ease preoccupation, insomnia, fatigue, pain, depression and drug-dependence.[716] Numerous scientific researches demonstrated that acts of caring for others are like exercise and/or meditation. They make patients fare better than self-centered others who are not involved in those activities.[717] We do not deny all the benefits deriving from the altruistic experiences. However we argue that, far from being truly self-abnegating, they are tinted with selfishness. An Italian old proverb says: "*To have a drag companion lessens the pain.*"[718] In fact, that altruistic wellbeing may derive from the sense of security offered by sharing in any form of *selfish-cooperation*. Besides, an altruistic act may become a self-image-buster. It may unleash a sense of superiority. It may make one feel luckier when compared to the disadvantage of the neighbor in need of benevolent attention. Even human babies feel an innate compassion, namely "pain at the pain of others."[719] Furthermore, altruism may alleviate the uncomfortable feeling of compassion, the sympathetic suffering-with deriving from the identification with the disadvantaged.[720] However, we should strongly clarify, here, that this feeling is different from the Buddhist compassion (*karúṇā*). This one is the serene, disengaged empathic awareness of what others go through while they are in the state of suffering and dissatisfaction (*duḥkhá/duṣ-kha*).

Psychologist Paul Bloom, Professor at the Infant Cognition Center, Yale University, recognizes a "naïve morality" in human babies. There is, he says, a primordial sense of justice in them. They "prefer the good guy and show an aversion to the bad guy." They prefer "those who act nicely." Dr. Bloom relates of many psychological studies proving his assertions. This is his account of one of such experiments. He and his

> "team of researchers watched a 1-year-old boy take justice into his own hands. The boy had just seen a puppet show in which one puppet played with a ball while interacting with two other puppets. The center puppet would slide the ball to the puppet on the right, who would pass it back. And the center puppet would slide the ball to the puppet on the left ... who would run away with it. Then the two puppets on the ends were brought down from the stage and set before the toddler. Each was placed next to a pile of treats. At this point, the toddler was asked to take a treat away from one puppet. Like most children in this situation, the boy took it from the pile of the 'naughty' one. But this punishment wasn't enough — he then leaned over and smacked the puppet in the head."[721]

It is not clear that this experiment demonstrates an innate sense of justice in babies. We argue that, on the contrary, it reinforces a sense of selfishness. Our first immediate observation is the *left* position of the *naughty* puppet. In fact, if the infant in question was a right-hander, he could have prejudged negatively the puppet as being on *wrong* side. Nonetheless, let us look at the dynamic of the puppets' game. The child is enjoying the ball going from one player to the other. The infant identifies with the game. But, all of a sudden… the fun and the game are interrupted by one puppet taking the ball away; end of the match and end of the fun. The *bad* puppet had taken away that baby's selfish pleasure. The infant's reaction towards the *naughty* puppet is that of revenge, not of justice. It is as if, while watching a gripping film… the power goes off. We immediately *blame* the Electric Power Company.

Laws, Guilt and Sins

Choosing an action over another implies will. In any case, a person always chooses the deed which s/he perceives as being good and/or beneficial at that moment. The will may follow or contradict moral injunctions. Nevertheless, the present choice is perceived as the best one to pursue. Moral assessments refer always to past events. Morals are present evaluating projections into the past. The action to evaluate, even if performed a instant ago, is still the past. Moral codes evaluate only something which already has been accomplished by thoughts and/or actions.

> "*Whosoever looketh on a woman to lust after her, **already** hath committed adultery with her in his heart.*"[722]

Laws are present pro-visions for actions once they have occurred. Moral codes are meaningless when referred to deeds that did not take place yet. Laws provide[723] forthcoming judgments for future completed action. Thoughts and/or deeds not already implemented or executed cannot be judged. Rewards and/or punishments are programed in the present for future events when they will be established as having been performed. A law becomes effective only after having been followed and/or enforced by deeds. The compensations for actions are projected towards the future. Laws are promulgated as provisions to judge future *past* deeds. In other words, morals evaluate now past actions and laws provide now rewards and/or punishments for future accomplished actions.

Neuroscientist Dr. Escobedo, from the California Institute of Technology, Division of Biology, conducted a study on "moral memories."[724] She found that the majority of the people interviewed and participating in the research recognized their misdeeds. Nonetheless, they referred that their wrongdoings happened in the very far past. On the contrary, those same persons, remembering their moral and good deeds, related that all occurred in the near past. Also, they declared of having evolved into better moral beings. In addition, they foresaw their future as foreboding of positive good behavior. However, all of them felt also quite guilty for their crimes.

<"*Even if one be a great sinner, one should not worry and weep 'O! I am a sinner, how can I be saved?' One should completely renounce the thought 'I am a sinner' and concentrate keenly on meditation on the Self; then, one would surely succeed.*"[725]

"*Verily so, one who thus knows even if s/he*
commits very much evil, s/he consumes all that
and becomes pure, clean, ever young and
immortal."[726]

Metaphysically, the sense of guilt derives from the epistemic impossibility to objectify Transcendence and its Apodictic Certitude. That is the reason for the mythical Biblical injunction not to eat the fruit of the tree of knowledge. Eating of that fruit, in fact, produces an epistemic sin leading, first, to the knowledge of the objective world as different from oneself, then, to fear in light of the law transgression and, finally, to a sense of naked vulnerability.[727] By eating that fruit, the Certitude, which makes knowledge possible in the first place, is not evident or is lost for the enjoyment derived from the object itself. In other words, knowledge produces a sort of identification with the object, which leaves the subject decentralized from the Absolute Certitude from which it departed. At the same time, the subject attempts to reach, through the object, the impossible objectification and unattainable quantification of that Original Certitude. This is the universal-unconscious-epistemic guilt that produces the whole sub-lunar world of punishments and rewards. Obviously, by withdrawing into the Original Certitude, any epistemic guilt would dissolve in the metaphysical realm. In other words, that Original Certitude becomes the savior, the epistemic redemption from the original epistemic sin.

Psychologically, the sense of guilt derives from personal, family and society-dictated codes relative only to the historical and geographic locations of their origins. Therefore, it is impossible to ascribe an absolute validity to those regulations. As an extreme example, a cannibal's behavior finds its justification in local norms that legitimize it, which leaves also its practitioners with a feeling of meritorious accomplishment. Conversely, that same act, in a different cultural environment generates a profound sense of guilt. Furthermore, a catastrophic act of Nature that kills hundreds of people is, obviously, beyond guilt or moral condemnation. However, it is common to the ethical mind to morally interpret such events and, therefore, to ascribe them to a divine mythical will that allows and sanctions those cataclysms. Then, the mind assumes that those calamities are divine punishments to reinstate a lost moral order. Similarly, the Biblical justification for the universal flood was because

> "*God saw that the wickedness of man* [was] *great in the earth... it repented...* [and sent a] *flood of waters upon the earth, to destroy all flesh, wherein* [is] *the breath of life, from under heaven.*"[728]

To overcome the guilt-mind obstacle traditional societies of all ages envisioned a hero going against the current of the general trend. Aleister Crowley declares, "Do what thou wilt shall be the whole of the Low."[729] Consequently, one becomes the breaker of codes, of all accepted moral order leading to a Transcendent beyond the dichotomy of good or evil. Therefore, Jesus

> "*rebuked Peter, saying, Get thee behind me, Satan: for thou are reasoning not as The Transcendent, but as men.* ***You are thinking not as The Transcendent does, but as human beings do.***"[730]

That divine thought was proclaimed by

> "*the scandal of the Cross.*"[731]

That *scandal* reappears with the Indian saṃnyāsins or sadhus... the Aghorīs...[732] the Japanese Ronins...[733] the Native American Heyókhas[734]... The ancient Romans dedicated on December 17 a feast to the god Saturn, thus named Saturnalia,[735] which reversed all social order. The Medieval knight, the troubadours and the Faithful-of-Love, in their frenzy for their spiritual quest, were beyond any constructed moral order; an example of this is the adulterous relationship between Lancelot and Guinevere, who was married to Arthur, his King and friend.

Ultimately, we are our own judges and we judge our actions according to the laws that society or ourselves historically construe. Truthfully, therefore, they are not absolute, and, as the *Kaṭha Upanishad* proclaims,

> "*If the slayer thinks that he slays, if the slain thinks that he is killed, both these do not understand. This One does not slay nor It is slain.*"[736]

And This One is the Apodictical-Certitude foundation of the entire Universe.>[737]

CHAPTER 4

HEDONISM and UTILITARIAN MORALS

Once, a young man stated, "There is nothing after death!" Hearing that, zí Paulin'e' Pone, a small bronze weathered farmworker from the rural inland of San Paolo Belsito (Naples, Italy), replied,
"You are right. I may agree with you. But, once you pass-over and you reach the *other side of the great divide* and you witness that there is an Eternal Justice, then, what do you do? Do you say, 'I am sorry, send me back; I want to return to life and fix everything the way it should have been?'"[738]

The helpful advice that the wrinkled rustic gave the boy was also a self-reminder. It was useful and advantageous to think in those terms, not only for the lad but mainly for that spirited ancient man. It was a utilitarian thought, a safety net for an unknown eventuality. As Schopenhauer states, there is "undeniable fact that, with the approach of death, everyone's train of thought assumes a moral trend, whether or not he has been a follower of religious dogmas."[739] However, the seemingly moral approach does not derive from an absolute universal ethic, but only from a relative selfishness. It is not out of altruistic concerns that he gave the advice, but out of fear and bitterness towards life's mystery.

Utilitarianism is "that principle which approves or disapproves of every action whatsoever, according to the tendency... to augment or diminish the happiness of the party whose interest is in question... to promote or to oppose that happiness... not only of every action of a private individual, but of every measure of government."[740] Furthermore, utilitarianism states "that pleasure, and freedom from pain, are the only things desirable as ends... or as means to the promotion of pleasure and the prevention of pain."[741] It is Hedonism,[742] which recognizes pleasure as an intrinsic good fulfilling our Pursuit of Happiness, the third Natural Law. This search for pleasure had been proclaimed in India by Cārvāka in his materialist and atheist *Lokāyata* philosophical system expounded in the *Bārhaspatya-sūtras.*[743] In China, Yang Zhu, established a school founded on ethical egoism[744] and Epicurus, in Greece thought an ethic based on the research for pleasure.[745]

Pleasure cannot be the foundation for a universal law. In fact, happiness deriving from pleasure ends with the advent of death and no one is delivered from it. At the time of birth we are condemned to die. Death or *Mort* is the Sovereign of kings before whom all monarchs are *mort*ified.[746] Nevertheless, in 1909, an Italian song was composed and after ten years became a very popular hymn of the Italian National Fascist Party. The refrain hailed,

"Youth, Youth, / Spring of beauty,"[747]

echoing a renaissance ballade. In 1490, two years before his death, the Magnificent Lord of Florence, Lorenzo de'Medici, wrote a Carnival Ballade titled *Triumph of Bacchus and Arianna*. The recurring verses are,

"How beautiful is youth,
Yet, this, so swiftly flees away.
Let, whosoever wants, be joyful:
About tomorrow there is no certainty."[748]

Lorenzo's statement is as old as life itself. One-thousand five-hundred years earlier, the Roman poet Quintus Horatius Flaccus wrote,

"Don't ask, it is forbidden for you and me to know
what final destiny the gods have reserved ...
drink wine... envious time will flee, therefore
seize the day and place little faith in tomorrow."[749]

The Bible declares that those without light encourage each other saying,

"*Let us eat and drink; for to morrow we shall die.*"[750]

In the general acceptance, heath, love and money-power are conceived as bestowing pleasure and happiness. However, this is not always the case. When pain and loss become intolerable, death may appear as more desirable. Suicide is never a negation of pleasure seeking life. That insane act is an escape from an unbearable situation. It is the quest for a new status. Then, death is seen as liberation. Almost as bestowing a more *pleasurable* condition than the one in which s/he was suffering the loss of those pleasures. This was the case of Miss Callie Rogers, an English teenager. In 2003 she won a two million pounds lottery. However, the lucky event brought her "nothing but unhappiness." It ruined her life. "She attempted suicide twice." And by the age of 22 she was broke.[751]

1) Humans lose heath and/or youth. This loss my lead some to suicidal desires. The physical sufferer may beg for the end of an agonizing life.
2) Smitten individuals may experience the *pains* deriving from a possessive love or by its inevitable end. Like Romeo and Juliet they may prefer death to a life without the other.
3) Powerful leaders, upon losing their authority, may seek, like Cleopatra, their own death instead of the humiliation of defeat.

<u>*Happiness*</u>

Hedonism and utilitarianism have nothing to do with Ethic. They are human selfish tendencies. Nevertheless, selfishness can never become universal. Namely, individual interest cannot become a law valid for everyone since it will always set individual gain against the profit of others.

The Dalai Lama, during his *Nobel Peace Prize Acceptance Speech*, delivered on December 10, 1989, at the University Aula, Oslo (Norway), said,

"*I believe all suffering is caused by ignorance. People inflict pain on others in the selfish pursuit of their happiness or satisfaction. Yet true happiness comes from a sense of brotherhood and sisterhood... I am convinced that everyone can develop a good heart and a sense of universal responsibility with or without religion... There is... the fundamental unity of all things...I believe all religions pursue the same goals, that of cultivating human goodness and bringing happiness to all human beings. Though the means might appear different the ends are the same.*"

However,

"*Happiness is the very nature of the Self; happiness and the Self are not different. There is no happiness in any object of the world. We imagine through our ignorance that we derive happiness from objects. When the mind goes out, it experiences misery. In truth, when its desires are fulfilled, it returns to its own place and enjoys the happiness that is the Self. Similarly, in the states of sleep, 'samadhi' and fainting, and when the object desired is obtained or the object disliked is removed, the mind becomes inward-turned, and enjoys pure Self-happiness. Thus the mind moves without rest alternately going out of the Self and returning to it. Under the tree the shade is pleasant; out in the open the heat is scorching. A person who has been going about in the sun feels cool when he reaches the shade. Someone who keeps on going from the shade into the sun and then back into the shade is a fool. A wise man stays permanently in the shade. Similarly, the mind of the one who knows the truth does not leave 'Brahman.' The mind of the ignorant, on the contrary, revolves in the world, feeling miserable, and for a little time returns to 'Brahman' to experience happiness. In fact, what is called the world is only thought. When the world disappears, i.e., when there is no thought, the mind experiences happiness; and when the world appears, it goes through misery."*[752]

CHAPTER 5

THE GOLDEN RULE

Ethic is Apodictic Awareness. It is the Foundation of being and non-being. There is no duty or commandment to be what we already are. There is nothing that *must be done*. We are Apodictic-Awareness. The only difference is that we do not identify with it and we are epistemically dissatisfied (*duḥkham*). Only when consciousness sheds its *consciousness-of something*, then it realizes Aware-Certitude as its own Reality. Then our neighbor becomes our Self and the Universe our own backyard.

> "*Love your neighbor as yourself,*"

commands the Bible.[753] And Lao Tzu declares,

> "*The Sage...makes the self of the people his self,*"[754]
>
> "*therefore, neither does he cause violence to others nor does he make others do so,*"

teaches Jainism.[755] Then we reach Pure Happiness and *Truth makes us free*. It is not the truth of an objective conception, but it is Certain-Faith that underlines all Reality.

From this point of view we should say whatever one does, does it to oneself. At first glance, it may appear that this Ethical realization refers to *reciprocity*. But it is not so. The Golden Rule, among all moral laws, seems to be really universal. All religious and non-religious texts refer to this imperative mutual exchange. Jesus affirms,

> "*As ye would that men should do to you, do ye also to them likewise.*"[756]

Confucius states

> "*Do not do to others what you do not want them to do to you.*"[757]

And, again, Jainism commands that

> "*A man should wander about treating all creatures as he himself would be treated.*"[758]

The Islamic tradition affirms,

> "*None of you* [truly] *believes until he wishes for his brother what he wishes for himself.*"[759]

And the Hindu epic poem confirms,

> "*This is the sum of duty: do not do to others what would cause pain if done to you.*"[760]

All religious and secular traditions, from the ancient Egyptian to the Native American wisdom, from Socrates the Roman Pagan Religion, from the Baha'i to the Buddhist, from Gandhi to Martin Luther King Jr., from Shinto to Sikhism, from Taoism to Wiccan, from Unitarian to Yoruba and Zoroastrianism, all recognize the great moral power of the Golden rule. Even Humanists recognize that this rule does not need any Divine intervention. They advocate: "mutual respect and... a spirit of empathy for all living beings."[761] And affirm, "Don't do things you wouldn't want to have done to you."[762]

The Golden Rule is regarded as a true universal moral code. In fact, on November 12, 2009, Prof. Dr. Karen Armstrong helped in the creation and the propagation of a beautiful and commendable *Charter for Compassion.*[763]

> "The Charter for Compassion is a document that transcends religious, ideological, and national differences. Supported by leading thinkers from many traditions, the Charter activates the Golden Rule around the world.
>
> The Charter for Compassion is a cooperative effort to restore not only compassionate thinking but, more importantly, compassionate action to the center of religious, moral and political life. Compassion is the principled determination to put ourselves in the shoes of the other, and lies at the heart of all religious and ethical systems.
>
> The principle of compassion lies at the heart of all religious, ethical and spiritual traditions, calling us always to treat all others as we wish to be treated ourselves. Compassion impels us to work tirelessly to alleviate the suffering of our fellow creatures, to dethrone ourselves from the centre of our world and put another there, and to honour the inviolable sanctity of every single human being, treating everybody, without exception, with absolute justice, equity and respect.
>
> It is also necessary in both public and private life to refrain consistently and empathically from inflicting pain. To act or speak violently out of spite, chauvinism, or self-interest, to impoverish, exploit or deny basic rights to anybody, and to incite hatred by denigrating others -even our enemies- is a denial of our

> common humanity. We acknowledge that we have failed to live compassionately and that some have even increased the sum of human misery in the name of religion.
>
> We therefore call upon all men and women ~ to restore compassion to the centre of morality and religion ~ to return to the ancient principle that any interpretation of scripture that breeds violence, hatred or disdain is illegitimate ~ to ensure that youth are given accurate and respectful information about other traditions, religions and cultures ~ to encourage a positive appreciation of cultural and religious diversity ~ to cultivate an informed empathy with the suffering of all human beings - even those regarded as enemies."[764]

On Buddhist assumptions, Schopenhauer asserts that "Boundless compassion for all living beings is the firmest and surest guarantee of pure moral conduct."[765] Nevertheless, he did not live up his compassion, as demonstrated by his anti-Semitic stereotyping. *Compassion* (*karúṇā*), in a Buddhist sense, does not judge. It is *sympathy* that does not feel pain. It is Awareness in the field of distress. It is dispassionate *pity* for the others' suffering. And, definitely, *karúṇā* is too serenely disengaged to *activate* the Golden Rule, which wants for others what one wishes for him/herself. Then, the reciprocity rule becomes subtly revengeful as in the saying, "I wish you what you wish me."[766]

A Franciscan poet of the XIII Century wrote,

"*death I am seeking.*"[767]

Nevertheless, with a different intent, during the first half of the IV Century, bands of heretical fanatical Christian Berbers roamed North Africa, in present Algeria and Tunis. They called themselves *Agonistici* (Fighters) in the name of Christ. In fact they fought at the war cry of "Praise God" (*Laudes Deo). The other Christians called them* Circumcellions, for their practice of loitering (*iēns*) around (*circum*) slave farmers' cells (*cellae*) hoping to convert them to their Donatist cause. They followed the schismatic Donatus Magnus of Casae Nigra (313). In a Church plagued by weak clergy scared by persecutions, he emphasized the necessity of martyrdom and consequent sainthood. Therefore, the Agonistici became the armed hand of Donatus' followers. They sought martyrdom by assaulting

Roman troops and armed caravans to kill and be killed as *saints.*[768]

They, as modern day suicide terrorist bombers, inflicted on others the death they wanted for themselves in order to achieve martyrdom for the glory of their god. Based on the principle of the Golden Rule, "Do or not do to others what you want them to do or not do to you," the action of these type of suicide becomes legitimate, if not meritorious. In fact, s/he is giving to others what he wants for her/himself.

Other types of suicide do not refer to any god, but still may be viewed from the perspective of reciprocity. This is the case of a "*Suicide by Cop.*"[769] The will-be suicide, who attacks or even kills police officers to be killed in response, is doing to others what s/he wants others to do to him or her. The same observation goes for the very numerous cases in which the one committing a massacre, in a school, in a theatre or in a market-store, then turns the weapon upon him/herself. S/he delivers on others what s/he self-inflicts. If we hold the Golden Rule to be true, we must admit that all the above cases are examples of high moral actions. In fact, those executors do to others what they want them to do to their own selves. It is similar to those religious ceremonies of penitents, where flagellants flagellate others to be flagellated.[770]

In addition, since no judge wants to be sentenced to any form of punishment, a magistrate following the Golden Rule can never inflict a lawful penalty. On a lighter note, with the rule of reciprocity we should recognize as true the paradox of the masochist who loves to receive pain. To be morally correct, s/he must become a sadist, loving to inflict pain. In fact, the masochist must inflict on *others* the pain that s/he *wants them to* inflict on him or herself.[771]

CHAPTER 6

CONCLUSION OF PART II

The search for universal morals turns out to be without solution. Postulating regional and dogmatic answers can lead to laws thought to be universal, but not effective as such. Only the realization of the Ethical Certitude in Awareness opens the avenue to Universality and Freedom.

Nevertheless, when the average person is confronted with everyday life while living away from the light of Certain-Bliss, what is s/he to do?

The third part of this book will address this question. To which, the best answer can be found with the help of the Golden Rule. In fact, when a wealthy person came to Jesus and asked him,

> "*Good Master, what good thing shall I do, that I may have eternal life?*"

Jesus

> "*said unto him... if thou wilt enter into life, keep the commandments.*"[772]

In other words, he advises to follow the Golden Rule. And the rich man

> "*said, All these have I kept from my youth up. Now when Jesus heard these things, he said unto him, Yet lackest thou one thing: sell all that thou hast, and distribute unto the poor, and thou shalt have treasure in heaven: and come, follow me*"[773]

in the Transcendent Pure Self Apodictical Awareness. However, Jesus continues,

> "*it is easier for a camel to go through the eye of a needle, than for a man rich* [with the consciousness-*of* worldly thoughts] *to enter into the kingdom of Transcendence.*"[774]

PART III

THE BOOK OF BEHAVIOR

PREMISE

"People say that what we're all seeking is a meaning for life... I think what we're seeking is an experience of being alive... so that we actually feel the rapture of being alive," states Joseph Campbell.[775] Nevertheless, "*being alive*" means to have brain activity, to have thoughts that conceptualize the world. In other words, what we are really seeking is the Transcendent as *food for thoughts*. Indeed, *seeking* becomes desire, *hunger* to *eat* and reduce this Transcendent Awareness to an object of thought. So that

> "*eyes shall be opened, and ye shall be as God, knowing good and evil.*"[776]

The Freudian *ego*, the conscious person living now in this world, realistically understands that s/he is torn between *good and evil*, laws and personal desires. The *id*, as forces of nature, is in contrast with the moral *super-ego*. Therefore, we should make ours the paraphrased inscription on the pillar before the Jokhang shrine, "*People* shall live happily in *their* great land, as *the others* will live happily in *their* great land."[777] Not always what we hope for is provided or allowed by relative social norms. Our behavior may be in contrast with the rules of the country we live in. Basic socializing relationship needs may be at odd with governmental statutes. Fascist dictatorships censor divergent ideas. Racist countries outlaw interracial marriages. Dogmatic theocracies place free thinking on fire. Homophobic states ban homosexual relationships. Non-conformity is frowned upon and marginalized in everyday life. Bigot-societies burn *witches* at the stake. Irrational mentalities silence the evidence of science with myopic preconceived ideas. Mafia associations impose organized criminality. Radical communist cultures view free enterprise as antisocial. Extreme capitalist viewpoints cut or negate basic social benefits. Realistically, therefore, which course of action should be followed? Which one is the *best* behavior?

At the behavioral levels, humans are whipped around by three interacting vortexes. In order of the importance attributed to them, the first one is health and life, the second one is love and libido and the third one is wealth and power. They are currents of thought that grip and captivate the mind. The spell of these whirlpools does not allow the mind to move above the navel.

Let it be clear, in this third part of our book we are not establishing new morals. We are only trying to establish the best way to behave from an Ethical standpoint. If our behavior should be different there are no metaphysical punishments or rewards. There will be only consequences based on physical and/or current public laws.

The best way to follow is that of the philosopher. It is Gandhi's search for freedom through truth-realization (*satyā-graha*).[778] Mahatma Gandhi recognized that

"*Man cannot for a moment live without consciously or unconsciously committing outward 'himsa'* [injury]. *The very fact of living – eating, drinking and moving about – necessarily involves 'himsa,' destruction of life, be it ever so minute. A votary of 'ahimsa'* [non-injury] *therefore remains true to his faith if the spring of all his actions is compassion... but he can never become entirely free from outward 'himsa.'*"[779]

The only recourse, then, is Compassion. Pure-Compassion, however, as we have seen, is *not of this world of duality*. Therefore, the best evaluator of behavior in the sublunar realm remains, even with all its faults, the Golden Rule. We will analyze behavior from that moral point of view knowing very well that it does not reach the Height of Ethic. With all the reservation analyzed in the second part of this book, the best approach for everyday life is the reciprocity of the Golden Rule.

> "*Do or don't do to others what you want or do not want being done to you.*"

We will investigate human behavior having this principle in mind and we will try to determine the best course of action.

Behavioral congregation

"*Peers with peers very easily congregate* [says] *an old* [Latin] *proverb.*"[780] A similar Italian adage, "*Tell me with whom you mingle and I will tell you who you are,*"[781] is echoed by the English "*Birds of a feather flock together.*"[782] In other words, *good* or *bad behaviors* spread among friends. Like socially transmitted viruses, networks influence each other. Nevertheless, these networks derive from the fundamental human tendency and the evolutionary necessity to find safety and security among similar associates.

The psychiatrist Jacob Moreno mapped out those connecting networks and called them "*sociograms.*"[783] Sociologist Paul Lazarsfeld applied them to the analysis of commercial and political propaganda. A new type of publicity became known as "word-of-mouth promotion" *or, better, as buzz* marketing. In any case, researches stated that human congregations produce not only psychological, but also physical contagious effects on social groups. So that social changes are considered *epidemics* relative to particular socio-cultural geographical and temporal structure.[784]

The social scientists Christakis and Fowler discovered that "Friends' Friends' Friends Affect Everything You Feel, Think, and Do... There are all sorts of social ties, thus, all sorts of social networks... There is *contagion*, which pertains to what... flows across the ties... [like] germs, money, violence, fashions, donor organs, happiness" loneliness and even health. Behavior, then, becomes contagious. That "contagious may be the so-called *mirror neuron systems* in the human brain [which] practice doing actions we merely observe in others." [785] Think about obesity. It was considered to be a sign of wealth and social status, like the rich fat Roman Gaius Pompeius Trimalchio Maecenatianus indulging in his dinner party banquet.[786] Up to the beginning of last century, corpulence was emulated as a sign of wealth in a world plagued by undernourishment. Today overweight is an indication of poor heath and bad dietary habits. In any case, it was and is a learned trait affected by the patterns of others.[787]

Shared actions or reactions are perceived as normal behaviors so that we can be accepted by the peers with whom we feel safe and secure. It is the example that is instinctively put into practice under the assumption that it should be followed for personal wellbeing. It is like animal behavior which is individually learned and performed following the others' examples. Similar to a stampede, we pick up subconscious signals from others for what we perceive as being the appropriate behavior. An example is the tendency that loving spouses have to depart this life following the death of their partners. And, if that did not happen naturally, the best behavior for an Indian widow was to become a true-*satī*. Namely, she had to sacrifice herself on the husband's funeral pyre.

The first and most determining element in human relationships is the political and religious leadership under which s/he happens to live. Both, religion and politics set the tone of human behavior.

CHAPTER 1

POWER IN THE POLITICAL AND RELIGIOUS ARENA

The Ancient Indian *Laws of Manu* declared "the King an Incarnation of the Gods... a great divinity under human shape."[788] Sovereigns, under all latitudes, were and are recognized Monarchs by "*grace of God*." We define such rulership as Traditional. Whereas, we call Hedonistic the leadership founded on free-democratic-consensus or on imposed-dictatorial-fear. There is a religious quality in every political choice, as there is a political structure in every religious institution.

In his novel *Satyricon,* the Roman author Gaius Petronius Arbiter (27 - 66 A.D.) states, "What's the benefit of laws where only money matters?"[789] After two millennia, this rhetorical question is still very poignant. Money matters to both Religion and Politics. Both blend into one another. Religion refers not only to behaviors connected to metaphysical realms, but also to spiritual interactions with political or social institutions. *Politics*, in Greek, means the *business* of the *city-dwellers*.[790] The leading-power, among them, is money, the *god in* which *we trust*.[791] It is the luring power of the people.[792] Money is that which makes people rejoice and/or sadden. It is placed like a carrot before headless donkeys. They "seem to care about riches, or anything, more than about virtue."[793] And "money and loss of character... are... the doctrines of the multitude," declared Socrates.[794]

Power, then, becomes the oppressive dictatorial regime. From Fascism[795] to Nazism, from Socialism to Communism, Totalitarianism in general plunges the world into pain, torture, massacres and holocaust. Dictators become idols. Hysterical crowds of destitute and breech-less *sans-culottes* salute them as gods and saviors of their *mother*-country. Then, all political views convert into religions. Nevertheless, those beliefs are not connected to metaphysical realms, but to political interactions. Resistance to the regime is punished by death. Like ancient Roman *Divine* Emperors,[796] leaders appease plebeians by keeping them in check with *bread and entertainments*[797] and, we add, with their indoctrination.[798] Also political managers reward intimate supporters by sharing crumbs of their power.

As a general rule, we must accept the laws of the country in which we live, states Socrates. This does not imply approval of particular rules as such. It only means acceptance of their deliberation. Serenely disengaged as Socrates, one should affirm his/her opposition to laws deprived of ethic by peacefully bearing its sentence.[799] Through history, that martyrdom becomes the most powerful force to oppose preexisting laws and social structures. "*Better... to endure anything, rather than think as they do and live after their manner,*" says Plato[800] quoting Homer.[801] Namely, that is the manner of those who are enslaved to subterranean laws.

When we leave the political struggles and we go back to the realm of the Supreme Ethic, then, according to the traditional (*hadith*) saying of the Prophet Muhammad,

> "*We return from the little jihād* (*el-jihādul-açghar*) *to the greater jihad* (*el-jihādul-akbar*)."[802]

The only true political perspective "Is Apoliteia,[803] the inner irrevocable distance from this society and its *values*; it is not consenting to be attached to it for some spiritual or moral connection... The disengaged attitude cannot be the same for both sides, which now contend for world domination, [*viz.*] the democratic capitalist *West* and the communist *East*. In fact, this contention, from a spiritual point of view, is devoid of any meaning. The *West* is not an expression of any superior idea. Its own civilization, based on an essential negation of traditional values, has the same destruction and the same nihilistic background that is featured in the Marxist and Communist area, albeit in various forms and degrees... At best, for the differentiated man it will be a practical problem. That specific margin of material freedom which the democratic world still leaves in some external activities, for those who not let it affect them inwardly, would certainly be abolished under a communist regime. Simply in view of this, one can take a stand against the Soviet-Communist front: for reasons that one might almost define as purely physical, not because we believe in some higher idea that the opposite side has on its own."[804]

In addition, we would argue that besides Communism and Capitalism, two more elements denote the *Modern World*, bigot Reformism and fundamental Extremism. Without any distinction we should apply apoliteia to both. The reformist's continuous updating makes the essential aspect of Ethic fade away. The Extremist's deadly bombs do not reach the heart of the system. Both are hedonistic attacks that hit the exterior surface without reaching a spiritual transformation. Both are lost in their own consciousness-*of* a world that becomes a dogmatic idol of their own imagination. The Pure-Ethical person is the one who really restores the connecting identification with the Transcendent. S/he is, then, the philosopher sovereign. S/he becomes the real silent *pontifex,*[805] the bridge-maker who restores the connection between True-Ethic with the relative-morals. The struggle of political power, then, becomes Gandhi's non-violent respect-for-life (*a-hiṃsā*) and beholding-Truth/Certitude (*satyā-graha*).[806]

Philosophers form and model history and its evolving moral principles. The various world views become the hallmarks of different historical periods. Christianity, the Enlightenment, Positivism, Romanticism, Communism, just to mention a few, produced and impacted world's events. Each of those weltanschauungs is the philosophical system of thinkers behind them. Nations and ideologists, shaped by them, enforce those ideas on people through education, sentences and wars.

War, namely a political action carried out with killing instruments, ushers death. The threat and/or the fear of death are the *hard power* that every political and ideological institution has to impose its will. In ancient times, war was seen as having sacred dimensions. It connected with the divine light of life's victory[807] or with the metaphysical dimension of death. Death, however, is the human dimension of Transcendence. It becomes *visible* under the threat of death or after the effects of death. Therefore, juridical entities like states summon that metaphysical to resolve conflicts. They deliver the force of death through terrorism, wars and capital punishments. Nevertheless, beside the *hard* one, there is a not so new type of strength employed by political organizations, it is called *soft power.*

Taoism speaks about the powerful softness of the *Ocean of Awareness,*

"*Nothing under heaven is softer or weaker than water,*
and yet nothing is better
for attacking what is hard and strong,
because of its immutability.

The defeat of the hard by the soft,
the defeat of the strong by the weak –
this is known to all under heaven,
yet no one is able to practice it."[808]

Nevertheless, the power of Awareness has been transformed. It has become political soft power. It is the smile of the merchant that is polite to the customers because s/he is after their money. Luc de Clapiers, marquis de Vauvenargues stated correctly that "There are no people bitterer than those who are sweet for interest."[809]

Joseph Nye, a political scientist at Harvard University describes "Soft power" as "the ability to shape the preference of others... If I can get you to want to do what I want, then I do not have to use carrots or sticks to make you do it."[810] We recognize the pragmatic validity of this political strategy as the best political alternative. However, *soft power* is a Trojan horse. Virgil in the *Aeneid* makes Laocoön, Poseidon's priest, cry out,

"Oh, miserable citizen, what is such insanity?
You believe the enemy sailed away? Or do you think
That Greeks' gifts bare no harm?...
Some trickery lurks in it. Trojan, don't trust the horse.
Whatever it is, I fear Greeks even when they bring gifts."[811]

Similarly, *Soft power* creates a need. Better still, it co-opts rather than coerce. It neutralizes oppositions and assimilates its own original will into the cultural mainstream. In other words, it generates a market and, consequently, imposes it by making it indispensable. The national interest of each world country sponsors its culture (*i.e.* life-styles like *the-American-way, Yoga-indic-centres, etc.*), global markets (with slogans and ads like *Coca Cola, McDonald, etc.*) and entertainment industry (with its role models filmed in *Hollywood, Bollywood, etc.*).[812] These, then, become the forerunner *Trojan-horses* of their true original county's political will and interests. Nevertheless, soft power is not so *soft*, in that it intends to promote and sponsor an utilitarian will, which, if not successfully accepted by others, must enforce itself with military and/or *terrorist* interventions. As an example, the idea of democracy, not accepted with *softness*, will be imposed necessarily by force.[813]

Ideological power

The real political power is not the *hard* or *soft* one, it is the *Ideological power*. It is the only one which imposes itself at any cost, namely with *hard* and/or *soft* interventions. The *Ideological power* is called Reason of State (*Raison d'État)*. The States aims and ambitions are its Political Will. Each will is shaped by its own view of the world or weltanschauung. The religious *God's Will*, the economic *National Interest*, the socialist *Economic Structure* and the pragmatic *Realpolitik* are the

"*beasts full of eyes*"[814]

of the *Ideological power*, which takes over the mind of the leaders in an *ideal-conspiratory-like* grip. Namely it creates a mind of its own that imposes itself on all participants. In fact, ideas, when set in motion, continue endlessly until stopped and checked by another contrary idea. Therefore, politicians, leaders or CEOs cannot escape the compelling self-preserving *Raison d'État. If a leader* should break away from it, then s/he would start a revolution generating *a new, fresh coercing and, again, conspiratory Reason of State*. The circle never ends.

> *Ideologies are self-preserving conspirators.*

Education

In general education is viewed as a mean to riches. A *biblical* proverb states,

"*A man of knowledge increaseth strength.*"[815]

In most cases, learning is not carried out to quench the natural human hunger for the fruit of knowledge, but to pursue a career or a well remunerating activity. Therefore, it becomes easy to educate masses and whip them around according to the current political ideology. In fact, in average, majors are chosen based on the demand and opportunity that they may offer. Science and business courses are preferred because of their practical applications. Philosophy, on the contrary, can be dangerous since it encourages free thinking.

Today students follow what they like. They learn what they want to hear. School classes are full with annoyed students awakening only at the sound of familiar tunes. What is missing is the spirit of objectivity that bans all preconceived ideas. There is no openness. There are no ears or eyes for the art of different eras because the present cacophony is blinding and deafening. Magnanimously astute demagogues offer crumbs of *bread and entertainments* to the crowds. In the meanwhile, they keep the real delicacies for their own palates. They teach the crowds what will keep them subjugated.

It is not by outlawing the consumption of alcohol that a nation becomes sober. The failure of American *prohibitionism* proves it. It is not by banning the sales of guns that we prevent murders. We would have to ban also knives, clubs, stones and pressure-cookers for homemade bombs. A gun does not fire by itself, as a knife does not wield on its own. Both need a brain to fire and to wield. Perhaps we should then ban brains. It is only by educating the brain that drunkenness, addiction and violence are curbed.

Education must lead to the discovery of universal absolute Ethic. But this becomes impossible where any value is measured by money and power. And this is true also, as we have seen, in the field of morality, religion and ideology. There one idea wants to predominate over all the others.

CHAPTER 2

LOVE

Love's strength

"There is One-Pure-Love. It is when one loves without wanting anything from the person loved." However, very few admit the existence of such love. "Who does not experience Passion, Hate, Greed, Anger, etc... No one would deny them. Actually, if anyone says that Desire, War and the others do not exist, s/he would immediately be considered mad and countless historical proofs would be offered... Each... is a strong impulse, which, like a wind, blows the mind away." However, to ask if love exists, the answer may be negative. Nevertheless, "You feel love... but you cannot see that love. This does not mean it does not exist... Today, people think they can buy everything... Therefore, if they do not find love... they immediately say that it does not exist." They say so because they are distracted, distant from Pure Awareness, "the truly existing Gentle-Wind-of-Pure-Love that asks nothing in return."[816]

Pure love is when we silence our thoughts in the stillness of Awareness' Apodicticity.

Therefore, the closer we can come to describe true love is to refer it metaphorically to our dreamless sleep or to the thoughtless instant of orgasm. We should clarify that the orgasm we refer here is different from the pleasurable thought of it. On the contrary, the orgasm we talk about is the Tantric ineffable and thoughtless quivering and instantaneous Present of Awareness during which the *world-stops*. It is Awareness during the blissful silence of the dreamless sleep. When we move away from it, then the *fruit of knowledge* is being *eaten*. Then, the world starts moving again. Then, we have only the memory or the thought of that ineffable-ecstatic-shivering-stillness of Apodictical-Awareness. Subsequently, that lost moment is perceived as pleasurable and the desire to repeat it or to *know* it again ensues.

Apart from the two moments of dreamless sleep and orgasm, what we call love is only egotistical polyamory. In fact, how can we be monogamous when our thoughts are continuously enamored with the varied world? The consciousness-*of*-the-objects takes us away from the stillness of Awareness. The objects seduce us and *love* becomes synonym of its contrary, namely, personal pleasure.

With daily negative actions, we pollute the society in which we live. With thoughts of dislike, we affect those who surround us. We spread *germs* of hate among close and distant people. Eventually, someone will be infected and will harbor the contagious disease. It is meaningless to be a conscience-objector and oppose a declared war when we pay taxes in the same belligerent country. Every tax dollar paid puts us on the front line of fire. Similarly, every sentiment of hate makes us guilty alongside the felon. The criminal is the executioner of our mental impulses. Each one of us has empowered and gives power to the tyrants, mass murderers and monsters of history. Our hate impulses end up embodying a person that will lead them to fulfillment.

Human society is like conjoined twins.[817] If one commits a crime the other one is accountable, even if s/he did not commit it. Since, one could have stopped the other. Each one of us, even those who opposed them, in different degrees is collectively responsible, for the Hittler*s* and Stalin*s* that stepped and will step on this earth. Our responsibility rests in our thoughts that in a way or the other generate them. Ultimately, as Thoreau states, we have "*the duty of civil disobedience.*"[818]

> "*Whatsoever ye shall bind on earth shall be bound in heaven: and whatsoever ye shall loose on earth shall be loosed in heaven.*
>
> "*Peter... said, Lord, how oft shall my brother sin against me, and I forgive him? till seven times? Jesus saith unto him, I say not unto thee, Until seven times: but, Until seventy times seven.*"[819]

Therefore, Love, Forgive and Forget always!

The Nature of Love[820]

Transcendent is synonym of God and Transcendence is synonym of Love. God is Love and Love is God. Nothing can be said about God, Love or Transcendence; these are thought but never known. Love is always one or, better still, is zero because even *one* is a quality that cannot express Transcendence. In this sense, we cannot state that Love exists, because even that existence would qualify the un-qualifiable Transcendence of Love. We may feel Love, but we cannot conceptualize it without stating that which is different from Love itself. In fact, Love can be felt not thought. The feeling of Love is its effect not its cause. We can never know that cause as an object. We can only conceptualize it mythologically, metaphorically and poetically as

"the love that moves the sun and the other stars."[821]

We can love many because each one is a reflection of that Transcendent Love, towards which we incessantly tend. Therefore, we are likely to recognize that Love in the beloved one. This one becomes the mask, the face, or the veil that covers Transcendent Love. When the veil, the *True-icon* (*Vera-icona*) transpires that Transcendence, then the beloved is recognized in its Loving Purity,[822]

"benignantly robed in modesty;
and seems to be something that came
from heaven to earth to show a miracle.
She shows herself so pleasant to her admirer,
that she conveys by eyes sweetness to the hearth,
not understood by him who does not feel it."[823]

However, when the mask or the veil covers and obscures the *nakedness* of that Love, then only its objectivity is experienced obfuscating the light, which we are really seeking for. In this immanent objective world,

"*the place called facing God* (*peniel*),"

Jacob saw

"*God face to face.*"

Therefore, as subject, he lived to know his God as his own object, not as God in-Itself.[824]

"*And the Lord spake*[825] *unto Moses face to face, as a man speaketh unto his friend... And he said, Thou canst not see my face: for there shall no man see me, and live*"[826]

a subject-object relationship.

Von Hildebrand in his *The Nature of Love* speaks about different degrees or orders of love.[827] However, based on Biblical scriptural injunctions, we must distinguish love under the human aspect (*sub specie humanitatis*) from the one under the divine aspect (*sub specie divinitatis*). From this last point of view, we must admit that no degree of love can be present. If this were the case, Redemption would have been obsolete. God does not love because "the other reciprocates"[828] His love. God loves because He is Love.

If God is love, could He have loved Adam and Eve less after they sinned? God's love for Abel was not different from the one He had for Cain. What

"*He did not accept*"

was Cain's "*offering.*"[829] Cain, in Hebrew *Qayin* (קין), means *possession*, namely that which is *mine.* Therefore, God did not accept the fruits of that possession, not Cain as His creature. The creative-love of God towards human beings does not have a degree or an *order*. God does not *have a change of heart*, namely love in one degree at the time of creation and reconsider it when the creature sins. God's projecting act is the *fiat* creating out of love to the point of Self-sacrifice. In fact, a lack or a lesser degree of that creative-love would result inevitably in non-existence or in a *minor* existence for the creature, if that could be conceivable at all. By its own nature, God's creative-love must always be there untarnished, identical for a saint or a Socrates[830] as well as for a sinner. For this last one, in fact, God promises the advent of the Messiah's Redeeming Sacrifice of the Cross.[831]

It could be argued that the two orders cannot be reconciled on their own account; because one is divine, the other is human. However, from the perspective of a "value response"[832] we must remember Jesus' injunction,

"*Be perfect, therefore, as your heavenly Father is perfect.*"[833]

This is a value, a precise commandment says von Hildebrand, a "message from God in all created goods and exist[s] as an ultimate reality in God Himself, who is, after all Justice itself, Goodness itself, Love itself."[834] Therefore, the *perfect* parent does not have favoritism, as instead von Hildebrand suggests. S/he should not condone misbehavior but should not love less an offspring who is "a superficial egotist, an unreliable scoundrel," based on the assumption that only "the gracious, noble child *deserves* to be loved more" or, as in the parable of the prodigal son, for the "unique significance of his deep repentance."[835] On the contrary, in that parable, the father loved his prodigal son even before he repented. The father, unselfishly and out of love, gave him his

"*share of the estate.*"[836]

Furthermore, the parent continued to love and look out for him even while he was a sinner, so that

> "*while he was still a long way off, his father saw him.*"[837]

Is it necessary "that the other reciprocates my love"[838] in order to be called friend? Jesus, after being

> "*osculatus,*"[839]

kissed by Judas, called him "*amice.*"[840] He called Judas friend even when he knew that

> "*One of you will betray me, one who is eating with me.*"[841]

Jesus knew that his love was not only unreciprocated but that he was being betrayed by his friend. Nevertheless, he called him friend and added,

> "*Judas, are you betraying the Son of Man with a kiss?*"[842]

God does not love more or less; there cannot be any "value hierarchy"[843] in His Love and, to be "perfect" as He is, we must love equally. God always loves the sinner, even when in Hell, but not the sin, which is negation of love. God does not distance Himself from the sinner, but it is this last one who rejects God's love. Never let the guard down,

> "*If you want to be perfect, go, sell your possessions and give to the poor, and you will have treasure in heaven. Then come, follow me.*"[844]

To engage in a true Christian friendship it is not necessary to be "understood by the other."[845] On the contrary, the "*Prayer for Peace,*"[846] attributed to Saint Francis and established as the morning recitation for the *Missionaries of Charity* of Mother Theresa of Calcutta, says

> "O divine Master,
> grant that I may not so much seek
> to be consoled as to console;
> to be understood, as to understand;
> to be loved, as to love."

Furthermore, in the presence of "the incomparable love for God,"[847] all other loves fade in nothingness. Thus,

> "*Love the Lord your God with all your heart and with all your soul and with all your strength.*"[848]

Contrary to von Hildebrand's view, "the famous statements of the saints" must be "understood as a formulation of the enduring nature of their love" and they do "constitute a formulation of the enduring nature of their love. This is why they" must "be cited as constituting proof for the sublimity of *amour desinteressé*"[849] (disinterested love). In fact, when the freed Platonic cave slave "approaches the light his eyes will be dazzled, and he will not be able to see anything at all of what are now called realities."[850] In that condition, how could he then be able to *see* his own subjectivity (*eigenleben*) without obfuscating that light of love by exalting himself? And

> "*For whoever exalts himself will be humbled, and whoever humbles himself will be exalted.*"[851]

In fact, the former Platonic slave returns to the cave. "Coming suddenly out of the sun to be replaced in his old situation; would he not be certain to have his eyes full of darkness?"[852] And, again, would he not give little or no importance to his own subjectivity during the virtual shadow competitions in which the other slaves find exaltation?

> "*But many who are first will be last, and many who are last will be first.*"[853]

Recognizing these truths, Saint Francis declares to Brother Leo that in sanctity or performing great miracles, even astonishing ones, like resurrecting the dead, "*there is not perfect happiness.*" However, when drenched, cold, tired, hungry and slandered, we are denied hospitality and we are beaten to a pulp and "*all these things we will endure... for his love... in this is perfect joy... Christ grants... to win oneself... I do not want to glorify myself, if not in the cross of our lord Jesus Christ.*"[854] In fact, nothing is truly mine that does not come from the Transcendent. The ultimate self-transcending cannot leave space for my *personal* happiness.[855] Jesus said:

> "*If anyone would come after me, he must deny himself and take up his cross daily and follow me.*"[856]

No one can follow Christ if s/he does not deny, renounce and renege himself/herself.[857] Even that which is "*mine,*" deriving from conjugal love, in the sense of "Your life is my life,"[858] even that must be given up.

> "*In fact, in the resurrection they neither marry nor are married, but are like angels in heaven.*"[859]

Jesus has very precise words regarding all "Kinds of 'Mine,'"[860] in fact,

> "*Everyone who has left houses or brothers or sisters or father or mother or children or fields for my sake will receive a hundred times as much and will inherit eternal life.*"[861]

The reason for this abnegation is that

> "*No one can serve two masters. Either he will hate the one and love the other, or he will be devoted to the one and despise the other. You cannot serve both God and selfish interest.*"[862]

Paul confirms,

> "*I want you to be without care. He who is unmarried cares for the things of the Lord, how he may please the Lord... instead he who is married cares about the things of the world, how he may please his wife... The unmarried woman cares about the things of the Lord, that she may be holy both in body and in spirit. But she who is married cares about the things of the world, how she may please her husband.*"[863]

In fact, those who were invited to God's banquet, declined the invitation and

> "*said, 'I just got married, so I can't come,*'"[864]

says Jesus in the parable of the great supper. In addition, to confirm this, he stresses,

> "*If anyone comes to me and does not hate his father and mother, his wife and children, his brothers and sisters -yes, even his own life- he cannot be my disciple.*"[865]

These very hard and unmistakable words,

> "*who does not hate his own,*"

support *l'amour desinteressé*. This can explain Abraham's obedience to God and his readiness to *sacri-fice* his beloved son Isaac

> "*as a burnt offering*"[866]

to the Lord. Because of this willingness to fulfill His

> "*jealous*"[867]

injunction, God blessed Abraham and his descendants,[868] as He had blessed Abel.

> "*For whoever does the will of my Father in heaven is my brother and sister and mother.*"[869]

In other words, ultimately all loves disappear without any residue in the light of God's will "that takes away any memory of sin."[870] Any other way of reasoning would not be according to

> "*the things that are of the Transcendent, but the things that are of men.*"[871]

In fact,

> "*For whoever wants to save his life*[872] *will lose it, but whoever loses his life for me will save it.*"[873]

Therefore, if we want to find what our real "personal concern" is, we find that it is not our concern at all, because we must renounce to ourselves. In fact,

> "*do not worry about your life... consider the ravens, who do not sow... yet God feeds them... the lilies grow, they do not labor... do not worry about it... For where your treasure is, there your heart will be also.*"[874]

If you love your Transcendent-Certain-Awareness with whole your heart, which part of it can be left out for your earthly beloved one?

Self-transcending must be transcendence without any residual immanence in which subjectivity, as purified as it may be, may leave its mark. The the subjectivity (*eigenleben*) "not confined to the sphere of immanence,"[875] would, as Capaneo "with the heart negating,"[876] or, at best, as the prodigal son, demand to receive that which is '*mine*.' However, my true concern must be God Awareness and Awareness only,

> "*But seek his kingdom, and these things will be given to you as well.*"[877]

Von Hildebrand, after recognizing that we must seek "*first* the Kingdom of God," affirms that "the human persons... should possess a full subjectivity... in second place."[878] However, once hunger and thirst have been quenched by

> "*Bread... eternal,*" "*living water*"[879] **and**
> "*everything that proceeds out of the mouth of the Lord,*"[880]

received first during the "great supper," how can there be left, in second place, any appetite for the *beloved* world?

The "dissolution of subjectivity" is not "annihilation of personal existence"[881] because the eternal creative act of God, which is the ineffable essence of our most intimate reality, establishes it. The *moment* of creation must be here and now. Placing creation in a different time or space would imply a temporality or a spatiality that would contradict God's Eternal Presence. The presence of God's creative act is the most fundamental core of our own being, without which we would not be.

Satcitānanda is the Divine (√*div*) Splendid Transcendent (*brahman*) Apodicticity. It generates Itself as the Real (*sat*), Mindfulness-*Son*, who is Pure-Consciousness (*cit*) returning instantly to the Bliss (*ānanda*) of the *Spirit*-of-Awareness.

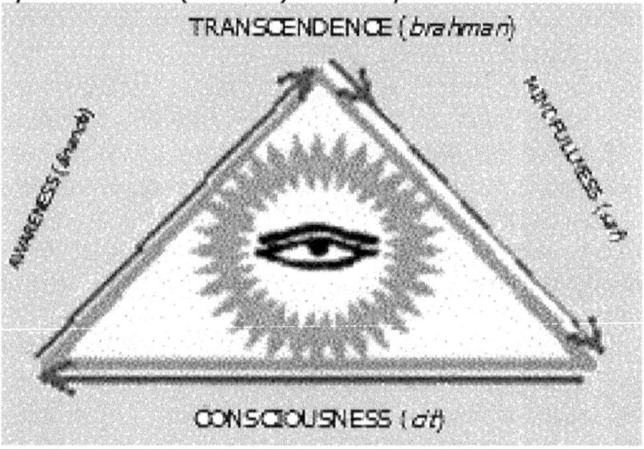

What von Hildebrand considers to be our personality and our subjectivity, must be, in essence, the image of the presence of God. That reflection is our true essence. It is our 'I' and our own true way of being in life.[882] Ontologically, our subjectivity must be

"*the image*[883] *of God.*"[884]

This likeness[885] radiates the unique individuality of our own-life (*eigen-leben*), "all those things that are of concern to me."[886] This is the 'I' that, in a "Super Value-Response,"[887] must reflect the light of Awareness[888] of God's creation. However, how can one distinguish a pure mirror made *of* Light, *by* the Light, *for* the Light, *with* the Light and *in* the Light from Light itself?[889] "This dialogue with God"[890] finds our true happiness with love, in Its love for us and through our love for It. What catches our love must be the Transcendent Beauty of the image of God, the "*imago Dei*,"[891] discovered by both lovers in each other, and, in turn, transcended by God Himself.

Epistemologically, the subject inevitably sees the other always as an object. However, an interpersonal subject-object relation distinguishes an object from a thing.[892] The thing is that which is placed *there* for my use, like when I reach out for my pen, with no further consideration. When, however, we reflect on the ontological nature of the object, then it is always referred "in relation to the I."[893] In this case, there is an interpersonal relationship caracterized by a transcendent quality conferred to the object. This interpersonal relation may refer to a person as well as a thing. Verga's short story of Mazzarò portrays a self-made, very wealthy Sicilian owner, who, facing death went on a rampage killing all his poultry, and screaming, "My things, come away with me!"[894] In this case, *things* were viewed as having an internal, inherent quality conceived vital and essential for the person, as if the *things* had become a metaphysical extension of the person itself. The objective world, however, enters in a much deeper and mystical interpersonal relation in St. Francis' *Canticle of the Sun* or *Praise of the Creatures*.[895] There, Francis of Assisi addresses the elements of nature with a brotherly embrace, which glorifies the creative power of God.

In a subjectivity devoid of transcendent afflatus, one finds the other only as an object *per-se*. There, obfuscated by the enigmatic mirror[896] of the objective immanent world, the divine image dims into egotism. On the other hand, if we dissolve and annihilate our subjectivity in total otherness, then, we would negate ourselves as the likeness *of the*

> "*The true light that illuminates every man who comes into the world.*"[897]

Therefore, we would negate God Himself, separating Him from the life of our self.

One does not need to go out of its own subjectivity to find the other, because the other is found in "the *intentio unionis* [intention of the union]... of the self-donation of love,"[898] where the 'Thou' becomes "the 'lord' of our subjectivity." In turn, that love is a reflection of the highest love that the 'I' has "for Christ and through Christ for God... the 'king of my existence.'"[899]

Subjectivity must self-transcend, reverting to its true source, "the mysterious center," where it finds its own true being and its "dignity as person."[900] In truth, only when the "whole person" commits with "full value-response"[901] to the highest moral "obedience to the divine will,"[902] then, subjectivity transcends into "the acceptance of the yoke, the actualization of the *similitudo Dei* [likeness, of God]."[903] Therefore, to love Christ is "to walk in His path."[904] This is the mystical journey of the return to Christ. Real love is to choke in ecstasy. Love is a journey that never relaxes during its voyage, not even at the arrival point. In fact, at the end of the trip, the lover discovers that s/he is not the same person who started the crossing, but s/he is the loved one. Forgetting also the departure station, s/he is reborn to true life. This crossing leads us to transcend our life, our subjectivity (*eigenleben*), the face or the veil of God. In the heart of that mask, resides Transcendence, our true happiness. He, as creator of that subjective image, must be more intimate to that image, namely to us, than we, as image, are to our own self. In other words, the intimate reality of my reflected image in the mirror is my true self.

"i carry your heart with me (i carry it in
my heart) i am never without it (anywhere
i go you go, my dear; and whatever is done
by only me is your doing, my darling)
i fear
no fate (for you are my fate, my sweet) i want
no world (for beautiful you are my world, my true)
and it's you are whatever a moon has always meant
and whatever a sun will always sing is you
here is the deepest secret nobody knows
(here is the root of the root and the bud of the bud
and the sky of the sky of a tree called life; which grows
higher than soul can hope or mind can hide)
and this is the wonder that's keeping the stars apart
i carry your heart (i carry it in my heart)"[905]

From this perspective, the nature of love is always monogamous.

"*That they all may be one; as thou, Father,* [art] *in me, and I in thee, that they also may be one in us: that the world may believe that thou hast sent me.*"[906]

The faces, the veils, the images, the subjects, the masks, the personalities may vary and they do change, however the Transcendent within each of those facades remains Unaltered, Unchanged, Immutable, Eternal Love.

> "*For in the resurrection they neither marry, nor are given in marriage, but are as the angels of God in heaven.*"[907]

When we identify and objectify that Ineffable Monogamic Reality with one or more persons here and now, we are in danger of losing Love Itself. Then a never-ending search for the *true* love, the *charming prince/ss* ensues, ending, most of the time, in disillusion, adultery, separation and/or divorce.

CHAPTER 3

LIFE, SEX AND FAMILY

Respect for life

Life is an extension of Awareness and Love. If we live in that dimension, then, there can never be any *interest* in taking someone's life. Rather, the preservation of life, from its most elementary levels on, would be the outcome of Love itself. Killing, when executed by egotism, self-interest or utilitarian reasons can never be ethical. By its own disengaged reality, Awareness is never desirous of death. On the contrary, it is always participating in Life. Therefore, it is the sustainer of life. It does not *want* abortion. It does not *desire* the death of another. Nor it *hungers* for food that implies the elimination of life.

Life is the outcome of a sexual act. All sexual acts have two drives, one hormonal, the other epistemic. By hormone, we mean a cell's chemical reaction conferring a drive or an impetus[908] to another cell in a different part of the organism. By epistemic, we mean the process of knowledge[909] reaching its informative goal. Therefore, the sexual act is, a) hormonally, the Blind Will[910] of Nature driving the evolutionary continuation of the specie. b) Epistemically, it is the conscious or unconscious urge or desire of the perceiving-subject to reach, beyond its objectivity, the other as a transcendent being in-itself. This last characteristic drive is that which always confers sacredness to the act. However, when we act upon the sexual impulse only for the attainment of our own pleasure, we destroy for our consciousness that sacred intent by reducing the other to an immanent object for-our-own-self. By transcendent, we mean that which is thought but not known, hence is intended beyond the subject-object epistemic relationship. By immanent, we mean that which finds its being in the subject-object relationship. Therefore, the sexual act is always sacred in its drive. Nevertheless that potential sacredness may be realized or unrealized depending of our intentional transcending towards the other or reverting to the immanence of the object for-our-own-self. A true fulfilling sexual mutual encounter is timeless even if never repeated again. When that instant is lived in reference to the partner, then it becomes a transcending event. This unit, which may be repeated with the same person/s during the course of a lifetime, derives, as we described, from a natural impulse created by hormonal and epistemic impulses.

Gender

The subject/object duality creates gender distinction. Gender is the mental response to the sex male/female biological foundation and to environmental-adapting behaviors. This masculine/feminine distinction could be expressed as knower/known. The knower is actively conscious-of knowing and the known is passively known. Both satisfy and complement the epistemic synthesis. Furthermore, the known can be a general object. In that case it is passively unconscious-of being known. Or it can be another knower. In that case s/he is passively conscious-of being known. However, we must understand that only the objective side of the known confers *knowledge* to the knower, without which it would not be a knower. The *feminine-object*, in other words, has a power without which the *masculine-subject* would be impotent. The Hindu pantheon is very well aware of her power; in fact, every god (*deva*) is paired with his goddess-consort (*devī*), a synthesis graphically expressed by the *yoni-liṅga*, vagina-phallus symbol.[911] Without her power (*śakti*) he would be unable to be a god. The Tantric literature says,

Woman is the creator of the universe
the universe is her form;
woman is the foundation of the world,
she is the true form of the body.
Whatever form she takes
whether the form of a man or a woman,
is the superior form.
In woman is the form of all things,
of all that lives and moves in the world.
There is no jewel rarer than woman,
no condition superior to that of a woman.
There is not, nor has been, nor will be
any destiny to equal that of a woman;
there is no kingdom, no wealth,

to be compared to that of a woman;
there is not, nor has been, nor will be
any holy place like unto a woman.
There is no prayer to equal a woman.
There is not, nor has been, nor will be
any yoga to compare with a woman,
no mystical formula nor asceticism
to match a woman.
There are not, nor have been, nor will be
any riches more valuable than woman."[912]

From the beginning, when not engaged in selfish, egotistical pursuits, we are holy temples,[913] beautiful child-like innocent, radiant, creatures. "However, our story of the Fall in the Garden sees nature as corrupt; and that myth corrupts the whole world for us. Because nature is thought of as corrupt, every spontaneous act is sinful and must not be yielded to. You get a totally different civilization and a totally different way of living according to whether your myth presents nature as fallen or whether nature is in itself a manifestation of divinity, and the spirit is the revelation of the divinity that is inherent in nature."[914]

Our hunger for knowledge transforms itself into limitless capacity to love. This epistemic characteristic, with its consequent common-union or communal-intent, may turn willing sex into a realized sacred act. In any case, all sexual acts confer, to the partners involved, an indelible exchange of positive and/or negative subliminal psychophysical fluid responses. However, this epistemic need remains unrealized because, ultimately, the sexual act reverts on the perceiving-subject and transforms it in objective pleasure for the perceiver. In addition, that pleasure may generate another Ego. It is to this new Ego that we ought to render our dutiful family service. Truthfully, the individual sexual act becomes an instrument for the generation of a new Ego. This new comer is that same Blind Will of Nature which forced the parental partners' union in order to achieve, with a new birth, individualized fresh possibilities through world-objectifying gazing eyes.

Homosexuality

The Dalai Lama affirms, "If you are not a religious believer and wish to have a sexual relationship with someone of the same sex, with mutual consent, without there being rape or abuse of any kind, and if you find in this a non-violent satisfaction, there is nothing I can say against it... It is unfair for homosexuals to be rejected by society... or to be punished and lose their jobs."[915]

Gender differences take their role also in homosexual couples, when the partners, although attracted by their own biological sex, identify one as more masculine and the other as more feminine. This diversity constitutes the harmonious oneness of all relationships. Paula Abdul sings, "*When we get together/ It just all work out...Things in common/ Just ain't a one...We come together/ Cuz opposites attract... Don't think we'll ever/ Get our differences patched/ Don't really matter/ Cuz we're perfectly matched.*"[916] The elements for a successful relationship are the same, regardless of the couple's biological-sex structure. Kurdek recognizes[917] that the general models, for a successful heterosexual and/or homosexual long-term committed relationship, are personality traits, supportive community, effective communication and dependence on the intimate relationship between partners. A supportive community acceptance of homosexual partnership is essential for its success. Conflicts arise when there is a lack of support from family, friends and society in general deriving from ignorance and misunderstanding. What is misunderstood is that in homosexual relationships there are opposite gender-roles and identities. The *hijra* Indian "third sex" distinguishes among themselves the more masculine penetrating *panthis* from the more feminine penetrated *kothis.*[918] Although the biological sex of the two persons may be the same, both, like in the song, will assume different relationship responsibilities that coincide with their personality, gender-identity and role.

Role switch is also present in sadomasochism.[919] From a gender perspective, the medieval tale of Phyllis, the beautiful wife of Alexander, tempting Aristotle clearly shows that she is the male while the Philosopher is the female in a sadomasochist role play. In fact, "riding on the Master's back, Phyllis loudly sang a song of triumph: "Master Silly carries me. / 'Love leads on, and so he goes, / by Love's authority'."[920]

Marriage

> "*God said; Let us make man* (Adam) *in our image, after our likeness... So God created man* (Adam) *in his* [own] *image, in the image of God created he him*; ***male and female*** *created he them... **And** called their name Adam... And the Lord God formed man* [of] *the dust of the ground, and ... man became a living soul.*"[921]

Joseph Campbell, alluding to a Platonic myth,[922] describes marriage as "the reunion of the separated duad. Originally you were one. You are now two in the world, but the recognition of the spiritual identity is what marriage is... Marriage is recognition of a spiritual identity... By marrying the right person, we reconstruct the image of the incarnate God, and that's what marriage is... There's a flash that comes, and something in you knows that this is the one... Marriage means the two that are one, the two become one flesh... the two really are one... spiritually... When you make the sacrifice in marriage, you're sacrificing not to each other but to unity in a relationship... You're no longer this one alone; your identity is in a relationship. Marriage is not a simple love affair, it's an ordeal, and the ordeal is the sacrifice of ego to a relationship in which two have become one... And that's a purely mythological image signifying the sacrifice of the visible entity for a transcendent good... the two experiencing that they are one... Marriage... is... primarily a spiritual exercise, and the society is supposed to help us have the realization."[923] It must be clear that marriage takes place upon the onset of any transcending sexual union.

*Marr*iage, from Latin *marītāre*, to unite with a husband (*maritus*), is the *marit*al union of a husband and a wife. It is a public social acknowledgement of a religious, civil and/or cohabitation union of two or more heterosexual and/or homosexual adult partners not related through adoption or blood expressing their will to live sexually together. This union should also include the social legal acknowledgement of a de-facto ascertained sexual cohabitation of two or more heterosexual and/or homosexual adult partners not related through adoption or blood, which becomes to all intents and purposes a marriage. In the absence of biological or adopted underage offspring and/or dependents in general, such unions can be dissolved.

George Bernard Shaw, to highlight the absurdity of a legally inseparable marriage, satirically argues, "When two people are under the influence of the most violent, most insane, most delusive, and most transient of passions, they are required to swear that they will remain in that excited, abnormal, and exhausting condition until death do them part."[924] In any case, Civil Laws, legalizing heterosexual and/or homosexual marriages/cohabitations, should ensue to regulate family management, finance security, health and mutual care, old age relations, divorce and alimony. Even von Hildebrand, the philosopher who was recognized by the Popes Pius XII, John Paul II and Benedict XVI as a prominent figure of "the intellectual history of the Catholic Church in the twentieth century,"[925] argues that in a marriage "a certain degree of immorality, lovelessness, and abuse objectively makes a separation absolutely desirable."[926]

In November 2009, at a Washington press conference, Justin Rigali, Catholic Cardinal of Philadelphia, declared, "Sexual relations outside the marital bond are contrary not only to the will of God but to the good of man. Indeed, they are contrary to the will of God precisely because they are against the good of man." [927] For the same principle, Robert P. George, Princeton University jurisprudence professor and a conservative Roman Catholic, rejected homosexual marriage on the basis that it violates human reason, which understands sex as having only the purpose of strengthening marital union and of procreating through vaginal intercourse.[928] Extending the implication of this myopic restrictive view, we can declare that eating a nut or a seed is against human reason and natural law since seeds are intended, by the creative will of God, to generate plants. In addition, those restrictive perspectives pass under silence female orgasm, not essential for procreation, including lesbian intercourse with oral stimulation[929] and/or use of sex toys. Furthermore, if the sexual act is intended only to procreate, it would not offer periods of infertility during which, different from other mammals, the sexual stimuli for humans is still present. Besides, if vaginal intercourse is intended to be the only avenue for procreation, why is artificial insemination possible? Finally, why the pre-conception choice of an offspring genetic characteristic should be considered unnatural, when, as suggested by the research of Sarah Robertson, professor at the University of Adelaide, Australia, it seems that the woman's body may unconsciously select or reject the man's seminal fluid's changes for the timing and activation of pregnancy.[930]

Furthermore, it is not clear why artificial insemination is consider by some religions as a sin only when used for generating humans and not for generating other animals. If sin means subversion of the present *natural* order of things, then all types of artificial insemination, including animal breeding, should be considered sinful acts, which they are not. Therefore, sexual relations are for the good of man because they are intended by the *will of God* also as the joyous interplay of epistemic unity.

Same-sex marriage rejection demonstrates the stubborn refusal to observe the incredible diversity of nature, like the human presence of intersex or hermaphrodites, having female and male genitalia,[931] of chimeras, having different genetic cells' types, and of intersexuality, having features common to both female and male.

"*For there are some eunuchs, which were so born from* [their] *mother's womb*,"

declares Jesus.[932] If Nature offers such diversity, which therefore, cannot be labeled *against* the principles of nature or reason, there is no fundamental natural law why homosexuality or same sex marriage should be rejected as *unnatural*. Nature displays homosexual behavior among various species of animals.[933] Consequently, that which is natural must also be rational, unless we want to define *unnatural* all *natural* diversities. Furthermore, religion in general does not necessarily exclude homosexuality or same sex marriage. On the contrary, some Animistic religions considered the homosexual double nature of a shaman a trait for the ecstatic ascension to Heaven.[934] The Male Cults of Melanesia,[935] the two-spirits *berdache* of North-American tribes[936] and the transgender Hindu *hijras*,[937] all practice/d ritualized homosexual behavior.

Matrimony

Matrimony, namely reaching the *mat*ernal condition,[938] should be distinguished from marriage in structure and nature.

Matrimony, in fact, implies the irreversible consensual bond, between two or more heterosexual and/or homosexual adult partners not related through adoption or blood, created by the presence of biological and/or adopted maternal/paternal offspring. There are two circumstances when divorce cannot be lawful. The first one is when at least one living offspring is underage and under educational obligation, the second one is when one of the partners is under the responsibility of the other because dependent or handicapped. This second reason is always binding, also in case of simple marriage, unless both childless partners consensually opt to divorce. In other words, in both cases, assumed responsibilities have precedence over the right of divorce. The duchess of Devonshire, commenting on her 62 years of marriage with Andrew, the 11th Duke of Devonshire, said, despite his alcoholism and dalliances "It was absolutely fixed that we shouldn't divorce or get rid of each other in any way. It's completely different to Americans, who all divorce each other the whole time. Such a bore for everyone, having to say who's going to have the dogs, who's going to have the photograph books."[939] Even in the case of domestic abuse, the abuser should remain tied to the married obligation, while serving the penalties imposed by the law for his/her abusiveness. At the same time, on the other hand, the abused one can legally marry another person.

All Civil Laws regulating marriage must regulate matrimony and outlaw divorce. Bertrand Russell takes a similar view declaring, "I take this view because I regard marriage not primarily as a sexual partnership, but above all as an undertaking to co-operate in the procreation and rearing of children."[940] The permanent offspring-bond, in fact, impedes it. The bond is irreversible because, in spite of any type of divorce, nobody can undo the biological and/or adoption bond created by the presence of maternal/paternal offspring. In case of adoption, the social contract undertaken is irrevocable because it recognizes the legal presence of the irreversible biological bond with another human being. The cases of an American mother, refusing to parent a legally adopted Russian child on the basis that certain disorders of the infant were not disclosed by the orphanage originally housing the boy, is inadmissible. In fact, no one can rescind the tie to a natural offspring because the baby suffered of a previously unknown prenatal condition.[941]

Extended-family

How can one expect my passionate mistress to act differently? She, is like

"that infected and ruffled maid
who with fetid nails scratches herself there...
is Thais the harlot."[942]

She is the daughter of a drug-pusher father who was killed in jail. Her mother was a nymphomaniac who was slaughtered by one of her jealous lovers, who had raped her older sister. She was eleven years old when all this took place.

Virginia Satir says,

"I want to love you without clutching,
Appreciate you without judging,
Join you without invading,
Invite you without demanding,
Leave you without guilt,
Criticize you without blaming,
And help you without insulting.
If I can have the same from you,
then we can truly meet and enrich each other."[943]

Any transcending sexual union is a small embryonic unit of the family structure. When both partners live that event, in a mutual self-giving of one to the other, then that becomes the nucleus of a family. Generally, a family starts when one is in somebody's heart and when that someone is in the other's heart. In any sexual relationship, the family starts in the *timeless very short in*stant of *la petite mort*, the little death awakened in the flash of orgasm, the moment here and now in which the flow of time is unperceived and suspended.

The word family derives from the Latin *famulus*, meaning servant. Therefore, we could try to define a family as the mutual serving or helping relationship between one or more persons based on connective bonds of blood, love and common interest. Traditionally and in some parts of the world today, families extend to include all relatives. More often, these relatives, or a good number of them, live together to forms one household. Everyone takes care of each other and defends their good family name and honor. The problem or the achievement of one is the problem or the achievement of all. This communal sharing gives a sense of belonging, warmth and security that elsewhere in these days has been forgotten or is not felt in atomized immediate family. The present (2013) family, consciously or unconsciously, feels the need for those interconnections. There is a hunger for closeness and interpersonal relationship, which are not satisfied by the socioeconomic reality of today. For a member of an extended-family, while away or at work, it is comforting and assuring to know that all basic needs of the loved ones will be taken care by concerned relatives. It is the good feeling of belonging to a household referred to as the "ancestral home." Today, *unfamiliar* day-care givers have taken up the role of those family members. In today's atomic families, differences, divergences, incomprehension must be resolved only by the two spouses or, at best, by a cold, distant *foreign* family counselor. Rarely, relatives intervene. All this generates a sense of loneliness that affects the couple damaging their offspring. Hence, there is a need to look elsewhere for the missing family warmth.

Monogamy and polygamy

There is no absolute natural reason and, therefore, no moral reason, why marriage and/or matrimony should be necessarily monogamous. We are not saying that polygamy should be imposed. Monogamy and/or polygamy are choices of equal rights. If a couple desires to remain monogamous, it is good. However, the claim that *mono*-gamy, namely having only one marriage,[944] has a moral superiority over *poly*-gamy, namely many[945] marriages, either with many wives (*i.e.*: poly-*gyny*)[946] and/or with many husbands (*i.e.*: poly-*andry*)[947] has no absolute foundation. In fact, any legal acknowledgement of divorces and remarriages constitutes, at best, a serial-monogamy, therefore a type of polygamy not taking place concomitantly. Examples of it are the serial-marriages of "Warren Beatty... an Israeli man... who... has... been granted his 11th divorce... [He] usually divorces after two years and immediately goes out... bride reeling... The rabbinical court... praised the man's adherence to religious procedure. Under Jewish law, a man seeking a divorce grants his wife a 'get,' which declares, 'You are hereby permitted to all men.'"[948] Furthermore, a divorce may be such from the perspective of the two spouses, not from that of the offspring. In fact, the children of a divorced couple live in a de-facto *open-*

family, in which they call father and/or mother the husband and/or wife of their respective biological parents.

Polygyny

Polygyny should take place only when there is a free mutual consent between all partners. Case in point is that of Nanette Sexton Bailey, who filed for *divorce* in 2000 at the Palm Beach County Circuit Court, accusing her husband Richard Bailey of *adultery* with his previous wife Anita Bailey, whom he had cheated on with Nanette, his current wife.[949]

Some religious texts permit polygyny. Besides the *Bible*, that recognizes multiple wives for a number of patriarchs and kings,[950] also the *Koran* allows it, stating,

> "*Marry from among* [other] *women such as are lawful to you* – [even] *two, or three, or four: but if you have reason to fear that you might not be able to treat them with equal fairness, then* [only] *one.*"[951]

In the Hindu tradition, "a Brahmin has only one wife, although he is not restricted to one by law."[952] However, it is always a pious duty to honor women;[953] therefore, polygyny must take place only when there is a mutual consent between all partners. A joyous, affectionate and mutual accepting polygyny relationship was portrayed in Kleiser's 1982 film *Summer Lovers*, set in the island of Santorini, Greece, where an American couple falls in love with a French woman accepting her as part of their marriage.

Certain groups may consider all marriage practices, different from the ones described before, as aberrations deserving to be stoned according to the Biblical condemnation. In fact,

> "*the LORD spake unto Moses, saying... the people of the land shall* ***stone...*** *the adulterer and the adulteress* [they] *shall surely be put to death... with stones: their blood* [shall be] *upon them... And the children... did as the LORD commanded.*"[954]

Nevertheless, Abraham, the Patriarch of the Judeo-Christian-Muslim tradition had a son with his wife's *handmaid*,

"*Now Sarai Abram's wife bare him no children: and she had an handmaid, an Egyptian, whose name* [was] *Hagar.*
And Sarai said unto Abram, Behold now, the LORD hath restrained me from bearing: I pray thee, go in unto my maid; it may be that I may obtain children by her. And Abram hearkened to the voice of Sarai.
And Sarai Abram's wife took Hagar her maid the Egyptian, after Abram had dwelt ten years in the land of Canaan, and gave her to her husband Abram to be his wife.
And he went in unto Hagar, and she conceived: and when she [Sarah] *saw that she had conceived,* [she became jealous and] *her mistress was despised in her eyes.*
And Sarai said unto Abram, My wrong [be] *upon thee: I have given my maid into thy bosom; and when she saw that she had conceived, I was despised in her eyes: the LORD judge between me and thee.*
But Abram said unto Sarai, Behold, thy maid [is] *in thy hand; do to her as it pleaseth thee. And when Sarai dealt hardly with her, she fled from her face.*
And the angel of the LORD found her by a fountain of water in the wilderness, by the fountain in the way to Shur.
And he said, Hagar, Sarai's maid, whence camest thou? and whither wilt thou go? And she said, I flee from the face of my mistress Sarai.
And the angel of the LORD said unto her, Return to thy mistress, and submit thyself under her hands.
And the angel of the LORD said unto her, I will multiply thy seed exceedingly, that it shall not be numbered for multitude.
And the angel of the LORD said unto her, Behold, thou [art] *with child, and shalt bear a son, and shalt call his name Ishmael; because the LORD hath heard thy affliction.*

[Therefore God is blessing her and the fruit of her union with Abraham.]
And he will be a wild man; his hand [will be] *against every man, and every man's hand against him; and he shall dwell in the presence of all his brethren.*
And she called the name of the LORD that spake unto her, Thou God seest me: for she said, Have I also here looked after him that seeth me? Wherefore the well was called Beerlahairoi; behold, [it is] *between Kadesh and Bered.*
And Hagar bare Abram a son: and Abram called his son's name, which Hagar bare, Ishmael.
And Abram [was] *fourscore and six years old, when Hagar bare Ishmael to Abram."*[955]

However, we must examine other marriages and partnership arrangements as practiced in the world.

Polyandry

Polyandry should takes place only when there is a free mutual consent between all partners. Cases of polyandry can be found in various traditions. In fact, in the ancient Indian epic poem *Mahābhārata,*[956] Draupadī[957] was wedded to five husbands. Today, fraternal polyandry is found in the Canadian Arctic, Mongolia, Tibet, Nepal, Bhutan, Sri Lanka, among the Mosuo people in China and in some parts of India. There, although "the wife's voice is the dominant voice in the household," its matriarchal setting is fading.[958] Furthermore, with the current disproportionate male-to-women birth rate in China, that country should resort to polyandry to allow each man to marry and have a wife. Other populations around the world, like the Maasai,[959] in Kenya-Tanzania, legalize the marriage of multiple husbands. Recently, many films celebrate polyandric settings; like "*Threesome,*"[960] set in a college dormitory suite shared by a woman and two men, and the latest film of Nancy Meyers, "*It's Complicated,*" where a divorced couple *adulterously* reunites while the former wife engages also in a new relationship. A fan of Meyers and of that film was a bride who appeared on a photo in the *Wedding/Celebrations* section of *The New York Times,* with two men. The marriage, officiated by her grandfather, who for the event became a minister of the Universal Life, was "very traditional for a nontraditional" couple in which she "spice[s] things up for him."[961]

Paradoxically and relative to a Catholic perspective, the reunion of a divorced couple, while engaged in a second legal marriage, would not be adulterous, on the contrary, the second legal marriage would be regarded as such. On the contrary, should we consider adulterous any sexual act committed with a wife, prior to a marriage annulment by the Apostolic Tribunal of the Sacred Roman Rota? If not adulterous, then, was it sanctified? How can something be holy once and sinful the next?

Given the present deterioration of family nucleus, the economic hardship, the loneliness of old age, William Safire, in a New York Times essay, admits that "The Polyandry Movement... the two-husband home may be the bedrock of the newest morality and the salvation of what's left of the American family."[962]

A recent television series, Showtime Polyamory episodes: Married and Dating presents, in a type of reality show, controversial ideas of Polyamory.[963]

Polyamory

The combination of both polygyny and polyandry, in the same household cohabitation, constitutes poly-*amory*, namely many-loves.[964] Morning Glory Zell created the term in 1990. She stated that for an "Open Relationship to be successful" it must abide by "two principles... Honesty and Openness about the *polyamorous* lifestyle" and "All partners involved in the Multiple Relations must fully and willingly embrace the basic commitment to a *polyamorous* lifestyle."[965] We can say that they all become "brothers and sisters in *love*." This type of love should never be confused with promiscuity or simply lascivious intent, of which we see innumerable examples in the media today. A number of elements characterize polyamory, namely honesty, openness, faithfulness, sharing and healthiness. The same way infidelity is the negation of monogamy, so the lack of one of those characteristics nullifies polyamory. One cannot be deceitful, or secretive, or disloyal, or possessive or unsanitary and claim, at the same time, to be polyamorous. Trust, openness, constant communication, sincerity and honesty are the hallmark for a polyamorous relationship.[966] We are not saying that a Polyamory relationship is easier than other relations, but the effects and rewards are superior to any other. For one it breaks away from the confinement of egoity making us realize a wider horizon beyond the immediate need. "When you say you love God what does it mean? It means that you love a projection of your own imagination... [Furthermore] is love of the one and not of the many? If I say, `I love you', does that exclude the love of the other? Is love personal or impersonal?... If you love mankind can you love the particular?... You say you love your wife. In that love is involved sexual pleasure, the pleasure of having someone in the house to look after your children, to cook. You depend on her; she has given you her body, her emotions, her encouragement, a certain feeling of security and well-being. Then she turns away from you; she gets bored or goes off with someone else, and your whole emotional balance is destroyed, and this disturbance, which you don't like, is called jealousy. There is pain in it, anxiety, hate and violence. So what you are really saying is, `As long as you belong to me I love you but the moment you don't I begin to hate you. As long as I can rely on you to satisfy my demands, sexual and otherwise, I love you, but the moment you cease to supply what I want I don't like you.' So there is antagonism between you, there is separation, and when you feel separate from another there is no love. But if you can live with your wife without thought creating all these contradictory states, these endless quarrels in yourself, then perhaps - perhaps - you will know what love is. Then you are completely free and so is she, whereas if you depend on her for all your pleasure you are a slave to her. So when one loves there must be freedom, not only from the other person but from oneself... Love is not the product of thought which is the past. Thought cannot possibly cultivate love. Love is not hedged about and caught in jealousy, for jealousy is of the past. Love is always active present... When you love there is neither respect nor disrespect. Don't you know what it means really to love somebody - to love without hate, without jealousy, without anger, without wanting to interfere with what he is doing or thinking, without condemning, without comparing - don't you know what it means? Where there is love is there comparison? When you love someone with all your heart, with all your mind, with all your body, with your entire being, is there comparison?

When you totally abandon yourself to that love there is not the other."[967]

We can infer certain human behavior from the study of the primate world. While collaboration amongst the male dominated aggressive chimpanzees takes place only under certain circumstances, among the very strong matriarchal bonobos their sharing and wide spread very frequent sexual interrelations allows them to refrain from killing each other, be very peaceful and tolerant.[968] The interaction on all levels with more than one person prepares us to look at neighboring human beings with a kinder eye, bringing them in a sphere of possibility that is not present when the maximum extent of our identity does not go beyond the single wife/husband boundary. Characteristic of the open-family must be complete mental intimacy. "If we can begin to relate to others on the basis of such equanimity, our compassion will not depend on the fact that so and so is my husband, my wife, my relative, my friend. Rather, a feeling of closeness toward all others can be developed based on the simple recognition that, just like myself, all wish to be happy and to avoid suffering. In other words, we will start to relate to others on the basis of their sentient nature."[969] This is the divine love of Jesus, who loves each individual soul equally to the point of self-sacrifice, and is the infinite love of Kṛshṇa for his metaphoric thousand Gopī. Furthermore, unequivocally Jesus gives

> *"a new commandment... That ye love one another; as I have loved you, that ye also love one another."*[970]

According to those who believe in Jesus, His love for all of us is equal and unchanged for each one of us. Therefore, if we must love one another *as He has loved us*, this is Polyamory. If this affirmation can sound offensive to some ears, it must be clear that polyamory is not only about sex. Sex comes into the equation as it comes into monogamous relations, in a pure altruistic giving of oneself to the other. Only then, the sexual act becomes unconditional love.

At times, honesty finds obstacles in monogamous relationships. If a partner does not intend to end a spousal relationship, but at the same time has new sentimental and sexual interests for another person, the monogamous preconception may hinder any honest disclosure of those new attractions. Current society imposes monogamous relationship as the only *proper* avenue to create a family. Therefore, monogamy becomes the preconceived way of life that may hinder honesty. In any monogamous marriage, there is an imposed seed of dishonesty, both towards the partner and towards oneself. Society, then, becomes co-responsible with the individual's lack of honesty. In fact, no true physical union can take place without true total mental communicative union. However, no one wants to reveal secrets when a condemning judgment follows that communication.

When we promise exclusive faithfulness
"*till death do us part,*"[971]
in effect we are anticipating blindly an unknown sentimental future that cannot be foretold. This contradiction prompts the necessity to legalize divorce. However, when one of the committed partners meets another significant one, while desiring to continue preserving the previous original relationship, because still in love, then it would be *sinful* to impose a separation. On the other hand, if polyamorous possibilities were present alongside monogamy, the emergence of *another* in a marriage setting would not come as a surprise for the couple. Therefore, no need for untruthfulness would ensue.

"No individual has the right to forbid the partner either a temporary or a permanent sexual relationship with another."[972] There is no reason why true polyamory should be considered an immoral behavior. On the contrary, it is an acceptable consensual open-ended union.[973] Examples of polyamory can be found in the multiple partner erotic sculptures of the medieval *Kandariyā Mahādeva* Śiva temple in Khajurāho, Madhya Pradesh, India.[974] The practice is established among many Amazonian cultures,[975] like the Zo'e, small hunter gatherers and horticulturalists groups of the Tupi-Guarani people (Cuminapanema river), of the state of Para in the rain forest of Northern Brazil.[976] "Among the Zo'e aggression is extremely rare. Close physical contact between adult and children is part of everyday life... It is common for a woman to have more than one husband and for a man to have several wives."[977] The practice of physical contact promotes a bond among the participants that is nurturing. In societies where such practices are discouraged, the emergence of "*Cuddle Parties*, a place where consenting adults, often strangers, dressed in their pajamas, pay to actually touch each other," prove the need that humans have to feel physically the others in a friendly, safe and "non-sexual space."[978]

Polyamory is a valid and moral behavior, involving mind, emotions and body, as any of the other ones previously described. Today, it is common to read in periodicals and newspapers ethical questions such as, "My husband and I practice polyamory... We are open about this to friends but are unsure what to disclose to others... I don't want to hide my affection for my boyfriend or make anyone uncomfortable."[979] Such statements demonstrate a growing persistence of this perspective promoted by countless websites[980] and a number of workshops, activities, and entertainment celebrating the polyamory lifestyle.[981]

Renate Ogilvie, the German-Australian existential Psychotherapist and Lecturer on Buddhist Philosophy, *In Praise of Polyandry*, describes that lifestyle as "A road less travelled... But surely worth pursuing in these multi-cultural times."[982] Furthermore, the accredited Graduate Institute of Transpersonal Psychology (ITP), in Palo Alto, CA, conducts researches on polyamory, like the poly-sex-positive doctoral dissertation project, "*Study on Multiply Partnered People*,"[983] exploring sexual identities and spirituality.

Having multiple partners is not *against nature*. In fact, *heteropaternal superfecundation* is biologically possible. That is to say, two different sperms from two different persons may impregnate two ova during the same female cycle, thus fathering twins each being an offspring of a different male parent.[984] The contrary, namely eggs from different persons producing one offspring, is possible with the "spindle–chromosomal complex transfer," a new gene therapy method of fertility for the cure of inherited maternal diseases.[985] These methods, which are currently used on *monkeys but* will be made available also for human therapies, consist in fertilizing eggs, with removed exchanged chromosomes, from two females and transplanted from one mother to another.

In both marriage and matrimony, extramarital relationships should never be cause for dispute among partners.[986] Those relationships should be viewed as temporary marriages, which must be ratified into matrimony only when generating offspring. Among many Brazilian cultures, it was unusual if one "did not have multiple sexual partners."[987] The anthropologist W. Crocker, in his studies of the Canela, a Brazilian population stationed 400 miles southeast of Belém, explains that some of the reasons for those peoples' stability in marriage were their widespread extramarital sexual customs[988] and great focus on the children's wellbeing promoting in them a sense of family unity for the sake of raising individuals.[989]

Open-family

Anyone, wishing to bring a new adult husband/wife not related through adoption or blood into a polyamorous family, could do so with the unanimous approval of all the common spouses. The new spouse becomes immediately the wife/husband of all the other spouses, but not requiring necessarily consummation with everyone. Furthermore, the new spouse becomes immediately the adopted father/mother of all the offspring of the family. We find a similar practice among certain Amazonian cultures, where all multiple partners of a woman, who consequently becomes a mother, are considered the biological fathers of the child born from those relationships.[990] In addition, the new husband/wife must pool all her/is economic possessions with all the other members as well as share the common wealth with all the others, establishing a communal-family. Furthermore, since census has found that "married couples are no longer a majority,"[991] all non-conventional family settings, including polyamory, must be regulated by the mentioned Civil Laws with the distinction between the described reversibility of marriage and irreversibility of matrimony.

The open-family should regulate all aspect of communal living security, from family management to finances, from kid's day care[992] to old age and from health care to mutual protection. On April 27, 2010, in New York City, "Open Love NY" sponsored a discussion of Diana Adams, Esq. on "*Charting the Legal Future for Poly and Alternative Families,*"[993] A legal system must be in place to regulate these new family structures. Diana, a "Family Law Attorney for Traditional and Non-traditional Families,... believes that 'family' extends beyond the traditional nuclear family... to include other loving, mutually supporting families.

Other valid 'non-traditional families' include grandparents raising grandkids, friends living together and sharing finances longterm, couples choosing not to marry, same-sex couples, polyamorous families, and intentional communities. All of these families deserve the ability to form stable legally binding ties, and deserve to have their rights represented in court when necessary."[994]

At stake, here are not the natural and justifiable sexual rights of the partners, which are important. We are not concerned so much for the satisfaction of the *lovers*, which it seems to be the primary concern in our society, as much as we are for the wellbeing of the offspring. This concern is an innate instinct by which parents look after and fend their offspring. It is not a possessive principle; it is the way of nature to assure the preservation of the specie. In the new open-family the young will find that security and family care enjoyed by the extended-family. It is the security children had in pristine *tribe-setting* based on kinship, where the common interest and safety was the primary concern beyond the fluidity of its structural organization.[995]

In multi-partnership, there cannot be relationship neglect. In fact, the presence of another person will overcome the sense of abandonment. The fundamental, basic total openness and communication of the community will excuse, understand and justify the blindness of a new love. Obviously, secretiveness, deceit, untruthfulness can never be excused in an open-family. All genders will be important, equal partners in this new family, with no ranks but different fluid roles equal, interchangeable and indispensable. This structure and behavior should ease or eradicate completely any type of envy among a group or towards other groups. In fact, alliances, trough matrimonies, would be an avenue for strengthening and enlarging the original family. We are not suggesting that an open-family will solve all problems. We are saying that all problems will be addressed as a community, taking away the exclusive burden from the individual.

Un-divorce

Nevertheless, reasons for separation among open-families could be many and varied. For whatever reason, there should be a possibility for a person or persons, within a matrimonial setting, to separate from the rest of the family in a spirit of openness, honesty, sincerity and loyalty. However, for the foretold reasons, this separation cannot be a radical divorce. S/he or they should always be allowed and able to come back and reestablish the original position. The entire family's council should unanimously deliberate on financial matters and obligations for both groups. All components of the open-family must always take care of one another and their offspring. Even if not living together, they all should be considered as one united family.[996] Since in the open-family there will always be the physical presence and unity of a mother and a farther, the offspring will always find them taking care of their needs and giving the necessary support they have always enjoyed.

Communal organizations

The communal council must unanimously elect a member of the open-family as a renewable *ceremonial* chief, who will preside and moderate, for an allotted time, the council itself according to the rules collectively and freely established by the community itself. For its socio-economic structure, the new open-family-organization could take example from historical communal organizations. The French utopian socialist Charles Fourier (1772-1837)[997] inspired the establishment of such constitutions, as *Community Place* (1830) in New York, the *North American Phalanx* (1844) in New Jersey, a successful "cooperative agricultural community founded by Albert Brisbane,"[998] and *La Reunion* (1855) in Texas. In New York State, John Humphrey Noyes in 1848 founded the Oneida spiritual Community, which, in 1881, became the Oneida Limited Corporation, based on love for "one another, not by pairs... but en masse."[999] In Palestine, one of the first "communal gathering," the kibbutz of Degania,[1000] was created around 1909. It established an example for the flourishing of numerous other kibbutzim, which were instrumental for the formation and establishment of the State of Israel in 1948.

Sex education

"Nowadays the family is reduced to the father and mother and their younger children, by the decree of the State, spend most of their time at school, and learn there what the State thinks good for them, not what their parents desire."[1001] However, the unsuccessful Federal supported abstinence-only sex education, started in the Eighties, ended in 2009. The program restricted young people from receiving accurate information regarding pregnancy, sexually transmitted diseases, and contraceptives. A valid medical sex education, intended to reduce teenage pregnancy, replaced it. Currently, Western pedagogical view expects young person to follow the instructions received; they should accomplish their scholastic duties, become successful moneymakers, marry and educate children in a similar manner.

Until recently, there were places in southern Italy where the honor of a man was proven by the virginal bloodstains on linens hung on the balcony the day following the first night of marriage. It was also not honorable to marry a girl that previously had been engaged without the vigil constant supervision of her entire family. In a number of nations, these costumes are changing through education. However, other countries, still trailing behind, require women never to go out alone and to dress from head to toe covering also their eyes. Furthermore, the overall most common lesson imparted is that there is only one true heterosexual love for each person and a degree of jealousy is synonymous of spousal care. However, how can jealousy be construed as love?

In reality, jealousy takes place when deceit sets in, when a mind lies to another mind and uncertainty sets in. Then, truly, there is a sense of displacement, non-connection with that love which was realized as Transcendence. In this sense, God declares in the Bible,

"*For I the LORD thy God [am] a jealous God.*"[1002]

Namely, the Transcendent requires from Its children total mind dedication.

> "*For I am jealous over you with godly jealousy: for I have espoused you to one husband, that I may present* [you as] *a chaste virgin to Christ.*"[1003]

Jealousy, as loss of possession, is socially taught and has no relation to love. In many pristine cultures it does not appear. It is

> "*when the spirit of jealousy cometh upon him, and he be jealous over his wife.*"[1004]

According to Ryan and Jethá, the onset of agriculture, with its consequent concept of ownership, led humans to connect property with sexuality only to insure paternity.[1005] Columbus, describing the natives of Cuba, writes that they were not jealous.[1006] And H.P.C. Melville, who lived for twenty-five years in Northern Brazil and Southern British Guiana, had observed that among the Arawaks "there is no cause for jealousy."[1007] "In some Amazonian cultures, it was bad manners for a husband to be jealous of his wife's extramarital partners."[1008] However, Russell argues, "Jealousy of brothers and sisters is very common in families, and is sometimes a cause, in later life, of homicidal mania as well as of less serious nervous disorders."[1009] In fact, that was the case of Gianciotto Malatesta, lord of Rimini, when, in a rage of jealousy *to save his honor*, he stabbed to death (1285?) his own wife Francesca da Polenta and his own brother Paolo, both caught in amorous embrace. Describing those adulterous partners and recognizing the ineluctability of their love's drive, Dante compares them to "doves by desire called on" who "fly through the air led by their volition"[1010]

Jealousy as possession can be curbed and transformed in love. This happens naturally among siblings. Through example and nurturing, family and school can instill in the young minds a true social behavior that recognizes love, caring and honesty as paramount among human relations. The bliss of the parents, their happiness and satisfactory monogamous and/or polygamous life style, resolving in a "lifelong friendship," should be in the first place, then that happiness will reflect on the offspring making them joyful children.[1011]

Any form of jealousy as possession has nothing in common with love. Paul declares,

> "*If I could speak in any language... If I had the gift of prophecy, and if I knew all the mysteries... If I had the gift of faith... If I gave everything... to the poor and even sacrificed my body... but... didn't love others, I would be of no value whatsoever... <u>Love is not jealous</u>... <u>Love does not</u>*

demand its own way... and it keeps no record of when it has been wronged."[1012]

A common cliché states that love and hate go hand in hand. How many heart-broken lovers and/or divorcees can testify to the fact that their *enduring* love became an all-out hate. The pain deriving from separation may generate hate. In reality, there was never love in the first place. Love is the contrary of hate and if hatred ensues it means that at the origin of the fancied affair there was only the pursuit of selfish happiness.

The opposite of jealousy as possession are *polyfidelity* and *compersion*, terms invented by the Kerista Commune "based in the Haight-Ashbury of San Francisco from 1971-1991."[1013] For the first term, we mean the practice of remaining sexually faithful within one's family. This observance, besides creating a bond for love relationships, would also prevent spouses from bringing sexually transmitted diseases in the family. This does not mean that a new husband/wife cannot be added to the family, but this would happen only with the unanimous approval of the community. Furthermore, it does not mean that a family member cannot have a marriage relationship outside her/his home, but this must take place with the knowledge and hygienic precautions of the entire household. In this openness, sincerity and trust consists *polyfidelity*. *Compersion*, then, means the happiness and joy felt by somebody for the delight and pleasure, caused by any event whatsoever including erotic, experienced by the loved one.

There is an important social-pedagogical side imparted within an open-family. In an extended and/or a single couple family, which we may call atomized structures, there is a perpetuation and enforcement of possession. "Most parents unfortunately think they are responsible for their children and their sense of responsibility takes the form of telling them what they should do and what they should not do, what they should become and what they should not become. The parents want their children to have a secure position in society. What they call responsibility is part of that respectability they worship; and it seems to me that where there is respectability there is no order; they are concerned only with becoming a perfect bourgeois. When they prepare their children to fit into society they are perpetuating war, conflict and brutality. Do you call that care and love?"[1014]

An example of that is the *business* interest proclaimed by the mafia crime *families*. That too is named family and demands loyalty, but it is based on hate and personal interest. The open-family, on the other hand, implicitly teaches love and openness toward others and eliminates the danger of xenophobia, hate and individualistic possession. With the atomized family structures of today, we perpetuate that which belongs to us unconcerned about others. There is a tiered expansion of selfish possessive interest. It goes from the Individual to the Family, from here to the Group, then to the Nation. All this takes place disregarding the humanistic aspect and the wellbeing of the World as a whole.

SELECTED CONCISE PHILOSOPHICAL TERMINOLOGIES

Apodictic (*adj.* **Apodictical**): clear and necessary self-evident truth.

A-posteriori: that which follows experience.

A-priori: that which precedes experience logically, but not actually.

Art: potentially universal language synthesis of form and idea.

Atmanism: the view that the Supreme Spirit or Self (*ātman*) is the only Reality.

Autoctisi: the self-constructed spark igniting itself.

Autochthonous: Self-generated.

Autogenous: Self-made, Self-born.

Awareness: is the fundamental apodictical presence of the certitude, which underlines and makes possible the consciousness-*of* the world.

Beauty: dawn of knowledge.

Being-for-itself: the continuous circular reference of a *subject* to its correlated inseparable *object*.

Being-in-itself: the absolute independent center of the *immanent* circle set apart from the inseparable *subject-object* circular correlation.

Conscience: the only immanent condition that states *existence*.

Consciousness-*of*: is the grasping and apprehension *of* the world in its objective reality.

Creation: the concept of a divine act *pro*ducing everything out of nothing.

***Darśana*:** six philosophical points of views:

- ***Mīmāṃsā́***: ritual examination;
- ***Nyāyá*:** logical argument;
- ***Sāṃkhya*:** enumeration;
- ***Vaiśeshika*:** distinct nature of substances;
- ***Vedānta*:** end of the *Veda*;
- ***Yoga*:** union.

Deontological:

Discursiveness: the process of a temporal procession ranging over the wide field of juxtaposed events and Experiences; the spreading out of a sequence.

Emanation: the process of emission from a higher source into a lower status, which in turn radiates into another position.

Epoché (ἐποχή)**:** suspending judgment in reference to reality *in-itself*; placing the world between brackets.

Episteme: knowledge, intellectually certain (*adj.* **Epistemic:** capable of knowledge or related to knowledge).

Epistemic loneliness: (see **Solipsism**) the impossibility of the I to know itself as I in-itself or to know another I as I.

Epistemology (*adj.* **Epistemological**)**:** the study of how we know what we know and its validity.

Ethic: search for apodictic moral laws.

Existence: that which is established by *conscience* within the *subject-object* correlation.

For-itself: see Being-for-itself.

Future: projection towards the reduction to consciousness' data.

Gnoseology (*adj.* **Gnoseological**)**:** see Epistemology.

Gnosticism (*adj.* **Gnostic**)**:** spiritual realization, knowledge deriving from mysticism.

Hedonism (*adj.* **Hedonistic**)**:** ethical doctrine that considers the pursuit of pleasure as the ultimate good.

History: weltanschauung's present actualization.

History: weltanschauung's present actualization.

Hypostasis (*pl.* **Hypostases**)**:** principle or substance deriving from another one and at the same time generating an inferior one.

Immanent: that which is inherent or characterizes the circle of the inseparable *subject-object* correlation; the relationship by which the mind, in the epistemic process, reduces the world to an *object for-itself*.

In-itself: see Being-in-itself.

In-se: see Being-in-itself.

Intentionality: experience as stream of consciousness directed toward something.

Intuition: the state of immediate and total com-prehension or in-sight of the objective world without any temporal of spatial juxtaposition.

I-think: the *a-priori* subject constantly united with its object.

Knowledge: the epistemic synthetic correlation of subject and object, which intentions objectivity as otherness.

Liberty: autonomous innate unalloyed permanent state of the self.

Life: satisfying the hunger for representation.

Love: unselfish tension toward the other in-itself
Monism: there is only one reality.
Myth: echo of the Ineffable.
Mythology: a many faceted prism, each side representing a relative omni-comprehensive paradigm of the inner human reality, tracing the generating process of the psycho-cosmological world and denoting a tension *in-itself* that announces and echoes the *Transcendent.*
Mythologem: recurrent fabulous tale repeating itself during different times and places.
Noema (*adj.* **Noematic**)**:** the objective aspect of experience in its modes-of-being-given.
Noesis (*adj.* **Noetic**)**:** the subjective aspect of experience as act-of-perception aiming to grasp the object.
Noumenon (*pl.* **Noumena**, *adj.* **Noumenal**): that which is thought but not known.
Numinous: mysterious; relating to the spirits or gods.
Object: the known as such. The passive one to *whom* the action indicated by the verb is directed.
Oneiric: pertaining to dreams.
Ontological: the essence or nature of the existent.
Past: consciousness' data.
***Per-se*:** see Being-for-itself.
Philosophy: constantly updated critical holistic rethinking of the World with intentional objectivity and History's mover.
Present: continuum perceptive awareness.
Quantum (*pl.* **Quanta**)**:** elementary particle/s, as a *quantum/a* [Latin: certain amount/s] *of energy* or mass.
Real: is not confutable Certitude and Certitude is Real.
Realization: the Apodictical-Certitude that does not necessitate an object, but intuitively reaches Reality In-Itself beyond any duality.
Religion: dogmatic bondage of a creed, vehicle to the Transcendent.
Science: mathematical intelligibility of nature's blind pro-ject.
Solipsism: (see **Epistemic loneliness**) the loneliness of the 'I' as such.
Subject: the knower as such. The one ***who*** does the action indicated by the verb.
Tautology (*adj.* **Tautological**): a repeating circular reasoning.
Transcendent (*n.* **Transcendence**)**:** that which is never

experienced or known *in-itself*, but it can be conceived as that which is beyond the subject-object correlation, thus, becoming an *immanent* thought. *Viz.*: God, Goddess, Lord of hosts, Unknown, Fourth state, Non-existent, Death, Future.

Transcendental: the manner in which *objects* are known, as this is possible *a-priori*.

Utilitarian (*n.* Utilitarianism):

Weltanschauung: World view.

INDEX

Abortion, 185
Adam, 85
Agni, 60, 109
ahaṃkāra, 120
ahiṃsā, 212
Allah, 103
Amritabindu Upanishad, 12
Ānandamayī Mā, 33, 38, 65, 81, 113, 118, 121, 124
Animist, 171
Anselm, 71
a-priori, 253, 254, 256
Aquinas, 72
Aristotle, 11
Armstrong, 201
Āshūrā, 184
Ataraxia, 160, 196
atheism, 70, 71, 72
ātman, 253
Augustine, 102, 154
AUM, 90
Auto da fé, 171, 178
Autochthonous, 253
Awareness, 3, 22, 28, 30, 31, 32, 33, 34, 35, 36, 37, 38, 40, 41, 45, 46, 47, 49, 50, 51, 52, 53, 54, 55, 56, 57, 58, 59, 60, 61, 62, 63, 65, 67, 68, 69, 70, 72, 73, 74, 75, 84, 85, 86, 87, 88, 89, 91, 92, 93, 96, 97, 100, 101, 102, 103, 104, 110, 111, 115, 118, 122, 124, 126, 127, 128, 129, 132, 133, 134, 137, 139, 140, 141, 143, 144, 145, 146, 147, 148, 149, 151, 152, 153, 154, 155, 156, 157, 158, 159, 160, 161, 162, 175, 253
Bamyan, 184
Being, 27, 100, 121, 253, 254, 255
Belief, 75
Bellarmine, 69
Bentham, 164
Bhagavad-Gītā, 4, 6, 37, 76, 103, 107, 109, 120, 154
Bible, 11, 47, 59, 73, 85, 88, 91, 175, 263
Big-Bang, 175
Biology, 24
Bloom, 191
Bodhisattva, 189
brahman, 110
Brahman, 120
Brāhmaṇa, 6, 7, 29, 112
Breath, 120
Brecht, 11, 263
Brennus, 186
Bṛhadāraṇyaka, 6, 64
Bṛhadāraṇyaka Upanishad, 12, 23, 45, 48, 54, 103, 116, 136
Bruno, 57, 69
Buddha, 51, 74, 135
Buddhist, 135
Bushido, 102
Campbell, 12, 31, 70, 137, 171, 263
Canela, 172
Capaneus, 181
caste, 38, 111, 112
Catholic Kings, 171
Celestial Waters, 47, 175
Certitude, 28, 32, 34, 41, 51, 52, 53, 58, 59, 60,

68, 69, 72, 74, 75, 86, 89, 91, 94, 97, 111, 117, 137, 143, 147, 156, 159, 160, 162, 176, 255
Chāndogya, 6, 73, 84
Charisma, 169
Charter for Compassion, 201
child, 73, 105, 162
Chingiz Khan, 186
concentration, 135
Confucius, 125
consciousness, 26, 120, 122, 135, 144, 253, 254, 255
Constitution, 15
creation, 120, 121
Creation, 175
Crowley, 102
Cult of Reason, 15
Dalit, 110
Dante, 263
Dawkins, 188
De Waal, 190
Death, 64, 212, 256
Declaration of the thirteen united States of America, 174
Descartes, 50, 51, 52, 68, 148
desire, 38, 64, 97
destiny, 136
dissolution, 33, 135
Divine-flame, 121
DNA, 24, 65, 156
dogma, 11, 34, 68, 69, 75
dvija, 110
Eden, 22, 23
effect, 112
emanation, 253
Emotions, 151, 152
Enlightenment, 174
Epicurus, 160, 196
epistemic, 120, 144, 254
epistemological, 254
epistemology, 254
equality, 175, 178, 179, 181
Ethic, 3, 10, 14, 18, 20, 59, 146, 155, 160
evil, 39
existence, 83, 111, 253
experience, 26, 253, 254, 255
Fascist, 186
Fête de la Liberté, 15
Fig Tree, 184
flood, 62
flowing seed, 64
food, 120
force, 212
for-itself, 27, 64, 253, 254, 255
Freemasons, 175
French National Convention, 15
Freud, 43, 44, 48, 115, 135
future, 22
Galilei, 11, 69, 146, 263
Gandhi, 207, 212
Gaṇeśa, 33
God, 48, 85, 86, 90, 102, 169, 170, 171, 173, 174, 175, 176, 177, 180, 181, 186, 256
Goddess of Reason, 15
Goddess Reason, 15
gods, 12, 13, 23, 53, 83, 84, 86, 93, 110, 116, 117, 120, 121, 151, 255, 263
Golden Rule, 200, 203
good, 38

good and evil, 23, 78, 98, 104, 131, 133, 137, 150, 155
Grand Unified Theory, 17
Greek, 98
heart, 26, 55, 73, 77, 84, 93, 97, 99, 100, 109, 117, 135
Hedonism, 196
Heidegger, 49, 114
Heyókhas, 102
Hindu, 171, 200
Hirohito, 170
History, 254, 255
Homer, 211
hunger, 64, 254
Husayn ibn Ali, 184
I AM THAT I AM, 56, 61, 62
immortality, 63
Indra, 83, 120
indriya, 83, 114, 120
Ineffable, 255
in-itself, 27, 87, 111, 176, 253, 254, 255, 256
intelligent design, 175
intelligibility, 255
intentionality, 64
intuition, 254
Īśa, 6
I-think, 254
Ius Suprēmum, 3, 10, 14, 16, 155, 160, 161, 162
Iusnaturalism, 173, 174
Jesus, 23, 30, 31, 32, 34, 35, 36, 37, 39, 56, 57, 61, 66, 67, 71, 80, 89, 94, 107, 123, 133, 135, 136, 143, 152, 153, 154, 155, 158, 170, 171, 173, 194
John, 102
John of the Cross, 102
Jones, 172
Jung, 33, 73
Kabul, 184
Kailāsa, 86
Kaivalya Upanishad, 76, 100, 101, 102, 105
Kālī, 172
Kant, 20, 23, 27, 45, 71, 126, 127
Karbala, 184
Kena, 6
kingdom of God, 73, 204
Knowledge, 254
Koran, 53, 94, 134, 135
Kṛshṇa, 87
kshatriya, 110
Lao Tzu, 63
Laocoön, 213
Latin, 255
Lavoisier, 175
Liberty, 3, 15, 22, 174, 178, 181, 254
life, 22, 23, 24, 25, 26, 27, 28, 29, 30, 36, 38, 39, 42, 44, 56, 58, 62, 65, 80, 82, 83, 89, 90, 91, 92, 93, 94, 100, 103, 107, 108, 111, 112, 113, 114, 115, 119, 123, 133, 135, 136, 138
Life, 174, 254
Love, 102, 154, 255
Mahā Bhārata, 6
Maitrī, 6
Māṇḍūkya, 46
Māṇḍūkya, 6
Marx, 180
mathematics, 146
meditation, 90, 193
Medusa, 29

Meister Eckhart, 102
merchant, 112
Midas, 179
mīmāṃsā́, 253
mind, 12, 17, 20, 27, 29, 35, 36, 39, 42, 47, 48, 50, 52, 56, 57, 58, 62, 64, 65, 67, 68, 69, 71, 74, 75, 79, 86, 89, 93, 94, 103, 113, 114, 119, 120, 129, 132, 134, 139, 140, 153, 156, 157, 254
Monier-Williams, 7
Morals, 3, 18, 19, 23
Moses, 20, 53, 56, 59, 60, 61, 64, 85, 169, 171
Mount Carmel, 102
mouse, 33
mush-aka, 33
Muslims, 171, 184
Mythology, 12, 13, 255
Nature, 174
Nazi, 186
New World Order, 15, 16
New York, 16
Nīlakaṇṭha, 87
nirvāṇa, 136
noematic, 255
noetic, 255
Notre-Dame, 16
noumenon, 22, 33, 70, 71, 75, 126, 155
NREM, 46, 53, 121, 144
Nyāyá, 253
Nye, 213
object, 27, 73, 193, 253, 254, 256
One, 38, 47, 62, 63, 84, 86, 91, 100, 117, 120
oneiric, 255
Paul, 105, 108
Peter, 170, 194
phenomenic, 72
Philistines, 183
Philosophy, 3, 17, 18, 51, 85, 148, 255
Physics, 24
Pietro Micca, 183
Pio, 3, 35, 36
Plato, 263
Pope, 16, 69
prājña, 90, 144
present, 121, 135, 136, 254
Present, 22, 58, 61, 62, 63, 65, 67, 74, 82, 87, 89, 114, 155, 160, 255
Price George, 188
Protagoras, 187
Psychology, 25, 44
Psychopaths, 160
Pursuit of Happiness, 15, 16, 174
Pyrrho, 160
quantum, 255
Rabia, 103
Ramana Maharshi, 3, 33, 37, 56, 58, 65, 101, 103, 113, 114, 123, 125, 130, 139
Rasputin, 102
Reality, 253
Realization, 255
Relativism, 183, 185
Religion, 171, 255
REM, 44, 45, 46, 53, 122, 144
Ṛg, 7, 63, 110
Romans, 170, 186
Romantic Movement, 174
Ronins, 102
ṛshi, 77
Russell, 146, 148

sacrifice, 121
sādhu, 38
Saint Pio, 120
śakti, 144
sāṃkhya, 253
saṃnyāsin, 38, 162
Samson, 183
Śaṅkara, 3, 39
Sanskrit, 7
Sartre, 110, 111
satyāgraha, 207, 212
Schopenhauer, 20, 263
Science, 20, 22, 60, 146, 148, 149, 255
Second World War, 186
seed, 64, 72, 73
Self, 22, 26, 29, 30, 31, 32, 33, 34, 35, 37, 38, 52, 55, 56, 59, 61, 73, 80, 86, 89, 91, 93, 94, 95, 96, 97, 99, 100, 101, 102, 103, 110, 112, 113, 114, 123, 124, 126, 127, 128, 130, 133, 134, 136, 137, 140, 141, 143, 144, 147, 149, 151, 152, 155, 159, 160, 161, 162, 193, 253
senses, 83, 84, 117, 120, 121
Shi'a, 184
Shinto, 170, 171, 201
sin, 75
Skeptic, 160
Soft power, 213
soul, 60, 85, 102, 120
Statue of Liberty, 16
subject, 27, 193, 253, 254, 255, 256
śūdra, 110
Suffering, 135
Sufi, 103
Supreme Spirit, 55, 253
Suzuki, 173
Śvetāśvatara, 7, 90
taijasa, 89, 90, 144
Taittirīya, 7
Taliban, 184
Taoist, 171
terrorist, 165, 166, 184
The Golden-Rule, 21
The Peoples Temple, 172
Thermodynamics, 175
Thoreau, 60
Thugs, 172
Tolle, 30, 70, 80, 118
Tomasello, 190
Totò, 179
Traditional Leaderships, 170
Transcendent, 12, 21, 22, 26, 30, 31, 32, 33, 34, 38, 60, 65, 68, 72, 74, 75, 77, 79, 84, 85, 86, 87, 89, 97, 107, 109, 120, 122, 123, 126, 127, 143, 144, 147, 149, 152, 153, 155, 161, 162, 194, 212, 255
Transcendental, 121
truth, 12, 32, 73, 112, 207, 253
Turin, 183
Unknown, 256
Upanishad, 6, 7, 13, 65, 73, 84, 95, 112, 195, 263
  Kaṭha, 6, 34
  Māṇḍūkya, 90
Uśan, 34
Utilitarianism, 21, 196, 256
Vaiśeshika, 253
vaiśya, 110
value, 15, 18, 21, 131, 143

Value, 3, 10, 18, 20, 21, 147
Vauvenargues, 213
Veda, 4, 7, 12, 31, 62, 63, 77, 84, 96, 105, 110, 120, 121, 175, 253
  Atharva, 77
  Ṛig, 77
  Sāma, 7, 77
  Yajur, 7, 77
Viśva, 89, 90, 144
waking, 144
Will, 3, 20, 26, 143
World War, 16
Yājñavalkya, 54
yoga, 7, 95, 135
Zen, 173

NOTES

[1] Brecht, *Life of Galileo*, Scene 4 and 6.

[2] Dalai Lama, *The Art of Happiness*, p. 197.

[3] *UB* IV.3.22. *devā* (the gods) *adevāḥ* (not the gods) *vedā* (the Vedas) *avedāḥ* (not the Vedas).

[4] *UAb.* 18.

[5] Pp. 56-57.

[6] deZayas, Picasso Speaks, 315.

[7] Campbell, *The Flight of the Wild Gander*, p.33.

[8] *Cf.* Plato, *Statesman* 277d.

[9] *Bible,* Matthew 11:15.

[10] Dante Alighieri, *La divina commedia, Inferno* IX, 61-63 "*O voi ch'avete li'ntelletti sani / mirate la dottrina che s'asconde / sotto il velame de li versi strani.*"

[11] *UA Aitareya* (descendent of the other) *Upanishad* I. 3. 14. *paroksha-* (mystery behind the range of sight) *priyā* (lovers) *iva* (indeed) *hi* (because) *devāḥ* (gods).

[12] *Cf.* Schopenhauer, *The basic of morality*, p. 171.

[13] Stark, *Knights of the Cross. The Epic of the Crusades*, p. 3. As example, *cf.* the *Ottoman Turkish Janissarian march, Ceddin, deden* (Your ancestors, your grandfathers) (*Ottomans.org.* accessed 2012) and the *Pontifical Anthem, O felix Roma* (O blissful Rome) (*Vatican official* site accessed 2012).

[14] As example, *cf.* the French National Anthem, *La Marseillaise, Allons enfants de la Patrie* (Arise, children of the Motherland) (*Assemblée Nationale* site accessed 2012) and the Italian National Anthem, *Inno di Mameli, Fratelli d'Italia* (Italian brothers) (*Presidenza della Repubblica* site accessed 2012).

[15] *Cf.* MGH, 1.117.

[16] Ius-naturalism, *cf.* Grotius (1583-1645), *De Jure Belli Ac Pacis*, Prolegomena IX.

[17] *New Order of the Centuries Novus Ordo Seclorum*, on the Great Seal of the USA and on the One Dollar bill.

[18] *Cf.* Jefferson and *Declaration of Independence.*

[19] *Liberté, égalité, fraternité.*

[20] 20 *Brumaire, Fête de la Liberté* or *Culte de la Raison.*

[21] Carlyle, *The French revolution*, p. 293-294.  Auguste Christian Fleischmann, print, *The Goddess of Reason in Notre-Dame*, 1793	*Cf.* The Postal service, *Guide...*, 1599 & 2147.  Frédéric Auguste Bartholdi's *Statue of Liberty Enlightening the World* (*La liberté éclairant le monde*).

[22] "*La filosofia è il ripensamento del mondo,*" taught Prof. Cleto Carbonara (1904-1998, cattedra di *Storia della filosofia*, Università degli studi di Napoli, Italy).

[23] *Cf.* Weinberg, *Dreams of a Final Theory*.

[24] Simonelli, *Philosophy as a Path to Education for Leadership*, p. 29. Proof of this technology is the *Bach-y-Rita*'s system where a television camera linked to 400 skin stimulators enables blind to *see* (*cf.* Restak, *The brain*, p. 403 fol.). *Cf.* Sebastian, *Stanford creates biological transistors*, "Dubbed the 'transcriptor,' this biological transistor is the final component required to build biological computers that operate inside living cells. We are now tantalizingly close to biological computers that can detect changes in a cell's environment, store a record of that change in memory made of DNA, and then trigger some kind of response — say, commanding a cell to stop producing insulin, or to self-destruct if cancer is detected."

[25] Ethic in Greek *hethiká* (ἠθικά) is related to *hèthos* (ἦθος) = custom. Moral in Latin *moralia* is related to *mores* = custom.

[26] *Bible*, Luke 12:33

[27] *Bible*, Matthew 13:44-46.

[28] *Bible*, Luke 6:45, distinguished, wellbeing, good = ἀγαθός *agathos*; evil causing pain and trouble, evil = πονηρός *ponēros*;

[29] *Bible*, Luke 12:34.

[30] *Bible*, John 8:5.

[31] *Cf.* Crocker, *Extramarital sexual practices...*, pp. 184–94.

[32] Kant, Emmanuel (1724-1804), *Fundamental Principles of the Metaphysic of Morals*, p. 268.

[33] *On the Basis of Morality*, p. 170.

[34] *Cf.* the Kantian noumena. For an explanation see Chapter 2 – Religion, b).

---

35 *God, Soul, Mother-Nature* ? ...

Is this what we think when we talk about God, Soul or Nature?

36 *Bible*, Matthew 7:12, "*Do to others as you would have them do to you,*" (Luke 6:31).

37 Confucius, *Analects* XV.24.

38 Scaligero, *Manuale...*, pp.58-59. "*La scienza della moralità è anzitutto una Scienza della Libertà, ossia una scienza dell'Io.*"

39 Malory, XXI, VII. Here lies Arthur, once King, and future King "*Hic jacet Arthurus, Rex quondam, Rexque futurus.*"

40 *Bible*, Genesis 2:8. עֵדֶן *eden* – delight.

41 *Cf. UB* IV,3,22.

42 *Bible*, Genesis 3:7.

43 *Cf. Bible*, Genesis 3:3.

44 *Cf. Bible*, Genesis 3:5. אֱלֹהִים *'elohiym.*

45 *Prolegomena to any future metaphysics*, §22.

46 Genesis 2:9. וְעֵץ הַדַּעַת טוֹב וָרָע: (דַּעַת *da`ath knowledge*- discernment - *judgement* ), (טוב *towb* good), (רע *ra`*. evil), (עץ *`ets* tree*),* (חי *chay* life), (תוך *tavek* midst) (גן *gan* garden).

47 Think concerning right and wrong (κρίνω *krinō); cf. Rocci, "penso," p. 1090a.*

48 *Bible*, John 8:15, craving senses (σάρξ *sarx).*

49 Light (φῶς *phōs*) as awareness; *cf.* Rocci, "*luce, per vita... della verità,*" p. 1998b.

50 *Bible*, John 8:12.

51 *Bible*, Genesis 2:9.

[52] *Cf.* the two directions↑→:
the tree of life ↑ upwards as *sushumnā*
(Simonelli, *Beyond immortality*, pp. 15, 41, 198, 211, 213) and
the tree of knowledge→ externally as *liṅga*
(*Synonyms and Analogies in the East and West*, The Asiatic journal and monthly miscellany, vol. 14, p. 181. *Cf.* Paramahansa Yogananda, *Autobiography*, p. 196).

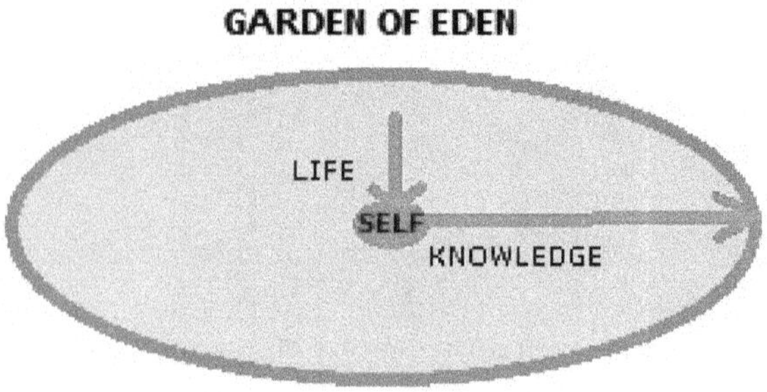

[53] *Cf.* Penrose, *The Road to Reality: A Complete Guide to the Laws of the Universe.*

[54] Systematic identifying and taxonomy naming.

[55] Hominidae evolution: Chimpanzee, Homo *neanderthalensis* and Homo sapiens.

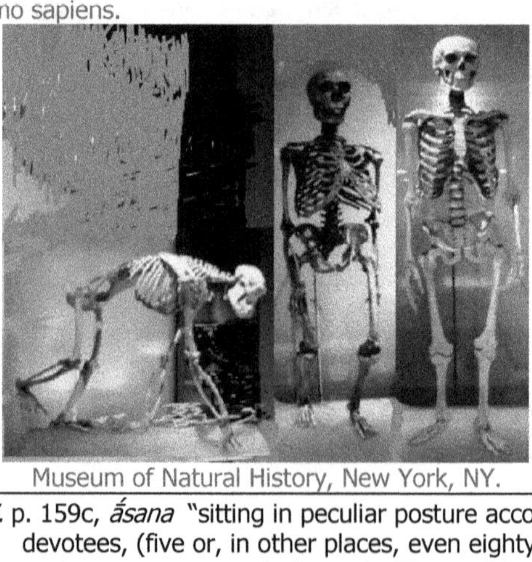

Museum of Natural History, New York, NY.

[56] *Cf. W.* p. 159c, *ā́sana* "sitting in peculiar posture according to the custom of devotees, (five or, in other places, even eighty-four postures are enumerated;» padmā*sana, bhadrā*sana, vajrā*sana, vīrā*sana, svastikā*sana: the manner of sitting forming part of the eightfold observances of ascetics)."

[57] *Cf.* Schopenhauer, *The world as will and representation.*

[58] *Cf. UB* V. 15. 3 and *Īśa* (Lord) *Upanishad* 17.

[59] *Cf. VṚ* I.1.5.

[60] *UB* IV.11.3. *tvád* (from you) *agne* (o Divine fire) *kā́vyā* (prophetic inspirations)

tván (from you) *manīshās* (thoughts) *tvád* (from you) *ukthā* (hymns) *jāyante* (spring) *rādhyāni* (propitiating). *Cf.* Vidyananda Videh, p. 1 and 13.

[61] *UC* III. 14. 1. *Sarvam* (all) *khalv* (verily) *īdaṃ* (this) *brahma* (the Supreme Transcendent Spirit) *taj-* (in that) *-ja-* (produced) *-l* - (absorbed) – *ān* (breathing √*jan*, √*lī*, √*an*.) *iti* (thus) *śānta* (in peace) *upāsīta* (one should meditate) *atha* (for) *khalu* (verily) *kratu-* (intention) – *mayaḥ* (made of) *purushaḥ* (a person) *yathā-* (as) *-kratur* (intention) *asminl* (in this) *loke* (world) *purusho* (a person) *bhavati* (is) *tathetaḥ* (thus) *pretya* (after death *Cf. BG.* VIII. 6.) *bhavati* (becomes) *sa* (one) *kratuṃ* (intention) *kurvīta* (let shape). *Cf. UMaitrī*. II. 3.

[62] *Bible,* Proverbs 23:7.

[63] Lanza (1956), *Biocentrism...*, V Principle, p. 93. (I Principle, p. 23.

[64] Kant, *The Critique of Pure Reason,* §21, p. 57.

[65] Lanza, *Biocentrism...*, pp. 23 (I Pr.), 39 (II Pr.), 59 (III Pr.), 81 (IV Pr.), 110 (VI Pr.), 127 (VII Pr.).

[66] *Bible,* John 4:14.

[67] In Sanskrit: heart *hṛdaya*; power *liṅgaṃ*.

[68] Campbell, *The Power of Myth,* p. 5-6.

[69] "*Transcend*"

base detail

Brad & Tammy Spencer, Tara Thullner Sculptors - McGee Brother Co. Carolina Ceramic Brick Company City of Greenville public works, Triangle Construction Co., 421 S. Main St., Greenville SC. *The Greenville News* 2009

[70] 4 *Veda,* 19 (?)*Brāhmaṇa* and 108 (?) *Upanishad.*

[71] *UB* III.4.2 (*bṛhad-āraṇyaka* - vast-forest - VII century BC) *na* (not) *dṛshṭer* (see) *drashṭāram* (the seer) *paśyeḥ* (of seeing) / *na* (not) *śruter* (hear) *śrotāraṁ* (the hearer) *śṛṇuyāḥ* (of hearing) *na* (not) *mater* (think) *mantāraṁ* (the thinker) *manvīthāḥ* (of thinking) *na* (not) *vijñāter* (understand) *vijñātāraṁ* (the understander) *vijānīūyāḥ* (of understanding) *esha* (this) *ta ātmā* (your Self) *arvāntaraḥ* (in everything) *ato'* (this) *nyad* (other than) *ārtam* (suffering - Hume and Radhakrishnan translate it as *evil*).

[72] *UB* IV.4.18 *prāṇasya* (of life) *prāṇam* (life) *uta* (and) *cakshushaś* (of eye)

cakshuḥ (eye) *uta* (and) *śrotrasya* (of ear) *śrotram* (ear) *manaso* (of mind) *ye* (who) *mano* (mind) *viduḥ* (know) *te* (they) *nicikyur* (have realized) *brahma* (transcendent) *purāṇam* (ancient) *agryam* (primordial). *Cf. UKe* I,2.

[73] African Two Heads Janus Bronze - Benin, Nigeria, 1950.

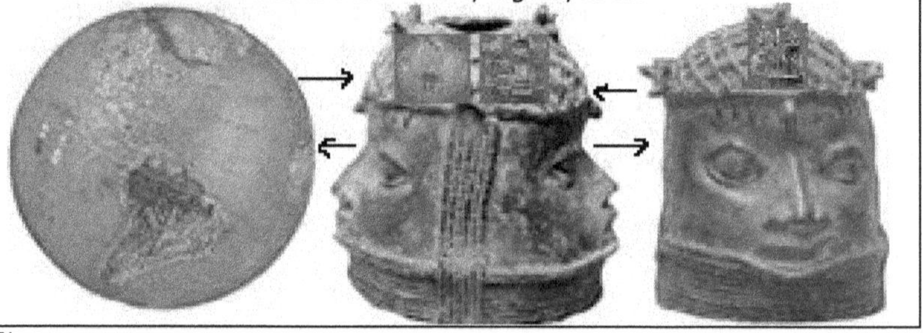

[74] *UB* IV.3.32 *salila* (as water) *eko* (one) *drashṭā-* (who sees) *dvaito* (non dual) *bhavati* (becomes).

[75] *Cf.* Carbonara, *Introduzione alla filosofia*, p. 75, "*non deve pensar di pensare... perchè ... é presente a se stesso, senza bisogno di mediarsi, cioè di vedersi inanzi a sè medesimo come oggetto del proprio conoscere.*" *Cf. Vedānta-Sūtras,* II. 3. 7; vol.

[76] Tolle, *The Power of Now*, p. 93. *Cf.* Mahadevan, *Ramana Maharshi*, It. tr. p. 39.

[77] *Bible*, John 8:14.

[78] *Bible*, John 8:19.

[79] Think concerning right and wrong (κρίνω *krinō).*

[80] Craving senses (σάρξ *sarx).*

[81] *Bible*, John 8:15, nothing (οὐδείς *oudeis).*

[82] *Bible*, John 8:16, ἀληθής *alēthēs* Pure-Awareness *from* α-λανθάνω *a-lanthanō* = not-unaware.

[83] Belonging to the κόσμος *kosmos.*

[84] φῶς *phōs = light, from* φημί *phēmi* to make thoughts known, and φαίνω *phainō* to be evident, to be viewed into light, to appear, shine, resplend, to be manifest.

[85] *Bible*, John 8:12.

[86] *Bible*, John 8:16.

[87] *Bible*, John 10:30.

[88] The sapient pharmacist Isaac Baulot, depicts immanence and Transcendence in the plates of his hermetic alchemic treatise *Mutus Liber* (1677, Latin: *Mute Book*), *Trésor Hermétique.*

3

4

5

8

15

(3) From the subject-object-world, (4) rinse-out the consciousness-*of.* (5) The distillation of that consciousness (8) leads to the Transcendent-Apodictic-Awareness. Having learned in this manner, and (15) *oculatus abis* "having seen, depart" towards the Transcendent.

[89] *Bible*, John 8:34.

[90] *Bible*, John 8: 35-36

[91] *Bible*, 1John 3:2.

[92] Campbell, *The Hero with a Thousand Faces*, p. 205.

[93] *VṚ* X.129.1. *n-* (no) *āsad* (non-being) *āsīn* (was) *nó* (nor) *sád* (being) *āsīt* (was) *tadānīṃ* (then). *Cf. Chāndogya* (relating to knowledge) *Upanisad*, VI, 2, 1

[94] Usually translated as sin. ἁμαρτία *hamartia* from ἁμαρτάνω *hamartanō*, to do wrong, to err, to miss the mark wondering away from the path of righteousness, to sin; also *cf. Bible*, John 8:34.

[95] *Bible*, John 8:21.

[96] *Bible*, John 8:52.

[97] *Bible*, John 8:24 Certain = πιστεύω *pisteuō.*

[98] *Bible*, John 8:23. Beneath temporal succession κάτω *katō;* above beyond time ἄνω *anō.*

[99] *Bible*, John 8:18.

[100] Plato, *Charmides* 164, γνῶθι σαυτόν (*gnṓthi sautón*).

[101] *Bible*, John, 8:32. Latin *cognosco*, from Greek *ginōskō* γινώσκω, from Sanskrit √ *jñā* = to realize.

[102] *UĪśa* 15 *hiraṇmayena* (with a golden) *pātreṇa* (dish) *satyasya* (of truth) *āpihitam* (is covered) *mukham* (the mouth) *tat* (that) *tvaṃ* (you) *pūshan* (bringer of prosperity) *apāvṛṇu* (remove) *satyadharmāya* (for me devoted to the law of truth) *dṛshṭaye* (I may behold) This same verse is in *UMa.* VI.35 (differing: *vishnave* instead of *dṛshṭaye*). In addition, verses 15 to 18 are identical in *UB* V.15.1-4. *Cf.* "*La bocca della vertà*" The Mouth of Truth *lie detector.*

I century Pavonazzetto marble sculpture of a man-bearded-face fountain of the god Oceanus or river Tiber (XVII century Santa Maria in Cosmedin church, Rome, Italy).

[103] *Bible*, Matthew 6:33, βασιλεία *basileia* = kingdom; δικαιοσύνη *dikaiosynē* = *righteousness.*

[104] *Bible*, John 8:16.

[105] *Cf.* *Samyutta Nikāya* (*Dhammacakkappavattana Sutta* The First Discourse of the Buddha Setting the Wheel of Dhamma in Motion) 56:11, pp. 1843-47, and sutta 12.2.1. Middle-path (*madhyamá pratipad*), austerity (*tapas*), sensual delight (*kāma sukha*), dissolves (*nirodha*) all extinguishes (*nirvāṇa*).

[106] *Cf.* Hermann, *Jaina Sutras.*

[107] Lipski, *The Essential Śrī Ānandamayī Mā*, p. 86.

[108] Jung, *Psychology*, p. 57.

[109] *Cf.* Kant, *Prolegomena* § 45 and *Critique of Pure Reason*, B3 09, P270.

[110] Natarajan, *Timeless in Time*, p.108[n.9].

[111] *eka-danta. Cf.* Simonelli, *Beyond Immortality*, *Gaṇapati Upanishad* 6. "You transcend the three qualities. You transcend the three states of consciousness. You transcend the three bodies and transcend the three times." *ṭvaṃ* (you) *guṇatrayā-* (qualities three) *tītas* (transcend) *tvaṃ* (you) *avasthā-* (states of consciousness) *trayā-* (three) *tītas* (transcend) *tvaṃ* (you) *dehatrayā-* (bodies three) *tītas* (transcend) *kālatrayā-* (times three) *tītaḥ* (transcend).

[112] *Bible*, 1 Timothy 5:2. "I come as a thief," says Revelation 16:15. *Cf.* also 1 Thessalonians 5:4; 2 Peter 3:10 and Revelation 3:3.

---

[113] *Cf. W.* p. 108c "(in *vedānta* philosophy) illusion (personified as *māyā*); ignorance together with non-existence Buddhist literature."

[114] *Sciencia muy* sabrosa, *The Poems...*, 27, p. 8. (San Juan de la Cruz, 1542 – 1591, a Spanish Catholic mystic who founded the Order of the Discalced Carmelites with Saint Teresa of Ávila).

[115] *Cf. W. abhyupagama* (78c); *satyá* (1135c); *adhikaraṇa* (20c); *siddhānta* (1216a); *pratitantram* (662a); *sárvatantra* (1185c).

[116] *Bible*, John 8:26.

[117] *Bible*, John 8:28.

[118] *Cf. UK* I.1 (I.I.1) (*kaṭha* = distress; VII century BC) ; *cf.* also Simonelli, *Beyond Immortality*, pp. 114 fol.

[119] *Cf. Bible*, John 8:19; exalted = ὑψόω *hypsoō*. Son = υἱός *huios*, of = τοῦ *tou*, man = ἀνθρώπου *anthrōpou*.

[120] *Bible*, John 8:29.

[121] *Bible*, John 8:37-38 & 44.

[122] Sicari, *Il secondo grande libro...*, p. 791."*Il cuore di Gesù ed il mio, permettetemi l'espressione, si fusero. Non erano più due i cuori che battevano, ma uno solo. Il mio cuore era scomparso, come una goccia d'acqua che si smarrisce in un mare.*"

[123] *Kaṭha Upanishad* (VIII cent. BC) IV.15. *yath-* (as) *odakaṁ* (water) *śuddhe* (into pure) *śuddham* (pure) *āsiktaṁ* (poured) *tādṛgeva* (the same one) *bhavati* (becomes) / *evaṁ* (in the same manner) *muner-* (of the sage) *vijānata* (who has right contemplation) *ātmā* (the self) *bhavati* (becomes).

[124] Sanskrit *pratyāhāra Cf.* Patañjali, *Yoga Sutras* 2,41-55.

[125] Reminiscent of the yogic *indriya*.

[126] Pio, *Epistolario* Letters vol I, 22 ottobre 1918 "*Tutti i sensi interni ed esterni, non che le stesse facoltà dell'anima si trovarono in una quiete indescrivibile. In tutto questo vi fu totale silenzio intorno a me e dentro di me; vi subentrò subito una gran pace ed abbandono alla completa privazione del tutto e una posa nella stessa rovina. Tutto questo avvenne in un baleno.*"

Photograph of Padre Pio da Pietrelcina in the Convent of San Giovanni Rotondo.

[127] Here is an allusion to Padre Pio's stigmata.

[128] Pio, *Epistolario* Letters vol I, 1 Novembre, 1913 "*La maniera ordinaria della mia orazione è questa. Non appena mi pongo a pregare, subito sento che l'anima incomincia a raccogliersi in una pace e tranquillità da non potersi esprimere con le parole. I sensi restano sospesi, ad eccezione dell'udito, il quale alcune volte non viene sospeso; però ordinariamente questo senso non mi dà fastidio, e debbo confessare che se anche a me intorno si facesse del grandissimo rumore, non per questo riesce a molestarmi minimamente. Il pensiero che in ogni istante posso perdere Gesù mi dà un affanno che non so spiegarlo; solo l'anima che ama sinceramente Gesù può saperlo. Quante volte, mi ha detto Gesù, mi avresti abbandonato figlio mio se non ti avessi crocefisso (allusione alle*

stimmate). Sotto la croce si impara ad amare e io la croce non la do a tutti, ma solo a quelli che mi sono più cari. Ecco, vorrei che la mia mente non pensasse che a Gesù, ma mi accorgo che spesso si smarrisce! Io, da parte mia, non saprei negarmi a nessuno. E come potrei se il Signore stesso lo vuole e nulla mi nega di ciò che gli chiedo? Tengo a dirvi che mi sacrifico volentieri per la speranza che ho di potere un giorno in questa vita mortale cantare con il profeta: "Signore hai finalmente spezzato i miei legami e io per questa ragione ti offrirò un sacrificio di lodi per l'eternità. AMEN! ALLELUIA!" (*Bible*, Psalms 115:18).

[129] *Santi e Sante* ..., p. 343.

[130] *bodhi* = enlightenment-full = *sattva.*

[131] *Cf*. Śāntideva, *A Guide to the Bodhisattva...* .

[132] *Bible*, John 18:38 Τί ἐστιν ἀλήθεια

[133] *Bible*, John 18:37 είς τοῦτο ἐλήλυθα είς τὸν κόσμον ἵνα μαρτυρήσω τῇ ἀληθείᾳ πᾶς ὁ ὢν ἐκ τῆς ἀληθείας ἀκούει μου τῆς φωνῆς.
ad hoc veni in mundum ut testimonium perhibeam veritati omnis qui est ex veritate audit meam vocem.

[53] Bhagavan, Sri Ramana Maharshi, Venerable Lovable Great-Seer (December 30, 1879 – April 14, 1950). Sri Ramanasramam, Tiruvannamalai, Tamil Nadu, 606 603 India 91-4175-237200, ashram@sriramanamaharshi.org, http://www.sriramanamaharshi.org/index.html. *Cf.* Natarajan, *Timeless in Time...*, pp. 16-19 and 36-46. *Cf.* Brunton, *A Search in Secret India*, p. 137.

Ramana Maharshi with Mt. Arunachala (1998 Indian Rs 2.^{00} stamp).

[135] Natarajan, *Timeless in Time*, p. 80.

[136] *BG* IX.22 *ananyāḥ* (having no other) *cintayantaḥ* (absorbed) *mām* (in me) *ye* (to those) *janāḥ* (beings) *paryupāsate* (worship) / *teṣām* (of them) *nitya* (always) *abhiyuktānām* (in permanent devotion) *yoga* (yoked) *kṣemam* (shelter) *vahāmi* (bring) *aham* (I).

[137] *neti neti* continuous refrain throughout most of the *Upanishads*.

[138] *Spiritual teaching*, pp. 3 (2), 42.

[139] Natarajan, *Timeless in Time*, p. $13^{n.5}$.

[140] Natarajan, *Timeless in Time*, pp. $13^{n.4 \& 8}$ and $14^{n.9}$.

---

[141] Lipski, *The Essential Śrī Ānandamayī Mā*, p. 95.

[142] *Bible*, Deuteronomy 6:5. Long, breathe after (אהב *'ahab*) the Transcendent (יהוה *Yĕhovah*) True Certain Awareness (אלהים *'elohiym God*) וְאָהַבְתָּ אֵת יְהוָה אֱלֹהֶיךָ בְּכָל־לְבָבְךָ וּבְכָל־ נַפְשְׁךָ וּבְכָל־מְאֹדֶךָ׃ *Cf.* Matthew, 22:37,39, 5:43; 19:19; 22:39; Mark 12:30-31; Luke 10:27.

[143] *UB* IV.4.22. *esha* (this) *mahān* (great) *aja* (unborn) *ātmā* (Self)... *sa* (he) *na* (not) *sādhunā* (by means of good) *karmaṇā* (action) *bhūyān* (does become greater) *no* (not) *ev-* (indeed) *-āsādhunā* (by means of bad) *kanīyān* (smaller) *esha* (this) *sarve-* (all) *-śvaraḥ* (Lord)... *esha* (this) *bhūtā -* (of every living being) *-dhipatiḥ* (Sovereign) *esha* (this) *bhūta-* (of every living being) *-pālaḥ* (Protector) *esha* (this) *setur* (the bridge, as boundary and passage way)[143] *vidharaṇa* (confining) *eshāṃ* (of these) *lokānām* (universes) *asambhedāya* (to be separated) *tam* (him) *etaṃ* (here) *vedā-* (the Sacred Books of Knowledge) – *nuvacanena* (by reciting) *brāhmaṇā* (those who have divine knowledge) *vividishanti* (they seek to know) *yajñena* (by sacrificing) *dānena* (by giving gifts) *tapasā-* (by practicing religious austerity) *-nāśakena* (by fasting)[143] *etam* (this one) *eva* (verily) *viditvā* (being conscious of) *munir* (ascetic) *bhavati* (becomes) *etam* (this) *eva* (verily) *pravrājino* (the religious mendicants) *lokam* (dimension) *icchantaḥ* (striving to obtain) *pravrajanti* (leave home and wonder forth as eremites) *etadd* (this) *ha* (indeed) *sma* (always) *vai* (verily) *tat* (then) *pūrve* (with the ancient) *vidvāṃsaḥ* (knowing) *prajāṃ* (offspring) *na* (not) *kāmayante* (did desire) *kiṃ* (why) *prajayā* (family, procreation) *karishyāmaḥ* (should we build) *yeshāṃ* (*of whom*) *no'* (not) *yam* (this) *ātmā-* (the Self) - *yaṃ* (this) *loka* (dimension) *iti* (therefore) *te* (they) *ha* (indeed) *sma-* (indeed) *-putraishaṇāyāś* (the desire for a son) *ca* (and) *vittaishaṇāyāś* (the desire for wealth) *ca* (and) *lokaishaṇāyaś* (the desire for worldly affairs) *ca* (and) *vyutthāya* (having turned away from) *atha* (then) *bhikshā-* (begging) – *caryaṃ* (going about) *caranti* (walk) *yā* (what) *hy* (verily) *eva* (indeed) *putraishaṇā* (the desire for a son) *sā* (that) *vittaishaṇā* (the desire for wealth) *yā* (what) *vittaishaṇā* (the desire for wealth) *sā* (that) *lokaishaṇā* (the desire for worldly affairs) *ubhe* (both) *hy* (verily) *ete* (these) *eshaṇe* (desires) *eva* (verily) *bhvataḥ* (both are) *sa* (he) *esha* (this) *neti* (not so) *nety* (not so) *ātmā* (Self) *agṛhyaḥ* (incomprehensible) *na* (not) *hi* (thus) *gṛhate* (be comprehended) *aśīryah* (imperishable) *na* (not) *hi* (thus) *śīryate* (destroyed) *esaṅgaḥ* (unattached) *na* (not) *hi* (thus) *sajyate* (does not attach himself) *asito* (unbound) *na* (not) *vyathate* (agitated in the mind) *na* (not) *rishyati* (harmed) *etam* (this one) *u* (furthermore) *haivaite* (indeed these two) *na* (not) *tarata* (subdue) *iti* (thus) *ataḥ* (certainly) *pāpam* (evil) *akaravam* (I have done) *iti* (thus) *ataḥ* (certainly) *kalyāṇam* (good) *akaravam* (I have done) *iti* (thus) *ubhe* (both) *u* (also) *haivaisha* (indeed he) *ete* (these) *tarati* (overcomes) *nainaṃ* (not this) *kṛtākṛte* (he has done and not done) *tapataḥ* (torment).

[144] *Bible*, Matthew 19:29.

[145] *Cf. UMaitrī* VI.28. "If a person is attached to the son, the wife and to the family never at any time goes onward to liberation*dehinaḥ* (if a person) ... *pravartate* (goes onward) ... *putra-*(to son) *dāra-*(to wife)

kuṭumbeshu (to family) *saktasya* (is attached) *na* (not) *kadācana* (never at any time).

[146] *Bible*, Luke 14:26 οὐ μισεῖ [*ou* (not) *misei* (hate)] and John 12:25 μισῶν [*misoon* (hateth)]. & *cf. Koran*, *Repentance*, 9:24 & *BG* IX.22.

[147] del-Vasto, *Return to the Source*, p.93.

[148] superimposition (*adhyāsa*) and confutation (*bādha*).

[149] *Cf. Vedānta-Sūtra.* I. 1, vol. I p, 5 and c*f.* Nikhilānanda, *Māṇḍūkyopaniṣad* II. 17 fol.

[150] *satyasya satyam UB.* II.1.20.

[151] מאֱלֹהִי (*'elohiym God*) ראה (*ra'ah saw*), *Bible*, Genesis 1:4,10,12,18,21,25,31.

[152] *Bible*, Genesis 1:26-27 and 31. Persons (אדם *'adam*), image (צלם *tselem*), likeness (דמות *dĕmuwth*), dominion (רָדָה *radah*)... male (זכר *zakar*) consciousness (from זָכַר *zakar* to record) and female נקבה *nĕqebah*) intentionality (from נָקַב *naqab* to pierce, appoint, to prick off, designate). aware (אֵת *'eth* from אוֹת *'owth* miracle, proof) saw (רָאָה *ra'ah*).

[153] Publius Vergilius Maro (70 - 19 BC), *Aeneis,* I.604 "*mens conscia sibi recti.*" "Conscious" derives from the Latin verb *con-scio* = *scio*, to know, from which derives "*sci*ence" (Latin *sci-entia*), and *con* meaning "together" with the object. Rescind = Latin *sci-ndo. Cf.* Simonelli, *Beyond Immortality*, p. 25.

[154] Freud, *The problem of lay-analyses*, p. 62, emphasis is ours.

Freud's couch,
20 Maresfield Gardens, Hampstead, North London.

[155] *Cf.* Halberg, *Phase relations of 24-hour.* From Latin *circa* (around) *diem* (the day).

[156] *UB.* IV.3.15-16-17 *punaḥ* (again) *pratinyāyam* (in inverted order) *pratiyony* (to source of origin) *ādravati* (hastens towards).

[157] *REM sleep and dreaming.* Allan Hobson, from 1968 to 2003, was the director of the Massachusetts Mental Health Center Laboratory of Neurophysiology in Boston, Massachusetts, USA.

[158] Kant, *The Critique of Pure Reason*, § 12, p. 49.

[159] Aurobindo, *The Life Divine*, p. 344.

---

160 Aurobindo, *The Life Divine*, p. 478.

161 Dream, the state of Rapid Eye Movement (REM) and Deep Sleep, the state of No Rapid Eye Movement (NREM). *Cf.* Borbély, A. (1986). *Secrets of Sleep*, 55, 57, 202.

162 *UB* IV.3.30. *na* (not) {[*paśyati* (does see) (23)], [*jighrati* (does smell) (24)]}, [*rasayati* (does taste) (25)], [*vadati* (does speak) (26)], [*śṛṇoti* (does hear) (27)], [*manute* (does think) (28)]} *vijānāti* (does know) [*paśyan* (seeing) (23), [*jighran* (smelling) (24)], [*rasayan* (tasting) (25)], [*vadan* (speaking) (26)], [*śṛṇvan* (hearing) (27], [*manvāno* (thinking) (28)]} *vijānan* (knowing) *vai* (verily) *tan* (that) *na* (not) {[*paśyati* (does see) (23)], [*jighrati* (does smell) (24)], [*rasayati* (does taste) (25)], [*vadati* (does speek) (26)], [*śṛṇoti* (does hear) (27)], [*manute* (does think) (28)]} *vijānāti* (does know) *na* (not) *hi* (verily) {[*drashṭur* (the seer) (23), [*ghrātur* (the smeller) (24)], [*rasayitū* (the taster) (25)], [*vakṭur* (the speaker) (26)], [*śrotuḥ* (the hearer) (27)], [*mantur* (the thinker) (28)]} *vijñātur* (the knower) {[*dṛshṭer* (seen) (23), [*ghrāter* (smelled) (24)], [*rasayater* (tasted) (25)], [*vakṭer* (spoken) (26)], [*śruter* (heard) (27)], [*mater* (thought) (28)]} *vijñāter* (knower) *viparilopo* (separation) *vidyate* (there is) *avināśitvāt* (imperishable) *na* (not) *tu* (however) *tad* (that) *dvitīyam* (second) *asti* (is) *tato'* (therefore) *nyad* (opposit) *vibhaktam* (divided) *yad* (that) {[*paśyet* (he may see) (23), [*jighret* (he may smell) (24)], [*rasayet* (he may taste) (25)], [*vadet* (he may speak) (26)], [*śṛṇuyāt* (he may hear) (27], [*manvīta* (he may think) (28)]} *vijānīyāt* (he may know).

163 *Cf.* *Śvetāśvatara* (having better white horses) *Upanishad*. *UŚ* IV. 6 fol.

164 *Cf.* תרדמה *tardemah* deep sleep, *Torah*: - Genesis, 2:1.

165 *Māṇḍūkya* (The frog-like cyclical composition) *Upanishad*. *UM* 5. *yatra* (where) *supto* (one asleep) *na* (not) *kaṁcana* (any) *kāmaṁ* (desire) *kāmayate* (does desire) *na* (not) *kaṁcana* (any) *svapnaṁ* (dream) *paśyati* (does see) *tat* (that) *sushuptam* (deep unconscious sleep) *sushupta* (deep unconscious sleep) *sthāna* (state) *ekī -bhūtaḥ* (one-become) *prajñāna-ghana* (knowledge-compact) *evānanda-mayo* (alone-bliss-made) *hyānanda-bhuk* (verily-bliss-enjoyer) *ceto-mukhaḥ* (consciousness-mouth-source) *prājñas-* (the knower) *tṛtīyaḥ* (third) *pādaḥ* (quadrant).

166 Christakis, *Connected*, pp. XII and 106.

167 *Cf.* the deep (תהום - *tehowm*) & the waters (מים - *mayim*) in *Bible*, Genesis 1:2 and (*gahana* = deep) & (*ámbhas* = celestial waters) in *VṚ* X.129.1.

168 רוּח *ruwach* wind, breath, spirit, *Bible*, Genesis 1:1 and 7.

169 *Cf.* *Ṛg Veda* (sacred verse knowledge - III millennium B.C.?) *VṚ* X.129.1. *n-* (no) *āsad* (non-being) *āsīn* (was) *nó* (nor) *sád* (being) *āsīt* (was) *tadānīṁ* (then)... *ámbhaḥ* (Celestial Waters) ... *āsīd* (was) *gahanaṁ* (depth) *gabhīráṁ* (of inscrutable) //

2. *ānīd* (was breathing) *avātáṃ* (windless) *svadháyā* (by self-power) *tád* (that) *ékaṃ* (One Thing)

3. *táma* (darkness) *āsīt* (was) *támasā* (by darkness) *gūḷhám* (covered) *ágre'* (in the beginning) *praketáṁ* (indiscriminate) *saliláṁ* (flowing flood) *sárvam* (all) *ā* (only) *idám* (this) */tuchyénābhv* (in emptiness) *ápihitaṁ* (hidden) *yád* (which) *āsīt* (was) *tápasas* (of

sacrificial heat) *tán* (that) *mahinā-* (by the great power) *jāyata-* (was generated) *íkam* (One Thing) //

170 *Bible*, Genesis, 1:2.

171 Freud, *The standard edition..., Beyond the Pleasure Principle*, p. 42.

172 *UB* I.2.1. *na-* (no) *iv-* (verily) *eha* (here) *kiṁcan-* (nothing at all?) *āgra* (in the beginning) *āsīt* (was) *mṛtyuna-* (by death) *iv-* (verily) *edam* (this) *āvṛtam* (concealed) *āsīt* (was) *aśanāyayā* (by hunger) *aśanāyā* (hunger) *hi* (because) *mṛtyuh* (death) *tan* (this) *mano* (the mind) *kuruta* (he projected) *ātmanvī* (a being for-itself) *syām* (let me be) *iti* (thus).

173 Farkas Simon, *Camilla*, p. 142.

174 *śūnyátā cf. W.* p. 1085b "*f.* emptiness, loneliness, desolateness ... absence of mind ... absence or want of ... nothingness, non-existence ... illusory nature (of all worldly phenomena)...

śūnyá mf(ā)n. empty, void ... (as a look or stare) ... absentminded ... possessing nothing ... wholly alone or solitary ... non-existent ... nonsensical ... void of result ..._ insensible ... vacuum, empty or deserted place, ... (in phil.) vacuity, nonentity, absolute non-existence (esp. with Buddhists) ... (in arithm.) nought, [zero] a cypher ... space N. of *brahma* ... a partic. phenomenon in the sky."

nirvāṇa cf. W. p. 557c "*mfn.* blown or put out, extinguished (as a lamp or fire), set (as the sun), calmed, quieted, tamed ... dead, deceased (*lit.* having the fire of life extinguished), lost, disappeared ... final emancipation from matter and re-union with the Supreme Spirit ... absolute extinction or annihilation (= *śūnya*...) of individual existence or of all desires and passions ... perfect calm or repose or happiness, highest bliss or beatitude."

175 Dawkins, *The Selfish Gene*, p. 35.

176 Francis, *Scritti di S. Francesco...*, p. 121, *Cantico di frate sole* or *Laude delle creature* 13: "*Beati quelli ke trovarà / ne le tue sanctissime voluntati, / ka la morte secunda nol farà male.*"

St. Francis of Assisi preaching to the birds
(750th Anniversary bronze plaque, Germany).

177 (*Sein zum Tode*), Heidegger, *Being and time*, II, I, H. 235-267, pp. 279-311.

178 Leopardi, *Tutte le opere*, *L'Infinito*, "*E'l naufragar m'è dolce in questo mare.*"

[179] *Cf.* Overbye, *CERN Physicists See Higgs Boson in New Particle.*
[180] *Cf. Māṇḍūkya Upanishad* in Simonelli, *Beyond Immortality.*
[181] Proto-Germanic *or* Old English *ge-wær = collective (ge) and on-guard-vigilance (wær).*
[182] *Bible,* Matthew 5:13. *Latin, sapere-sapor = flavor.*
[183] *E.g.* Architect Miguel Rosales of Boston, eastern pylon of Liberty Bridge.

Reedy River Falls, Greenville, SC, USA.

[184] *Bible,* Isaiah 28:16.
[185] *Bible,* 1 Peter 2:6. Is certain πιστεύων from πιστεύω *pisteuō.*
[186] *Bible,* Matthew 5:14-16.
[187] Descartes, René (1596-1650), *Discourse on Method,* pp. 1 (I), 15 (II).
[188] In Latin, *cogito ergo sum.*
[189] (Emphasis is ours) *si ferme et si assurée,* Descartes, *Discours de la méthode...,* IV.
[190] Descartes, *Discourse on Method,* pp. 34-35 (IV).
[191] *bhūmi-sparśa.*
[192] *Cf.* Warren, *Buddhism in translations...,* p. 81. Cf. *Jātaka* I.74.[25]

detail

Buddha *bhūmisparśa,* Tibetan votive Tsa Tsa clay tablet, Chinese Yuan Dynasty (1271-1368).

[193] *Bible*, Romans 1:20 ποιήμασιν (*poieémasin* by the things that are made) νοούμενα (*nooúmena* being understood) καθορᾶται (*kathorãtai* are clearly seen).

[194] Attibuted to Pawnee Eagle Chief (Letakos-Lesa). Campbell, *The Power of Myth*, Cp. III. The First Storytellers, p. 79.

[195] Descartes' Notebook entry, 11/11, 1620, *Descartes...*, Anscombe Ed., p. 3.

[196] *Cf.* Watson, *Cogito* ..., p. 115 and Clarke, *Descartes...*, p. 64.

[197] Descartes, *The Philosophical Works...*, Reply to Objection II, 3rd, p. 38.

[198] To exist, from the Latin *exsistere* = (*ex*) out-from-to-stay (*sistere*), from the Sanskrit "*sthā... cl.1 P. A1... tíshṭhati...* to stay," *cf. W.* p. 1262c). To extract, from the Latin *extrahere* = (*ex*) out-from-to-trail (*trahere*).

[199] *Cogito* = co-agitation (*a-gito*) with (*co* = *cum*).

[200] Descartes, Anscombe Ed., *Descartes...*, Second Meditation, p. 70. co-agitation (*a-gito*) of the thought with (*co* = *cum*) itself Latin text: in *Renati Des Cartes Meditationes...*, II (7) "*Jam autem* ***certò*** *scio me esse*," French text: in *Les Méditations...*, II (7) "*Or je sais déjà* ***certainement*** *que je suis.*" Emphasis is ours.

[201] Descartes, Anscombe Ed., *Descartes...*, Second Meditation, p. 70. Latin text: in *Renati Des Cartes Meditationes...*, II (7) [it is Absolute-Aware-Certitude, Latin: *certissimum est*, French: *il est très certain* (7)], [thought, Latin: *cogitatione*, French: *penser* (6), [thought is existent, Latin: *cogitatio est*, French: *la pensée est* (6)], [recognize, Latin: *novi*, French: *reconnu* (7)]. The emphasis is ours.

[202] Schopenhauer (1788-1860), *The basic of morality*, p. 176.

[203] *Luciferic*, Latin: light = *lucem* – *ferre* = to carry. *Cf.* *Bible*, Isaiah 14:12, "*How art thou fallen from heaven, O Lucifer* (הילל *heylel*), *son of the morning!* [how] *art thou cut down to the ground, which didst weaken the nations!... I will be like the most High* [Transcendent]."

Statue of Liberty carrying the light. 2001 USA FIRST CLASS MAIL

[204] *Bible*, John 1:7-8-9.

[205] *Bible*, Genesis 1:1 and 10, *emphasis is ours,* אֱלֹהִים וַיִּקְרָא ... כִּי־טוֹב: .... וַיַּרְא ... אֶרֶץ (קרא *qara' to name,* ארץ *'erets World,* ראה *ra'ah to see),*

[206] *Koran*, Ta Ha, 20:110.

[207] Lack of knowledge, ignorance and *no awareness* (تَجْهَلُونَ *tajhalwana*), (Italic is ours) *Koran*, The Battlements 7:138l; in this context, it refers to 'the children of Israel' who had no true awareness of the nature of God. *Cf.* The Ant, 27:55; The Battlements, 7:138; Hood, 11:29.

[208] *Koran*, Al-'Ankabut [The Spider] 29:45 وَلَذِكْرُ اللَّهِ أَكْبَرُ وَاللَّهُ يَعْلَمُ مَا تَصْنَعُونَ
Ladhikru Allahi 'Akbaru Wa Allahu Ya`lamu Ma Taṣna`ūna.

[209] *Bṛhad-āraṇyaka* (vast-forest), one of the oldest sacred *Upanishads* (I millennia B.C.?). *UB* IV.3.1. *janakam̐* (to King Janaka-the-progenitor) *ha* (indeed) *vaideham* (of Videha- incorporeal) *vājñavalkyo* Sacrifice-Speaker) *jagāma* (came) ... *agni-*(at a fire) *hotre* (oblation) ... *tam̐* (him) *ha* (indeed) *samrāḍ* (the supreme ruler) *eva* (verily) *pūrvaḥ* (with formal speech accompanied by smiles) *papraccha* (asked). 2. *yājñavalkya* (o Sacrifice-Speaker) *kim̐-* (what) *jyotir* (light) *ayam* (this) *purusha* (person) *iti* (truly) *āditya-* (of the sun) *jyotih* (light) *samrāṭ* (supreme king) *iti* (truly) *hovāca* (said) *ādityenaivāyam̐* (with the sun verily this) *jyotish-* (light) *āste* (one stays) *palyayate* (moves) *karma* (work) *kurute* (performs) *vipalyet* - (returns back) *īti* (thus) *evam* (so) *evaitat* (verity this) *yājñavalkya* (Sacrifice-Speaker). 3. *astam* (has set) *ita* (when) *āditye* (the sun) *yājñavalkya* (o Sacrifice-Speaker) *kim̐-* (what) *jyotir* (light) *evāyam* (verily this) *purusha* (person) *iti* (truly) *candramā* (the moon) *evāsya* (verily his) *jyotir* (light) *bhavati* (is) *candramasaivāyam̐* (with the moon verily this) *jyotish-* (light) *āste* (one stays) *palyayate* (moves) *karma* (work) *kurute* (performs) *vipalyet* (returns back) *īti* (thus) *evam* (so) *evaitat* (verity this) *yājñavalkya* (Sacrifice-Speaker). 4. *astam* (has set) *ita* (when) *āditye* (the sun) *yājñavalkya* (o Sacrifice-Speaker) *candramasy* (the moon) *astam* (has set) *ite* (thus) *kim̐-* (what) *jyotir* (light) *evāyam* (verily this) *purusha* (person) *iti* (truly) *agnir* (fire) *evāsya* (verily his) *jyotir* (light) *bhavati* (is) *agnin-* (with fire) *aivāyam* (verily this) *jyotish-* (light) *āste* (one stays) *palyayate* (moves) *karma* (work) *kurute* (performs) *vipalyet-* (returns back) *īti* (thus) *evam* (so) *evaitat* (verity this) *yājñavalkya* (Sacrifice-Speaker). 5. *astam* (has set) *ita* (when) *āditye* (the sun) *yājñavalkya* (o Sacrifice-Speaker) *candramasi* (the moon) *astam* (has set) *ite* (thus) *śānte* (extinguished) *agnau* (the fire) *kim̐-* (what) *jyotir* (light) *evāyam* (verily this) *purusha* (person) *iti* (truly) *vāg* (the word-idea) *evāsya* (verily his) *jyotir* (light) *bhavati* (is) *vāc-* (with the word-idea) *aivāyam̐* (verily this) *jyotish-* (light) *āste* (one stays) *palyayate* (moves) *karma* (work) *kurute* (performs) *vipalyeti* (returns back) *tasmād* (therefore) *vai* (verily) *samrāḍ* (supreme king) *api* (also) *yatra* (where) *pāṇir* (the hand) *na* (not) *vinirjñāyate* (is discerned) *atha* (then) *yatra* (when) *vāg* (the word-idea) *uccarati* (is uttered) *upaiva* (therefore truly) *tatra* (there) *nyet-* (leads towards) *īti* (thus) *evam* (so) *evaitat* (verity this)*yājñavalkya* (o Sacrifice-Speaker). 6. *astam* (has set) *ita* (when) *āditye* (the sun) *yājñavalkya* (o Sacrifice-Speaker) *candramasy* (the moon) *astam* (has set) *ite* (thus) *śānte* (extinguished) *agnau* (the fire) *śāntāyām̐* (has quieted) *vāci* (the word) *kim̐-*(what) *jyotir* (light) *evāyam* (indeed this) *purusha* (person) *iti* (thus) *ātmaivāsya* (the Self his) *jyotir*

(light) *bhavati* (is) *ātmanaivāyam* (due to the Self indeed this) *jyotish-* (the light of intelligence which is placed in the heart – *Cf. jyotir hṛdaya āhitam yat Vṛ* VI.9.6-) *āste* (exists) *palyayate* (moves perceiving - *Cf. W.* p. 605b "*parī*... to perceive, ponder,... to move round or in a circle."-) *karma* (work) *kurute* (performs) *vipalyeti* (returns back - *Cf. W.* p. 974a "*vi-parī*... to turn around or back, return."-) *iti* (thus). 7. *katama* (which one) *ātmeti* (the self then) *yo* (who) *yaṁ* (this) *vijñānamayaḥ* (composed of knowledge) *prāṇeshu* (among the vital senses) *hṛdy* (heart) *antarjyotiḥ* (the light within) *purushaḥ* (person) *sa* (he) *samānaḥ* (serenely centered in itself) *sann* (being) *ubhau* (both) *lokāv* (worlds) *anusañcarati* (penetrates) *dhyāyatīva* (thinking as if) *lelāyatīva* (moving to and fro as if) *sa* (he) *hi* (upon) *svapno* (dream state) *bhūtvā* - (becoming) *imaṁ* (this) *lokam* (dimension) *atikrāmati* (beyond goes) *mṛtyo* (death) *rūpāṇi* (the forms). 9. *svena* (by his own) *bhāsā* (light) *svena* (by his own) *jyotishā* (brightness) *prasvapiti* (he sleeps dreaming) *atrāyam* (in this state) *purushaḥ* (person) *svayaṁ* (self-) *jyotir* (illuminated) *bhavati* (becomes).... 4,6 *Brahma-* (Being Supreme Awareness*)* *iva* (verily) *san* (obtains) *brahmā-* (to Brahman-Awareness) *payeti* (goes)... 7 *yadā* (when) *sarve* (all) *pramucyante* (are shed) *kāmā* (desires) *ye'* (which) *sya* (one's) *hṛdi* (in heart) *śritāḥ* (fastened)/ *atha* (then) *martyo'* (the mortal) *mṛto* (immortal) *bhavaty-* (becomes) *atra* (in this manner) *brahma* (Supreme Spirit) *samaśnute* (one reaches) [identical verse in *UK* VI.14 (II.3.14)].

210 *Bible*, John 8:12.

211 *Bible*, John 1:5.

212 Ramana Maharshi, *The Spiritual Teaching...*, p. 3 (1-2) emphasis is ours.

213 *Bible*, Exodus 3:14 אֶהְיֶה אֲשֶׁר אֶהְיֶה (היה *hayah to be* אֲשֶׁר *'ashér* that).

214 *Bible*, John 12:46, (our translation) ἐγὼ φῶς εἰς τὸν κόσμον ἐλήλυθα ἵνα πᾶς ὁ πιστεύων εἰς ἐμὲ ἐν τῇ σκοτίᾳ μὴ μείνῃ, (πιστεύων *pisteúōn*, credit)*ego lux in mundum veni ut omnis qui credit in me in tenebris non maneat.*

215 *good understanding*" as intellectual capability (טוב *towb*).

216 To see, perceive (ראה *ra'ah*) *Bible*, Genesis 1:4,10,12,18,21,25.

217 *Bible*, Genesis 1:3, 4 and 31. וַיֹּאמֶר אֱלֹהִים יְהִי אוֹר וַיְהִי־אוֹר: (אור *'owr light* of day, of dawn, of life, of God itself; היה *hayah to be*); 4. אוֹר כִּי־טוֹב וַיַּבְדֵּל אֱלֹהִים (ראה *ra'ah* to see, perceive; *cf.* also 10, 12, 18, 21, 25).

218 *Bible*, Genesis 1:5,8,13,19,23,31. "Let there be (היה *hayah*) light (אור *'owr*)... saw, *light* (אור *'owr*), saw (ראה *ra'ah*)... perceives (ראה *ra'ah*)... good understanding" (טוב *towb*)."

219 *Bible*, Genesis 2:2, he rested שבת *shabath*.

220 *Bible*, John 9:5.

221 (1548-1600) in *Lo Spaccio de la bestia trionfante* (Paris 1584) and in *De la causa, principio e uno* (Venice 1584).

222 Bruno, *Opere italiane*, *Spaccio*, I, 3, Mercury explaining to Sophia.

223 *Bible*, Luke 15:8.

224 *Cf.* Bruno, *Opera Italiane*, *De la causa*, II, Teofilo.

225 *Cf.* Bruno, *Opere italiane*, II, 75-7, n. 5 and Spampanato, *Vita di G. B.....*

[226] *Cf.* Bruno, *Opere italiane, Spaccio,* I, 3, Mercury reporting to Sophia.

[227] [√ά (intensive) + τλα *a+tla*], τλῆναι-*tlénai* to sustain.

OB-JECT

SUB-JECT

Lee Oscar Lawrie (1877-1963), Atlas 1936

(New York City, 630 Rockefeller Center, 5th Ave & 51-50 Street).

[228] Genesis 2:9.

[229] Natarajan, *Timeless in Time...*, p. 13 n. 3 quoted from Mudaliar, A. Devaraja: *Day by Day*, entry dt.22.11.45 and p. 14 n. 9 entry dt. 4.10.46.

[230] *Cf. UK* IV.1 (II.I.1) *svayam-bhū́.*

[231] *Bible*, Genesis, 1:3. וַיֹּאמֶר אֱלֹהִים יְהִי אוֹר וַיְהִי־אוֹר׃ (אור *'owr* light).

[232] *Cf.* Exodus, 2:10, משה *Mosheh Moses,* משה *mashah* to draw, מים *mayim* water of transitory things. *Cf.* "he drew me out of many waters," 2 Samuel 22:17 and Psalms 18:16.

[233] יִתְרוֹ *Yithrow* his abundance יֶתֶר *yether* abundance.

[234] *Cf.* Wealthy-famous *Vājaśravas*, (*Kaṭha Upanishad* I.1) famous (*śrávas*) for wealth or *gain* (*vāja*) (*W.* 938a-b) father of Desirous (Uśan), Simonelli, *Beyond Immortality*, p. 114.

[235] מדין *Midyan,*מִדְיָן *midyan*

[236] צאן *tso'n* of multitude (metaphor).

[237] אַחַר *'achar*

[238] Exodus, 3:1, הַר *har mountain,* אלהים *'elohiym* God, חרב c*horeb* desert.

[239] Exodus, 3:2, "לבה *labbah* flashing point of spear... he intently looked (רָאָה *ra'ah*), and, behold, the **bush** (סְנֶה *cĕnah*) burned (בָּעַר *ba`ar*) with supernatural fire (אֵשׁ *'esh*), and the **bush** [was] not consumed or devoured (אָכַל *'akal*)."

[240] *VṚ* X.45.1. *divas* (the sky) *pari* (from) *prathamaṃ* (the first time) *jajñe* (was born) *agnir* (fire).

[241] Exodus, 3:3 סור *cuwr* to reject and turn away from.

[242] Thoreau, *A Year...*, July 16, 1851.

[243] *Bible*, Deuteronomy 5:11 and Exodus 20:7.

[244] *Bible*, Exodus, 3:4.

[245] Exodus, 3:5 קרב *qarab* to bring near, approach, קֹדֶשׁ *qodesh Sacred set-apart,* קָדַשׁ *qadash that which is separated, namely transcendent.*

[246] *Bible*, Matthew 5:3 & 8. *The poor in ego-spirit* (οἱ πτωχοὶ τῷ πνεύματι *oi ptōchoi tō pneumati*) refers to the spirit (πνεῦμα *pneuma*, - *cf.* Sanskrit *prāṇa*

vital-principal) as the *principium individuationis*. Heart καρδία *kardia*, mind and thought.

[247] *Bible*, John 18:36. κόσμος *kosmos* cosmos, world; νῦν *nyn* now, present; ἐντεῦθεν *enteuthen* this place.

[248] Exodus, 3:6.

[249] *UB* III.4.2.

[250] *Bible*, Exodus, 3:13.

[251] אֶהְיֶה אֲשֶׁר אֶהְיֶה *hayah asher hayah*

[252] *Bible*, Exodus, 3:14.

[253] *Bible*, Exodus, 3:11.

[254] *Bible*, Exodus, 3:12. כִּי הָאוֹת: אות *'owth* miraculous sign or proof; כי *kiy* because, certainly, surely. מִצְרַיִם *mitsrayim Egypt, d*ual of מָצוֹר *matsowr Egypt* siege, entrenchment The same as מָצוֹר *matsowr* in the sense of a limit, enclosure צוּר *tsuwr* to bind, besiege, confine, to shut in, enclose, to be an adversary.

[255] *Cf. Bible*, 1 John 2:16.

[256] ערב *'ereb the evening of the day* יום *yowm Bible*, Genesis 1:5.

[257] *Cf. day* יום *yowm* from the root יָחַם *yacham* meaning to be hot.

[258] *VR* X.129.3. *táma* (darkness) *āsīt* (was) *támasā* (by darkness) *gūḷhám* (covered) *ágre'* (in the beginning) *praketáṃ* (indiscriminate) *salilám* (flowing flood) *sárvam* (all) *ā* (only) *idám* (this) */tuchyénābhv* (in emptiness) *ápihitaṃ* (hidden) *yád* (which) *āsīt* (was) *tápasas* (of sacrificial heat) *tán* (that) *mahinā-* (by the great power) *jāyata-* (was generated) *íkam* (One Thing) *//*

[259] *Bible*, Luke 12:3.

[260] *Cf.* Susskind, *The Black Hole War.*

[261] 爲無爲 *wei wu wei,Tao Te Ching,* 6 (43).

[262] *Cf.* the "wind (רוח- *ruach*) from God" *Genisis* 1:2.

[263] *Cf VR Die Hymned des Rigveda*, ed. Aufrecht, II, p. 430 n. 2 "*ha anyát.*" And *W.* "2. *ha* ... m. ... water; a cipher (i.e. the arithmetical figure which symbolizes 0) ... sky, heaven, ... n. the Supreme Spirit; ... 3. ... ind. ... indeed" (1286a) and "*anyá,* ... other ... another; another person" (45b); "*dhānyá* ... n. corn, grain ... a measure = 4 sesamum seeds" (514b).

[264] *VR* X.129.2. *ná* (nor) *mṛtyúr* (death) *āsīd* (was) *amṛtaṃ* (immortality) *ná* (nor) *tárhi* (then) *ná* (no) *rātryā* (night) *áhna* (day) *āsīt* (was) *praketáḥ* (knowledge) / *ānīd* (was breathing) *avātáṃ* (windless) *svadháyā* (by self-power) *tád* (that) *ékaṃ* (One Thing) *tásmād* (therefore) *dhānyán* (indeed other seed) *ná* (no) *paráḥ* (beyond) *kíṃ ca-* (further) *n-* (none) *āsa* (was) *//*

[265] *Cf.* a May 1971 letter to a disciple of Massimo Scaligero.

[266] *VR* X.129.4. *kāmas* (desire, intention) *tád* (consequently) *ágre* (in the beginning) *sám avartatādhi* (sprung about) *mánaso* (of the mind) *rétaḥ* (flowing seed) *prathamáṃ* (the original) *yád* (that) *āsīt* (was)

[267] Freud, *The Ego and the Id*, p. 22.

[268] *UB* I.2.1. *na-* (no) *iv-* (verily) *eha* (here) *kiṃcan-* (nothing at all?) *āgra* (in the beginning) *āsīt* (was) *mṛtyuna-* [by death, name of the god of love (*kāma, W.* 128a)] *iv-* (verily) *edam* (this) *āvṛtam* (concealed) *āsīt* (was) *aśanāyayā* (by hunger) *aśanāyā* (hunger) *hi* (because) *mṛtyuh*

(death) *tan* (this) *mano* (the mind) *kuruta* (he projected) *ātmanvī* (a being for-itself) *syām* (let me be) *iti* (thus).

[269] Genesis, 3:7, *cf.* 17.

[270] *UB* I.2.7. *anavarudhya*-non restraining-*ivā*-thus-*manyata*-he thought.

[271] *W.* 783c., "Mind (in its widest sense as applied to all the mental powers), intellect, intelligence, understanding, perception, sense, conscience, will... the internal organ... of perception and cognition, the faculty or instrument through which thoughts enter or by which objects of sense affect the soul... distinct from *ātman* and *puruṣa*, 'spirit or soul.'"

[272] *Bible*, Matthew 21:42; Mark 12:10; Luke 20:17.

Graphic rendering of the corner stone (oil on canvas 1990).

[273] *Bible*, John 6:35, is certain in me πιστεύων εἰς ἐμὲ *pisteuōn eis eme*.

[274] *Spiritual teaching*, pp. 3 (2), 42. *Cf.* similar mining in *Bible*, 1Chronicles 21:1, "*Satan* (שטן *satan* = adversary) *stood up against.*" Also Job 1:6 fol., Psalms 109:6, Zechariah 3:1 fol. and in *New Testament* (σατανᾶς *satanas*).

[275] Grant Steen, *Dna & Destiny*, p. 3.

[276] The action (*karma*) which begun (*ārabdha*) in previous (*pra*) lives thus it.

[277] Ramana Maharshi, *The Spiritual Teaching...*, p. 27.

[278] Quoted in Osborne, *The Mind of Ramana Maharshi...*, p. 34.

[279] Lipski, *The Essential Śrī Ānandamayī Mā*, p. 57.

[280] Eyes of a buck during the rut season.

[281] *Bible*, Matthew 8:21-22 (underlining is ours) and Luke 9:58.

[282] UB IV.4.6. *tad* (to that) *eva* (indeed) *saktaḥ* (is attached) *saha* (together

with) *karmaṇa-* (with the deeds) *iti* (thus) *liṅgam* (subtle self) *mano* (mind) *yatra* (in which) *nishaktam* (fastened to) *asya* (it).

[283] *Bible*, Matthew 8:13.

[284] *Sees* (*εἶδον eidov*) that idea (*εἶδος eidos*) as a deified idol (*εἴδωλον eidōlon (from εἶδος* <u>*eidos*</u>). *Cf. Bible*, Genesis 1:4.

ABOVE

BELOW

Mesmerized by thought, as if a *goddess* (below), the mind ignores Awareness (above) that *certifies* that idea.

[285] *Deus vult. Cf.* Phillips, *Holy Warriors A Modern History of the Crusades.*

[286] (English) Robert Bellarmine (1542-1621), now Saint. *Cf.* Mercati, *Il sommario del processo di Giordano Bruno.* Vol. 101.

[287] *Cf.* Bruno, *De l'infinito, universo e mondi*, in *Opere italiane.* Giordano Bruno (born in Nola in 1548) was condemned for his free thought by the Roman Inquisition and consequently burnt at the stake in Rome (1600). Schopenhauer, in his *The world as will and representation* (I, 422, n. 2), recognized that the Nolan Philosopher did not belong to the Occidental "part of the globe... [His] death in this Western world... [was] like that of a tropical plant in Europe. The banks of the sacred Ganges were... [his] true spiritual home; where... [he] would have led a peaceful and honored life among men of like mind." In fact, he would not have been condemned, but he would have been invited to the public interfaith theological discussions sponsored, at the time, by the Mughal Emperor Akbar (1556-1605). Today, however, in Bengal, India, a new Western materialistic inquisition, not less vicious and dogmatic than the old European ones, hounds Tantric practitioners, who find themselves "under threat from the ruling Communist Party... 'Anti-Superstition Committees'... There have been reports of the persecution of poor... accused of practicing witchcraft and... occasionally put to death" (Dalrymple, *Nine Lives...*, pp. 201-2).

1) 

2) 

1) Nola, Naples, Italy, statue of the astronomer, mathematician and philosopher Giordano Bruno. 2) Campo de' Fiori, Rome, Italy, bronze plaque on the base of Bruno's statue, written by Giovanni Bovio:
"9 GIUGNO 1889- A BRUNO- IL SECOLO DA LUI DIVINATO- QUI - DOVE IL ROGO ARSE- AUSPICE LA GIOVENTÙ DELL'ATENEO DI ROMA- CONCORRENTI LE NAZIONI CIVILI."
"June 9, 1889- to Bruno- the century foretold by him – here – where the stake burned – Under the patronage of the University of Rome youth - concurrent the civil nations."

[288] *Cf.* Sobel, *Galileo's Daughter*, p. 347.
[289] *Cf.* D'Souza *What's So Great About America*, p. 7.
[290] *W.* p. 1a, 3.
[291] Rocci, p. 1.
[292] Angelini, p. 2, 14; also the prepositional prefix "*in*," "in composition with names, adjectives, participles and adverbs gives them generally a negative meaning," *ibid.* p. 713.
[293] *Cf.* also "*in - im*" or "*un*" (*i.e. im*moral, *un*moral = *without*-moral).
[294] *The Power of Myth*, p. 49.
[295] Tolle, *The Power of Now*, p. 13.
[296] *Cf.* Saint Anselm (*Proslogion*, IV), ontological proof: the idea of a perfect being implies existence to be perfect.
[297] *Bible*, Matthew, 22:37,39 and *cf.* 5:43; 19:19; 22:39; Leviticus 19:18; Mark 12:30-31; Luke 10:27 yourself= σεαυτόν *seautón. Cf.* Deuteronomy 6:5 מאד *ma`od* = might ≠ διάνοια *dianoia* = mind.
[298] *Cf.* Saint Thomas (*Summa Theologica*, Iª, q. 2 a. 3 co.), *a-posteriori* proofs: a) from motion, b) from cause, c) from necessity, d) from perfection and e) from order.
[299] *In* Hebrew אֱמוּנָה *'emuwnah* derives *from* √אָמַן *'aman* = to be certain. In Greek πίστις *pístis* means assurance, proof, testimonial. Rocci, p.1503b *sicurtà*.
[300] Latin *fides*.
[301] *Bible*, Habakkuk 2:4 and Hebrew 11:1, certitude, conviction, certainty, faith (πίστις *pístis*), *foundation, substance* (ὑπόστασις *hypostasis*), *to trust* (ἐλπίζω *elpizō*), *evidence,* conviction (ἔλεγχος *elegchos*), *to see, to* discern mentally (βλέπω *blepō*).

[302] That fulguration is symbolically represented by the thunderbolt in the Tibetan *rdo-rje* or Indian *vajra.Cf. UB* I.2.1. *Cf. W.* pp. 47c, 53a, 143a. *Cf. Vajra mudrā.*

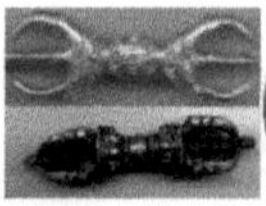
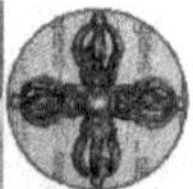

Sanskrit *vajra*, Tibetan *rdo-rje*, 19th Century, brass.

"*vájra* ... "the hard or mighty one," a thunderbolt (esp. that of Indra [*cf.* Greek Zeus or Roman Thundering Jupiter *pluvius*], said to have been formed out of the bones of the ṛṣi Dadhīca or Dadhīci [q.v.], and shaped like a circular discus [*cf.* the circularity of consciousness], or in later times regarded as having the form of two transverse bolts crossing each other thus x; sometimes also applied to similar weapons used by various gods or superhuman beings, or to any mythical weapon destructive of spells or charms, also... the lightning evolved from the centrifugal energy of the circular thunderbolt of Indra when launched at a foe; in Northern Buddhist countries it is shaped like a dumb-bell and called Dorje)" (*W.* p. 115a).

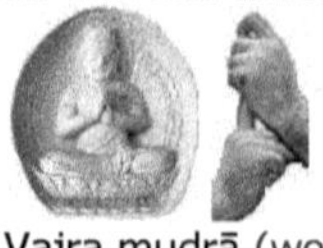

Cf. Buddha Mahāvairocana in Vajra mudrā (wood incense container, Japan).

[303] *Bible*, Hebrew 11:3. utterance (ῥῆμα *rhēma), see also to flow* (ῥέω *réō)*; to

appear (φαίνω *phaínō).*

304 *Bible,* Matthew 17:20.

305 *Bible*, Mark 11:24.

306 *Bible*, John 11:25 & *cf.* 26 (also 3:18, 36; 6:35, 47; 7:38; 12:44; 14:12; & Mark 16:16). I am certain = πιστεύω (*pisteúō*) see note below.

307 *UC* III.14.3 (Indian sacred text, VII cent. BC), *esha* (this *esha* [*vai prathamaḥ*] this [before mentioned]) *ma* (my) *ātmā-* (Self) *-ntar* (within) *hṛdaye'* (the heart) *ṇīyān* (smaller than) *vrīher* (a grain of rice) *vā* (or) *yavād* (a barley-corn) *vā* (or) *sarshapād* (a mustard seed) *vā* (or) *śyāmākād* (a grain of millet) *vā* (or) *śyāmāka-* (of a grain of millet) *-taṇḍulād* (a kernel) *vā* (or) *esha* (this) *ma* (my) *ātmā-* (Self) *-ntar* (within) *hṛdaye* (the heart) *jyāyān* (greater than) *pṛthivyāḥ* (the earth) *jyāyān* (greater than) *antarikshāj* (the sky) *jyāyān* (greater than) *divaḥ* (heaven) *jyāyān* (greater than) *ebhyo* (these) *lokebhyaḥ* (universes)

308 Jung, *Psyche and Symbol*, pp. 80 and 120.

309 *Bible*, Mark 9:37, Luke 18:17.

310 *Bible*, Habakkuk 2:4.

311 *Bible*, Romans 1:17.

312 *UK* I.2 (I.I.2) (*kaṭha* = distress, Indian sacred text, VII cent. BC). *śraddhā*, *W.* p. 1095c "*śrad-√dhā...* to have faith,... believe... *śraddhā ...* faith,... belief ... *Śraddhā*, f. ... reverential homage." *śrát* or *śrád*, ind. ... = *satya*, 'truth...' Lat. *credo* for *cred-do*; *cor*, *cord-is*; Gk. Καρδία ... Eng. 'heart;'" (p. 513c "*dhā* ... holding"). See *śrāddha* (fr. *śrad-dhā*) p. 1097c.

313 *Bible*, John, 12:46; believeth = πιστεύω (*pisteúō*): to be certain, *verb of the* feminine noun πίστις (*pístis*): certitude. My ἐμέ (*eme*).

314 *I.e.* the Gospel εὐαγγελίζω *euaggelizō, Romans 1:16.*

315 *Bible*, Romans 1:19-20.

316 *bhūmi-sparśa cf. Jātaka* I.74.25 (Buddhist text, IV cent. BC).

317 *Bible*, Romans 1:8, to proclaim = καταγγέλλω *kataggellō, universally =* κόσμος *kosmos.* And *cf.* 12, to strengthen = συμπαρακαλέω *symparakaleō, you* = ὑμῶν *hymōn, both* = τε *te, and* = καὶ *kai*, me = ἐμοῦ *emou.*

318 Saint Anselm ontological proof and Saint Thomas *a-posteriori* proofs.

319 Simonelli, *Beyond Immortality*, p. 119.

320 *Bible*, Romans 1:21, *Transcendent* [*viz.* God] θεός *theos... become empty* ματαιόω *mataioō... thinking process* διαλογισμός *dialogismos.*

321 *Ibid.* 23, *image of things* εἰκών *eikōn.*

322 *Ibid.* 25, *certain truth* ἀλήθεια *alētheia... lie* ψεῦδος *pseudos.*

323 *Ibid.* 21-25, Paul ends chapter I with the word ἀμήν *amen* (25). The verses that follow (26 to 32) seem to have been a later interpolation against homosexuality. However, Paul could be following Leviticus' injunction against male homosexuality (18:22 and 20:13). However, if we take those passages literally, we must also follow the next Biblical injunctions (25:44 fol. & Exodus 21:21) that promote slavery.

324 √1 *vid* to know.

325 *VṚ* X.129.4. *hṛdí* (in the heart) *pratíshyā* (searching) *kaváyo* (the seers) *manīshā* (with reflection).

326 *Upa-* (by the side of) *ni-* (down) *shad* (sitting).

[327] √*kévala* = isolation.

Loneliness.

[328] *Śunaka*, dog; *śaunaka*, related to a dog; *śaunika*, hunting dog.

[329] *Ṛg-Veda sūtra Cf.* W. pp. 116a and 159b.

[330] His name [equestrian (*āśva*) approaching (*ā́yana*) horse (*aśva*) staying (*layana*) on the road (*áyana*)] derives from Aśvala, the fire priest of *Janaka*, the Generator, King of *Videha*, the Incorporeal, [perhaps identified with the Southern Nepali city of Janakpur (*cf.* the epic poems *Mahābhārata* (VI,9) and *Rāmāyaṇa* (I,2)].

[331] *Cf.* Simonelli, *Beyond Immortality*, pp. 53-57.

[332] *Bible*, Luke 18:22 and 29-30.

[333] Tolle, *The Power of Now*, pp. 134 and 217.

[334] *Bible*, Acts 8:20.

[335] *U-The Principal Upanishads*, Radhakrishnan reads *bibhrājad etad.*

[336] *Cf. BG* 8,11.

[337] *Cf. UMu* III.2.6.

[338] Lipski, *The Essential Śrī Ānandamayī Mā*, p. 49.

[339] *padmā-sana.*

[340] *Cf.* Simonelli, *Beyond Immortality*, p 109.

---

[341] *Cf. ibid.* pp.30-1.

[342] Metastasio, *L'Olimpiade*, Act II, scene 7, "*Conservate questa bell'opera vostra, eterni dei.*"

[343] *UMu.* III.2.7. *devāś-* (senses) *ca* (and) *sarve* (all) *prati-* (in corresponding) *devatāsu* (deities) *karmāṇi* (the deeds) *vijñānamayaś-* (intellectual) *ca* (and) *ātmā* (self) *pare'* (the Supreme) *vyaye* (Imperishable One) *sarva* (all) *ekī-* (one) *bhavanti* (they become).

[344] *UC.* III.13.1. *tasya*(of this) *ha vā-*(verily) *etasya* (here) *hṛdayasya* (heart) *pañca* (five) *deva-*(gods) *sushayaḥ* (channels).

[345] *VṚ* X.129.6. *arvāg* (after) *devā* (the resplendent beings) *asyá* (of this) *visárjanenā-* (the reation) *thā* (then) *kó* (who) *veda* (knows) *yáta* (from what) *ābabhūva* (began to exist).

[346] *UB* III.4.2.

[347] *VṚ* X.129.4. *sató* (being) *bándhum* (connection) *ásati* (in being) *nír* (non) *avindan* (found) *hṛdí* (in the heart) *pratíshyā* (searching) *kaváyo* (the seers) *manīshā* (with reflection) //

[348] *Bible, Genesis, 1:26,* וַיֹּאמֶר אֱלֹהִים נַעֲשֶׂה אָדָם בְּצַלְמֵנוּ כִּדְמוּתֵנוּ (man, Adam, אדם *'adam;* image = צלם *tselem* - εἰκών eikōn – *imago*; likeness דמות *dĕmuwth);*
27, וַיִּבְרָא אֱלֹהִים אֶת־הָאָדָם בְּצַלְמוֹ בְּצֶלֶם אֱלֹהִים בָּרָא אֹתוֹ זָכָר וּנְקֵבָה בָּרָא אֹתָם׃ (**male =** זכר *zakar*) **and (female** = נקבה *nĕqebah*);
5:2 וַיִּקְרָא אֶת־שְׁמָם אָדָם;
2:7, נפש *nephesh* breathing being; *dust =* עפר *`aphar; inhabited ground =* אדמה *'adamah (cf. Adam,* אדם & אָדָם *'adam red connected to white, cf. Arjuna).*

[349] *Cf.* Pernety, *Dictionnaire Mytho-Hermétique*, Rebis.

[350] *Cf.* Simonelli, *Beyond Immortality*, p. 50 fol.

[351] *UKena* (VII cent. BC) III.2 *na* (not) *vyajānata* (know) *kim* (what) *idam* (this) *ysksham* (spirit).
11abhyadravat (he ran towards) *tasmāt* (from him) *tirodadhe* (disappeared).

[352] Exodus, 3:5 קרב *qarab* to bring near, approach, קֹדֶשׁ *qodesh Sacred set-apart,* קָדַשׁ *qadash that which is separated, namely transcendent.*

[353] The god of Himā-laya (meaning Snow-receptacle), also known as Mount Kailāsa-Śiva's-Pleasure-Seat.

[354] *UKena* III.12 *sa* (he) *tasminn* (in that) *ev-* (same) *ākāśe* (vacuity) *striyam* (woman) *ājagāma* (- Indra - met) *bahu* - (very) *śobhamānām* (beautiful) *umāṁ* (umā) *haimavatīṁ* (daughter of Himavat-the-frost-cladded) [Himalaya = *himá* = snow - *ā-laya* = receptacle. Kailāsa = *kaila* pleasure *āsa* seat] *tāṁ* (her) *ho-* (indeed) *vāca* (asked) *kim* (what) *etad* (this) *yaksham* (supernatural being) *iti* (thus).

[355] *úmā* (*W.* p. 217a) "splendour , light." Also, Pārvatī, the Mountainous, Kālī, the black form of Durgā, the Inaccessible, Gaurī, the Shining, or Satī.

[356] The name Umā may stem from her mother's warning, "*u mā*," meaning "*O* (*u*) [little daughter], *don't* (*mā*) [practice yogic austerities]."

[357] *úmā* (*w.* p. 217a) "perhaps fr. √*ve* (p. 1013b), cf. √*ūy* (p. 221b), to weave, ... (fig. to string ... together artificially... make into a ... web-like covering)."

[358] *UKena* 4.1 *sā* (she) *brahmeti* (Brahman thus) *hovāca* (said) *brahmaṇo* (of

Brahman) *vā* (for sure) *etad* (this) *vijaye* (in the superiority) *mahīyadhvam* (you have been exalted) *iti* (indeed).

[359] "The gods are the five channels of perception of this heart." *UC.* III.13.1.

[360] *UKena* 4.4 *vyadyutadā* (lightning) *itīn* (like) *nyamīmishadā* (the winking of an eye) *ity* (like) *adhidaivatam* (as in regards to the gods).
5 *ath-* (now) *ādhyātmam* (in regards to the self) *yadedtat* (namely) *gacchatīva* (tends towards) *ca* (and) *manaḥ* (mind) *anena* (because) *caitad* (and this) *upasmaraty* (remembers) *abhīkshṇaṁ* (always) *saṁkalpaḥ* (intentions).

[361] Müller, *The Six* ... p. 53.

[362] *UB* III.4.2.

[363] *kāla-kūṭa cf.* Simonelli, *Beyond Immortality*, p. 60 fol.

[364] *Naṭa Rāja*, Dancer King or *Nāṭa Rāja*, Dance King

[365] *Kāla,* Death, the black Poisonous-serpent-of-Time. *Cf. W*. p. 278a, 2.

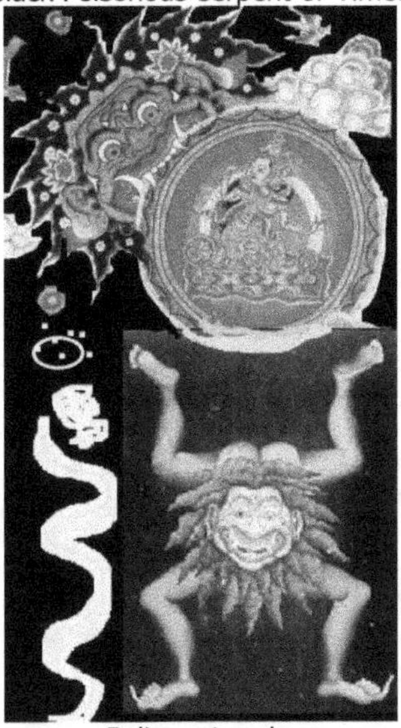

Bali, postcards.

[366] Jonah 1:17.

[367] דָּג *dag* = fish, from דָּגָה *dagah = to cover.*

[368] The moon *Candra,* reflecting the light of the Sun, reflects on the Ocean of possibilities.

[369] *Bible*, John 8:23.

[370] *Bible*, John 14:6.

[371] *Bible,* Matthew 22:37, cf. Luke 10:27.

[372] *Bible*, Matthew 19:19 and 22:39, also Mark 12:31.

373 *Cf. UK* IV.8.

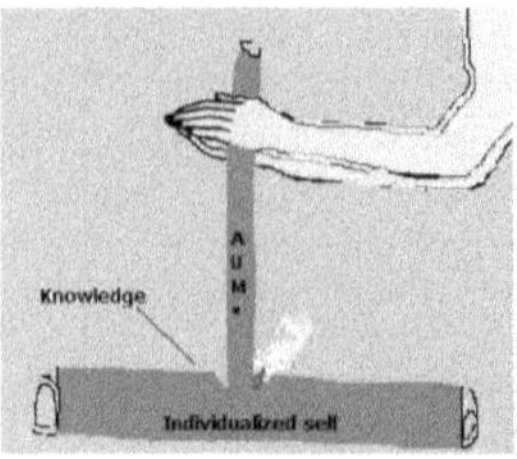

1

2

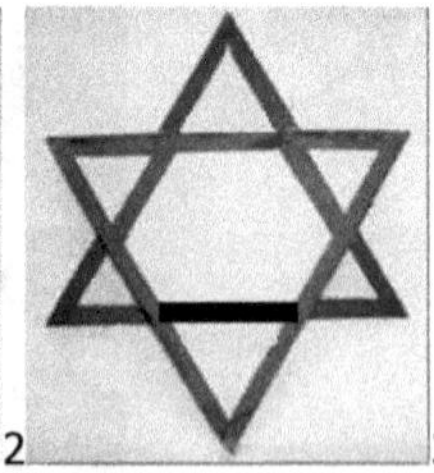
3

1. The stick (*araṇi*) were produced by the woods of the *samī* (labor) tree, *Prosopis Spicigera* or *Mimosa Suma* and the *aśvattha* tree, the holy fig tree, *Ficus religiosa – Pipal.*
2. Erotic metaphor: Tantric figures of consciousness-sub-ject (Śiva) – consciousness-*of*-ob-ject (Kālī) synthesis. Brass (China 2002).
3. Geometrical metaphor: the hexagram as the union of the pair.

374 *UŚ* I.14. *sva*-(one's own) *deham* (body) *araṇiṃ* (the fire friction stick) *kṛtvā* (making) *praṇavam* (the syllable AUM) *co'* (and) *ttarāraṇim* (the upper fire friction stick) / *dhyāna*- (profound meditation) *nirmathanābhyāsāt* (churning being in the center) *devam* (transcendent) *paśyen* (one may see) *nigūḍhavat* (as hidden).

375 *Cf.* Simonelli, *Beyond Immortality,* Chapter *Māṇḍūkya Upanishad.*

376 *UK* IV.8 (II.I.8) Same verse in *VṚ* III.29.2. (*sudhitogarbhiṇīshu*); *cf. VS* I.II.3.7.*araṇyor*- (within both fire-sticks) *nihito* (placed) *jāta*- (all) *vedā* (knower) *garbha* (foetus) *iva* (like) *subhṛto* (well borne) *garbhiṇībhiḥ* (by pregnant women) / *dive* (day) *diva* (after day) *īḍyo* (to be praised) *jāgṛvadbhir*- (by the awakened) *havishmadbhir*- (offering oblations) *manushyebhir*- (by men) *agniḥ* (fire of knowledge) /
etad (this) *vai* (verily) *tat* (that) /

377 *Cf. UKai* 1, 2.

378 πονηρός *ponēros translated as evil i.e.* "deliver us from evil" *Bible,* Luke 11:4.

379 Experimentation πειρασμός *peirasmos (commonly translated as temptation).*

380 *Bible,* Matthew 26:41 and Mark 14:38, pay attention γρηγορέω *grēgoreō,* from ἐγείρω *egeirō* to arouse from the sleep of death; experience πειρασμός *peirasmos,* from πειράζω *peirazō to experiment.*

381 *Bible,* Luke 18:1.

382 *UC.* III.13.1. *tasya*(of this) *ha vā*-(verily) *etasya* (here) *hṛdayasya* (heart) *pañca* (five) *deva*-(gods) *sushayaḥ* (channels).

383 *Cf. Bible,* Matthew 13:31, 17:20; Mark 4:31; Luke 13:19, 17:6; *UC* III.14.3.

384 *Cf. UMaitrī* VI.38; *UB* V.6.1; *UC* III.14.3 & VIII.1.1; *UK* IV.12 (II.I.12).

385 *UB* III.4.2. *Cf. Ibid.* IV.4.18 and *UKe* I.2.

386 Witness *sākṣin. W.* p. 1198a.

387 *Cf. W.,* 397c *cin-mātra, cin* "in compound for *cit.*" *cit*" *cl.1.* ... to perceive, fix the mind upon, attend to, be attentive, observe ... to aim at, intend, to... care for... to understand, comprehend, know... to cause to comprehend... to observe... be intent upon... *A1.* ... to form an idea in the mind, **be conscious of**, understand, comprehend, think, reflect upon... **to... have consciousness of**... *mfn....* thinking... *f.* thought, intellect... pure Thought" (394-7 bold is ours). *mātra* "elementary matter... measure... *n.* the full or simple measure

of anything, the whole or totality, the one thing and no more, often = nothing but, entirely, only" (804bc).

[388] *Bible*, Revelation 1:5 Ἰησοῦ Χριστοῦ ὁ μάρτυς ὁ πιστός ὁ πρωτότοκος ἐκ τῶν νεκρῶν καὶ ὁ ἄρχων τῶν βασιλέων τῆς γῆς faithful [πιστός *pistòs*] witness [μάρτυς *mártus*]

[389] *Ibid.* 3:14 ὁ Ἀμήν ὁ μάρτυς ὁ πιστὸς καὶ ἀληθινός ἡ ἀρχὴ τῆς κτίσεως τοῦ θεοῦ. faithful [πιστός *pistòs*], true [ἀληθινός *alhethinòs*] witness [μάρτυς *mártus*].

[390] *Koran*, The Constellations 85:9, وَاللَّهُ عَلَىٰ كُلِّ شَيْءٍ شَهِيدٌ. God (*Allah*) witness (*shahid*) unto everything (*ala kul shi*)

[391] *Koran*, Women 4:3, لَّٰكِنِ اللَّهُ يَشْهَدُ بِمَا أَنْزَلَ إِلَيْكَ أَنْزَلَهُ بِعِلْمِهِ وَمَشْهُودٍ وَشَاهِدٍ وَالْمَلَائِكَةُ يَشْهَدُونَ وَكَفَىٰ بِاللَّهِ شَهِيدًا (166).

[392] *UY* 10.6 in Varenne, *Yoga..*, p. 221.

[393] del Vasto, *Return to the Source*, p. 93.

[394] *Cf. UKai* 1&2.

[395] *UK* II.20 (I.2.20) *aṇor-* (of the subtle) *anīyān* (smaller) *mahato* (of the great) *mahīyān* (greater) *ātmāsya* (Self this) *jantor-* (of the creature) *nihito* (fixed) *guhāyām* (in the secret of the heart) /

[396] *UB* IV.3.36 *purusha* (person) *ebhyo'* (these) *ṅgebhyaḥ* (from limbs) *sampramucya* (being free from)

[397] *UK* II.20 (I.2.20) *am-* (that) *akratuḥ* (desireless) *paśyati* (realizes) *vīta-* (free from) *śoko* (sorrow) *dhātu-* (of the five senses and of the properties of the elements perceived by them) *prasādān-* (through the stillness) *mahimānam-* (majesty) *ātmanaḥ* (of the Self)

[398] *ámbara*.

[399] *Cf.* Joshi: *Gravitational collapse ...*

[400] Dante Alighieri, *La divina commedia*, Inferno, V, 4-6, p. 41. *Cf.* Yama in *W.* p. 846a.

Gustave Doré, illustration of Minos.

[401] Dante Alighieri, *La divina commedia*, Inferno, VII, 11 fol., p. 109.

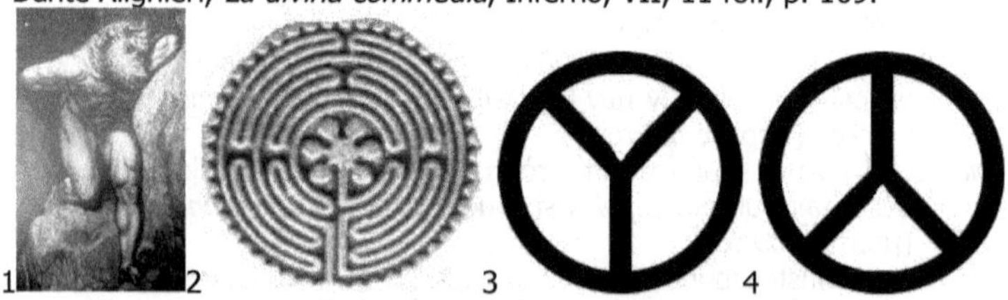

1) Gustave Doré, illustration of the Minotaur. 2) The Labyrinth. 2) Life's symbol. 3) Death's symbol.

[402] *Bible*, Luke 24:5.

[403] Chevalier, *Dictionnaire des Symboles*, vol. 4, p. 401. "*Visita Interiora Terrae Rectificando Invenies Occultum Lapidem*" (V.I.T.R.I.O.L.)

[404] Scaligero, *La forza della resurrezione*. "*Forza... il nostro essere liberi ci dà la possibilità di essere... dalla parte dell'essere che in noi sceglie la Verità di contro alla menzogna. La scelta è importante perché apre il varco alla forza del Principio che sceglie: la Forza di Colui che 'avanza senza combattere,' in quanto ha scelto non secondo la brama, ma secondo relazione d'Amore. È escluso Lucifero dall'anima: questa esclusione è la possibilità dell'anima cosciente che nella percezione sensoria ha lo schema della massima indipendenza dell'Io dal mondo sensibile.*"

[405] Luther, *Luther's Works, Volume 48: Letters I*, p. 282, August 1, 1521 Letter 501 to Melanchthon "*Esto peccator et pecca fortiter, sed fortius fide et gaude in Christo, qui victor est peccati, mortis et mundi (be a sinner and sin strongly, but believe even more strongly and rejoice in Christ, who is victor over sin, death and the world).*"

[406] Scaligero, *La forza della resurrezione*, "*infatti i processi sensibili dell'organo della percezione non hanno nulla a che fare con il percepire medesimo. Ma le deità luciferiche operano a che l'uomo ascenda dal sensibile, non discenda in esso... è invece la forza che discende... Questa capacità di discendere porta ad affrontare la tenebra sino ad un esaurimento di lotta, da cui scaturisce, come prima virtú di relazione, la compassione. Noi possiamo dire il Sacro Amore.*"

[407] *Cf.* Schaff, *Creeds of Christendom*. "*Descendit ad inferna; tertia die resurrexit a mortuis.*"

[408] Scaligero, *La forza della resurrezione*. "*Possiamo discendere nel profondo di noi, sprofondarci, sino a toccare le basi della vita... Cosí, con determinati pensieri intensamente vissuti, scendiamo nelle profondità di noi stessi: questi pensieri conducono in sé le forze che vincono l'egoismo.*"

[409] *UK* I.14 (I.I.14) *atho* (and) *pratishṭhāṃ* (the state of rest) *viddhi* (know) *tvam-* (you) *etaṃ* (this) *nihitaṃ* (placed) *guhāyām* (in the cave of the heart).

[410] *VṚ* X.129.1. *n-āsad āsīn nó sád āsīt*

[411] *UT.* II. 7. *ānīd* (was breathing) *avātáṃ* (windless) *svadháyā* (by self-power) *tád* (that) *ékaṃ* (One Thing)

[412] *VṚ* X.129.2. *ná* (nor) *mṛtyúr* (death) *āsīd* (was) *amṛtaṃ* (immortality) *ná*

(nor) *tárhi* (then) *ná* (no) *rātryā* (night) *áhna* (day) *āsīt* (was) *praketáḥ* (knowledge) / *ānīd* (was breathing) *avātáṃ* (windless) *svadháyā* (by self-power) *tád* (that) *ékaṃ* (One Thing) *tásmād* (therefore) *dhānyán* (indeed other seed) *ná* (no) *paráḥ* (beyond) *kíṃ ca-* (further) *n-* (none) *āsa* (was) // *Cf.* the "wind (רוח- *ruach*) from God" *Genisis* 1:2.

413 *VṚ* X.129.4. *sató* (being) *bándhum* (connection) *ásati* (in being) *nír* (non) *avindan* (found) *hṛdí* (in the heart) *pratíshyā* (searching) *kaváyo* (the seers) *manīshā* (with reflection) //

The "Priest King," *ṛshi-kavi* seer, Mohenjo-daro (Mound of the Dead) in the Indus Valley (2600–1900 BC), National Museum, Karachi, Pakistan (Wikipedia image: Creative Commons Attribution-Share Alike 3.0 Unported license. http://en.wikipedia.org/wiki/File:Mohenjo-daro_Priesterk%C3%B6nig.jpeg).

414 *Bible*, Luke 23: 32-33, 39, 42-43, the malefactor, [Greek: κακοῦργος *kakourgos* (κακός *kakos* = evil + ἔργον *ergon* = deed)] - (Latin: *malum* = evil + *factor* = doer) the evil-doer becomes a *Good thief* (Latin: *Bonus latro*) [*cf.* Vulgate: *nequam* (32) = dishonest and *latrones* (33) = thieves]. However, this Saint is not officially commemorated as such in the Catholic calendars. Transcendent heaven = παράδεισος *paradeisos*.

Pedro de Orrente, La crucifixión, óleo sobre lienzo (Madrid, Museo del Prado). Wikimedia Commons Public domain , File: Orrente-crucifixion.jpg, Source http://www.museodelprado.es/coleccion/galeria-on-line/galeria-on-line/obra/la-crucifixion-7/; http://commons.wikimedia.org/wiki/File:Orrente-crucifixion.jpg.

415 *W.* 883a.

416 Natarajan, *Timeless in Time*, p. 1$^{n. 3 \& 6}$.

417 *saṃnyāsins*, also called *sādhus* or *śramaṇas*

[418] *W.* pp. 7a, 485b and 767a.
There are two branches of Aghorī:
1) a subdivision of the Gorakhnāthīs [(Cowherd-lord) established by Gorakshanātha [Cow-ray (*go*) eye (*aksha*) powerful-master (*nāth*) (XI century?)] who carry a skull (***kapāla***) as a bowl, and
2) the independent Bābās (father) who carry a coconut bowl.

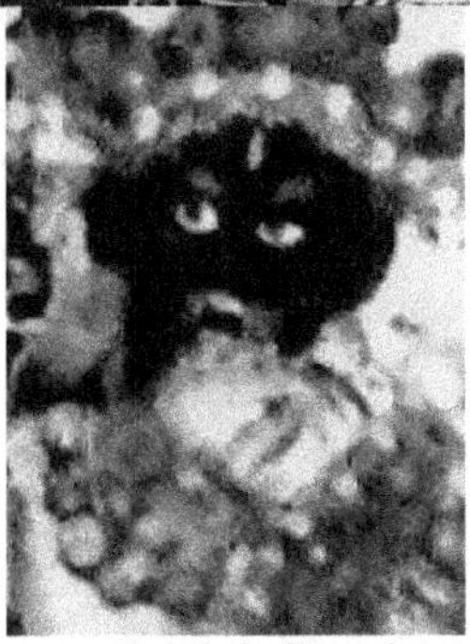

Bhairava, and details (Nepal Art 1970)

[419] Hartsuiker, *Sādhus*, pp. 36 and *cf.* 17.
[420] *Cf.* Ratti, *Secrets of the Samurai*, pp. 118-125.
[421] *Cf.* Gill, *Dictionary of Native American Mythology*, pp.121-22.
[422] The Great Beast 666, English occultist (1875-1947) Crowley, *Confessions*, p. 3.
[423] (1869-1916) *Cf.* Moynahan, *Rasputin: The Saint Who Sinned.*
[424] Already quoted: Augustine, *In Epistolam Joannis Ad Parthos Tractatus Decem*, VII, 8. "*Dilige* (love), *et* (and) *quod* (that which) *vis* (you want) *fac* (do)."
[425] Eckhart, *Meister Eckhart: A Modern translation*, p. 130.
[426] *UAb Amṛta*-(immortal-nectar)-*bindu* (point-drop) *Upanishad*, mantra 18.

[427] John of the Cross, "*ya por aquí no hay camino, que para el justo no'ay ley*" on the attached 1) engraving.

1  2 

1) John of the Cross, engraving of "The Mount of Perfection."
2) *Cf.* Tibet, Mt. Kailāsa (*kaila* pleasure *āsa* seat?), 19th century Tibetan embroidery depiction on silk (public domain photo, Wikipedia). Corresponding to the mythical Axis Mundi (Hindu: Mt. Su-Meru "Great-Mountain," Tibetan, Bön: Kang Tise "Snow water peak," Buddhist: Kang Rimpoche "Precious Snow"), abode of Lord Śiva and his consort Pārvatī with nearby lakes Rakshastal (*rakshas* demon *tal* accomplish) and Manasarovar (*mānasa* spiritual *sarovara* lake).

[428] Ramana Maharshi, *The Spiritual teaching ...*, p. 36.

[429] *UB* IV.4.22. *etam* (this one) *eva* (verily) *viditvā* (being conscious of) *munir* (ascetic) *bhavati* (becomes) *etam... eshaṇe* (desires) *eva* (verily)... *neti* (not so) *nety* (not so) *ātmā* (Self) *agṛhyaḥ* (incomprehensible) *na* (not) *hi* (thus) *gṛhate* (be comprehended) *aśīryah* (imperishable) *na* (not) *hi* (thus) *śīryate* (destroyed) *esaṅgaḥ* (unattached) *na* (not) *hi* (thus) *sajyate* (does not attach himself) *asito* (unbound) *na* (not) *vyathate* (agitated in the mind) *na* (not) *rishyati* (harmed) *etam* (this one) *u* (furthermore) *haivaite* (indeed these two) *na* (not) *tarata* (subdue) *iti* (thus) *ataḥ* (certainly) *pāpam* (evil) *akaravam* (I have done) *iti* (thus) *ataḥ* (certainly) *kalyāṇam* (good) *akaravam* (I have done) *iti* (thus) *ubhe* (both) *u* (also) *haivaisha* (indeed he) *ete* (these) *tarati* (overcomes) *nainam̊* (not this) *kṛtākṛte* (he has done and not done) *tapataḥ* (torment).

[430] *UB* V.14.8 *evaṁ* (indeed) haivaivaṁ- (thus as if indeed) *vid* (knows) *yady* (if) *api* (although) *bahv* (many) *iva* (as) *pāpaṁ* (evil sins) *kurute* (commits) *sarvam* (all) eva (certainly) *tat* (it) *sampsāya* (consumes) *śuddhaḥ* (cleansed) *pūto'* (pure) *jaro'* (ageless) *mṛtaḥ* (immortal) *sambhavati* (becomes). *gāyatrī-vid* = the knower of the hymn of life (*gāyatra cf. UC* II.11.1-2)

[431] III.17. *tasya* (of him) *kāryaṃ* (duty) *na* (not) *vidyate* (exists)

[432] Scaligero, *Manuale...*, p. 58. "*Un impulso di bontà o di moralità, quando è*

autentico, non domina l'Io, perché è espressione dell'Io... Anche l'uso di un impulso morale può divenire illecito, se non è la decisione dell'io, bensì della brama del corpo."

433 Fadiman, *Essential Sufism*, p. 86. *Cf.* identical expressions in St. Francis Xavier, Caswall, *Hymns...*, VIX, p. 152.

434 *Bible*, Romans 3:19-20.

435 *Bible*, Matthew 22:13; *cf.* 8:12; 13:42, 50; 24:51; 25:30; & Luke 13:28.

436 *Bible*, 1Corinthians 13:11.

437 *W.* 311c

438 By Vyasa, *Mahā-bhārata = The Great War of the Descendants of the Bearer of Oblation*," 9th c. BC.

439 *Bible*, Matthew 8:22.

440 *BG* II.19 *ya* (he) *enaṃ* (this) *vetti* (views) *hantāraṃ* (killer) *yaś* (he) *cainaṃ* (and this) *manyate* (considers) *hatam* (killed) / *ubhau* (the two) *tau* (those) *na* (not) *vijānīto* (know) *nāyaṃ* (not this) *haṃti* (kills) *na* (not) *hanyate* (is killed) //

441 *Bible*, I Corinthians 7, 30.

442 *Cf. W.* p. 90a.

443 *VṚ* X.45.1. *divas* (the sky) *pari* (from) *prathamaṃ* (the first time) *jajñe* (was born) *agnir* (fire).

444 Augustine, *Confessions*, 1.1.1 "*inquietum est cor nostrum donec requiescat in te.*"

445 Sartre, *Being and Nothingness*, p. 549 & *cf.* 509.

446 *VṚ* X. 90. *Cf. Bible*, Daniel 2:32 to 45.

447 *BG* 4.13 *cātur-* (the four) *varṇyaṃ* (castes) *mayā* (by me) *sṛshṭaṃ* (were projected) *guṇa-* (of quality) *karma-* (of actions) *vibhāgaśaḥ* (by division) / *tasya* (of it) *kartāram-* (maker) *api* (also) *māṃ* (me) *viddhy-* (know) *akartāram-* (non-acting) *avyayam* (unchangeable)
14 *na* (no) *māṃ* (me) *karmāṇi* (actions) *liṃpanti* (do affect) *na* (no) *me* (of me) *karma-* (of action) *phale* (for the fruit) *spṛhā* (desire).

448 Sartre, *Being and Nothingness*, p. 60.

449 See § 1; *cf. Bible*, John 18:38 Τί ἐστιν ἀλήθεια *Quid est veritas.*

450 *Chi fuor li maggior tui?* Who were your ancestors? Asks proudly Farinata degli Uberti to Dante, La d*ivina commedia*, Inferno X, 42

451 *UC.* IV.4.1 *satya-kāmo* (Longing-after-truth) *ha* (verily, then) *jābālo* (son of Girly) *ja-* (born) *bālām* (Girl of sixteen) *mātaram* (mother) *āmantrayāṁ* (address) *cakre* (he did) *brahmacaryam* (the life of a celibate religious student) *bhavati* (revered one) *vivatsyāmi* (I wish to live)
3 *sa* (he) *ha* (then) *haridrumataṁ* (in-light-dissolving-exultant) *gautamam* (highest-cow-herder) *ety-* (went) *ovāca* (said) *brahmacaryam* (the life of a celibate religious student) *bhagavati* (o holy one) *vatsyāmi* (I wish to live) *upeyām* (may I approach you) *bhagavantam* (reverend sir) *iti* (thus)
4 *ta* (he) *hovāca* (said) *kiṁ-* (of what) *gotro* (ancestry) *nu* (now then) *saumya* (my dear) *asīti* (are) *sa* (he) *hovāca* (replied) *nā-* (not) *ham* (I) *etad* (this) *veda* (know) *bhoḥ* (Sir) *yad-* (of what) *gotro'* (ancestry) *ham* (I) *asmi* (am) *apṛccham* (I asked) *mātaram* (mother) *sā* (she) mā (me) *pratyabravīt* (answered) *bahv* (in many) *ahaṁ* (I) *carantī* (works) *paricāriṇī* (serving others) *yauvane* (in my youth) *tvām* (you) *alabhe* (I got) *sā-* (such) *ham* (I) *etan* (this) *na* (not) *veda* (know) *yad-* (of

what) *gotras* (ancestry) tvam (you) *asi* (are) *jabālā* (Girly) *tu* (however) *nāmā-* (by name) *ham* (I) *asmi* (am) *satyakāmo* (Longing-after-truth) *nāma* (named) *tvam* (you) *asīti* (are) *so'* (thus) *haṁ* (I) *satyakāmo* (Longing-after-truth) *jābālo'* (son of Girly) *smi* (am) *bhoḥ* (Sir) *iti* (thus)
5 *taṁ* (to him) *hovāca* (he said) *naitad* (not so) *abrāhmaṇo* (not a Brahmin) *vivaktum* (to speak) *arhati* (can) *samidham* (sacrificial fire) *saumya* (my dear) *āhara* (bring) *upa* (by the side) *tvā* (you) *neshye* (initiate) *na* (not) *satyād* (from the truth) *agā* (deviated) *iti* (thus).

452 Dalrymple, *Nine Lives...*, pp. 55.

453 *Vajrasūcika* (Pinpointed thunderbolt) *Upanishad UV* 3. *na* (not) *jīva* (the living being) – 4. *deho* (a physical individual) – 5. *jātir* (birth) – 6. *jñānam* (knowledge) -7. *karma* (work) – 9. *dhārmiko* (pious acts) *brāhmaṇa* (Brāhmaṇa, one who has divine knowledge) *iti* (therefore)... vā (verily) *brāhmaṇo* (the Brāhmaṇa) ... *ātmānam* (the Self) *advitīyam* (without a second) *jāti-* (birth) *guṇa-* (quality) *kriyā-* (action) *hīnam* (devoid of difference). Meaningful is the case of the Dalit Hari Das, an untouchable dancer in Kerala who, every year, for a period of three months, is worshipped by Brahmins while he dances representing an incarnation of Vishṇu (*cf.* Dalrymple, *Nine Lives...*, pp. 50-53).

454 Natarajan, *Timeless in Time*, p. 104-5 and 109[n.V-4], 14; and Brunton, *A Search in Secret India*, pp. 290-1.

455 Lipski, *The Essential Śrī Ānandamayī Mā*, pp. 104-105.

456 Heidegger, *Being and Time*, II, I, H. 235-267, pp. 279-311.

457 Natarajan, *Timeless in Time*, pp. 81 and 107-108[n.8].

458 *UK* III. 5-8 (I.3.5-8).

459 Plato, *Phaedrus* , 246.

460 For this concept *cf.* Simonelli, *Beyond Immortality*, PART III Epistemology and Cosmology

461 *Bible*, Genesis, 1:28.

462 *Cf.* Schopenhauer, *The world as will and representation.*

463 *UMu.* III.2.7. *devāś-* (senses) *ca* (and) *sarve* (all) *prati-* (in corresponding) *devatāsu* (deities) ... *ekī-* (one) *bhavanti* (they become).

464 *UC.* III.13.1.

465 Lipski, *The Essential Śrī Ānandamayī Mā*, p. 95.

466 *Cf. Bible*, Genesis 4:4.

467 Lipski, *The Essential Śrī Ānandamayī Mā*, p. 19.

468 *Cf. Bible*, Genesis, 4:1-25.

[469] Tolle, *The power of Now*," p. 195.

At Lincoln Center, NY City, from the play, within the Metropolitan Opera, to Manhattan's stage offered by the Moon.

[470] *Cf. VṚ* V.63.1 *vṛshṭír* (rain) *madhumat* (rich in honey) *pinvate* (overflows) *divaḥ* (from heaven); 2. *rādho* (gift) *amṛtatvam* (immortality); 5. *payasyā* (milk).

[471] *Cf. UC* II.3.1 & 15.1 "One should acknowledge as rain the fivefold song... while it rains, it is the upper-song *vṛshṭau* (in rain) *pañcavidhaṃ* (fivefold) *sāmo-* (song) *pāsīta* (one should acknowledge)... *varshati* (while it rains) *sa* (he) *udgītha* (upper-song)." *Cf. UMaitrī*, VI.4 "The upper-song is the syllable... AUM *udgīthaḥ* (upper-song) *sa* (he) *praṇavo* (syllable)... *aum* (AUM)."

[472] *W.* p. 1011c.

[473] *Cf. W.* p, 606b, *parjánya*, "rain... rain personified or the god of rain (... Indra)," from √*pṛc* "to mix, mingle, put together with... unite, join... to increase, augment" (p. 645b).
Cf. UMaitrī, VI.4 "The upper-song is the syllable... AUM *udgīthaḥ* (upper-song) *sa* (he) *praṇavo* (syllable)... *aum* (AUM)."

[474] *VṚ* X.29.4 and *VA* 20.76.4 *indra* (Indra)... *āgan* (came) *mitro* (friend) *na* (like) *satya* (true) *urugāya* (wide-striding) *bhṛtyā* (to support) *anne* (in food) *samasya* (made entirely) yad- (since) *asanmanīshāḥ* (every thought).

[475] *Cf. W.* p. 167b. *Indriyá*, the senses, the organs of the senses, the "power, force, the quality which belongs especially to the mighty indra."

[476] *UB.* 12. *prāṇo* (the vital breath) ... *sa* (he) *indraḥ* (Indra, the Conqueror) *sa* (he) *esho'* (this no) *sapatnaḥ* (rival) *dvitīyo* (the second, the other) *vai* (verily) *sapatnaḥ* (rival).

[477] Damasio, *Self Comes to Mind*, p. 170. *Cf. UB* (I.3.1-7; I. 5. 22; VI.1-7), *UK* (III.3), *UM* (3 and 4), *UMaitrī* (2.6), *UP* (II.1 to 13).

[478] Pio, *Epistolario* Letters vol. I, 22 ottobre 1918 "*Tutti i sensi interni ed esterni, non che le stesse facoltà dell'anima si trovarono in una quiete indescrivibile.*"

[479] IV.24. *brahmā-* (the Transcendent Spirit) *rpaṇaṃ* (oblation) *brahma* (the Transcendent Spirit) *havir-* (the offered) *brahmā-* (of the Transcendent Spirit) *gnai* (in the fire) *brahmaṇā* (by the Transcendent Spirit) *hutam* (offered).

[480] *VṚ* X.90.6. *púrusheṇa* (with the Cosmic being) *havíshā* (as sacrificial butter)
7. *yajñám* (as oblation) ... *púrushaṃ* (the Cosmic being).
15. *púrusham* (the Cosmic being) *paśúm* (as sacrificial victim). & *cf.* 130. 1.

[481] *UC* III.16.1 *purosho* (the person) *vāva* (indeed) *yajñaḥ* (sacrifice).

[482] *UMaitrī* II.6. *purushaḥ* (the Cosmic being) *so* (he) *gnir* (the divine-flame) *vaiśvānaraḥ* (digestive-fire-common-to-all).

[483] *UB* I.4.5. *sṛshṭāṃ* (creation) *hāsyaitasyām* (indeed of this one in this) *bhavati* (becomes) *ya* (who) *evaṃ* (thus) *veda* (knows).

[484] *Cf.* Vidyananda Videh, p. 7 *fol.*

[485] Hindu saint and mystic (1896-1982).

[486] Lipski, *The Essential Śrī Ānandamayī Mā*, p. 15 and 19.

[487] *VṚ* I.1.5. *agnír* (Divine-flame) *hótā* (sacrificer) *kaví-*(of the wise bard) *kratuḥ* (power) *satyáś* (the truthful) *citrá-* (bright) *śravas-* (glory) *amaḥ* (most)/ *devó* (resplendent being) *devébhir* (with the resplendent beings) *ā-* (here) *gamat* (may come).

[488] *VṚ* X.7.6. *svayáṃ* (to yourself) *yajasva* (sacrifice)... *deva* (o resplendent being).

[489] *Cf. UB* I.2.1-7 & 4.1-3.

[490] *W.* p. 887c. *UB* I.2.3.

[491] Genesis 1:5.

[492] Plato, *The Apology*, 28.38a, p.132. ὁ (*o-* an) δὲ (*dè* - thus) ἀνεξέταστος (*avexétastos* - unexamined) βίος (*bíos* - life) οὐ (*ou* - not) βιωτὸς (*biōtòs* - is living) ἀνθρώπῳ (*anthrṓpǭ* - for a human).

[493] *Bible*, Exodus 21:23-25, *cf.* Matthew 5:38.

[494] Natarajan, *Timeless in Time*, p. 85.

[495] *Bible*, Matthew 5:44.

[496] *Bible*, Luke 23:34.

[497] Plato, *Four texts on Socrates... Citro*, 49.

[498] *W. pārtha* (fr. *pṛthā*) metron.[ymic]... of Arjuna (621c); *pṛthā* mother of... Arjuna (645c) = *pṛth* to extend... (cf. √ prath) (645c); *pṛthi* (621c, 646a); *prath* "to extend over i.e. shine upon, give light to" (678c); *cf. pṛthu* extensive, fire (646b).

[499] Lipski, *The Essential Śrī Ānandamayī Mā*, p. 105.

[500] *W.* p. 301a, √*kṛ* to act, to do, to *cr*-eate, "[cf. Hib. *caraim*, "I perform..." Old Germ. *karawan*, "to prepare"; Mod. Germ. *gar*, "prepared (as food)"; Lat. *creo...*, ceremonia; κραίνω, κρόνος]" Greek *krainō*, to do *kronos*, old.

[501] Natarajan, *Timeless in Time...*, p. 13[n. 4] quoted from Narasimmha Swami B.V.: *Papers*.

[502] *Cf. UB* IV.3.1[(n.99)] and *UKai* 1. *Cf. Mahābhārata* VI,9 and *Rāmāyaṇa* I,2.

[503] Confucius [*Kǒng* (孔) Master (*Fūzǐ* 子): *Kǒngfūzǐ* (孔夫子)], *The Analects*, 2..22 and 12..7.

[504] The three Pyramids of Giza in Egypt.

(Sphinx and Pyramids, detail on a 2002 Egyptian 10 Piastres banknote).

[505] Kant, *Grundlegung zur Metaphysik,* Zweiter Abschnitt. Übergang von der populären sittlichen Weltweisheit zur Metaphysik der Sitten, *"Handle nur nach derjenigen Maxime, durch die du zugleich wollen kannst, dass sie ein allgemeines Gesetz werde"* (AA IV, 421/ GMS, BA 52) and *"Handle nach der Maxime, die sich selbst zugleich zum allgemeinen Gesetze machen kann* (AA IV, 436/ GMS, BA 81). *Cf. Fundamental Principles of the Metaphysic of Morals,* p. 268.

[506] *varteyaṃ* optative √ vṛt *W.* p. 1009a "to be or exist or live at a partic. time, be alive or present."

[507] *W. vártman* p. 925c "*n.* the track or rut of a wheel , path , road way , course (lit. and fig.)." √ *vṛt.*

[508] *anuvartante W.* "anu- √ vṛt p, 39a to obey, respect, imitate."

[509] See our *Beyond Immortality.* Some narrowly interpret this stanza as referring only to specific Vedic sacrifices.

[510] *W. saṃ-graha* p. 1129b.

[511] *cikīrshur W.* p. 301a √ *kṛ* to do "Desid... to wish to make or do, intend to do, design, intend, begin, strive after.

[512] *dhyāna – chán – seon - zen.*

[513] *Cf.* Cleary, *Instant Zen,* p. 136.

[514] *Bible,* Romans 3:27-28.

[515] Nagamma, *Letters from Sri Ramanasramam,* (48) JAPA, TAPA AND THE LIKE, The Forty Verses, Supplement, verse 33, pp. 81-82. *Cf. UKai* 24.

[516] pra-kṛti (*W.* p. 654a) *f.* "making... before...", the original... form or... substance... nature... which evolve the whole visible world... a goddess, the personified will of the Supreme in the creation... (...*śakti* or personified energy or wife of ... the Supreme Being)... (in *sāṃkhya* phil.) an ingredient or constituent of *prakṛti* [the original producer of (or rather passive power of creating) the material world ... Nature (distinguished from *puruṣa* , Spirit...), chief quality of all existing beings (viz. *sattva, rajas,* and *tamas* i.e. goodness, passion, and darkness, or virtue, foulness, and ignorance."

[517] *púruṣa* (*W.* p. 637a) "the Supreme Being or Soul of the universe... mount *meru."*

[518] *guṇá* (*W.* p. 357a) "quality, peculiarity, attribute or property... attribute of the 5 elements (each ... has its own ... quality ... as well as organ of sense; thus 1. ether ... sound ... ear... 2... air... tangibility...skin... 3. Fire... shape... eye... 4. water ... flavour ... tongue... 5. earth ... smell... nose... characteristic of all created things (... twenty-four guṇas ... shape... savour... odour... tangibility... number,,, dimension... severalty... conjunction... disjunction... remoteness... proximity... weight... fluidity...

viscidity... sound... knowledge... pleasure... pain... desire... aversion... effort... merit... demerit... self-reproductive quality)... good quality, virtue... 'power, might'... (consistency , elegance of expression , &c).

519 *Sattva W.* p. 1135b, "*n.* ... being, existence, entity, reality ... true essence, nature, disposition of mind, character... spiritual essence, spirit, mind... good sense, wisdom, magnanimity."

520 *rájas* (W. p= 863b) "*n...* coloured or dim space... the sphere of vapour or mist, region of clouds, atmosphere, air, firmament... the whole expanse of heaven or sky, divided into a lower and upper stratum... darkness... impurity... 'darkening' quality, passion, emotion, affection."
tejas (*W.* p. 454b) "= *rajas* (passion)."

521 *támas* (*W.* p. 438a) "*n.* darkness, gloom... 'led into darkness', deprived of the eye's light or sight... the darkness of hell, hell or a particular division of hell... the obscuration of the sun or moon."
a-vidyā (*W.* p. 108c) "spiritual ignorance."

522 *kárman* (W. p. 258c) "n. ... √*kṛ* ... act, action... special duty... religious act or rite (as sacrifice, oblation...)... work, labour, activity... action consisting in motion... product , result , effect... organ of sense... (or of action» *karme*ndriya*)... former act as leading to inevitable results, fate (as the certain consequence of acts in a previous life)."

523 *Cf.* Leopardi, *Tutte le opere, La ginestra,"Qui su l'arida schiena / Del formidabil monte / Sterminator Vesevo, /La qual null'altro allegra arbor né fiore,"* "Here on the arid back / of the formidable mountain / Vesuvian Exterminator, / which nothing else cheers neither flower nor tree."

Top: Inside of the Vesuvius' crater. Bottom: Ruins of Herculaneum destroyed by that volcano during the eruption of 79 AD.

524 Hume, *An abstract of A treatise*, p. 468f.

525 *Bible*, Matthew 18:6-7, σκανδαλίζω *skandalizō = I scandalize.*

526 *Bible*, Matthew, 6:25, 27, 32, 34.

527 *BG.* II.48 *yogasthaḥ* (in a state of union) *kurū* (perform) *karmāṇī* (actions)

saṃgaṃ (attachment) *tyaktvā* (having rejected *siddhayasiddhayoḥ* (in success in non success) *samo* (same) *bhūtvā* (be).

[528] *Bible*, Matthew, 22:37.

[529] Martin Luther, 5.311. "*Fides enim in Christum facit eum in me vivere et moveri et agere.*"

[530] *Koran*, The Table, 5:35 يَا أَيُّهَا الَّذِينَ آمَنُوا اتَّقُوا اللَّهَ وَابْتَغُوا إِلَيْهِ الْوَسِيلَةَ وَجَاهِدُوا فِي سَبِيلِهِ لَعَلَّكُمْ تُفْلِحُونَ

[531] Dante Alighieri, *La divina commedia, Inferno* III, 60 "*che fece per viltade il gran rifiuto.*" The hermit Pietro Angelieri da Morrone (1215-1296), acclaimed pope in 1294 with the name of Celestine V, resigned after five months of reign.

[532] *Ibid.*, 3, 35-36, "*tegnon l'anime triste di coloro/ che visser sanza 'nfamia e sanza lodo.*"

[533] Joseph Aloisius Ratzinger, Pope Benedict XVI (2005-2013).

Pope Benedict XVI blessing well-wishers at the 12 PM *Angelus* Saint Peter's Square, Vatican City on Sunday May 30, 2010.

Ratzinger, having abdicated the pontificate of Benedict XVI, undermined the whole Roman Catholic Apostolic Tradition. According to that, the *Pontiff, viz.* the *Bridge-maker* between humanity and God, is the Vicar of Jesus Christ. In fact, the Pope is designated as the successor of the apostle Simon. He was renamed *Peter*, namely, *Rock* to represent the *petri*fied foundation on which Jesus Christ builds his Church (Matthew 16:18). During the following millennia, all Popes were elected. As it was and as it always is "understood ... the electors elect the Supreme Pontiff *after having invoked the enlightenment of the Holy Spirit*" (Italic is ours) [Paul VI, *Constitutio Apostolica, Romano Pontifici Eligendo, De Conclavi Deque Iis, Qui Huius Partem Habent*, Caput II (42). "*accipitur... Spiritus Sancti lumine invocato,... electores Summum Pontificem eligunt*"]. This invocation is not taken as a metaphor. In fact, Catholics believe that anointed prelates, during the daily mass' offertory, make real the transubstantiation of bread and wine into the actual body and blood of Jesus Christ (Matthew 26:26 fol., Mark 14:22 fol., and Luke 22:17), *viz.* God as the second person of the Holy Trinity. Consequently, it is believed that the Holy Spirit, *viz.* God as the third person, really enlightens the electors to choose the Pope according to His Will. Naturally, as a man, a pope can sin. Nevertheless, as a Pope, when exercising his office from Peter's chair (*ex cathedra Petri*), his doctrine is infallible. This quality of the Papacy was declared a Catholic dogma by Pope Pius IX, at the First Vatican Council (1869-1870). Almost as a premonition, in 1994 Pope John Paul II declared that "There's no place for a Pope Emeritus" (Accattoli, "*non c'e' posto per un Papa emerito*"). Even if, as suggested, the abdication was prompted by the Vatican's internal scandals, nevertheless, Ratzinger's action ratifies that a Pope may go against the Holy Spirit, not as a sinful man may do, but as a Pope. In fact, his resignation is ether

a) admitting that he was never the vicar of Christ because he went against His injunction to do "*Not what I will, but what thou* [Father] *wilt*" (Mark 14:34-36; *cf.* Luke 22:42, Matthew 26:42); or
b) stating that the Holy Spirit does not truly mandate the Papacy. In this case the Institution itself loses any spiritual validity, doctrinal infallibility and teaching direction. To confirm this view in an interview on Bavarian television in 1997, Ratzinger stated "I would not say... that the Holy Spirit picks out the Pope... but... leaves us much space, much freedom... There are ... popes the Holy Spirit... would not have picked!" (Allen, *A quick course in 'Conclave 101'*). This is as if he would have said: 'God did not create Lucifer directly, because, knowing that angel's aftermath, He would not have done so.'

[534] *Bible*, Mark 13:16 ... Luke 9:62.
[535] *Koran*, The City, 90:4, لَقَدْ خَلَقْنَا الْإِنْسَانَ فِي كَبَدٍ
[536] *Cf.* Freud, *Five Lectures on Psycho-Analysis*, p. 28-9.
[537] *UMaitrī* I.2. *kāmān* (desires) *vṛṇīshveti* (choose).
[538] *Bible*, John 14:1.

[539] *Samyutta Nikāya* (*Dhammacakkappavattana Sutta* The First Discourse of the Buddha Setting the Wheel of Dhamma in Motion) 56:11, pp. 1843-47, and sutta 12.2.1.

The Middle Path to be Walked (*madhyamá pratipad*, pali *majjhimā paṭipadā*), Buddha in *vitarka mudrā* the teaching gesture.

[540] *BG* XIV.22. *srī-* (lord) *bhagavān* (blessed) *uvāca* (said) / *prakāśaṃ* (contemplative life or glory) *ca* (and) *pravṛttiṃ* (active life or his destiny) *ca* (and) *moham* (delusion) *eva* (even) *ca* (and) ... / *na* (not) *dveshṭi* (hates) *saṃpraVṚttāni* (present) *na* (not) *nivṛttāni* (absent) *kāṃkshati* (desires) //

23. *udāsīna-* (neutral) *vad* (as) *āsīno* (is seated) *guṇair* (by the qualities) *yo* (who) *na* (not) *vicālyate* (is troubled) / *guṇa* (the qualities) *vartaṃta* (change) *ity* (thus) *eva* (even) *yo'* (who) *vatishṭhati* (remains apart) *neṃgate* (unmoved) //

24. *sama-* (the same) *duḥkha-* (in sorrow) *sukhaḥ* (in happiness) *sva-* (in the self) *sthaḥ* (centered) *sama-* (equally) *loshṭāśma-* (a lump of dirt, a stone) *kāṃcanaḥ* (gold) / *tulya-* (equal) *priyāpriyo* (loved not loved) *dhīras* (firm) *tulya-* (equal) *niṃdātma-* (in defamation of self) *saṃstutiḥ* (praise) //

25. *mānāpamānayos* (in honor in dishonor) *tulyas* (equal) *tulyo* (equal) *mitrāri-* (of friend of enemy) *pakshayoḥ* (in sides) / *sarvāraṃbha-* (all endeavors) *parityāgī* (renouncing) *guṇātītaḥ* (gone beyond qualities) *sa* (he) *ucyate* (is said) //

[541] *Bible*, Luke 14:26 οὐ μισεῖ [*ou* (not) *misei* (hate)] and John 12:25 μισῶν [*misoon* (hateth)].

[542] *UB* IV,3,23. *atra* (there) *pitā'* (a father) *pitā* (not a father) *bhavati* (is) *matā'* (a mother) *māthā* (not a mother).

[543] *The Power of Myth*, Cp. III. The First Storytellers, p. 75.

[544] Laurentin, *La Vergine appare a Medjugorje?* (June 16, 1982) p. 99.

[545] Participle of √*jñā*.

[546] *Spiritual teaching*, pp. 3 (2), 42.

[547] *Bible*, Matthew 5:39.

[548] *Bible*, Matthew 26:42.

[549] *Bible*, Luke 11:2, Πάτερ (*páter* father-founder) ἡμῶν (*ēmōon* our) ὁ (*o* who) ἐν (*en* in) τοῖς (*toīs* the) οὐρανοις (*ouranois* heaven-transcendent),

[550] *ibid.*, ἁγιασθήτω (*agiasthētō* acknowledged be) τὸ (*to* the) ὄνομά {*onoma* name-power [according to the Hebrew usage (Rocci, p. 1339b – *d*)]} σου (*sou* your)

[551] *ibid.*, ἐλθέτω (*elthétō* may appear) ἡ (*ē* the) βασιλεία (*basileia* ruler-ship) σου (*sou* your)

[552] *Ibid.*, γενηθήτω (*genēthētō* may be manifest) τὸ (to the) θέλημά

(*thelēmá* purpose) σου (*sou* your) ὡς (*ōs* as) ἐν (*en* in) οὐρανῷ (*ouranō*ᵢ heaven-transcendent), καὶ (*kai* and) ἐπὶ (*epì* in) τῆς (*tēs* the) γῆς (*gēs* earth-immanent). *Cf.* Matthew 6:10.

[553] *Bible*, John, 8:32 ἀλήθεια *alētheia* = truth, from α-λανθάνω a-*lanthánō = non-unaware = aware.*

[554] Malory, *Le Morte d'Arthur*, 21:7, *Rex quondam, Rexque Futurus.* Arthur *cf.* Sanskrit *artham* = "aim, purpose... cause, motive, reason... the son of *dharma* [morality... law (510c)] ... affair, concern... (in law) lawsuit, action... prohibition" *W.* p. 90c.

[555] *Cf. Māṇḍūkya Upanishad* in Simonelli, *Beyond Immortality.*

[556] Galilei, *Assayer* VII, 232.

[557] Russell*, Our Knowledge of the External World,* ON THE NOTION OF CAUSE pp. 240-241.

[558] Rutherford, *Science for All Americans*, p. 7.

[559] *Bible*, Genesis 1:3-4.

See = Hebrew רָאָה *ra'ah, Greek εἶδον eidon (√Ϝιδ Ϝid), Latin video, Sanskrit vid.*

Light = Hebrew אור *'owr*, Greek φῶς *fōs*, Latin *lūx*, Sanskrit *bhā́sas – loká* (space).

[560] *Cf. UK* IV.1 (II.I.1).

[561] *UB* I.2.1. *naiveha kiṁcanāgra āsīt*

[562] *VṚ* X. 129.7 *ná véda... iyáṁ vísṛshṭir yáta ābabhūva.*

[563] *Bible*, Luke, 9:25, γὰρ (*gar* what) ὠφελεῖται (*ōpheitai is advantage*) ἄνθρωπος (*anthrōpos* men-person) κερδήσας (*kerdēsas* gains) τὸν (*ton* the) κόσμον (*kosmon* kosmos) ὅλον (*olon* whole) ἑαυτὸν (*eauton* one's self) δὲ (*de* but) ἀπολέσας (*apolesas* loses).

[564] *Cf.* also the systematic doubt of the Advaita Vedānta, *UB* IV. 4. 22, *neti* (not so) *neti* (not so).

[565] Russell*, Our Knowledge of the External World,* ON THE NOTION OF CAUSE pp. 241-243.

[566] Budge, *The Egyptian Book...*, p. civ.

London, Soane Museum: inside border of the coffin of Seti I (1318 - 1304 BC, XIX Dynasty).

[567] Gauch, *Scientific Method in Practice*, Figure 1.2, pp. 1-2.

[568] Rutherford, *Science for All Americans*, pp. 3-4 and 9.

[569] *On the Basis of Morality*, p. 201.

[570] *UB* IV.4.23. *na* (not) *vā* (verily) *are* (well) *patyuḥ* (for the husband) *kāmāya* (for love) *patiḥ* (the husband) *priyo* (beloved) *bhavati* (is) *ātmanas* (of the self) *tu* (but) *kāmāya* (for love) *patiḥ* (the husband) *priyo* (beloved) *bhavati* (is) *na* (not) *vā* (verily) *are* (well) *jāyāyai* (for the wife) *kāmāya* (for love) *jāyā* (the wife) *priyā* (beloved) *bhavati* (is) *ātmanas* (of the self) *tu* (but) *kāmāya* (for love) *jāyā* (the wife) *priyā* (beloved) *bhavati* (is) *na* (not) *vā* (verily) *are* (well) *putrāṇāṁ* (for the

sons) *kāmāya* (for love) *putrāḥ* (the sons) *priyā* (beloved) *bhavanti* (are) *ātmanas* (of the self) *tu* (but) *kāmāya* (for love) *putrāḥ* (the sons) *priyā* (beloved) *bhavanti* (are) *na* (not) *vā* (verily) *are* (well) *vittasya* (for wealth) *kāmāya* (for love) *vittam* (wealth) *priyām* (beloved) *bhavati* (is) *ātmanas* (of the self) *tu* (but) *kāmāya* (for love) *vittam* (wealth) *priyām* (beloved) *bhavati* (is) *na* (not) *vā* (verily) *are* (well) *paśūnāṁ* (for the cattle) *kāmāya* (for love) *paśavaḥ* (the cattle) *priyā* (beloved) *bhavanti* (are) *ātmanas* (of the self) *tu* (but) *kāmāya* (for love) *paśavaḥ* (the cattle) *priyā* (beloved) *bhavanti* (are) *na* (not) *vā* (verily) *are* (well) *brahmaṇaḥ* (for One who has divine knowledge) *kāmāya* (for love) *brahma* (One who has divine knowledge) *priyam* (beloved) *bhavati* (is) *ātmanas* (of the self) *tu* (but) *kāmāya* (for love) *brahma* (One who has divine knowledge) *priyam* (beloved) *bhavati* (is) *na* (not) *vā* (verily) *are* (well) *kshatrasya* (for the warrior) *kāmāya* (for love) *kshatram* (the warrior) *priyam* (beloved) *bhavati* (is) *ātmanas* (of the self) *tu* (but) *kāmāya* (for love) *kshatram* (the warrior) *priyam* (beloved) *bhavati* (is) *na* (not) *vā* (verily) *are* (well) *lokānāṁ* (for the words) *kāmāya* (for love) *lokāḥ* (the words) *priyāḥ* (beloved) *bhavanti* (are) *ātmanas* (of the self) *tu* (but) *kāmāya* (for love) *lokāḥ* (the words) *priyā* (beloved) *bhavanti* (are) *na* (not) *vā* (verily) *are* (well) *devānāṁ* (for the gods) *kāmāya* (for love) *devāḥ* (the gods) *priyā* (beloved) *bhavanti* (are) *ātmanas* (of the self) *tu* (but) *kāmāya* (for love) *devāḥ* (the gods) *priyā* (beloved) *bhavanti* (are) *na* (not) *vā* (verily) *are* (well) *vedānāṁ* (for the Sacred-verses-of-knowledge) *kāmāya* (for love) *vedāḥ* (the Sacred-verses-of-knowledge) *priyā* (beloved) *bhavanti* (are) *ātmanas* (of the self) *tu* (but) *kāmāya* (for love) *vedāḥ* (the Sacred-verses-of-knowledge) *priyā* (beloved) *bhavanti* (are) *na* (not) *vā* (verily) *are* (well) *bhūtānām* (for the beings) *kāmāya* (for love) *bhutāni* (the beings) *priyāṇi* (beloved) *bhavanti* (the beings) *ātmanas* (of the self) *tu* (but) *kāmāya* (for love) *bhūtāni* (the beings) *priyāṇi* (beloved) *bhavanti* (are) *na* (not) *vā* (verily) *are* (well) *sarvasya* (for everything) *kāmāya* (for love) *sarvam* (everything) *priyam* (beloved) *bhavati* (is) *ātmanas* (of the self) *tu* (but) *kāmāya* (for love) *sarvam* (everything) *priyam* (beloved) *bhavati* (is) *ātmā* (the Self) *vā* (verily) *are* (well) *drashṭavyaḥ* (is to be seen) *mantavyo* (is to be thought) *nididhyāsitavyaḥ* (is to be meditated upon) *maitreyi* (o Benevolent) *ātmani* (in the self) *khalv* (verily) *are* (well) *dṛshṭe* (seen) *śrute* (heard) *mate* (thought) *vijñāte* (discerned) *idaṁ* (this) *sarvaṁ* (all) *viditam* (is known).

[571] From Latin *e-movere* to out-move.

[572] *Bible*, John 14:27.

[573] *Bible*, Luke 22:44.

[574] *Bible*, Mark 14:34-36; *cf.* Luke 22:42, Matthew 26:42.

[575] *Bible*, Matthew 27:46 (*Eli, Eli, lama sabachthani*? ܐܠܝ ܐܠܝ ܠܡܢܐ ܫܒܩܬܢܝ) and Mark 15:34 (*Eloi*). *Cf.* Psalms 22:1 אֵלִי אֵלִי לָמָה עֲזַבְתָּנִי

[576] *Cf.* Kasser-Meyer-Wurst ed., *The Gospel of Judas.*

[577] Augustine, *Confessions,*1.1.1 "*inquietum est cor nostrum donec requiescat in te.*"

[578] Leopardi, *Tutte le opere*, L'infinito (1819), "*Sovrumani/ silenzi, e profondissima quïete/... infinito silenzio .../ e mi sovvien*

l'eterno."

[579] *Cf.* Croce, *Breviario di estetica.*

[580] *Cf. W. abhikhyā* 61c, *téjas* 454b; *rūpá* 886a; *várṇa* 924b.

[581] John 13:34 and 15:12, love ἀγαπᾶτε *agapate, cf.* 13:35; 15:17; 1John 3:11,23;4:7, 11-12; 2John 1:5; 2:5; Ephesians 4:2; Galathians 5:13; Hebrews 10:24; Romans 12:10, 13:8 & 35; 1Thessalonians 3:12, 4:9; 1Peter 1:22, 3:8.

[582] *Bible,* 1John 4:7,12.

[583] *Bible,* Galatians 5:13.

[584] *Cf.* Simonelli, *Transcendence - The Universal Quest.*

[585] Donida-Mogol, *Al Di Là,* (1961), *"Non credevo possibile, / si potessero dire queste parole: / al di là del bene più prezioso, ci sei tu. / Al di là del sogno più ambizioso, ci sei tu./ Al di là delle cose più belle./ Al di là delle stelle, ci sei tu./ Al di là, ci sei tu per me, per me, soltanto per me./ Al di là del mare più profondo, ci sei tu. / Al di là dei limiti del mondo, ci sei tu./ Al di là della volta infinita, al di là della vita./ Ci sei tu, al di la, ci sei tu per me." Cf.* *UKai* 3

[586] *Cf.* Dalai Lama, *Healing Anger,* p. 97.

[587] Augustine, *In Epistolam Joannis Ad Parthos Tractatus Decem,* VII, 8. "Dilige (love), et (and) quod (that which) vis (you want) fac (do)."

[588] III. 17. *tasya* (of him) *kāryaṃ* (duty) *na* (not) *vidyate* (exists).

[589] *Bible,* Matthew 5:34 & 37; *cf.* 2Corinthians 1:17.

[590] Here, we are representing (at times *verbatim*) part of the sub-chapter, *Outline for a future moral code*, as published in our *Beyond immortality*, because this book wants to be the continuation of that one.

[591] *Bible,* John 12:35-36 "be certain" (πιστεύετε *pisteúete, credite*); light (φῶς *phōs*).

[592] *UMu* III.1.3. *tadā* (then) *vidvān* (knower) *puṇya-* (good) *pāpe* (evil) *vidhūya* (shaking off) *nirañjanaḥ* (free from stain).

[593] *UT* II.9.1. *ānandam* (bliss) *brahmaṇo* (of Brahman) ...*etaṁ* (such a one) *ha* (naturally) *vāva* (verily) *na* (not) *tapati* (torments) *kim* (why) *ahaṁ* (I) *sādhu* (right) *nākaravam* (not have done) *kim* (why) *aham* (I) *pāpam* (evil) *akaravam* (have done) *iti* (thus) *sa* (he) *ya* (who) *evaṁ* (thus) *vidvān* (understands) *ete* (these) *ātmānam* (himself) *spṛṇute* (saves) *ubhe* (both) ... *ity* (so) *upanishat* (the secret teaching).

[594] *Bible,* Matthew 5:45.

[595] *Cf.* Vasubandhu, *Vijñaptimātratāsiddhi-Triṃśikā,* (Thirty stanzas only on consciousness), IV century BC Yogācāra (yoga-rule) Buddhism, v.3 and 5. *ālaya* - (receptacle) *vi-* (distinction) *jñāna* (knowledge).

[596] *Cf.* Saenger, *Principles of Nucleic Acid Structure.*

[597] Triceratops, horned dinosaur with Carnosaurus.

American Museum of Natural History, New York, NY.

[598] Ramana Maharshi, *The Spititual Teaching...*, pp. 7-8 (14) (italic is ours).
[599] *Bible*, Matthew 25:35-36.
[600] *Bible*, Mark 9:37.
[601] *Bible*, Matthew 25:40-45.
[602] *Bible*, Mark 9:41.
[603] *Bible*, Matthew 26:52.
[604] *Bible*, Matthew 7:2.
[605] *Bible*, Matthew 25:29.
[606] *Bible*, Genesis 2:17.
[607] *UB.* V.15.3. *aum krato* (o will's power) *smara* (remember) *kṛtaṃ* (the action) *smara* (remember) *krato* (o enlightenment) *smara* (remember) *kṛtaṃ* (the magic) *smara* (remember). Same in *UĪśa* 17.
[608] ἀταραξία *ataraxía* = tranquility from α+τάραξις *a+táraxis* = non+agitation. *Cf.* Diogenes Laërtius, *Lives of eminent philosophers*, Pyrrho (360 – 270 BC) Book IX, sections 61-108 and Epicurus (341 – 270 BC) Book X, sections 1-154.
[609] Dutton, *The Wisdom of Psychopaths*, ' 1, Scorpio Rising 6.
[610] *Bible*, Matthew 6:24; *cf.* Luke 16:13.
[611] *Bible*, Luke 16:9-11.
[612] Aramaic for riches, treasure.
[613] *Bible*, Luke 16:15.
[614] *UB* IV.5.3 *amṛtatvasya* (immortality) *tu* (but) nāśāsti (is no hope) *vittene-* (with wealth) *ti* (thus).
[615] *Bible*, Matthew 19:23.
[616] Gounod, *Faust*, Act II, Scene IV, p. 16, "*Le veau d'or est toujours debout!/ On encense/ Sa puissance,/... D'un bout du monde à l'autre bout!/ Pour fêter l'infàme idole,/ Peuples et rois confondus,/ Au tintement des écus,/ Forment une ronde folle / Autour de son piédestale!.../ Le veau d'or est vainqueur des dieux!/ Dans sa gloire / Dérisoire,/ Son front abject brave les cieux!/ Il contemple, ô rage étrange!/ A ses pieds le genre humain,/ Se ruant, le fer en main,/ Dans le sang et dans la fange/ Où brille l'ardent métal/... Et Satan conduit le bal!*"
[617] *Cf. W.* p. 100a.
[618] *Bible*, John 12:35.
[619] *Bible*, John 12:35-36 "be certain" (πιστεύετε *pisteúete, credite*); light (φῶς *phōs*).
[620] *Bible*, Luke 1:76.

[621] *Bible*, Mark 9:37, Luke 18:17.
[622] Francesco, *I fioretti*, cap. VIII, p. 34. "*non è ivi perfetta letizia.*" *Cf.* Paul, *Bible*, 1 Corinthians 13:1-3.
[623] Ramana Maharshi, *The Spiritual Teaching*..., p. 63. *jñāna* = realization of Self-Awareness.
[624] Jeremy Bentham (1748 - 1832), *Anarchical Fallacies.*
[625] *Bible*, Matthew 5:20.
[626] *Bible*, Matthew 5:48.
[627] *Bible*, John 8:3,4,5,7,9,10,11.
[628] *The Garuda purāṇa* III.
[629] *Bible*, Genesis 2:17.
[630] Greek, an-archy (ἀν-αρχία *an-archia*) = *without* (ἄν *an*) *leader* (ἀρχός *archos*).
[631] Etymology from the Latin verb *spiro* = I re*spir*e, I breathe.
[632] *Cf.* D'Souza, *What's So Great about Christianity.*
[633] *Cf.* Marx (1818–1883), *The Economic and Philosophic Manuscripts of 1844.*
[634] *Wer* = hero-tribute = *gild*. Sanskrit *vīrá*, Latin *vir*, Old Norse *ver*, Old Germanic *wer* = man & Sanskrit *yajñá* √*yaj* (worship with oblations), Old German *gield* and *gelt* (*cf.* yield), Gothic *gild* = tribute.
[635] The *wergild* of a woman was equal or even double that of a man of the same status or rank.
[636] Greek χάρισμα *khárisma* = divine gift.
[637] *Bible*, Exodus 34:1, 11, 29 & 35:1.

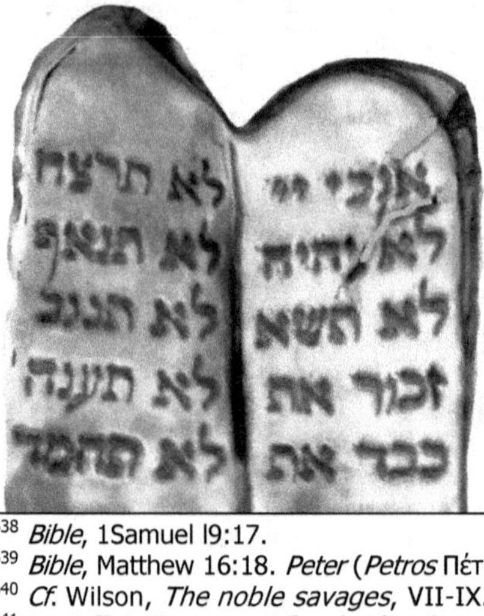

[638] *Bible*, 1Samuel l9:17.
[639] *Bible*, Matthew 16:18. *Peter* (*Petros* Πέτρος), *rock* (*petra* πέτρα).
[640] *Cf.* Wilson, *The noble savages*, VII-IX.
[641] Ponti-ff, Latin = *ponti-fex*, bridge (*pons*) maker (*facere*).
[642] Simonelli, *Philosophy as a path*..., p. 23.
[643] Kontzevich, *The mystical meaning*..., p. 327. ascetic struggle подвиг *podvig*, , great or heroic deed.

[644] *Cf.* 240 A.D. silver Roman Antoninianus of Emperor Gordian III with Goddess Roma

OB. IMP GORDIANVS PIVS FEL AVG. Right RE. ROMAE AETERNAE left, seated on a shield with idol of Victory and spear.

[645] Head of Constantine

Campidoglio, Rome, Italy.

[646] **Cf. 1059-67 AE Follis, Constantinople, of Constantine X with Christ**

OB. Christ standing with Gospels RE. left, Eudocia, right, Constantine

[647] Hilt of ***Los reyes católicos'*** sword.

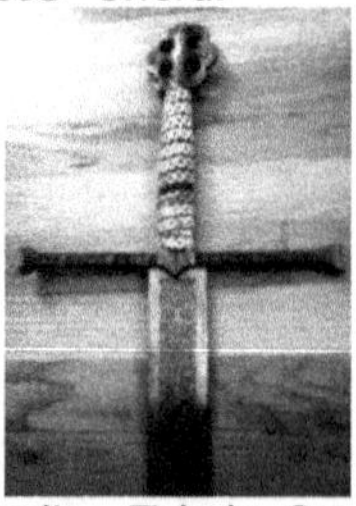

Replica, Toledo, Spain

[648] *Bible,* Exodus 20:3.
[649] Campbell (1904-1987), *The Power of Myth*, p. 21, 56 and 65.
[650] *Bible*, Exodus 20:13, Deuteronomy 5:17.

[651] *Bible*, Exodus 15:3 (LORD = יהוה *yĕhovah,* man = איש *'iysh*, war = מלחמה *milchamah*; יְהוָה אִיש מִלְחָמָה).

Cf. the Kabalistic rendering of the Tetragrammaton body of God: Y (י)10 for the head, H (ה)5 for the arms, W (ו)6 for the torso and H (ה)5 for the legs, with a Gematria value of 26.

[652] *Bible*, Exodus 15:15.
[653] *Bible*, Numbers 21:3 and 32:4, 32.
[654] Sanskrit: *sthaga*: "cunning, sly, fraudulent, dishonest" (*W.* p. 1261c), Hindi: *ṭhagī*, from *thag*: to rob, to cheat. *Cf.* Russell, *Thug*.
[655] *Bible*, Exodus 20:13, 15-16. Deuteronomy 5:17, 19-20.
[656] Kālī

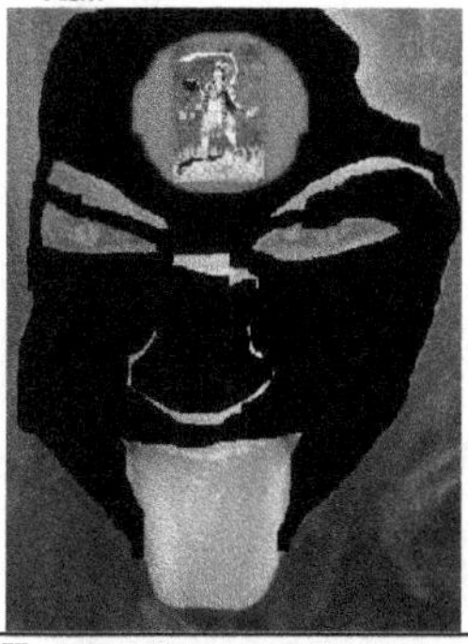

[657] *Bible*, Exodus 20:14, Deuteronomy 5:18, *cf.* Leviticus 18:20.
[658] *Cf.* Crocker, *Extramarital sexual practices of the Ramkókamekra-Canela Indians.*
[659] *Bible*, Matthew 10:34.
[660] *Bible*, Luke 12:51.
[661] *Bible*, Genesis 1:26.
[662] *The Power of Myth*, p. 99. Also *cf.* p. 24.
[663] (1870 - 1966) as reported by Campbell, *The Power of Myth*, p. 56.
[664] Laland, *How culture shaped the human genome*, Abstract, p. 137-148.
[665] *Cf.* Indian *Prakṛti, Mahāmāyā, Mahīdurga*, Mesopotamian *Inanna/ Ishtar*, Greco-Roman *Ma-Gaia, Demeter, Ceres, Persephone*, pre-Columbian *Pachamama, Nokomis*-Grandmother, *Tawantinsuyu*, South-East Asian *Phra Mae Thorani, Dewi Sri*, etc.
[666] *Cf.* Kant, *The Critique of Pure Reason*, p. 132 fol.
[667] *Declaration of Independence as Adopted by the Second Continental Congress.* In CONGRESS, July 4, 1776 (Thomas Jefferson).

"*Distinguished Masons of the Revolution*" (19th century Masonic print).

[668] Jefferson, *Letter to the Danbury Baptists,* January 1, 1802, Vol 57, No. 6.

[669] Freemasons' Great Architect of the Universe

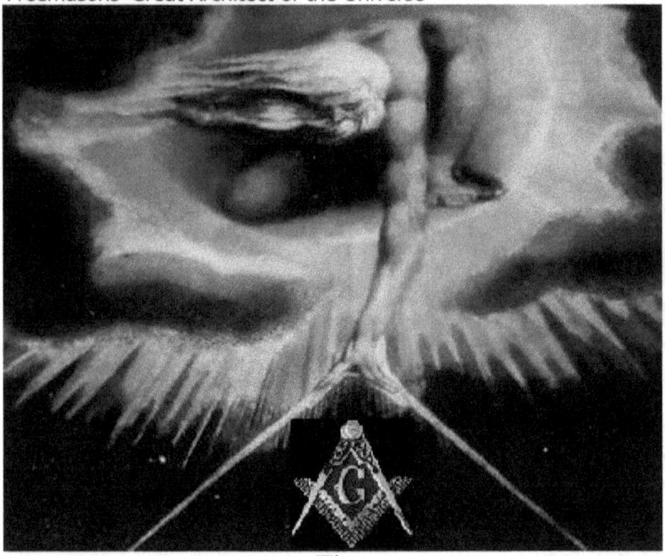

Tile

[670] <u>Create</u>, Sanskrit root √*kṛ*, to make. Creation out of nothing (*ex nihilo*), Hebrew, ברא *bara'* (*Bible,* Genesis 1:1, 21, 27 and 2:3). <u>Produce</u>, Latin, *pro-* (forward) *ducere* (lead).

[671] Genesis 1:2. Void (בהו *bohuw*).

[672] *Cf. Ṛg Veda* (sacred verse knowledge - III millennium B.C.?) *VṚ* X.129.1. *n-* (no) *āsad* (non-being) *āsīn* (was) *nó* (nor) *sád* (being) *āsīt* (was) *tadānīm̊* (then)... *ámbhaḥ* (Celestial Waters) ... *āsīd* (was) *gahanam̊* (depth) *gabhīrám̊* (of inscrutable) //

3. *táma* (darkness) *āsīt* (was) *támasā* (by darkness) *gūḷhám* (covered) *ágre'* (in the beginning) *praketám̊* (indiscriminate) *salilám̊* (flowing flood) *sárvam* (all) *ā* (only) *idám* (this).

[673] Lavoisier (1743-1794), *Elements of chemistry*, p. 187.

[674] From Greek κῦριᾶκός *kyriakos* = of the Lord = κύριος *kyrios.*

[675] *Cf.* Bellamy, *Pledge of Allegiance,* intended to be valid for any citizen in any country.

[676] Dante, *La Vita Nova*, Tanto gentile, "*ogni lingua divien tremando muta.*"

[677] *UKai* 19.

[678] Ramana Maharshi, *The Spiritual Teaching...*, p. 3 and 4 (2 and 4).

[679] *Cf.* Noble Wilford, *So Who Is Buried in Midas' Tomb?* at Gordion central Turkey.

[680] Totò, *'A livella,* "*'A morte 'o ssaje ched"e?...è una livella.../ 'Nu rre,'nu maggistrato,'nu grand'ommo.../ ha perzo tutto,'a vita e pure 'o nomme.../ Perciò ... / Sti ppagliacciate 'e ffanno sulo 'e vive:/ nuje simmo serie...appartenimmo à morte!*"

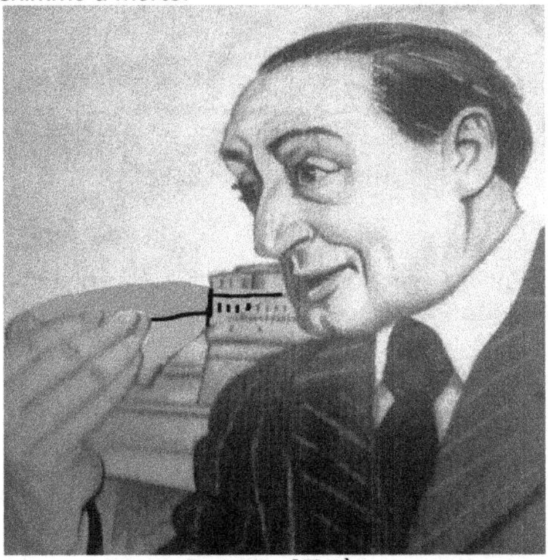

Portrait of Totò.

[681] *Cf.* Rae, p. 127 and 132 fol. From Sanskrit *sama* (*cf.* English same), Greek ἰσότης (*isotes*), Latin *aequitas*, French *égalité*, German *gleichheit*.

[682] *Cf.* Simonelli, *Beyond Immortality*, pp. 90 fol.

[683] Goddess AEQVITAS AVGG (*Aeqvitas Augusti* = Justice of Augustus) standing left with scales (*libra*) and cornucopia.

Re. Silver Antoninianus of Philip I (244-249 A.D.)

[684] Manual hand (*manus*) gesture to set (*mittere*) free.

[685] Phrygian cap.

1

2

3

1) Mithras with Phrygian cap and a halo, Re. Roman Æs detail, 161-169 AD, Lucius Verus, Trapezus (Pontus).
2) Liberty Phrygian cap, Ob. US 1878 silver Morgan dollar detail.
3) **Fasces with Phrygian cap, Re. French 1792 sols 2 detail, Louis XVI.**

[686] *Cf.* Calvin, Institutes, III, XIV, 2 & 19. *Cf.* also Simonelli, *Beyond Immortality*, pp. 92 fol.

[687] *Cf.* Engels, *Socialism*. Cf. also Marx, *Capital / Manifesto of the Communist Party.*

[688] Marx and Engels, *The German Ideology*, Part I, section A, pp. 47, 50.

[689] Dante, *Divina Commedia, Inferno*, XI, 46 "*negando e bestemmiando*"; XIV. 63-64, 69-70 "*non s'ammorza /la ... superbia... abbia / Dio in disdegno.*" Capaneus, one of the mythological seven kings of Thebes, deemed himself superior to God. While scaling the city's walls, Zeus' lighting struck him down.

Capaneus, illustration by Gustave Doré (detail).

[690] Dante, *La Divina Commedia*, Inferno, 7.23 *voltando pesi per forza di poppa.* 7.53-54 *la sconoscente vita che i fé sozzi / ad ogne conoscenza or li fa bruni.* 7.64-66 *ché tutto l'oro ch'è sotto la luna/ e che già fu, di quest' anime stanche/ non poterebbe farne posare una.*

Illustration by Gustave Doré.

[691] *Cf.* ***Pietro Micca*** *Museum*, Torino, via Guicciardini 7°.

[692] *Bible*, Judges 16:30.

[693] *Ficus aurea, Moraceae* and a *Casimiroa edulis Rutaceae.*

A "Strangler Fig Tree" (*Ficus aurea, Moraceae*) *strangling* its host, a "White sapote" (*Casimiroa edulis Rutaceae*) a tropical fruiting tree native to the cloud forest of Monteverde, Costa Rica.

[694] *Bible*, Romans 2:1.

[695] *Bible*, Matthew 5:22.

[696]

A man strangling a woman.

[697] "*Vae victis*," Livy, *Ab Urbe Condita*, V, 34–49.

[698] Lane, *Daily Life in the Mongol Empire*, p. 123.

[699] *De gustibus et coloribus non est disputandum*." Empiricist Bertrand Russell (1872-1970) and Catholic Frederick Copleston (1907-1994), 1948 Third Program broadcast of the British Broadcasting Corporation, Russell – Copleston, *Copleston vs. Bertrand Russell*, also Russell, *Bertrand Russell on God and Religion*.

[700] Plato, *Theaetetus* 152a.

[701] *Cf.* Indonesian Komodo Dragons feeding.

Museum of Natural History (New York)

[702] $\overline{w}\,\Delta\,\overline{z} = \mathrm{Cov}(w_i\,z_i) + E(w_i\Delta z_i)$, Harman. *The Price of Altruism: George Price and the Search for the Origins of Kindness*, p. 370.

[703] Dawkins, *The Selfish Gene*, p. 4.

[704] *Cf.* Roper, *A FAITHFUL dog has refused to move from his master's grave for SIX YEARS.*

[705] *Cf. UB* I.2.1.

[706] *Bible*, Luke 23:34.

[707] *Bible*, Matthew 5:44.

"Invitation to prayer," from businessman Jeremiha Lanphier (9-23-1857) Broadway and 61st Street (NYC 2007).

[708] *Cf.* Bodhisattva (One whose essence is perfect knowledge), *cf*. Śāntideva, *A Guide to the Bodhisattva...*

Seated Guanyin Bodhisattva,
(oil painting on canvas, China).
Cf. Liao Chinese Dynasty (907-1125).
Wood with paint
(The Nelson-Atkins Museum of Art,
Kansas City, Missouri, N. 460)

Standing Bodhisattva Maitreya
(Buddha of the Future),

Wikimedia Commons. public domain by its author, PHG at the Wikipedia project. http://en.wikipedia.org/wiki/File:KushanMaitreya.JPG
Cf. Pakistan (Gandhara), ca. 3rd century. Schist, Metropolitan Museum of Art, New York (91.75).

[709] *Cf.* De Waal (Emory University, Atlanta, GA), *The Bonobo and the Atheist.*
[710] Latin *infans* = not (*in*) talking (*fans*), participle present of *fari* = to talk.
[711] Tomasello (Leipzig, Germany), *Shared intentionality*, & *cf. Why We Cooperate*. *Cf.* also anthropologist Hillard S. Kaplan (University of New Mexico) for similar independent conclusion.
[712] Rousseau, *Du Contrat Social.*

[713] *Cf.* Keeley, *War Before Civilization.*
[714] *Cf.* Henrich, *Markets, Religion, Community Size, and the Evolution of Fairness and Punishment.*
[715] *Cf.* Post (director of the Center for Medical Humanities, Compassionate Care and Bioethics at Stony Brook University, Long Island, NY) *Why Good Things Happen to Good People.*
[716] *Cf.* Walker, 29 Gifts. Cf. also http://www.29gifts.org/.
[717] *Cf.* (2002 Boston College study) Arnstein, *From chronic pain patient to peer: Benefits and risks of volunteering.* & (Buck Center for Research in Aging, Novato, California, USA) Oman, *Volunteerism and Mortality among the Community-dwelling Elderly.* & (Miami study of patients with H.I.V.) Ironson, *Do Positive Psychosocial Factors Predict Disease Progression in HIV.* & (Study of 150 heart patients) Scherwitz, *Type A Behavior.*
[718] Aprile, *Vita Che Teatro*, p. 39. "*AVER COMPAGNO AL DUOL SCEMA LA PENA.*"
[719] Bloom, *The Moral Life of Babies.*
[720] *Cf.* Darwin, *The Expression of the Emotions in Man and Animals.*
[721] Bloom, *The Moral Life of Babies.*
[722] *Bible*, Matthew 5:28; ἤδη *ēdē* = *already* (emphasis is ours), as time *already* past.
[723] Latin = *pro-vidēre* = to see before.
[724] Escobedo, *Becoming a better person...*
[725] Ramana Maharshi, *The Spiritual Teaching...*, p. 7 (14).
UB V.14.8 *evaṃ* (even so) ***Error! Main Document Only.****haivaivaṃ-* (one who thus) *-vid* (knowing) yady (this) *api* (very) *bahv* (much) *iva* (verily) *pāpaṃ* (evil) *kurute*
(commits) *sarvam* (all) *eva* (verily) *tat* (that) *sampsāya* (consumes) ***Error! Main Document Only.****śuddhaḥ* (pure) *pūto'* (clean) *jaro'* (ever young) *mṛtaḥ* (immortal) *sambhavati* (becomes).
[727] *Bible*, Genesis, 3:7 ידע *yada`* *(to know),* 10, ירא *yare' (fear),* עירם *`eyrom (naked).*
[728] *Ibid.* 6:5, 6, 17.
[729] Crowley, *Confessions...*, p. 3.
[730] *Bible*, Mark 8:33, our translation is in italic ὅτι οὐ φρονεῖς τὰ τοῦ θεοῦ ἀλλὰ τὰ
τῶν ἀνθρώπων.
[731] *Ibid,* Galatians 5:11 *scandalum crucis.*
[732] Hartsuiker, *Sādhus...*, p. 36.
[733] *Cf.* Ratti, *Secrets of the Samurai*, pp. 118-125.
[734] *Cf.* Gill, *Dictionary of Native American Mythology*, pp.121-22.
[735] Cf. Dumézil, *La religione...*, p. 244.
[736] II.19.
[737] <Simonelli, *Beyond Immortality*, pp. 223-5.>
[738] *Cf.* Pascal's Gamble, *Pensées*, The Wager § 121 fol.
[739] *On the Basis of Morals*, p. 200.
[740] Bentham (1748-1832), *The Utilitarians*, pp. 17-18.
[741] Mill (1806-1873), *The Utilitarians*, p. 407.
[742] Greek *hēdonismós* (ἡδονισμός) from *hēdonhé* (ἡδονή) pleasure.
[743] *cf.* Bṛhaspati, *Bārhaspatya-sūtras.* Cārvāka 500 BC (*W.* 394a, *cārvāc* = "speaking nicely."), *Lokāyata* (*W.* 907b "world-extended").

---

[744] *Yangism* (475-221 BC), *cf.* Ivanhoe, *Readings in classical Chinese philosophy*, p. 369.
[745] *Cf.* Diogenes Laërtius, *Lives of eminent philosophers*, Epicurus (341 – 270 BC) Book X, sections 1-154.
[746] Outdated English term, present *mortal* (from Sanskrit *mṛtyu* = death; ṛ is a vowel as *or, ur* from √*mṛ* = to die, *cf.* murder). *Mortify* (from Latin *mors–mortis* = death + *facere* = to make).
[747] Fumagalli, *Chi l'ha detto*, p. 653, "*Giovinezza, giovinezza, primavera di bellezza.*"
[748] *Trionfo di Bacco e Arianna, Canto Carnevalesco.* Roscoe, *The life of Lorenzo de'Medici* (1449 – 1492), p. 129. "*Quant'è bella giovinezza,/ che si fugge tuttavia! / Chi vuol esser lieto, sia: / di doman non c'è certezza.*"
[749] Horace (65-8 BC), *Odes* 1.11, 1-2, 6-8, "*Tu ne quaesieris, scire nefas, quem mihi, quem tibi/ finem di dederint... vina liques... fugerit invida/ aetas: carpe diem quam minimum credula postero.*"
[750] *Bible*, Isaiah 22:13, Ecclesiastes 9:7–9 and 1 Corinthians 15:32.
[751] DAILY MAIL REPORTER, *Teenage lottery millionaire who won £1.9m broke at 22.*
[752] Ramana Maharshi, *Who am I? The Spiritual Teaching*, p. 11, 24. *What is happiness?*
[753] Leviticus, 19:18.
[754] Lao Tzu, Tao Te Ching, Chapter 49.
[755] Acaranga sutra, 5.101-2.
[756] Bible, Luke 6:31, Matthew 7:12.
[757] Confucius, *The Analects* 15:23.
[758] *Sutrakritanga* 1.11.33.
[759] Yahya al-Nawawi, "Al-Nawawi Forty Hadiths, 13.
[760] *Mahābhārata* 5:1517.
[761] Olsson, *Leaving Faith Behind*, p. 109 n.5 & 11.
[762] Weil, Most Good, p. 10. British Humanist Association, 1 Gower Street, London, UK. http://www.humanism.org.uk/
[763] Armstrong, *Twelve Steps to a Compassionate Life*, pp. 6, 8, 26, 56, 196, 198, 225.
[764] The Charter for Compassion, http://charterforcompassion.org/the-charter.
[765] *On the Basis of Morality*, p.172, *cf.* 171-8.
[766] Derrida, *The Work of Mourning*, p. 184.
[767] Ozanam, *I poeti francescani...*, p. 282, "*Tal morte vo cercando.*"
[768] *Cf.* Pierce, *The Donatist Circumcellions*, pp. 123–133.
[769] Brown, http://www.geocities.com/~halbrown/suicide_by_cop_1.html.

[770] Francisco Goya, *Flagellants* (1812-13).

Real Academia de Bellas Artes de San Fernando (Calle Alcalá 13, Madrid); File:Francisco de Goya y Lucientes 025.jpg; http://it.wikipedia.org/wiki/File:Francisco_de_Goya_y_Lucientes_025.jpg Zenodot Verlagsgesellschaft mbH GNU; Free Documentation License. *Cf.* Wakin, *Medieval Flagellation in an Italian Town* (Guardia Sanframondi, BE) every 7 years in August during the feast of the Assumption.

[771] "A sadist is a masochist who follows the golden rule," Cathcart, *Plato and a Platypus*, "The Supreme Categorical Imperative and the Olden Goldie."

[772] *Bible*, Matthew 19:16-17 fol. *Cf.* Mark 10:17 fol. & Luke 18:18 fol.

[773] *Bible*, Luke 18:21-22 fol.

[774] *Bible*, Mark 10:25, *cf.* Luke 18:25.

[775] Campbell, *The Power of Myth*, p. 5.

[776] *Bible*, Genesis 3:5, God אלהים *'elohiym.*

[777] "*Tibetans will live happily in the great land of Tibet, and the Chinese will live happily in the great land of China*," in Lhasa (Tibet, 823 A.D.)

http://commons.wikimedia.org/wiki/File%3ATreaty_pillar_outside_the_Jokhang_in_Lhasa.jpg; File:Treaty pillar outside the Jokhang in Lhasa.jpg http://upload.wikimedia.org/wikipedia/commons/6/6c/Treaty_pillar_outside_the_Jokhang_in_Lhasa.jpg; H. Richardson [Public domain].

[778] *Cf.* Gandhi (1869 - 1948), *An Autobiography.*
[779] Gandhi, *An Autobiography...*, pp. 291-2.
[780] "*Pares autem vetere proverbio cum paribus facillime congregantur*" Cicero, *De Senectute*, III, 7, p. 14.
[781] "*Dimmi con chi vai e ti dirò chi sei*" *De Pretis, Epistolarity...*, p. 92.
[782] *Cf.* first cited in Minsheu, *A Dictionarie in Spanish and English.*
[783] Moreno, *The Essential Moreno.*
[784] *Cf.* Gladwell, *The Tipping Point.*
[785] Christakis, *Connected*, p. 16 and 39.
[786] *Cf.* Petronius Arbiter, *Petronii Arbitri Cena Trimalchionis*, a I century A.D. character.
[787] *Cf.* Christakis, *Connected.*
[788] Manu, *The Laws of Manu*, VII.4,5,8.
[789] Petronius, *Petronii Arbitri Cena Trimalchionis*, 14.2 *quid faciunt leges ubi sola pecunia regnat.*
[790] Politics = τά πολιτικά *tá politiká* (pl. n.) = business of the citizen = πολίτης *polítes* = dweller of city = πόλις *polis*.
[791] One 2012 USA Dollar Reverse detail.

[792] Democracy = *demos* δῆμος = people's power = *kratos* κράτος.
[793] Plato, *The Apology*, 41e.
[794] Plato, *Four texts on Socrates... Citro*, 47.

[795] WW2 Italian Army Officer's MVSN Fascist Dagger with Scabbard & Hangers

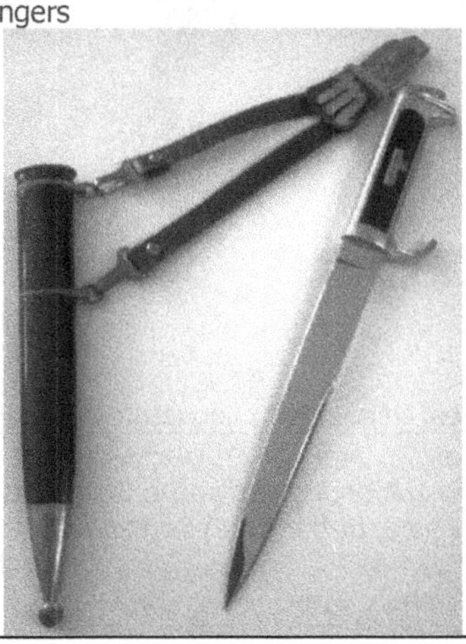

[796] First Roman Emperor from 27 B.C.
Gaius Julius Caesar Octavianus Divi Filius Augustus (63 B.C. - 14 A.D.)

His birthplace: Nola, Naples, Italy. (Photo Leonardo Avella, Fototeca nolana)

[797] *panem et circenses*, Juvenal, *Juvenal and Persius*, *Satires* IV.10.81.

[798] *Cf.* the German Hitler-Youth (*Hitler-Jugend*) or the Italian Fascist's Sons of the She-Wolf (*Figli della lupa*) or the North Korean Kim Il Sung Socialist Youth League (*김일성사회주의청년동맹*), just to mention a few.

[799] *Cf.* Plato, *Four texts on Socrates... Apology and Crito*.

[800] Plato, *The Republic*, VII, 514-521.
[801] *Odyssey*, 11, 489-491.
[802] Evola, *Rivolta contro il mondo moderno*, p. 153; *cf.* also Armstrong, *Muhammed...*
[803] Greek: α-πολιτεια (*a-politeia* non-citizenship), Sanskrit: *kaivalya.*
[804] Evola, *Cavalcare la tigre*, p. 152. "*L'apolitia è la distanza interiore irrevocabile da questa società e dai suoi 'valori'; è il non accettare di essere legati ad essa per un qualche vinvolo spirituale o morale... L'atteggiamento di distacco non può essere mantenuto negli stessi confronti di entrambi le parti che oggi si disputano il dominio del mondo, l' 'Occidente' democratico capitalista e l' 'Oriente' comunista. Infatti, questa lotta, dal punto di vista spirituale, è priva di ogni significato. L' 'Occidente' non è espressione di nessuna idea superiore. La sua stessa civiltà, basata su di una negazione essenziale dei valori tradizionali, presenta le stesse distruzioni e lo stesso sfondo nichilistico che è in evidenza nell'area marxista e comunista, sia pure in forme e gradi diversi... Per l'uomo differenziato potrà porsi, al massimo, un problema pratico. Quel certo margine di libertà materiale che ad alcune attività esterne il mondo della democrazia ancora lascia a chi non se ne lasci condizionare interiormente, sarebbe certamente abolito in regime colmunista. Semplicemente in vista di ciò si può prendere posizione contro lo schieramento sovietico-comunista: per motivi che si potrebbero quasi dire elementarmente fisici, non perché si creda in una qualche più alta idea che l'opposto schieramento abbia in proprio.*"
[805] Evola, *Rivolta contro il mondo moderno*, p. 23.
[806] *Cf.* Gandhi, *An Autobiography...*
[807] Divine light of Victory, Sanskrit *jyótis*, Greek φῶς *fōs* and Latin *lux* (*W.* p. 425a). Victory, Greek νίκη *nikē.*

Flying Nike crowning above victorious Acheloos, man-headed fertility bull, standing right facing (Neapolitan didrachmas *AR,* Reverse detail, 275-250 BC). *Cf.* Simonelli, *Hyria.*

[808] Lao Tzu, Tao Te Ching, II, 43 (78),1 天下莫柔弱于水，而攻堅強者，莫之能勝，以其無以易之。2) 弱之勝強，柔之勝剛，天下莫不知，莫能行。
[809] Vauvenargues (1715-1747), *Maxims and Thoughts*, 55. *Il n'y a guère de gens plus aigres que ceux qui sont doux par intérêt.*
[810] Nye, *Soft Power*, p. 5-6.
[811] Virgil, ... *Aeneid* II,42 "*o miseri, que tanta insania, cives?*/(43)*Creditis avectos hostis? Aut ulla putatis* /(44) *Dona carere dolis Danaum?...* /(48) *Aliquis latet error; equo ne credite, Teucri.*/(49) *Quidquid id est, timeo Danaos et dona ferentis.*"

---

[812] *Cf. Tharoor, Pax Indica (India);* Watanabe, *Soft Power Superpowers (Japan)*; Kurlantzick, *Charm Offensive* (China); McCormick, *The European Superpower*, Fraser, *Weapons of Mass Distraction* (USA).

[813] *Cf.* Lieven, *Imposing democracy and freedom, American-style.* & Kinzer, *Overthrow.*

[814] *Bible,* Revelation 4:6, 8.

[815] *Bible*, Proverbs 24:5.

[816] Pal, *SANTA CLAUS*, pp. 4-21.

[817] *Cf.* Kam (University of San Francisco School of Law, California State Bar), *Half* Guilty. Real XVII cent. Italian conjoined twin case. The guilty one was sentenced to death, but not executed since the death of one would have killed the innocent also.

[818] Thoreau, *Walden.*

[819] *Bible*, Matthew 18:18, 21-22.

[820] Simonelli, *Self-Transcendence, a Mystical Perspective in von Hildebrand's "The Nature of Love."* Part of a paper presented at the **Pontifical University of the Holy Cross, Rome, Italy,** for the "*Dietrich von Hildebrand Legacy Project.*" **Pope Benedict XVI imparted "*To all associated with*** *the work of the Project"* *the* **"*Apostolic Blessing as a pledge of wisdom, strength and peace in the Lord. From the Vatican 30 May 2007.*"**

[821] Dante, *La Divina Commedia*, Paradiso XXX,145 "*l'amor che move il sole e l'altre stelle.*"

[822] *Cf.* Campbell, *The Mask of God: Creative Mythology.*

"This image reproduces very faithfully the Holy Relic known as St. Veronica's Veil" or *The Holy Face*, with Latin certificate of authenticity (Autograph and seal of Pope Leo XIII, July 18, 1887).

[823] Dante Alighieri, *La Vita Nova, Tanto gentile...*, "***Error! Main Document Only.****benignamente d'umiltà vestuta; / e par che sia una cosa venuta / di cielo in terra a miracol mostrare. / Mostrasi sì piacente a chi la mira, / che dà per gli occhi una dolcezza al core, / che intender non la può chi non la prova.*"

[824] *Bible*, Genesis 32:30, פנואל *Pĕnuw'el* Peniel = facing God; פנים *paniym* = face; ראה *ra'ah* = to see.

[825] דבר *dabar* = to set things in order, to lead, to follow, to lay snares, to speak with one another, to put words in order.
[826] *Bible*, Exodus 33:11-20.
[827] *Ordo Amoris*, § 14.
[828] von Hildebrand, *The Nature of Love*, p. 353.
[829] *Bible*, Genesis 4:5; **קין** *Qayin = possession* **מנחה** *minchah = offering.*
[830] *Cf.* von Hildebrand, *The Nature of Love*, p. 352.
[831] *Cf. Bible*, Mark 9:12.
[832] *Cf.* von Hildebrand, *The Nature of Love*, § 1.
[833] *Bible*, Matthew 5:48. *Cf.* Mark 12:33. "*Estote ergo vos perfecti sicut et Pater vester caelestis perfectus est.*"
[834] von Hildebrand, *The Nature of Love*, p. 16, n. 1.
[835] von Hildebrand, *The Nature of Love*, p. 353, n. 3.
[836] *Bible*, Luke 15:12, "*portionem substantiae.*"
[837] *Ibid.* 20. "*cum autem adhuc longe esset vidit illum pater ipsius.*"
[838] von Hildebrand, *The Nature of Love*, p. 353.
[839] *Bible*, Matthew 26:49.
[840] *Ibid.* 50.
[841] *Bible*, Mark 14:18. "*unus ex vobis me tradet qui manducat mecum.*"
[842] *Bible*, Luke 22:48. "*Iuda osculo Filium hominis tradis.*"
[843] von Hildebrand, *The Nature of Love*, p.353.
[844] *Bible*, Matthew 19:21. "*Si vis perfectus esse vade vende quae habes et da pauperibus et habebis thesaurum in caelo et veni sequere me.*"
[845] von Hildebrand, *The Nature of Love*, p. 254.
[846] Renoux, *La preghiera per la pace...*; also *L'Osservatore Romano*, January 1916. "*O Maestro, fa ch'io non cerchi tanto:/ Essere consolato, quanto consolare./ Essere compreso, quanto comprendere. /Essere amato, quanto amare.*"
[847] von Hildebrand, *The Nature of Love*, p. 356.
[848] *Bible*, Deuteronomy 6:5; (*diliges*, ἀγαπήσεις, אהב *'ahab* = human love for another); וְאָהַבְתָּ אֵת יְהוָה אֱלֹהֶיךָ בְּכָל־לְבָבְךָ וּבְכָל־נַפְשְׁךָ וּבְכָל־מְאֹדֶךָ׃ καὶ ἀγαπήσεις κύριον τὸν θεόν σου ἐξ ὅλης τῆς καρδίας σου καὶ ἐξ ὅλης τῆς ψυχῆς σου καὶ ἐξ ὅλης τῆς δυνάμεώς σου *diliges Dominum Deum tuum ex toto corde tuo et ex tota anima tua et ex tota fortitudine tua.*
[849] von Hildebrand, *The Nature of Love*, p. 142, n. 13. Even the successful investor Warren Buffett recognized that, "*There is no power on earth like unconditional love*" (Bay, *Buffett recounts the best advice he's ever received*, *Yahoo! News*, Thu Jul 8, 12:55 am ET).
[850] Plato, *Republic*, VII. 516a.
[851] *Bible*, Matthew 23:12. "*qui autem se exaltaverit humiliabitur et qui se humiliaverit exaltabitur.*"
[852] Plato, *Republic*, VII. 516e.
[853] *Bible*, Matthew 19:30. "*Multi autem erunt primi novissimi et novissimi primi.*"
[854] Francesco, *I fioretti*, cap. VIII, p. 34. "*non è ivi perfetta letizia... tutte queste cosa sosterremmo... per suo amore... in questo è perfetta letizia... Cristo concede... di vincere se medesimo... Io non mi voglio gloriare, se non nella croce del nostro signore Gesù Cristo.*" *Cf.* Paul, 1 Corinthians 13:1-3.
[855] *Cf.* von Hildebrand, *The Nature of Love*, p. 141.
[856] *Bible*, Luke 9:23. *Cf.* Matthew 16:24 and Marc 8:34. "*si quis vult post me*

venire abneget se ipsum et tollat crucem suam cotidie et sequatur me.

[857] Renege (ἀπαρνησάσθω *aparnēsasthō- abneget*) himself/herself (ἑαυτὸν *esauton- se ipsum*).

[858] von Hildebrand, *The Nature of Love*, p. 195.

[859] *Bible*, Matthew 22:30. "*In resurrectione enim neque nubent neque nubentur sed sunt sicut angeli Dei in caelo.*"

[860] von Hildebrand, *The Nature of Love*, § 8.

[861] *Bible*, Matthew 19:29. "*Omnis qui reliquit domum vel fratres aut sorores aut patrem aut matrem aut uxorem aut filios aut agros propter nomen meum centuplum accipiet et vitam aeternam possidebit.*"

[862] *Bible*, Matthew 6:24 and *cf.* Luke 16:13. "*Nemo potest duobus dominis servire aut enim unum odio habebit et alterum diliget aut unum sustinebit et alterum contemnet non potestis Deo servire et mamonae.*"

[863] *Bible*, 1 Corinthians 7:32 to 34. *volo autem vos sine sollicitudine esse qui sine uxore est sollicitus est quae Domini sunt quomodo placeat Deo... qui autem cum uxore est sollicitus est quae sunt mundi quomodo placeat uxori et divisus est... mulier innupta et virgo cogitat quae Domini sunt ut sit sancta et corpore et spiritu quae autem nupta est cogitat quae sunt mundi quomodo placeat viro.*

[864] *Bible*, Luke 14:20. "*dixit uxorem duxi et ideo non possum venire.*"

[865] *Bible*, Luke 14:26. "*si quis venit ad me et non odit patrem suum et matrem et uxorem et filios et fratres et sorores adhuc autem et animam suam non potest esse meus discipulus.*" *hate* (μισεῖ *misei, odit*) *his own* (ἑαυτοῦ *eautou, suam*) *eigenleben* (ψυχή-ν *phsychē-n, anima-m*).

[866] *Bible*, Genesis 22:2, 6, 7, 13.

[867] *Bible*, Exodus 20:5; 34:14; Deuteronomy 4:24; 5:9; 6:15; Joshua 24:19; Ezekiel 39:25; Nahum 1:2. (קנא *qanna'*).

[868] *Bible*, Genesis 22:1 to 18.

[869] *Bible*, Matthew 12:50. "*Quicumque enim fecerit voluntatem Patris mei qui in caelis est ipse meus et frater et soror et mater est.*"

[870] Dante, *La Divina Commedia*, Purgatorio, XXVIII, 128. "*che toglie altrui memoria del peccato.*"

[871] *Bible*, Mark 8:33, ὅτι οὐ φρονεῖς τὰ τοῦ θεοῦ ἀλλὰ τὰ τῶν ἀνθρώπων. "*quae Dei sunt sed quae sunt hominum.*"

[872] Life = *anima-m, i.e.*: subjectivity = *eigenleben, cf.* von Hildebrand, *The Nature of Love*, pp. xxvii-xxx, 139, 141, 179, 194, 200-220 *passim*, 245, 255, 263 321, 362, 367n, 373-374.

[873] *Bible*, Luke 9:24 (*salvam facere*), and Matthew 10:39 (*invenire*). *Cf.* Matthew 16:25 and Marc 8:35. "*qui enim voluerit animam suam* (i.e. : *eigenleben*) *salvam facere* (or *invenit*) *perdet illam nam qui perdiderit animam suam* (i.e. : *eigenleben*) *propter me salvam faciet* (or *inveniet*) *illam.*"

[874] *Bible*, Luke 12:22, 24, 27, 29, 34. "*nolite solliciti esse animae* (i.e.: life, *eigenleben*)... *considerate corvos quia non seminant ... et Deus pascit illos... lilia quomodo crescunt non laborant... nolite in sublime tolli... ubi enim thesaurus vester est ibi et cor vestrum erit.*"

[875] von Hildebrand, *The Nature of Love*, p. 203.

[876] Dante, *La Divina Commedia*, Inferno, XI, 47. "*col cor negando.*"

[877] *Bible*, Luke 12:31; *cf.* Matthew 6:33. "*Verumtamen quaerite regnum Dei et*

haec omnia adicientur vobis."
[878] von Hildebrand, *The Nature of Love*, p. 215.
[879] *Bible*, John 6:58 and 4:10. "*panem... aeternum,*" "*aquam vivam.*"
[880] *Bible*, Deutheronomy 8:3 כִּי עַל־כָּל־מוֹצָא פִי־יְהוָה יִחְיֶה הָאָדָם:
παντὶ ῥήματι τῷ ἐκπορευομένῳ διὰ στόματος θεοῦ.
[881] von Hildebrand, *The Nature of Love*, p. 201.
[882] Own (*eigen*) being in life (*leben*).
[883] *Cf.* צלם *tselem* - εἰκών *eikÓn – imago* (*Genesis, 1:26).*
[884] von Hildebrand, *The Nature of Love*, p. 213.
[885] *Cf.* דמות *dĕmuwth* - **ὅ**μοιος ό*moios – similitudo (Ibid.*).
[886] von Hildebrand, *The Nature of Love*, p. 203.
[887] von Hildebrand, *The Nature of Love*, p. 146.
[888] *Cf.* אור *'owr* - φώς *phÓs – lux* (*Ibid.* 1:3).
[889] φῶς ἐκ φωτός *fōs ek fōtos* Apostles' Creed.
[890] von Hildebrand, *The Nature of Love*, p. 211.
[891] von Hildebrand, *The Nature of Love*, p. 70, 337.
[892] *Cf.* von Hildebrand, *The Nature of Love*, p. 145-6.
[893] von Hildebrand, *The Nature of Love*, p. 145.
[894] Verga, *Novelle rusticane*: *La roba*, p. 119. "*Roba mia, vientene con me*!"
[895] *Cf. Scritti di S. Francesco...* p. 121, *Cantico di frate sole or Laude delle creature* (*Laudes Creaturarum*).
[896] *Cf. per speculum in enigmate* (1 *Corinthians*, 13:12).
[897] *Bible*, John, 1:9. "*lux vera quae inluminat omnem hominem venientem in mundum.*"
[898] von Hildebrand, *The Nature of Love*, p. 131.
[899] von Hildebrand, *The Nature of Love*, p. 220.
[900] von Hildebrand, *The Nature of Love*, p. 206.
[901] von Hildebrand, *The Nature of Love*, p. 84.
[902] von Hildebrand, *The Nature of Love*, p. 215.
[903] von Hildebrand, *The Nature of Love*, p. 206.
[904] von Hildebrand, *The Nature of Love*, p. 217.
[905] Cummings (1894-1962), *Complete Poems*, "*I carry your heart with me,*" 1952.
[906] *Bible,* John 17:21, "*ut omnes unum sint sicut tu Pater in me et ego in te ut et ipsi in nobis unum sint ut mundus credat quia tu me misisti.* "
[907] *Bible*, Matthew 22:30, "*in resurrectione enim neque nubent neque nubentur sed sunt sicut angeli Dei in caelo.*"
[908] Greek: ὁρμή *orméh.*
[909] Greek: ἐπιστήμη *epistéhmeh.*
[910] *Cf.* Schopenhauer, *The world as will and representation.*
[911] The serpent *kuṇḍalinī* covering *yoni-liṅga* (XX century brass-work from India).

[912] *Śaktisaṅgama Tantra* II,52, in Mookerjee, *Kali...*, p. 6.

[913] *Cf. Bible*, 1 Corinthians 3:17, "the temple of God is holy, which [temple] ye are."

[914] Campbell, *The Power of* Myth, Ch. IV. p. 99.

[915] *365 Dalai Lama Daily Advices from the Heart*, Meditation on Homosexuality 131, p. 132.

[916] Leiber, *Opposites Attract*, in the album *Forever your Girl*.

[917] *Cf.* Kurdek, *A general model of relationship commitment...*, pp. 391-405.

[918] *Cf.* Patel, *India's Hijras*.

[919] *Cf.* Réage, *Histoire d'O*.

1995 Quagmyr © of the triskelion (three-legs) enigmatic symbol of circular BDSM divided in three sections meaning:

α) 1) B&D (Bondage-Discipline), 2) D&s (Dominance-submission), 3) S&M (Sadism-Masochism);

β) 1) Safe, 2) Sane, 3) Consensual;

γ) Each individual is one of the three holes representing incompleteness to be filled by another role player as:
1) Top, 2) Bottom or 3) Switch.

The curved lines represent:

I) the fluid border where each role begins and ends;
II) the whipping gesture of lashes.

Colors represent:

a) black, the dark side of sexuality;
b) metallic, the irons shackles of servitude and ownership.

920 Harrison, *Gallic Salt*, pp. 284-285.

Hans Baldung, Grien 1513; Woodcut Germanisches Nationalmuseum, Nuremberg, Germany public domain source http://www.ibiblio.org/wm/paint/auth/baldung/ and http://commons.wikimedia.org/wiki/File:Aristotle_and_Phyllis.jpg

[921] *Bible, Genesis, 1:2,* emphasis is ours (man, Adam, אדם *'adam;* image = צלם

tselem - εἰκών *eikÓn – imago*; likeness דמות *dĕmuwth); 27* (male = זכר *zakar*) and (female = נקבה *nĕqebah*); 5:2; 2:7, *dust* = עפר *'aphar; inhabited ground* = אדמה *'adamah (cf. Adam,* אדם).

[922] Plato, *Symposium*, 190a-c.

[923] Campbell, *The Power of Myth*, Cp. I. Myth and the modern world, pp. 7-8.

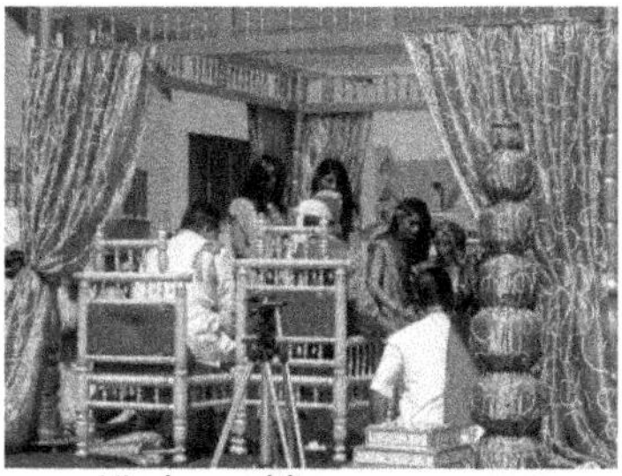

Hindu wedding ceremony
(Pier Village, Long Branch, NJ, USA 2008).

[924] *Getting Married*, Preface § FOR BETTER FOR WORSE.

[925] Legacy Project.

[926] *The Nature of Love*, p. 337 n. 7.

[927] Kirkpatrick, *The Conservative-Christian Big Thinker*.

[928] *Cf. Ibid.* Also George, *One Man, One Woman*, and *Utah will be whipped into line*.

[929] Interesting are the group statue of sculptor Evelyn Wilson

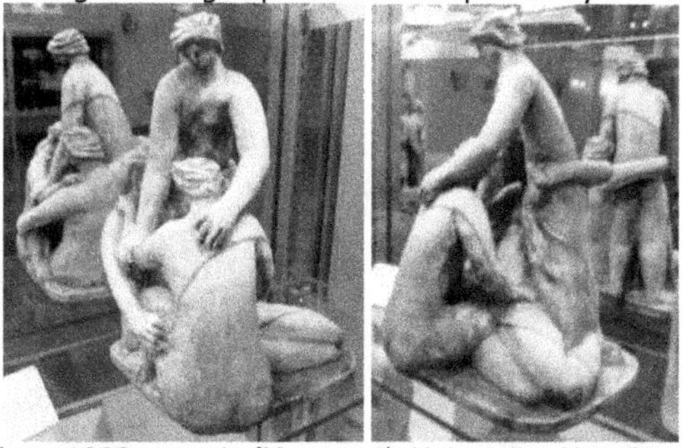

Bathers, 1990 ceramic (Monmouth University, New Jersey).

[930] *Cf.* White, *'Choosy' women set high standards for sperm*.

[931] *Cf.* Weil, *What if It's (Sort of) a Boy and (Sort of) a Girl?*

[932] *Bible*, Matthew 19:12.

[933] *Cf.* University of Wisconsin biologist, **Error! Main Document Only.**Bagemihl, *Biological Exuberance*.

Furthermore, homosexual behavior among non-human animals was observed by the University of Oslo zoologist Petter Böckman (**c**urator of the Norwegian Natural History Museum exhibition "*Against Nature's Order*"), by the University of Hawaii zoologist Lindsay Young (studying an albatross colony at Kaena Point), by Ohio Health and Science

University physiologist Charles Roselli (studying domestic rams), and others.

934 *Cf.* Eliade, *Lo sciamanesimo e le tecniche dell'estasi*, p. 201.

935 *Cf.* Herdt, *Ritualized Homosexuality in Melanesia*, Ritualized Homosexual Behavior in the Male Cults of Melanesia, 1862-1983: An Introduction, pp. 1-73.

936 *Cf.* Roscoe, *The Zuni Man-Woman*, p.5.

937 *Cf.* Nanda, *Neither Man Nor Woman: The Hijras of India*; also *cf.* Ardhanārīśvara, the Śiva-Pārvatī's androgynous form.

938 Latin, *māter–matrem,* mother, + suffix *monium*, condition.

Infant Kṛshṇa with his foster mother Yaśodā. (Tamil Nadu, *Pudukkottai* and *Thanjavur* district, India, Chola period, early 12th century. Copper alloy. Metropolitan Museum of Art, New York, N. 1982.220.8).

939 Lyall, *A Duchess With a Common Touch.*

940 *Marriage and Morals*, p. 224.

941 THE ASSOCIATED PRESS *Russia Furious Over Adopted Boy Sent Back From US.* Other adoptions ended in a similar way and some resulted with the death of the infant.

942 *Cf.* Dante, *La Divina Commedia*, Inferno, Eighth Circle, Malebolge: Fraudulent and Malicious, I Bolgia, XVIII v. 130-3 " *quella sozza e scapigliata fante/ che là si graffia con l'unghie merdose,.../ Taide è, la puttana.*"

Illustration by Gustave Doré (detail).

[943] Satir, *Making Contact*, Goals for Me.
[944] Greek, μονός *monós* = one - γάμος *gámos* = marriage.
[945] Greek, πολύ *polú* = many.
[946] Greek, γυνή *gyné* = woman.
[947] Greek, ανδρός *andrós* of man.
[948] *The New York Times, GRIST; I Don't...*
[949] *Cf.* CNN.com transcripts, *Burden of proof, DNA in Divorce Court.*
[950] Abraham (*Genesis* 16:1-4, 21:21), Esau (*Genesis* 26:34, 28:9), Jacob (*Genesis* 29:21-28, 37:2), Moses (*Exodus* 18:2, *Numbers* 12:1), David (*1 Samuel* 18:28, 25:22-23, (*2 Samuel* 3:2, 5:13, 11:26) and King Solomon (*1 Kings* 11:3).
[951] Women, 4:3.
[952] del-Vasto, *Return to the Source*, p, 247. *Cf.* Manu, *The Laws of Manu*, V.
[953] Manu, *The Laws of Manu*, III.55.6.
[954] *Bible*, Leviticus 20:1, 2, 10, 27 and 24:14, 16, 23.

Doré, Stoning of St. Stephen, Dante, *The Divine Commedy*, Purgatorio, XV 106-108, p. 389.

[955] *Bible*, Genesis 16:1-16.
[956] Book 1: *Adi Parva* II.88.
[957] *Cf. W.* p. 502a, *draupadī* "descendant from *drupada*," "a post (to which captives are tied)" (503a).

At the far right is Draupadī, to her left are her five Pāṇḍava husbands, in sequence: Arjuna, Bhima, Yudhishthira, Nakūla and Sahadeva. Dashavatar Vishṇu Temple, Lalitpur district, Deogarhm Uttar Pradesh, India. (Creative Commons Attribution 2.0 Generic, File:2716 PandavaDraupadifk.jpg.jpg).

[958] Polgreen, *One Bride for 2 Brothers: A Custom Fades in India.*
[959] *Cf.* Amin, *The Last of the Maasai*, pp. 86-87.
[960] Fleming, (1994).

---

[961] Mallozzi. *Cf.* also *Polyandry.org* at
http://www.solidstatelight.com/polyandry/index.htm.
[962] Safire, *Essay; A Polyandry Solution.*
[963] Showtime, *Polyamory: Married and Dating.*
[964] Latin, *amor* = love.

1

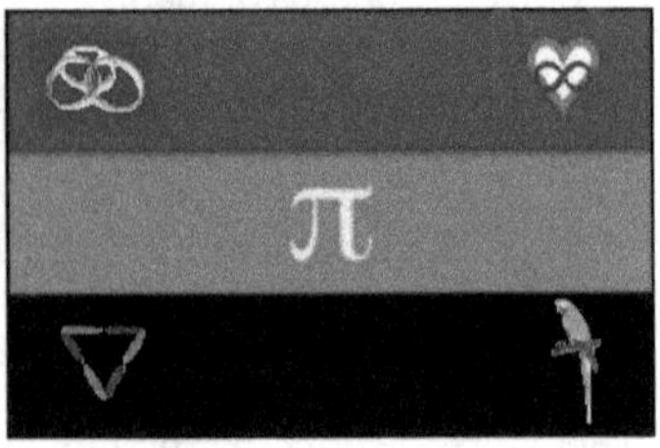
2

3

4

1) Poliamory pride in San Francisco 2004.jpg (800 × 556 pixels, file size: 113 KB, MIME type: image/jpeg), taken 6/27/04 by Pretzelpaws with a Casio QV-3000EX camera. Cropped 1/12/05 using the Gimp. (Source: Wikipedia http://en.wikipedia.org/wiki/File:Poliamory_pride_in_San_Francisco_2004.jpg).
2) and various symbols of polyamory:
a) Upper blue band with left symbol of multiple interlocked gold wedding bands and
b) with right symbol of a red heart with an infinity blue symbol in a white field.
c) Center red band with center gold Greek letter π *pi* for π-ολὐ *p-olý* = many *amores* = loves.
d) Lower black band with left symbol of a purple Möbius Strip symbolizing the interlocked variety of gender-orientations and
e) with right red and white mascot parrot commonly named *Poly*. The colors symbolize: black solidarity with those socially compelled to hide their nature, blue open honesty, gold emotional attachment, purple neutrality, red passionate love and white purity of sentiments.
3) The parrot Poly/Cupid grips the Mind (19th century polychrome ceramic sculpture).
4) <83 Emoticon and graphic symbol.

[965] *A Bouquet of Lovers* http://original.caw.org/articles/bouquet.htm (in *Green*

Egg, The official Journal published on-line of the Neo-pagan Church of All Worlds, Rogersville, TN), italic is ours.

[966] *Cf.* Error! Main Document Only.Mystic Life, *Welcome to Polyamory - An Unconditional Love!*

[967] Krishnamurti, *Total freedom...*, pp. 127 to 129.

[968] *Cf. Woods (scientist researcher at Duke University, Department of Evolutionary Anthropology), Bonobo Handshake... Cf.* Ryan, *Sex at Dawn...*, pp. 101 fol.).

[969] Dalai Lama, Ethics for the new millennium, p. 127.

[970] *Bible*, John 13:34 (Italic is our), *cf.* -35 & 15:12 & 17; 1John 4:7 & 11-12; 2John 1:5; Ephesians 4:2; Galathians 5:13; Hebrews 10:24; 1Peter 1:22, 3:8; Romans 12:10, 13:8 & 35; 1Thessalonians 3:12, 4:9.

[971] "*donec mors nos separaverit*" (*Liber Precum Publicarum*, § *De Solenni Matrimonio*).

[972] Reich, *The Sexual Revolution*, p. 27.

[973] *Cf.* Block, *Open.*

[974] *Cf. Anapol, Polyamory..., p. 192. Cf. Polyamory India group (http://groups.google.com/group/polyamory-india/web/email) and Polyamory: The New Love. Cf.* also Easton, Hardy, *The Ethical Slut*, Kaldera, *Pagan Polyamory*, Ravenscroft, *Polyamory* and Taormino, *Opening Up*.

1928 photogravure of the *Kandariyā Mahādeva.*

[975] *Cf.* Walker, *Evolutionary history...*

[976] *Cf.* Carelli-Gallois, *Meeting ancestors: The Zo'e.*

[977] Jillings, *The Zoé.*

[978] WBAL TV, *Cuddle Parties.*

[979] **Error! Main Document Only.**Cohen, ***Error! Main Document Only.****Open the Marriage, Close the Door*, p. 16.

[980] *Expanding the notion of family* (http://www.polyamoryonline.org/); *Human Awareness Institute*, (http://www.hai.org/); *Loving More, New Models for Relationships* (http://www.lovemore.com/); *Modern Poly <83* (http://www.modernpoly.com/); *Network for a New Culture* (http://www.cfnc.us/index.html); *Polyamory organization UK* (http://www.polyamory.org.uk/polyamory_guide.html); *Polyamory is Family commitment for Eternity* (http://www.4thefamily.us/); *Polyamory Links & Resources* (http://www.xeromag.com/fvpolylinks.html); *Polyamory-Related Books*

(http://www.polychromatic.com/); *Polyamory weekly* (www.polyweekly); *Poly Camping* (http://www.polycamp.net/); *Polymatchmaker* (http://polymatchmaker.com/); *Practical Polyamory* (http://www.practicalpolyamory.com/); *Spiritual Polyamory* (http://www.spiritualpolyamory.com/); *The Desire Curve* (http://www.thedesirecurve.com/); *The Polyamory Society, Serving the Polyamorous Community* (http://www.polyamorysociety.org/); Tilted Forum Project, The Evolution of Humanity, Sexuality and Philosophy (http://www.tfproject.org/tfp/); *UnificationDotCom, 'pathways to healing yourself'* (http://Unification.com); *Usenet newsgroup* (http://www.polyamory.org/); *World Polyamory Association* (http://www.worldpolyamoryassociation.org/) and others.

981 Like the one sponsored, on May 13-16, 2010, and presented by members of the polyamory community, the Southern Polyamory Gathering (SPG), at All World Acres (AWA, a not for profit polyamory sanctuary) in Florida, 4715 Bruton Rd., Plant City, Tampa Bay area, http://healingtoday.com/all_world_acres.htm; or Groups without web pages, like: The *Body Sacred* (*TBS*), a community in the region of NY State embracing sexuality, intimacy and spirituality by coming together in retreat space; *The Body Electric School programs*; *Network for a New Culture Summer Camp*; *PolyLiving*; and others.

[982] Ogilvie, *In Praise of Polyandry*.

[983] ITP, *New Psy.D. in Clinical Psychology Program*, (polyresearcher@yahoo.com).

[984] *Cf.* FOX 4 News Peter Daut, *Dallas Twins Have Different Dads*, and FOX News Network, *Doctors Discover Dallas Twins Have Two Different Dads*: May 2009, DNA scientists in Dallas, Texas, ascertained that the twins of Mia Washington had two different fathers.

[985] Developed at the Division of Reproductive Sciences and funded by the Oregon National Primate Research Center (ONPRC) of the Oregon Health & Science University (OHSU), the Oregon Stem Cell Center, the National Center for Research Resources, the National Institute of Child Health and Human evelopment of the National Institutes of Health. *Cf.* Masahito, *Mitochondrial gene replacement in primate offspring and embryonic stem cells*.

[986] The poly-geometry jargon illustration of relationship structures refers as: "V" = a relationship with two different persons who are not romantically or sexually involved with each other; "TRIAD, etc."= a relationship in which everyone is involved with each other; "N," "U," "Z," FOURSOME; "W," or "M," FIVE-SOME, etc. = a relationship with two people who, in turn, are involved each with other persons.

[987] Walker, *Evolutionary history...*

[988] *Cf.* Crocker, *Extramarital sexual practices...*, pp. 184–94.

[989] *Cf.* Crocker, *The Canela (Brazil) taboo system...* p. 326. *Cf.* Ryan, *Sex at Dawn...*, pp. 11-12.

[990] Walker, *Evolutionary history...*

[991] Tavernise, *Married Couples Are No Longer a Majority, Census Finds*.

[992] Child care in ancient Egypt.

Reproduction Cairo, Egypt.

[993] Open Love NY is an organization "open to ALL people interested in polyamory" since 2009.

[994] Diana Adams Law, *A Brooklyn attorney...* with offices in Brooklyn and Albany, NY, serves, since 2006, the "lesbian/ gay/ bisexual/ trans/ poly/ kink communities, clients in other nontraditional families such as grandparent child guardians, single parents, and blended families, and clients who seek more traditional family law support for divorce or child custody. *Cf.* Diana Adams (BA in Political Science from Yale and JD from Cornell Law School), *FEMINISTOUTLAW.COM.*; *cf.* Diana-Adams, *True Life "I'm Polyamorous*," *cf.* Polyamory in the News, *The Pansexual, Polyamorous, BDSM Law School Application*; *cf*, Current, *Sexual Civil Rights Lawyer*; and *cf.* *sex activist* Quinones, *Reader Beatdown...*

[995] *Cf.* Fried, *The Notion of Tribe*. *Cf.* Walker, *Evolutionary history...*

[996] *Cf.* Paul, *The Un-Divorced.*

[997] *Cf.* Fourier, *The theory of the four movements*, pp. 109-180.

Paris, France.

[998] "NORTH AMERICAN PHALANX Site of the 1844 cooperative agricultural community founded by Albert Brisbane and modeled after the philosophy of French Socialist Charles Fourier. This communal experiment was a success until it was destroyed by fire in 1854."

Phalanx Rd and Woodhollow Rd., Colts Neck Township, NJ USA

[999] Zellner, W. W., Kephart, W. M. *Extraordinary groups...*, p. 77. Barnard, *The Utopia of Sharing in Oneida, N.Y.*; criminal charges ended the Oneida experiment in 1879. For a brief "*History of Polyamory*," see *Anapol, Polyamory..., Chapter 3.*

1907 Post Card of the Oneida Community, Home Building (Public domain photo, source Wikipedia).

[1000] Hebrew דָּגָן *dagan* = grain of corn.
[1001] Russell, *Marriage and Morals*, p. 179.
[1002] Exodus 20:5; *cf.* 34:14; Deuteronomy 4:24; 5:9; Joshua 24:19 Nahum 1:2 Zechariah 1:14; 8:2.
[1003] *Bible*, 2Corinthians 11:2.
[1004] *Bible*, Numbers 5:14-30.
[1005] *Cf.* Ryan, *Sex at Dawn...*, pp. 13-15 and 166 fol.
[1006] *Cf.* Columbus, *The journal...*, p. 124.
[1007] Farabee, *The central Arawaks*, p. 95.
[1008] Walker, *Evolutionary history...*
[1009] Russell, *Marriage and Morals*, p. 193.
[1010] Dante, *The Divine Commedy*, Inferno, V. 82.84, p. 53 "*colombe dal disio chiamate... vegnon per l'aere, dal voler portate.*"

Doré, Paolo and Francesca stabbed by Gianciotto.

[1011] Code, *To Raise Happy Kids, Put Your Marriage First*, pp. 246 fol. *Cf.* Russell, *Marriage and Morals*, p. 191.
[1012] *Bible*, 1 Corinthians 1 to 8 (italic and emphasis are ours).
[1013] Winegar, *Kerista Home.*
[1014] Krishnamurti, *Total freedom...*, pp. 129-130.

SELECTED and QUOTED BIBLIOGRAPHY and FILMOGRAPHY

Acaranga Sutra. (1981). *Ayaro (Acaranga Sutra) The First Anga Agama (Canonical Text) of the Jainas : The Text in Devanagari and Roman Scripts with English Translation, Annotations, Notes, Glossary and Index.* (A. Tulsi, Trans.) New Delhi: Today & Tomorrow's Printers and Publishers.

Accattoli, L. (1994, maggio 18). "non c' e' posto per un Papa emerito". *Corriere della Sera*, p. 17.

Allen. J. L. Jr. (2013, Feb. 15). A quick course in 'Conclave 101'. *National Catholic Reporter.*

Amin, M., Willetts, D., Eames J.D. (1987). *The Last of the Maasai.* Nairobi: Camerapix Publishers International.

Anapol, D. (1997). *Polyamory: The New Love Without Limits.* San Rafael: IntiNet Resource Center.

Anapol, D. (2010). *Polyamory in the 21st Century Love and Intimacy with Multiple Partners.* Lanham, MD: Rowman & Littlefield .

Angelini, G. (1950). *NUOVO DIZIONARIO LATINO-ITALIANO* (IX ed.). Milano-Roma-Napoli-Città di Castello: Società Editrice Dante Alighieri p.a. (Albrighi, Segati e C,.

Aprile, S. (2001). *Vita Che Teatro.* Napoli: Lettere Italiane di Alfredo Guida Editore.

Armstrong, K. (1993). *Muhammed: A biography of the Prophet.* San Francisco: Harper.

Armstrong, K. (2010). *Twelve Steps to a Compassionate Life.* New York, Toronto: Borzoi Books Alfred A. Knopf and Alfred A. Knopf Canada.

Arnstein, P. et Al. (2002, September). From chronic pain patient to peer: Benefits and risks of volunteering. *Pain Management Nursing, Volume 3, Issue 3*, 94–103.

Augustine. (1965). *In Epistolam Joannis Ad Parthos Tractatus Decem PL 35, 1977-2062.* (Migne-Patrologia-Latina, Ed.) Upper Saddle River, New Jersey: Gregg Publishing.

Augustine. (1992). *Confessions, Latin text.* (J. J. O'Donnel, Ed.) Oxford: Clarendon Press.

Aurobindo, Sri Gosh. (1994). *The Life Divine.* Twin Lakes, WI: Lotus Light Publications.

Bagemihl, B. (1999). *Biological Exuberance: Animal Homosexuality and Natural Diversity.* New York: St. Martin's Press.

Barnard, B. Q. (2007, August 3). The Utopia of Sharing in Oneida, N.Y. . *The New York Times.*

Baulot, Isaac (?). (1677). *Mutus Liber.* La Rochelleunder, France: Pierre Savouret.

Bay, W. (2010, July 8, 12:55 am ET). Buffett recounts the best advice he's ever received. *Yahoo! News THE UPSHOT News Blog http://news.yahoo.com/s/yblog_upshot/20100708/bs_yblog_upshot/buffett-recounts-the-best-advice-hes-ever-received.*

Bellamy, F. (1892, September 8). Pledge of Allegiance. (PerryMason&Co., Ed.) *The Youth's Companion (Boston, Massachusetts).*

Benard, E. A. (1994). *Chinnamastā: The Aweful Buddhist and Hindu Tantric Goddess.* Delhi: Motilal Banarsidass Publishers Private Limited.

Bentham, J. (1838-1843). ANARCHICAL FALLACIES; BEING AN EXAMINATION OF THE DECLARATIONS OF RIGHTS ISSUED DURING THE FRENCH REVOLUTION (1843, Vol. 2, Part V). *The Works of Jeremy Bentham, published under the Superintendence of his Executor, John Bowring, 11.* Edinburgh, Scottland, UK: William Tait. Retrieved 1 27, 2013, from http://oll.libertyfund.org/title/1921/114226

Bentham, J. (1961). *The Utilitarians: an introduction to the principles of morals and legislation.* Garden City, N.Y.: Doubleday.

BG. (n.d.). *Bhagavad Gītā* (1926 text ed.). (Besant, Ed.) Adyar, Madras, India: Theosophical Publishing House.

BG. Bhagavad-Gītā. (1926 text ed.). *BG. Bhagavad-Gītā.* (Besant, Ed.) Adyar, Madras, India: Theosophical Publishing House.

Bible. (1958). *The Holy Bible.* (K. J. version, Ed.) Philadelphia, PA: The National Bible Press.

Bible. (1967). *New Testament: Η ΚΑΙΝΗ ΔΙΑΘΗΚΗ, ΒΙΒΛΙΚΗ ΕΤΑΙΡΙΑ.* Athens: Ancient text with Modern Greek tr.

Bible. (1970). *The New English Bible with the Apocrypha.* Oxford, Cambridge, USA: Cambridge University Press.
Bible. (n.d.). *Biblia sacra, vulgatae editionis* (1957 ed.). (Sixti-V-et-Clementis-VIII, Ed.) Romae: Editiones Paulinae.
Block, J. (2008). *Open: Love, Sex and Life in an Open Marriage.* Berkley CA: Seals Press.
Bloom, P. (2010 , May 3). The Moral Life of Babies. *The New York Times Magazine*, pp. 44-63.
Borbély, A. (1986). *Secrets of Sleep.* (Schneider, Trans.) New York: Basic Books, Inc.
Brecht, B. (2008). *Life of Galileo.* New York: Penguin Books.
Bṛhaspati. (1952). *Bārhaspatya-sūtra : with Malayālam commentary.* Madras: Govt. Oriental Manuscripts Library.
Brown, H. (1998-2003). *Suicide by Cop.* Retrieved April 14, 2013, from Police Stressline: http://www.geocities.com/~halbrown/suicide_by_cop_1.html
Bruno, G. (1925-7). *Opere italiane* (Vols. I, DIALOGHI METAFISICI, II, DIALOGHI MORALI, III, COMMEDIA). (G. G.-I. V. Spampanato (III), Ed.) Bari: Laterza.
Brunton, P. (1985). *A Search in Secret India.* York Beach, Maine: Samuel Weiser, Inc.
Budge, E. A. Wallis. (1967). *The Egyptian Book of the Dead, (The Papyrus of Ani) Egyptian Text Translitteration and Translation.* New York: Dover Publications, Inc.
Calvin, J. (1957). *Institutes of the Christian religion.* Grand Rapids: Eerdmans.
Campbell, J. (1968). *The Mask of God: Creative Mythology.* NY: The Viking Press.
Campbell, J. (1988). *The Power of Myth, with Bill Moyers.* New York: Doubleday.
Campbell, J. (1990). *The Flight of the Wild Gander. Explorations in the Mythological Dimensions of Fairy Tales, Legends and Symbols.* New York: Harper Perennial A Division of HarperCollins Publishers.
Campbell, J. (2008). *The Hero with a Thousand Faces.* Novaro, California: New World Library.
Carbonara, C. (1967). *Introduzione alla filosofia.* Napoli: L.S.E.

Carelli, V., Gallois, D. T. (1993). *Meeting ancestors The Zo'e.* Brasília: Centro de Trabalho Indigenista.

Carelli-Gallois (Director). (1993). *Meeting ancestors: The Zo'e /* [Motion Picture]. Brasilia: Latin American Video Archives & US Description: Visual Material.

Carlyle, T. (1899). *The French revolution; a history, by Thomas Carlyle; with a special introduction by Julian Hawthorne* (Vol. II). New York: The Colonial Press.

Caswall, E. (Ed.). (1873). *Hymns and poems, original and translated* (II ed.). (E. Caswall, Trans.) London: Burns, Oates, & Co.

Cathcart T. & Klein D. (2008). *Plato and a Platypus Walk into a Bar , Understanding Philosophy Through Jokes.* New York: Penguin Books.

Ceddin, deden. (2002). *Ottoman Turkish Janissarian march, Ceddin, deden.* Retrieved 12 21, 2012, from TheOttomans.org: http://www.theottomans.org/english/campaigns_army/mehter.asp

Charter for compassion. (2009, November 12). *The Charter for Compassion.* Retrieved April 13, 2013, from The Charter for Compassion http://charterforcompassion.org/: http://charterforcompassion.org/the-charter

Chevalier, Jean, & Gheerbrant, Alain . (1974). *Dictionnaire des Symboles.* Paris: Seghers.

Christakis, N., Fowler. J. (2009). *Connected: The Surprising Power of Our Social Networks and How They Shape Our Lives.* New York, NY: Little Brown and Company.

Cicero. (1992). *De Senectute, De Amicitia, De Divinatione. With an English Ranslation.* (Falconer, Trans.) Cambridge, MA: The Loweb Classical Library, Harvard University Press.

Clarke, D. M. (2006). *Descartes: a biography.* New York: Cambridge University Press.

Cleary, Thomas translator . (1994). *Instant Zen: Waking Up in the Present.* (T. Cleary, Trans.) Berkeley, CA: North Atlantic Books.

CNN.com. (2001, Aired January 2 - 12:30 p.m. ET). *CNN.com transcripts.* Retrieved May 13, 2010, from Burden of Proof, DNA in Divorce Court:

http://transcripts.cnn.com/TRANSCRIPTS/0101/02/bp.00.html

Code, D. (2009). *To Raise Happy Kids, Put Your Marriage First.* New York, NY: Crossroad Publishing Company.

Cohen, R. (2010, January 27). Open the Marriage, Close the Door. *The New York Times, The Times Magazine, The Ethicist*, p. 16.

Columbus, C. (1893). *The journal of Christopher Columbus etc.* . London: Chas. J. Clark for The Hakluyt Society.

Confucius. (1986). *The Analects (Lun yü).* (D. Lau, Trans.) Middlesex England, NY, USA, Bungay, Suffolk, G.B.: Penguin Books.

Croce, B. (1990). *Breviario di estetica - Aesthetica in nuce* (8 ed.). Milano: Adelphi.

Crocker, W. (1968). The Canela (Brazil) taboo system: A preliminary exploration of an anxiety-reducing device. *Verhandlungen 3:323–31, XXXVIII Internationalen Amerikansterkongresses*, 323–31.

Crocker, W. (1974). Extramarital sexual practices of the Ramkókamekra-Canela Indians: An analysis of socio-cultural factors. In P. J. Lyon (Ed.), *Native South Americans: Ethnology of* (pp. 184–94). Boston: Little, Brown.

Crowley, A. (1969). *The Confessions of Aleister Crowley : An Autobiography.* New York: Bantam Book.

Cummings, E. E. (1991). *Complete Poems: 1904-1962.* (G. J. Firmage, Ed.) New York: Liveright Publishing Corporation.

Current (Director). (2009). *Sexual Civil Rights Lawyer http://current.com/shows/max-and-jason-still-up/89808888_sexual-civil-rights-lawyer.htm* [Motion Picture].

DAILY MAIL REPORTER. (2009, August 24). Teenage lottery millionaire who won £1.9m broke at 22, http://www.dailymail.co.uk/news/article-1208498/Teenage-lottery-millionaire-Callie-Rogers-won-1-9m-broke-22.html#ixzz2PbpqIQfu. *Daily Mail, Associated Newspapers Ltd Part of the Daily Mail, The Mail on Sunday & Metro Media Group Daily Mail, http://www.dailymail.co.uk/ushome/index.html.*

Dalai Lama. (1989, December 10). *Nobel Peace Prize Acceptance Speech.* Retrieved April 11, 2013, from His Holiness The 14th Dalai Lama of Tibet: http://www.dalailama.com/messages/acceptance-speeches/nobel-peace-prize

Dalai Lama. (1997). *Healing Anger. The Power of Patience from a Buddhist Perspective.* (G. T. Jinpa, Trans.) Ithaca, New York: Snow Lion Publication.

Dalai Lama. (1999). *Ethics for the new millennium .* New York: The Berkley Publishing Group Penguin Putnam Inc.

Dalai Lama. (2007). *365 Dalai Lama Daily Advices from the Heart.* (M. Ricard, Ed., & C.Bruynt, Trans.) New York: Metro Books.

Dalai Lama, Cutler H. (1998). *The Art of Happiness. A Handbook for Living.* New York: Riverhead Book.

Dalrymple, W. (2010). *Nine Lives: In Search of the Sacred in Modern India.* New York: Alfred A. Knopf a division of Random House, Inc.

Damasio, A. (2010). *Self Comes to Mind: Constructing the Conscious Brain.* New York: Pantheon Books.

Dante Alighieri. (1930). *La divina commedia illustrata da Gustavo Doré.* Milano: Casa Editrice Sonzogno.

Dante Alighieri. (1999). *La Vita Nova .* Milano: Arnoldo Mondadori.

Darwin, C. (1913). *The Expression of the Emotions in Man and Animals.* New York: D. Appleton and Company.

Dawkins, R. (1976). *The Selfish Gene.* Oxford: Oxford University Press.

De Pretis, A. (2004). *Epistolarity in the First Book of Horace's Epistles.* Piscataway, NJ: Gorgias Press.

De Waal, F. (2013). *The Bonobo and the Atheist In Search of Humanism Among the Primates.* New York: W. W. Norton & Company.

Declaration of Independence. (2006). *The Declaration of Independence as Adopted by the Second Continental Congress.* Retrieved 12 21, 2012, from Declaring Independence - Digital History - http://www.digitalhistory.uh.edu/learning_history/revolution/revolution_declaringindependence.cfm:

http://www.digitalhistory.uh.edu/learning_history/revolution/declaration_of_independence.cfm

del-Vasto, L. (1972). *Return to the Source.* (J. Sidgwick, Trans.) New York: Schocken Books.

Derrida, J. (2001). *The Work of Mourning.* Chicago, London: The University of Chicago Press.

Descartes, R. (1664). *Renati Des Cartes Meditationes de prima philosophia in quibus Dei existentia, & animae humanae aì corpore distinctio demonstrantur : his adjungitur tractatus De initiis primae philosophiae juxta fundamenta clarissimi Cartesii, tradita in ipsius meditation.* Londini : Excudebat J.F. pro Jona Hart.

Descartes, R. (1673). *Les Méditations Métaphysiques De René Descartes Touchant La Première Philosophie. Dediées À Messieurs De Sorbone - Sic. Nouvellement Divisées Par Articles Avec Des Sommaires À Costé .* Paris: Théodore Girard.

Descartes, R. (1886). *Discours de la meìthode pour bien conduire sa raison et chercher la veìriteì dans les sciences.* Paris: Lib. de la Bibliotheìque nationale.

Descartes, R. (1966). *Descartes. Philosophical Writings.* (Anscombe&Geach, Ed.) London: Nelson.

Descartes, R. (1977). *The philosophical works of Descartes : rendered into English / by Elizabeth S. Haldane, and G.R.T. Ross.* (Haldane&Ross, Trans.) Cambridge: The University Press.

Descartes, R. (pref. 1899). *Discourse on the method of rightly conductiong the reason, and seeking truth in the sciences. Translated from the French and collated with the Latin by John Veitch.* (J. Veitch, Trans.) La Salle, Ill.: Open Court Pub. Co.

deZayas, M. (1932, May). Picasso Speaks. *The Arts, 3*(5).

Diana Adams. (2006). *FEMINISTOUTLAW.COM.* Retrieved April 16, 2010, from FeministOutlaw.com: http://feministoutlaw.com/

Diana Adams Law. (2006). *A Brooklyn attorney for traditional and nontraditional families.* Retrieved April 16, 2010, from DianaAdamsLaw.net: http://www.dianaadamslaw.net/

Diana-Adams (Director). (2010). *True Life "I'm Polyamorous"* [Motion Picture]. http://www.mtv.com/videos/true-life-im-polyamorous/1631509/playlist.jhtml.

Diana-Adams (Director). (2010). *True Life "I'm Polyamorous"* [Motion Picture]. http://www.mtv. com/videos/ true-life-im-polyamorous/ 1631509/playlist .jht\ml.

Diogenes Laërtius. (1958-59). *Lives of eminent philosophers text and English translation.* (R. D. Hicks, Trans.) Cambridge: Loeb classical library Harvard University Press.

Donida-Mogol. (1961). Al Di Là. *Sheet Music.* Harlow, Essex UK: Alfred Publishing Co.

D'Souza, D. (2002). *What's So Great About America.* Washington DC: Regnery Publishing, Inc.

D'Souza, D. (2007). *What's So Great about Christianity.* Washington, DC: Regnery Publishing Inc.

Dumézil, G. (1977). *La religione romana arcaica.* (F. Jesi, Trans.) Milano: Rizzoli Editore.

Dutton, K. (2012). *The Wisdom of Psychopaths: What Saints, Spies, and Serial Killers Can Teach Us About Success.* New York: Scientific American / Ferrar, Straus and Giroux.

Easton, D., Hardy, J. W. (2009). *The Ethical Slut: A Practical Guide to Polyamory, Open Relationships & Other Adventures.* Berkeley, CA: Celestial Arts.

Eckhart, M. (1941). *Meister Eckhart: A Modern translation.* (R.B.Blakney, Trans.) New York: Harper Torchbooks, Harper & Row.

Economist. (2010, October 2). Alien ambassador. *The Economist,* pp. 21, Economist.com/node/21011257.

Eliade, M. (1953 (En.) 1972). *Lo sciamanesimo e le tecniche dell'estasi (En. tr.) Shamanism: archaic techniques of ecstasy.* (Italian-d'Altavilla, Trans.) Roma-Milano (En.) Princeton, N.J.: Fr. Bocca Editori (En.) Princeton University Press.

Engels, F. (1999). *Socialism: Utopian and Scientific.* Sydney: Resistance Books NSW.

Escobedo JR, Adolphs R. (2010, August). Becoming a better person: temporal remoteness biases autobiographical memories for moral events. *Emotion 10(4), doi: 10.1037/a0018723,* 511-8.

Evola, J. (1969). *Rivolta contro il mondo moderno.* Roma: Edizioni Mediterranee.
Evola, J. (2008). *Cavalcare la tigre.* Roma: Edizioni Mediterranee.
Fadiman, James and Robert Frager. (1997). *Essential Sufism.* San Francisco: Harper.
Farabee, W. C. (1918). *The central Arawaks.* Philadelphia: University Museum.
Farkas Simon, A. (2011-2012). *Camilla the Siren The Daughter of Death's Love, the Siren's Call to Life And Her Love Coordinates.* Wilkes-Barre, PA: Kamadeva.
Fleming, A. (Writer), & Fleming, A. (Director). (1994). *Threesome* [Motion Picture].
Fourier, C. (1996). *The theory of the four movements.* (Stedman-Jones&Patterson, Ed.) Cambridge: Cambridge University Press.
FOX 4 News Peter Daut. (2009, May 11). *Dallas Twins Have Different Dads myfoxdfw.com.* Retrieved March 19, 2010, from http://www.myfoxdfw.com/dpp/news/weird/Dallas_Twins_Fathered_by_2_Men
FOX News Network. (2009, May 18). *Dads, Doctors Discover Dallas Twins Have Two Different.* Retrieved March 19, 2010, from Fox News.com http://www.foxnews.com/story/0,2933,520524,00.html: http://www.foxnews.com/story/0,2933,520524,00.html
Francesco. (1902). *I fioretti di San Francesco.* Firenze: G. Barbera Editore.
Fraser, M. (2005). *Weapons of Mass Distraction: Soft Power and American Empire.* New York: St. Martin's Press.
Frédéric Ozanam, Jean Jacques Ampère. (1854). *I poeti francescani in Italia nel secolo decimoterzo.* (Fanfani, Trans.) Firenze: F. Alberghetti e C.
Freud, S. (1927). *The problem of lay-analyses.* (A. P. Maerker-Branden, Trans.) New York: Brentano's Publisher.
Freud, S. (1962-1974, 1953-c1962). *The standard edition of the complete psychological works of Sigmund Freud* (Vol. 24). (A. Richards, Ed., & J. Strachey, Trans.) London: Hogarth Press and the Institute of Psycho-Analysis.
Freud, S. (2010). *The Ego and the Id.* Seattle, Washington: Pacific Publishing Studio.

Fried, M. H. (1975). *The Notion of Tribe.* Menlo Park, CA: Cummings Pub. Co.

Fumagall. (1989). *Chi l'ha detto.* Milano: Hoepli.

Galilei, G. (1960). *The Assayer. The Controversy on the comets of 1618.* Philadelphia: University of Pennsylvania Pres.

Gambari, O. (2009, giugno 1). Bramini, altari e canti come in India. Il rito del fuoco alla Fondazione Merz. *La Repubblica*.

Gandhi, M. (1993). *An Autobiography: The Story of My Experiments with Truth.* (M. H. Desai, Trans.) Boston, MA: Beacon Press.

Gauch, H. G. (2003). *Scientific Method in Practice.* Cambridge, UK: Cambridge University Press.

George, R. P. (2003, November 28). One Man, One Woman. The case for preserving the definition of marriage. *The Wall Street Journal*.

George, R. P. (2008, October 28). *NOM Chairman Robert P. George: "Utah will be whipped into line."*. Retrieved March 20, 2010, from Later-Day Chino: http://www.chinoblanco.com/2009/06/nom-chairman-robert-p-george-utah-will.html

Gill Sam D., Sullivan Irene F. (1992). *Dictionary of Native American Mythology.* New York, Oxford: Oxford University Press.

Gladwell, M. (2002). *The Tipping Point: How Little Things Can Make a Big Difference.* New York: Back Bay Books.

Gounod C.F., Barbier & Carré (librettists). (1859). *Faust: opéra en cinq actes.* Paris: Michel Lévy Frères, Libr.-Éditeurs.

Grant Steen R. . (2001). *DNA & Destiny: Nature & Nurture In Human Behavior.* Cambridge Center, Cambridge, MA: Da Capo Press, Perseus Publishing Group.

Grotius, H. (1853). *De Jure Belli Ac Pacis.* (W. Whewell, Trans.) Cambridge: John W. Parker, London.

Halberg F., Peterson R. E., Silber R. H. (1959). Phase relations of 24-hour periodicities in blood corticosterone, mitoses in cortical adrenal parenchyma and total body activity. *Endocrinology 64. [109]*, 222-230.

Harman, O. (2010). *The Price of Altruism: George Price and the Search for the Origins of Kindness.* New York, NY: W.W. Norton & Company Ltd.

Harrison, R. (1974). *Gallic Salt: Glimpses of the Hilarious Bawdy World of Old French Fabliaux.* Berkeley, Los Angeles: University of California Press.

Hartsuiker, D. (1993). *Sādhus. India's Mystic Holy Men.* Rochester, Vermont: Inner Traditions International.

Heidegger, M. (1996). *Being and time : a translation of Sein und Zei.* Albany, NY: State University of New York Press.

Henrich, J. et. Al. (2010, March 10). Markets, Religion, Community Size, and the Evolution of Fairness and Punishment. *Journal of Science, Vol. 327 no. 5972, DOI: 10.1126/science.1182238*, 1480-1484.

Herdt, G. H. (Ed.). (1984). *Ritualized Homosexuality in Melanesia.* Berkley and Los Angeles, California: University of California Press.

Hermann, G. J. (1884). *Jaina Sutras Part I (Akaranga Sutra & Kalpa Sutra) and Part II (Uttarâdhyayana Sutra & Sutrakritanga Sutra)* (Vol. 2). Oxford: The Clarendon press.

Hobson, J. A. (2009, November). REM sleep and dreaming: towards a theory of protoconsciousness. *Nature Reviews Neuroscience 10 n.11, doi:10.1038/nrn2716*, 803-813.

Homer. (1995). *Odyssey. English & Greek.* (A. Murray, Trans.) Cambridge, Mass: Harvard University Press, The Loeb classical library; L104-Ll05.

Horace. (1815). *Quinti Horatii Flacci Opera. Interpretatione et notis illustravit Ludovicus Desprez cardinalitius socius ac rhetor emeritus (1691).* Neapolis: Excudebat Cajetanus Raymundus.

Hume, D. (1965). *An abstract of A treatise of human nature.* Hamden, Conn.: Archon Books.

Husserl, E. (1958). *Ideas. General Introduction to Pure Phenomenology.* (W. B. Gibson, Trans.) London, New York: G. Allen & Unwin, The Macmillan Co.

Inno di Mameli. (2007, 6 12). *Italian National Anthem Inno di Mameli, Fratelli d'Italia (Italian brothers) (Residenza della Repubblica site accesseds 2012). http://www.quirinale.it/qrnw/statico/simboli/inno/inno.htm.* Retrieved 12 21, 2012, from Presidenza della Repubblica:

http://www.quirinale.it/qrnw/statico/simboli/inno/inno.htm
Ironson, G. H. et. Al. (2008, June). Do Positive Psychosocial Factors Predict Disease Progression in HIV-1? A Review of the Evidence. *Psychosom Med. 70(5) doi: 10.1097/PSY.0b013e318177216c*, 546–554.
ITP. (1975). *Institute of Transpersonal Psychology http://www.itp.edu/index.php*. Retrieved March 14, 2010, from ITP Announces New Psy.D. in Clinical Psychology Program: http://www.itp.edu/academics/resphd/tp.php
Ivanhoe, P.J.; Van Norden, B.W. (2005). *Readings in classical Chinese philosophy.* Indianapolis, IN: Hackett Publishing.
Jātaka. (1939, 2003 Reprint). *The Jataka : Or Stories of the Buddha's Former Births/edited* (Vol. VI). (E. Cowell, Ed., & Cowell-Rouse, Trans.) New Delhi: AES.
Jātaka. (1969). *The Jātaka.* London: Published for the Pali Text Society by Luzac & co.
Jefferson, T. (1998, June). *Letter to the Danbury Baptists. The Final Letter, as Sent Jan. 1. 1802*. Retrieved February 9, 2013, from Library of Congress/Ameritech National Digital Library Competition - Vol 57, No. 6 http://www.loc.gov/index.html: http://www.loc.gov/loc/lcib/9806/danpre.html
Jillings, A. (Director). (1999). *The Zoé: Marrying Tribe of the Amazon* [Motion Picture].
John of the Cross. (1957). *The Dark Night of the Soul.* (K.F.Reinhardt, Trans.) New York: F. Ungar.
John of the Cross, St. (1995). *The Poems of St. John of the Cross. A Bilingual Edition* . (J. F. Nims, Trans.) Chicago: The University of Chicago Press.
Joshi, P. S. (2007). *Gravitational collapse and spacetime singularities.* Cambridge: Cambridge Univ. Press.
Joyce, J. (2009). *Ulysses.* Middlesex TW: The Echo Library.
Jung, C. G. (1958). *Psyche and Symbol. A selection from the Writings of C. G. Jung Archetype, The Phenomenology of the Spirit in Fairy Tales, The Psychology of the Child.* (V. S. De Laszlo, Ed.) Garden Ciyy, NY: Doubleday Anchor Books.

Jung, C. G. (1978). *Psychology and the East.* (Hull, Trans.) Princeton, NJ: Bollingen Series, Princeton University Press.

Juvenal. (2004). *Juvenal and Persius.* (S. M. Braund, Ed., & S. M. Braund, Trans.) Cambridge, Mass: Harvard University Press, Loeb classical library; 91.

Kaldera, R. (2005). *Pagan Polyamory: Becoming a Tribe of Hearts.* Woodbury, MN: Llewellyn Publication.

Kam, N. (2009, 12 29). *Half Guilty.* Retrieved April 23, 2013, from http://nickkam.com/: http://nickkam.com/2009/12/29/half-guilty/

Kant, I. (1900ff). *Grundlegung zur Metaphysik der Sitten - I. Kant, AA IV: Kritik der reinen Vernunft – Prolegomena – Inhaltsverzeichnis - http://www.korpora.org/Kant/aa04/Inhalt4.html.* Berlin: Gesammelte Schriften, Ausgabe der Preußischen Akademie der Wissenschaften, Walter de Gruyter.

Kant, I. (1952). *Fundamental Principles of the Metaphysic of Morals (p. 253-90 of All three Critiques and Metaphysics of Morals)* (Vol. Vol. XLII of the Great Books of the Western World series). (T. Kingsmill-Abbott, Trans.) Chicago, London, Toronto, Geneva, Sydney, Tokyo: Encyclopaedia Britannica.

Kant, I. (1952). *The Critique of Pure Reason (All three Critiques and Metaphysics of Morals)* (Vol. XLII of the Great Books of the Western World series). (M. D. Meiklejohn, Trans.) Chicago, London, Toronto, Geneva, Sydney, Tokyo: Encyclopaedia Britannica.

Kant, I. (1953). *Prolegomena to any future metaphysics that will be able to present itself as a science.* Manchester : Manchester University Press.

Kasser-Meyer-Wurst (Ed.). (2006). *The Gospel of Judas, From Codex Tchacos* (II ed.). Washington, DC: National Geographic Society.

Keeley, L. H. (1996). *War Before Civilization : The Myth of the Peaceful Savage.* Oxford: Oxford University Press.

Kinzer, S. (2006). *Overthrow. America's Century of Regime Change From Hawaii to Iraq.* New York: New York Times Books/ Henry Holt & Company.

Kirkpatrick, D. D. (2009, December 16). The Conservative-Christian Big Thinker. *The New York Times Magazine* .
Kleiser, R. (Writer), & Kleiser, R. (Director). (1982). *Summer Lovers* [Motion Picture].
Kontzevich , Bishop N. (1988). The mystical meaning of the Tsar's martyrdom. *The Orthodox Word 24, n. 5&6.*
Koran. (1963). *The Koran.* (J. Rodwel, Trans.) London - NY: Everyman's Library.
Koran. (1977). *The Holy Qur'an, Arabic text.* (T. M. Association, Ed., & A. Yusuf-Ali, Trans.) USA: American Trust Publications.
Koran. (1995). *The Koran, Arabic text.* (Dawood, Trans.) London - NY, N.J.: Penguin Books.
Krishnamurti, J. (1996). *Total freedom: the essential Krishnamurti.* New York: HarperCollins Publishers.
Kugel, J. J. (1997). *The Bible as it was.* Cambridge, Mass: Harvard University Press.
Kurdek, L. (2008). A general model of relationship commitment: Evidence from same-sex partners. *Personal Relationships, 15*, 391-405.
Kurlantzic, J. (2007). *Charm Offensive: How China's Soft Power is Transforming the World.* New Haven, CT: Yale University Press.
La Marseillaise. (1999, 1 22). *French National Anthem, La Marseillaise.* Retrieved 12 21, 2012, from Assemblée nationale: http://www.assemblee-nationale.fr/english/la_marseillaise.asp
Laland K.N., John Odling-Smee J. Myles S. (2010, February). How culture shaped the human genome: bringing genetics and the human sciences together. *Nature Reviews Genetics 11, doi:10.1038/nrg2734*, 137-148.
Lane, G. (2006). *Daily Life in the Mongol Empire.* Westport, CT: Greenwood Press.
Lanza, Robert, Berman, Bob. (2009). *Biocentrism: How Life and Consciousness Are the Keys to Understanding the True Nature of the Universe.* Dallas: BenBella Books .
Lao Tzu. (1990). *Tao Te Ching, The Classic Book of Integrity and the Way. Based on the Ma-Wang-Tui manuscripts.* (V. Mair, Trans.) N.Y., Toronto, London, Sydney, Auckland: Bantam Books.

Laurentin, René, Rupčić, Ljudevit. (1984). *La Vergine appare a Medjugorje? Un messaggio urgente dato al mondo in un paese marxista.* (B. Pistocchi, Trans.) Brescia: Editrice Queriniana.

Lavoisier, A.-L. (1796). *Elements of chemistry: in a new systematic order, containing all the modern discoveries.* Edinburgh: William Creech.

Legacy Project. (2004). *What is the Legacy Project?* (J. H. Crosby, Editor) Retrieved March 11, 2010, from The Dietrich von Hildebrand Legacy Project: http://www.hildebrandlegacy.org/main.cfm?r1=2.00&ID=2&level=1

Leiber, O. (Composer). (June 13, 1988). Opposites Attract. [Paula Abdul, Performer] On *Forever your Girl.* New York, NY, USA: Virgin.

Leopardi, G. (1940). *Tutte le opere di Giacomo Leopardi* (1 ed.). Milano: A. Mondadori.

Liber Precum Publicarum. (1560 reprint 1847). *Liturgical Sources: Liturgies and Occasional Forms of Prayer Set Forth in the Reign of Queen Elizabeth.* (W. K. Clay, Ed.) London: Parker Society.

Lieven, A. (2006, April Friday,). Imposing democracy and freedom, American-style. *The New York Times.*

Lipski, A. (2007). *The Essential Śrī Ānandamayī Mā. Life and Teaching of a 20th Century Indian Saint.* Bloomington, Indiana: World Wisdom, Inc.

Livy, T. (1949-63). *Ab urbe condita. Text & translation* (Vol. 14). (Foster-Moore-Sage-Schlesinger-Geer, Trans.) Cambridge Mass., London: The Loeb Classical Library, Harvard University Press, William Heinemann Ltd.

Luther, M. (1963). *Luther's Works, Volume 48: Letters I.* (Krodel, Trans.) Philadelphia: Fortress.

Lyall, S. (2010, November 5). A Duchess With a Common Touch. *The New York Times, THE SATURDAY PROFILE.*

Mahābhārata. (1906 - 1910, II ed. 1985). *Sriman Mahābhāratam, According to the Southern Recension based on the South Indian Texts with Footnotes and reading.* (T. R. Krishnacharya and Vyasacharya, Ed.) Delhi - India: Sri Satguru Publications.

Mahadevan, T. (1977-1980). *Ramana Maharshi. The Sage of Arunacala.* (Italian, Trans.) London, Roma: Unwin, Mediterranee ed.

Mallozzi, V. M. (2009, December 19). Fuller/Rodgers. *The New York Times,* p. Wedding/Celebrations section and http://www.nytimes.com/2009/12/20/fashion/weddings/20FULLER.html?_r=1&scp=1&sq=Jessie%20Catherine%20Fuller%20&st=nyt .

Malory, T. (1961). *Le Morte Dārthur, The Book of King Arthur and his Knights of the Round Table* (Vol. 2). New York: University Book.

Manu. (1991). *The Laws of Manu.* (O'Flaherty-Smith, Trans.) London, New York, Toronto: Penguin Books.

Martin Luther. (1883-2009). *D. Martin Luthers Werke: Kritische Gesammtausgabe Weimarer Ausgabe.* Weimar: Hermann Böhlau.

Marx and Engels. (2004). *German Ideology, Part 1 and Selections from Parts 2 and 3.* (C. J. Arthur, Ed.) New York, NY: International Publishers Co.

Marx K., Engels F. (1988). *The Economic and Philosophic Manuscripts of 1844 and the ommunist Manifesto.* (M. Milligan, Trans.) Amherst, NY: Prometheus Books.

Marx, K. (1952). *Capital / Manifesto of the Communist Party.* (F. Engels, Ed.) Chicago: Encyclopaedia Britannica.

Masahito Tachibana, Michelle Sparman, Hathaitip Sritanaudomchai, Hong Ma, Lisa Clepper, Joy Woodward, Ying Li, Cathy Ramsey, Olena Kolotushkina, Shoukhrat Mitalipov. (2009, August 26). Mitochondrial gene replacement in primate offspring and embryonic stem cells. *Nature 461 doi:10.1038/nature08368 Article* , 367-372.

McCormick, J. (2006). *The European Superpower.* London, New York: Palgrave Macmillan.

Mercati, A. (1942). *Il sommario del processo di Giordano Bruno* (Vol. 101). Vaticano: Biblioteca Vaticana Studi e Testi.

Metastasio, Cimarosa. (2003). *L' Olimpiade. Dramma per musica di Pietro Metastasio. Musica di Domenico Cimarosa.* Roma: Artemide, collana Metastasiana.

Meyers, N. (Writer), & Meyers, N. (Director). (25 December 2009 (USA)). *It's Complicated* [Motion Picture].

MGH. (1900-1903). *Monumenta Germaniae Historica inde ab anno Christi quingentesimo usque ad annum millesimum et quingentesimum* (Vol. 1). Hannoverae: Societas Aperiendis Fontibus.

Mill, J. S. (1961). *The Utilitarians: Utilitarianism, and On liberty.* Garden City, N.Y.: Doubleday.

Minsheu, J. (1599-2000). *A Dictionarie in Spanish and English.* London-Malaga: Universidad De Málaga, Servicio De P, E Intercambio C,.

Mookerjee, A. (1988). *Kali. The Feminine Force.* New York: Destiny Books.

Moreno. Jacob Levy, Jonathan Fox. (1987). *The Essential Moreno: Writings on Psychodrama, Group Method, and Spontaneity.* New York: Springer Publishing Co.

Moynahan, B. (1997). *Rasputin: The Saint Who Sinned.* New York: Random House Press.

Müller, M. (1899). *The Six Systems of Indian Philosophy.* London, NY, Bombay: Longmans Green, and CO.

Mystic Life . (1998 - 2010). *Welcome to Polyamory - An Unconditional Love!* Retrieved April 16, 2010, from Polyamory - An Unconditional Love: http://www.anunconditionallove.org/

Nagamma, S. (2006). *Letters from Sri Ramanasramam, Letters from & Recollections of Sri Ramanasramam* (Vols. I-II). (D. Sastri, Trans.) Tiruvannamalai: Sri Ramanasramam.

Nanda, S. (1998). *Neither Man Nor Woman: The Hijras of India.* Belmont, CA: Wadsworth Publishing.

Natarajan, A. R. (2006). *Timeless in Time Sri Ramana Maharshi.* Bloomington, Indiana - Printed in China: World Wisdom.

Noble Wilford, J. (2001, December 25). So Who Is Buried in Midas' Tomb? *The New York Times.*

Nye, J. (2004). *Soft Power: The Means to Success in World Politics.* New York: Public Affairs.

O felix Roma. (2007). *Pontifical Anthem, O felix Roma*. Retrieved 12 21, 2012, from Vatican City State: http://www.vaticanstate.va/EN/State_and_Government/General_informations/Anthem.htm

Ogilvie, R. (2009). *In Praise of Polyandry.* (http://www.renateogilvie.com.au/, Producer, & homepageDAILY The World's First Global Student

Newspaper) Retrieved December 21, 2009, from http://www.homepagedaily.com/: http://webapp3.itechne.com/HomePageDaily/Pages/article5202-in-praise-of-polyandry.aspx

Olsson, J. (2009). *Leaving Faith Behind.* Bloomington, Indiana : Xlibris Corporation.

Oman,D. et Al. (1999, May). Volunteerism and Mortality among the Community-dwelling Elderly. *Journal of Health Psychology, vol. 4 no. 3, doi: 10.1177/135910539900400301*, 301-316.

Open Love NY. (2009). *Open Love NY.* Retrieved April 16, 2010, from Open Love NY on Facebook: http://www.facebook.com/group.php?gid=101879123434

Osborne, A. (1990). *The Mind of Ramana Maharshi and the Path of Self-Knowledge.* Ottawa, Canada: Laurier Books, Limited Pub.

Overbye, D. (2013, March 14). CERN Physicists See Higgs Boson in New Particle. *The New York Times*, p. Science.

Pal. (2012). *SANTA CLAUS EXISTS!* West Long Branch, NJ: Sacer Equestris Aureus Ordo, Children Books division.

Paramahansa Yogananda. (1993). *Autobiography of a Yogi.* Los Angeles, California: Self-Realization Fellowship.

Pascal, B. (1995). *Pensées.* (Krailsheimer, Trans.) London, New York: Penguin Classics.

Patañjali. (1955). *Yoga Sutras of Patanjali .* (Ballantyne&Sastri-Deva, Trans.) Calcutta: Susil Gupta.

Patel, A. R. (2010). India's Hijras: The Case for Transgender Rights. *The George Washington International Law Review*, 838-839.

Paul VI Pope. (1975-2013, Feb. 28). *The Apostolic Constitution - Paulus VI Constitutio Apostoli.* Retrieved March 8, 2013, from Vatican, Sancta Sedes, Documenta Latina http://www.vatican.va/index.htm: http://www.vatican.va/holy_father/paul_vi/apost_constitutions/documents/hf_p-vi_apc_19751001_romano-pontifici-eligendo_lt.html

Paul, P. (2010, July 30). The Un-Divorced. *The New York Times*, p. Fashion & Style.

Penrose, R. (2007). *The Road to Reality: A Complete Guide to the Laws of the Universe.* New York, NY: Vintage Books subdivision of Random House.

Pernety, D. A.-J. (1758). *Dictionnaire Mytho-Hermétique.* Paris: Chez Bauche, Libraire.

Petronius Arbiter. (1975). *Petronii Arbitri Cena Trimalchionis.* (M. S. Smith, Ed.) Oxford: Clarendon Press.

Phillips, J. (2010). *HOLY WARRIORS A Modern History of the Crusades.* New York: Random House.

Pierce, B. R. (1935). The Donatist Circumcellions. *Church History: Studies in Christianity and Culture, Vol.4, No.2,* 123-133.

Pietro Micca Museum. (2000). *Turin Pietro Micca Museum.* (L. C. Torino, Producer, & webmaster@tiscalinet.it) Retrieved Feb. 23, 2013, from www.museopietromicca.it: http://www.museopietromicca.it/html/episodio.html

Pio, Padre. (1991-1992-1994-1977). *Epistolario - Padre Pio da Pietrelcina* (Vols. I [terza ed.], II [seconda ed.], III, IV [seconda ed.]). (Melchiorre-da-Pobladura&Alessandro-da-Ripabottoni, Ed.) San Giovanni Rotondo, FG: Edizioni «Padre Pio da Pietrelcina».

Plato. (1955-63). *Text and English translations in Plato* (Vol. 10). (Loeb-classical-library, Ed.) Cambridge, London: Harvard University Press, W. Heinemann.

Plato. (1960). *The Apology* (Vol. 1). (H. NorthFowler, Trans.) Cambridge, London: Harvard University Press, W. Heinemann; Loeb classical library.

Plato, Aristophanes. (1998). *Four texts on Socrates: Plato's Euthyphro, Apology and Crito and Aristophanes' Clouds.* (Starry-West, Trans.) Ithaca, New York; London: Cornell University Press.

Polgreen, L. (2010, July 16). One Bride for 2 Brothers: A Custom Fades in India. *The New York Times.*

Polyamory in the News. (2009). *The Pansexual, Polyamorous, BDSM Law School Application.* Retrieved April 16, 2010, from Polyamorous Perculations Polyamory in the News: http://polyinthemedia.blogspot.com/

Post, S. G. (2007). *Why Good Things Happen to Good People.* New York: Broadway, A Division of Random House, Inc.

Postulazione Generale Cappuccini. (1982). *Santi e Sante nell'Ordine Cappuccino* (Vol. III). Roma: Postulazione Generale Cappuccini.

Quinones Martin, Hess Amanda. (2010, April 5). *Reader Beatdown: THE SEXIST, The Pansexual, Polyamorous, BDSM Law School Application.* Retrieved April 16, 2010, from Washington City Paper online http://www.washingtoncitypaper.com/ : http://www.washingtoncitypaper.com/blogs/sexist/2010/04/05/reader-beatdown-the-pansexual-polyamorous-bdsm-law-school-application/

Rae Rae, Douglas, et al. (1981). *Equalities.* Cambridge: Harvard University Press.

Ramana Maharshi. (1988). *Who am I? The Spiritual Teaching of Ramana Maharshi.* Boston & London: Shambhala.

Ratti, O. & Westbrook, A. (1973). *Secrets of the Samurai.* Rutland, Vermont; Tokyo, Japan: Charles E. Tuttle Company.

Ravenscroft, A. (2004). *Polyamory: Roadmaps for the Clueless & Hopeful.* Santa Fe, NM: Crossquarter Publishing Group.

Réage, P. (1973). *Histoire d'O.* (S. Estrée, Trans.) New York: Ballantine Books.

Reich, W. (1986). *The Sexual Revolution: Toward a Self-Regulating Character Structure.* (T. Pol, Trans.) New York: Farrar, Straus and Giroux.

Renoux, C. (2003). *La preghiera per la pace attribuita a san Francesco, un enigma da risolvere* (it. ed.). Padova: Edizioni Messagero.

Restak, R. (1979). *The brain. The last frontier.* New York, NY: Warner Books.

Rocci, L. (1952). *Vocabolario Greco - Italiano* (VII ed.). Roma, Napoli, Citta' di Castello: Dante Alighieri & S. Lapi Coeditori.

Roper, M. (2012, September 13). A FAITHFUL dog has refused to move from his master's grave for SIX YEARS, a family claims. *The Sun.*

Roscoe, W. (1797). *The life of Lorenzo de'Medici: called the Magnificent* (Vol. 1). London: Straman, Cadell, Davies and Edwards.

Roscoe, W. (1991). *The Zuni Man-Woman.* Albuquerque, NM: University of New Mexico Press.

Rousseau, J. J. (1762). *Du Contrat Social: ou Principes du Droit Politique.* Amsterdam: Marc Michel Rey .

Russell - Copleston. (1948). *Copleston vs. Bertrand Russell: The Famous 1948 BBC Radio Debate on the Existence of God.* Retrieved February 25, 2013, from Evangelical Catholic Apologetics: http://www.philvaz.com/apologetics/p20.htm

Russell, B. (1914). *Our Knowledge of the External World as a Field for Scientific Method in Philosophy.* George Allen & UnwiN LTD: London.

Russell, B. (1957). *Marriage and Morals.* New York: Liveright Publishing Corporation.

Russell, B. (1986). *Bertrand Russell on God and Religion.* (A. Seckel, Ed.) Amherst, New York: Prometheus Books.

Russell, R. V., Hira Lal. (1916). Thug. (Russell-Hira, Ed.) *The Tribes and Castes of the Central Provinces of India, 4,* 558-587, London: Macmillan.

Rutherford, F. J., Ahlgren, A. (2001). *Science for All Americans.* New York: American Association for the Advancement of Science, Oxford University Press.

Ryan, C., Jethá, C. (2010). *Sex at Dawn : The Prehistoric Origins of Modern Sexuality.* New York: HarperCollins Publishers.

Saenger, W. (1984). *Principles of Nucleic Acid Structure.* New York: Springer-Verlag.

Safire, W. (2001 , May 21). Essay; A Polyandry Solution. *The New York Times,* p. Opinion.

Saint Anselm. (2012). *Proslogion, With A Reply on Behalf of the Fool by Gaunilo and The Author's Reply to Gaunilo.* (M. J. Charlesworth, Trans.) Notre Dame, IN: University of Notre Dame Press.

Saint Thomas Aquinas. (1948). *Summa Theologica.* New York, NY: Benziger Bros.

Saṃyutta Nikāya. (1890). *Saṃyutta Nikāya of the Sutta Pitaka part III Khandha-Vāgga.* (Léon-Feer, Ed.) London: Published for the Pali Text Society by Oxford Univ. Press.

Śaṅkarācārya. (1904 - 1968). *The Vedānta-Sūtras, with the commentary by Śaṅkarācārya* (Delhi 1968 ed., Vol. I & II). (M. Muller, Ed., & G. Thibaut, Trans.) Oxford, Delhi,

Varanasi, Patna: The Sacred Books of the East, Motilal Banarsidass.
Śāntideva. (1979). *A Guide to the Bodhisattva's Way Of Life or Entering the Path of Enlightenment (Bodhisattvacaryāvatāra).* (S. Batchelor, Trans.) Dharamsala, India: Library of Tibetan Works and Archives.
Sartre, J.-P. (2000). *Being and Nothingness.* London: Routledge.
Satir, V. (1976). *Making Contact.* Millbrae, CA: Celestial Arts.
ŚB. (1964). *Śatapatha Brāhmaṇa* (Chowkhamba Sanskrit Series 96 ed.). (A. Weber, Ed.) Varanasi.
Scaligero, M. (1972). *Manuale pratico della Meditazione.* Roma: Teseo.
Scaligero, M. (2001, Aprile). La forza della resurrezione. *L'Archetipo Mensile di ispirazione antroposofica – Anno VI n. 6.*
Schaff, P. (1877). *Creeds of Christendom, with a History and Critical notes. The History of the Creeds* (Vol. I&II). New York: Harper & Brothers.
Scherwitz et al. (1983, March). Type A Behavior, Self-Involvement, and Coronary Atherosclerosis. *Psychosomatic Medicine Journal of Biobehavioral Medicine, Vol. 45, No. 1, 0033-3174/83/010047+11 $03.00,* 47-57.
Schopenhauer, A. (1958). *The world as will and representation* (Vol. 2). (Payne, Trans.) Indian Hills, Col.: Falcon's Wing Press.
Schopenhauer, A. (1965). *The basic of morality.* (Payne, Trans.) Indianapolis: Bobbs-Merrill.
Sebastian, A. (2013, March 29). *Stanford creates biological transistors, the final step towards computers inside living cells.* Retrieved March 29, 2013, from ExtremeTech, http://www.extremetech.com/: http://www.extremetech.com/extreme/152074-stanford-creates-biological-transistors-the-final-step-towards-computers-inside-living-cells
SETI (Search for Extraterrestrial Intelligence). (2010, October 3). *The science of SETI@home.* (UC Berkeley) Retrieved October 3, 2010, from SETI@home

http://setiathome.ssl.berkeley.edu/: http://setiathome.berkeley.edu/sah_about.php

Shaw, G. B. (1986). *Getting Married: A Disquisitory Play, with Preface and Press Cuttings.* New York: Penguin Books.

Showtime. (2012). *Polyamory: Married and Dating*. Retrieved April 29, 2013, from A Shotime Original Series : http://www.sho.com/sho/polyamory-married-and-dating/home

Sicari, A. (2006). *Il secondo grande libro dei ritratti di santi.* Milano: Jaca book.

Simonelli, P. J. (1996). Philosophy as a Path to Education for Leadership. In Sarsar (Ed.), *Education for Leadership and Social Responsibility* (pp. CHAPTER 3, 23-34). West Long Branch, NJ: Monmouth University, Center for the Study of Public Issues.

Simonelli, P. J. (2000). *HYRIA, A Lost City-State, Una Polis Scomparsa.* Charleston, SC: Sacer Equestris Aureus Ordo History division.

Simonelli, P. J. (2000). Transcendence - The Universal Quest. In F. Elders (Ed.), *Mythological Europe Revisited. Humanism and the Third Millennium III* (pp. 175-193). Brussels, Belgium: VUB University Press.

Simonelli, P. J. (2012). *Beyond Immortality. The Electron Frog-Jump Past the Edge of Death's Abyss.* Charleston, SC: Sacer Equestris Aureus Ordo ISBN-13: 978-0615637068 ISBN-10: 061563706X.

Simonelli, P. J. (May 27-29, 2010). Self-Transcendence, A Mystical Perspective in von Hildebrand's "The Nature of Love". *The Dietrich von Hildebrand Legacy Project, the Christian Personalism of Dietrich von Hildebrand: Exploring His Philosophy of Love,* (pp. 1-14). School of Philosophy of the Pontifical University of the Holy Cross Rome, Italy.

Sobel, D. (1999). *Galileo's Daughter.* New York: Walker & Company.

Spampanato, V. (1921). *Vita di Giordano Bruno, con documenti editi e inediti.* Messina: Principato.

Stark, R. (2008). *Knights of the Cross: The Epic of the Crusades.* Bloomington, IN: iUniverse.

Susskind, L. (2008). *The Black Hole War: My Battle with Stephen Hawking to Make the World Safe for Quantum Mechanics.* New York, Boston, London: Little, Brown & Company.
Taittirīya Āraṇyaka. (1985). *Taittirīya Āraṇyaka* (Vol. 3). (A. Mahadeva-Sastri, Ed.) New Delhi: Motilal Banarsidass Publishers Pvt. Ltd.
Taittirîya-Saṃhitâ. (1871-1872). *Die Taittirîya-Saṃhitâ.* (A. Weber, Ed.) Leipzig: Brockhaus (Indische Studien, 11-12).
Taormino, T. (2008). *Opening Up: A Guide to Creating and Sustaining Open Relationships.* Berkeley, CA: Cleis Press.
Tavernise, S. (2011, May 26). Married Couples Are No Longer a Majority, Census Finds. *The New York Times.*
Tharoor, S. (2012). *Pax Indica: India and the World of the 21st Century.* New Delhi: Penguin Books India.
The Asiatic journal and monthly miscellany. (1834). *Synonyms and Analogies in the East and West* (Vol. 14). London: Parbury, Allen, and Co.
THE ASSOCIATED PRESS. (2010, April 10). Russia Furious Over Adopted Boy Sent Back From US . *The New York Times.*
The Garuḍa purāṇa. (1911-1974). *The Garuḍa purāṇa (Sāroddhāra).* (Wood-Subrahmanyam, Trans.) New York: AMS Press.
The New York Times. (2010, January 10). GRIST; I Don't, I Don't, I Don't, I Don't, I Don't, I Don't. *The New York Times, Week in Review*, p. 4WK.
The Postal Service. (1987). *The Postal Service Guide to U.S. Stamps* (13 ed.). Washington D.C: United States Postal Service.
Thoreau, H. D. (1968). *Walden and On the Duty of Civil Disobedience.* New York: Collier Books.
Thoreau, H. D. (1993). *A Year in Thoreau's Journal: 1851.* New York: Penguin Books USA Inc.
Tolle, E. (2004). *The Power of Now: A Guide to Spiritual Enlightenment.* Vancouver, Canada: Namaste Publishing.
Tomasello, M. (2009). *Why We Cooperate.* Cambridge, Massachusetts: A Boston Review Book.
Tomasello, M. and Carpenter, M. (2007). Shared intentionality. *Developmental Science, Max Planck Institute for*

Evolutionary Anthropology, Leipzig, Germany, 10:1 DOI: 10.1111/j.1467-7687.2007.00573.x, 121–125.

Torah, Plaut. (n.d.). *The Torah. A modern commentary* (1981 ed.). (W. G. Plaut, Ed.) New York: Union of American Hebrew Congregation.

Totò. (1964). *'A Livella e poesie d'amore.* Roma: Grandi Tascabili Economici Newton.

Trésor Hermétique. (1920?). *Le Livre d'Images sans paroles (Mutus Liber) et Le Traité symbolique de la Pierre philosophale.* Lyon: Paul Derain.

UAb. (2005). *Amritabindu Upanishad in Krishna-Yajurvediya . In The Scriptural Commentaries of Yogiraj Sri Sri Shyama Charan Lahiri Mahasaya* (Vols. 1, pp. 209, Ch. 4). (Y. Niketan, Trans.) New York, Lincoln, Shanghai: iUnivese, Inc.

UB. (1889). *Bṛhadāraṇyaka Upanishad, in der Mādhyadina Recension.* St. Petersburg (and Leipzig): Herausgegeben und übersetzt von O. Böhtlingk.

UC. (1889). *Chāndogya Upanishad.* Leipzig: Kritisch herausgegeben und übersetzt von Otto Böhtlingk.

UG. (1965). *Gaṇapati Upanishad, text* (Vol. XVIII). (L. Renou, Ed., & J. Varenne, Trans.) Paris: Libraire d'Amérique et d'Orient Adrien-Maisonneuve.

UK. (1850). *Kaṭha Upanishad.* (E. Röer, Ed.) Calcutta: Bibliotheca Indica.

UKai. (1898). *Amritabindu and Kaivalya Upanishad (pp. 11-16) with commentaries.* (A. Mahadeva-Sastri, Trans.) Madras: Thompson and Co. Minerva Press.

UKai. (1952). *Kaivalyopaniṣad Texte et traduction.* (L. Renou, Ed., & B. Tubini, Trans.) Paris (VI): Librairie D'Amerique et d'Orient Adrien-Maisonneuve.

UKena. (1850). *Kena Upanishad.* (Röer, Ed.) Calcutta: Bibliotheca Indica.

UM. (1850). *Māṇḍūkya Upanishad.* (E. Röer, Ed.) Calcutta: Bibliotheca Indica.

UMaitrī. (1870). *Maitrī Upanishad.* (E. B. Cowell, Ed.) Calcutta, London: Bibliotheca Indica.

UMu. (1850). *Muṇdaka Upanishad.* (E. Röer, Ed.) Calcutta: Bibliotheca Indica.

UŚ. (1850). *Śvetāśvatara Upanishad, in Tāittirīya, Āitareya and Śvetāśvatara Upanishads.* (E. Röer, Ed.) Calcutta: Bibliotheca Indica.

UT. (1850). *Taittirīya Upanishad, in Tāittirīya, Āitareya and Śvetāśvatara Upanishads.* (E. Röer, Ed.) Calcutta: Bibliotheca Indica.

U-The Principal Upanishads. (1953). *U. The Principal Upanishads edited with Introduction, Text, Translitteration and Notes.* (S. Radhakrishnan, Ed.) London: George Allen & Unwin Ltd.

UV. (n.d.). *Vajrasūcika Upanishad, Text in The Principal Upanishad.*

UY. (n.d.). *Yoga Darshana Upanishad.* Translation in Varenne, Yoga...

Vālmīki. (2008). *Rāmāyaṇa of Vālmīki An Epic of Ancient India.* (R. P. Goldman, Trans.) New Delhi: Motilal Barnasidass.

Varenne, J. (1976). *Yoga And the Hindu Tradition.* (D. Coltman, Trans.) Chicago and London: The University of Chicago Press.

Vasubandhu and Asaṅga. (1925). *Vijñaptimātratāsiddhi-Triṃśikā with Sthiramati commentary.* (S. Lévi, Ed., & S. Lévi, Trans.) Paris: Librairie Ancienne Honoré Champion.

Vauvenargues, Luc de Clapiers, marquis de Vauvenargues. (1940-2012). *Maxims and Thoughts (The Works of Vauvenargues) [Kindle Edition DX version].* (T. Siniscalchi, Trans.) London: Humphrey Milford and Retrieved from Amazon.com http://www.amazon.com/Maxims-Thoughts-Works-Vauvenargues-ebook/dp/B009P8NGRW [Kindle version].

Vedānta-Sūtras. (1904 - 1968). *The Vedānta-Sūtras, with the commentary by Śaṅkarācārya* (Delhi 1968 ed., Vol. I & II). (M. Muller, Ed., & G. Thibaut, Trans.) Oxford, Delhi, Varanasi, Patna: The Sacred Books of the East, Motilal Banarsidass.

Verga, G. (1885). *Novelle rusticane* . Torino : F. Casanova, Editore .

Vergili, P. M. (1898, 1910). *Aeneis, Editio stereotypa, in usum scholarum iterum.* (O. Ribbeck, Ed.) Lipsiae: in aedibus B. G. Teubneri.

Virgil. (1986). *Eclogues, Georgics, Aeneid I-VI (I) & Aeneid VII-XII (II), The Minor Poems. With an English translation* (Vol. I & II). (Fairclough, Trans.) Cambridge, London: Harvard University Press, Loeb Classical Library.

Vishnu Purana. (2006). *The Vishnu Purana: A System of Hindu Mythology and Tradition.* (H. H. Wlson, Trans.) Cambridge: Read Country Books.

von Hildebrand, Dietrich. (2009). *The Nature of Love.* (J. F. Crosby, Trans.) South Bend, Indiana: St. Augustine's Press.

VṚ. (n.d.). *Die Hymnen des Ṛigveda* (1968 text ed., Vols. I-II). (T. Aufrecht, Ed.) Wiesbaden: Otto Harrassowitz.

W. (1899 - Reprint 1974). *Monier-Williams, A Sanskrit-English Dictionary.* London: Oxford University Press.

W. (1976). *Monier-Williams, English-Sanskrit Dictionary.* New Delhi: Munshiram Manoharlal Publishers Ovt. Ltd.

Wakin, D. J. (2010, September 9). The New York Times. *Medieval Flagellation in an Italian Town.*

Walker, C. (2009). *29 Gifts: How a Month of Giving Can Change Your Life.* Cambridge, Massachusetts: Da Capo Press.

Walker, Robert S., Flinn, Mark V., Hill, Kim R. (2010, October). Evolutionary history of partible paternity in lowland South America. *Proceedings of the National Academy of Science PNAS 2010 107 (45)* , 19195-19200.

Warren, H. C. (1922). *Buddhism in translations: passages selected from the Buddhist sacred books* (Harvard Oriental Series ed., Vol. Three Eighth Issue). Cambridge, Massachusetts: Harvard University Press .

Watanabe Y. and McConnell D., eds. (2008). *Soft Power Superpowers: Cultural and National Assets of Japan and the United States.* (Watanabe-McConnell, Ed.) London: M E Sharpe.

Watson, R. A. (2007). *Cogito, ergo sum : the life of René Descartes.* Boston: David R. Godine.

WBAL TV. (2010). *Cuddle Parties.* (CNN © 2010, Internet Broadcasting Systems, Inc.) Retrieved April 21, 2010, from WBAL TV NEWS http://www.wbaltv.com/index.html: http://www.wbaltv.com/video/10414311/index.html

Weil, E. (2006, September 24). What if It's (Sort of) a Boy and (Sort of) a Girl? *The New York Times*, p. Magazine.

Weil, Z. (2009). *Most Good, Least Harm: A Simple Principle for a Better World and Meaningful Life.* New York: Simon and Schuster.

Weinberg, S. (1993). *Dreams of a Final Theory: The Scientist's Search for the Ultimate Laws of Nature.* New York: Vintage Books a division of Random House, Inc.

White, C. (2010, June 23). 'Choosy' women set high standards for sperm. *ABC News*, p. http://www.abc.net.au/news/stories/2010/06/23/2935003.htm.

Wilde, O. (2003). *The Picture of Dorian Gray.* London: Collector's Library.

Wilson, B. R. (1975). *The noble savages. The primitive origins of charisma and its contemporary survival.* Berkeley, Los Angeles, London: University of California Press.

Winegar, T. (2002). *Kerista Home.* Retrieved September 24, 2010, from Kerista Commune: http://www.kerista.com/

Woods, V. (2010). *Bonobo Handshake: A Memoir of Love and Adventure in the Congo.* New York: Gotham Books, Penguin Group (USA).

Yahya al-Nawawi. (2010). *Al-Nawawi Forty Hadiths and Commentary.* New York: Arabic Virtual Translation Center.

Zellner, W. W., Kephart, W. M. (2001). *Extraordinary groups: an examination of unconventional lifestyles* (VII ed.). New York: Worth Publishers, Incorporated.

www.ingramcontent.com/pod-product-compliance
Lightning Source LLC
Chambersburg PA
CBHW071647090426
42738CB00009B/1451
* 9 7 8 0 6 1 5 7 5 4 2 6 0 *